ST. MARY'S
ST. MARY'S

THE LIBRARY

W9-ADS-991

The Road to
Post-Communism

The Road to Post-Communism

Independent Political Movements in
the Soviet Union, 1985-1991

Geoffrey A. Hosking
Jonathan Aves
and
Peter J. S. Duncan

Pinter Publishers
London and New York
Distributed exclusively in the USA and Canada by St. Martin's Press

Pinter Publishers
25 Floral Street, Covent Garden, London, WC2E 9DS, United Kingdom

First published in 1992

© School of Slavonic and East European Studies 1992

Apart from any fair dealing for the purposes of research or private study, or criticism or review, as permitted under the Copyright, Designs and Patents Act, 1988, this publication may not be reproduced, stored or transmitted in any form or by any means or process without the prior permission in writing of the copyright holders or their agents. Except for reproduction in accordance with the terms of licences issued by the Copyright Licencing Agency, photocopying of whole or part of this publication without the prior written permission of the copyright holders or their agents in single or multiple copies whether for gain or not is illegal and expressly forbidden. Please direct all enquiries concerning copyright to the Publishers at the address above.

Distributed exclusively in the USA and Canada by
St. Martin's Press, Inc., 175 Fifth Avenue, New York, NY 10010, USA

Geoffrey A. Hosking, Jonathan Aves and Peter J. S. Duncan are hereby identified as the authors of this work as provided under Section 77 of the Copyright, Designs and Patents Act, 1988.

British Library Cataloguing in Publication Data

A CIP catalogue record for this book is available from the British Library.
ISBN 185567 080 1 (hb)
      185567 081 X (pb)

Library of Congress Cataloging-in-Publication Data

Hosking, Geoffrey A.
  The road to post-Communism : independent political movements in the Soviet Union 1985–1991 / Geoffrey A. Hosking, Jonathan Aves, and Peter J. S. Duncan.
  p. cm.
  Includes bibliographical references and index.
  ISBN 1-85567-080-1, – ISBN 1-85567-081-X (pbk.)
  1. Soviet Union–Politics and government–1985-1991. 2. Soviet Union–History–Autonomy and independence movements. 3. Nationalism–Soviet Union–Republics. 4. Post-communism–Soviet Union. I. Aves, Jonathan. II. Duncan, Peter J. S., 1953-   III. Title.
DK286.5.H67 1992
322′.0947′09048–dc20   92-14811
                                                                              CIP

Typeset by Joshua Associates Limited, Oxford
Printed and bound in Great Britain by Biddles Ltd of Guildford and Kings Lynn

Contents

Notes on the authors

Geoffrey A. Hosking is Professor of Russian History at the School of Slavonic and East European Studies, University of London. He was the BBC Reith Lecturer in 1988, is the author of *The Awakening of the Soviet Union* (London, 1991), the *History of the Soviet Union* (3rd edn London, 1992), and has published widely on Russian history and contemporary Russian literature.

Jonathan Aves is Lecturer in Russian Government at the London School of Economics, University of London, and was formerly Leverhulme Research Fellow at the School of Slavonic and East European Studies. He is the author of *Paths to National Independence in Georgia, 1987–1990* (London, 1991) and has written on Russian and Soviet politics.

Peter J. S. Duncan is Lecturer in Contemporary Russian Politics and Society at the School of Slavonic and East European Studies, University of London. He is the author of *The Soviet Union and India* (London, 1989), co-editor of *Soviet-British Relations since the 1970s* (Cambridge, 1990), and the author of various chapters and articles concerning nationalism and religion in the Soviet Union.

Preface

The movements which form the subject of this book changed the face of world politics. At least, that does not seem an exaggerated claim to make about organisations which channelled the forces that destroyed the Communist Party and broke up the Soviet Union. Yet so far they have received remarkably little sustained scholarly attention, most of which has gone instead to Gorbachev and his reforms. Of course, without these reforms, our movements would probably not have existed and certainly could not have played a major role. But that does not mean they are not worth serious examination.

This study was first conceived in the course of work which Geoffrey Hosking was doing in his preparation of the 1988 BBC Reith Lectures and his subsequent book *The Awakening of the Soviet Union*. His interest was aroused in the independent political movements beginning to push shoots through the scorched earth of Soviet totalitarianism. It soon became clear, however, that it was quite beyond the powers of a single individual to follow the burgeoning variety of movements springing up amongst the peoples of the USSR.

Together with Pete Duncan, he submitted a research proposal to the Leverhulme Trust, as a result of which Jonathan Aves became full-time research fellow on a joint project based at the School of Slavonic and East European Studies of London University throughout 1990 and 1991. The name of the project kept changing as the subject blossomed and sprouted in all kinds of unexpected directions. We started by talking of 'informal' political associations, then of 'independent' ones, then finally simply of 'political movements'.

Following closely such rapid and bewildering developments has been at times exhausting and frustrating, but also exciting and intellectually challenging. The steadily growing archive of materials (which will be available to future researchers in the Library of the School of Slavonic and East European Studies) has been our delight and our despair: it periodically reminds us that even three scholars cannot really hope to do justice to the materials which the new political movements have generated.

This book attempts to explore the history of the last years of the Soviet Union between 1985 and 1991 through an examination of the development of independent political movements. They include the myriad of clubs and circles that sprang up after 1986 to discuss politics and campaign on specific issues independently of the CPSU, the popular fronts that began to be organised from the spring of 1988, the electoral blocs that were put together for the 1990 republican and city elections, and the putative political parties of various tendencies that were established between 1988 and 1991.

The book begins by looking at the roots of the independent political movements in the dissident circles of the 1970s and early 1980s and their emergence in 1986–7 in the form of clubs and single-issue campaigns. This is followed by a broad overview of the evolution of the political movements after 1988, showing their decisive role in the process which led to the disintegration of the Soviet Union at the end of 1991. We highlight, in particular, the unprecedented expansion of mass political activity and effective political participation in 1989–90, and the way in which, although the independent political movements continued to set the political agenda after the 1990 republican and city elections, new organisational initiatives, particularly the formation of political parties, tended to dissipate the movements' strength. Finally, we consider the role played by the independent political movements, and the politicians associated with them, in defeating the coup attempt of August 1991.

Case studies then examine the development of specific independent political movements. First and foremost, there is a detailed examination of the development of the democratic movement in the Russian Federation. Defying all expectations, the population of the Russian Federation for the most part supported radical democratisation. This turn of events ensured that independent political movements could emerge in the other republics. As Pete Duncan notes, the coup attempt of August 1991 was defeated principally within the Russian Federation. Leningrad is singled out as a city in which independent political movements played a particularly important role, reflecting a wide political spectrum, polarised between the 'conservative' apparat with its base in the local military–industrial complex and the city's radical intelligentsia, in both its predominant westernising guise and in its minority Russian nationalist guise. Also within the Russian Federation we examine the strengths and weaknesses of the new labour movement, particularly its potential role as a mass social base for the democratic movement on the model of Polish Solidarity. This is followed by accounts of the evolution of independent political movements in two non-Russian republics. In contrast to the situation in the Russian Federation, in both Georgia and Estonia, nationalism provided the slogans around which at least practically all the ethnically Georgian and Estonian population could rally. The two nations differ greatly in their history and traditions and in the manner in which the CPSU adapted to local conditions, including the high level of popular nationalism: these differences greatly influenced the way in which independent political movements in the two republics developed.

We believe that writing the history of the Soviet Union in this period from the perspective of the independent political movements is a useful way of showing the importance of changes in society as well as in the political élite in bringing about the unprecedented changes that occurred. Too often the study of the process of reform in the Soviet Union of the late 1980s has been written purely in terms of decisions made in the political élite, in terms of what Gorbachev said or did and in terms of battles between 'conservatives' and reformers in the Politburo. This book represents an attempt to reassert the importance of perestroika from below in shaping the course of events. It also represents an early attempt to analyse the forces that brought about the dis-integration of the Soviet Union at the end of 1991.

Taken together the independent movements that sprang up all over the Soviet Union after 1986 may not add up to a civil society, as it is usually conceived, but we should not disparage the role that they played in setting the political agenda and, in a number of crucial cases, actually wresting power from the CPSU, by the effectiveness of their organisation and the strength of their resolve. The chances for independent political movements to emerge and grow may have depended on decisions made in the central and republican bodies of the CPSU and on the choice made by many Communist Party members, often quite prominent members, to join them; but it is still the case that the new political agenda, the expansion of democratic and civil rights and the assertion of republican sovereignty and independence, was initiated from below and that the final result was the collapse of the USSR.

Each chapter has been written by the author indicated, but has been read and carefully discussed by all three, so that we feel ourselves jointly responsible for the errors and omissions which are perhaps inevitable in an early attempt to survey a huge and complex subject. The last chapter is a genuine joint effort.

We have accumulated an enormous debt of gratitude to the people who have helped us along the way. First of all, to the Leverhulme Trust, which has financed our research project, and to the School of Slavonic and East European Studies of the University of London, which gave us a home and administrative support; to the politicians who took time off in the midst of very busy lives to talk to us; to the British Academy, which supported part of Geoffrey Hosking's research; to Martin Dewhirst, who constantly and generously provided us with material, sometimes from very unexpected sources; to the SSEES Soviet Press Study Group, whose Wednesday lunchtime meetings kept us supplied with information and comment; to Radojka Miljević, the SSEES Publications and Conferences Officer; to Ursula Phillips of the SSEES Library; to Christine Thomas of the British Library; to Alexander Suetnov of the Centre for the Study of Social Movements in Moscow; to the Samizdat Archive and the Red Archive of Radio Liberty, Munich; to Dr Andrei Sakharov, Liudmila Kolodnikova and Valerii Solovei of the Institute of Russian History, Moscow; to Larissa Ryazanova of the University of Strathclyde; to Konstantin Kon'kov of the Urals State University, Ekaterinburg; to the Estonian Academy of Sciences; to Professor Heino Liiv and his colleagues of the English Faculty of Tartu University; to Anna Temkina and Vladimir Kostiushev of the Leningrad Branch of the Institute of Sociology of the Russian Academy of Sciences; to

Sergei and Natasha Belimov; to Sergo Naveriani, Guliko Margvelani and Rashid Kaplanov; to Elena Poliakova of the Institute of General History, of the Russian Academy of Sciences.

Geoffrey Hosking
Jonathan Aves
Pete Duncan
March 1992

1 The beginnings of independent political activity

Geoffrey A. Hosking

To all appearance, the Soviet Union in the mid-1980s offered a very unpromising soil for the development of civil society—of institutions and associations independent of the state and the ruling party. It was a uniquely centralised polity, in which the party-state apparatus governed not only the aspects of society normally associated with authority, but also the economy, culture, science, education and the media. Everyone's employment depended on the state, and senior appointments in all walks of life were decided under the nomenklatura patronage system controlled by the party.

This made the Soviet Union very different from Spain, Portugal, Greece or any of the Latin American countries feeling their way from authoritarianism to democracy in the 1970s and 1980s. In all those countries, there were social strata which long pre-dated the authoritarian regime and did not owe their existence to it; there was a market economy, distorted perhaps by the state but not entirely dominated by it; there were autonomous churches and religious associations, interest groups and ethnic movements, even sometimes opposition political parties, albeit underground. Such bodies either did not exist in the Soviet Union, or were totally dependent on the state.

Even this list does not quite grasp the peculiarity of the Soviet system (and other communist systems), for its essence lay not in the tightness and pervasiveness of its bureaucratic controls, important though they were, but rather in its adoption of a degenerated utopianism as an ideological adhesive to hold the system together. The fanaticism, brutality and terror of the Stalinist system had largely disappeared, to be replaced by a political charade. The population did not believe in the ideology, but signalled symbolic assent to it in a variety of public rituals. Václav Havel once summarised the spiritual consequences in the person of the greengrocer who displays in his shop-window a placard reading 'Workers of the World, Unite!', not because he believes in workers uniting, but because he wishes to convey to all and sundry that he is willing to assent to the system in order to stay out of trouble. Aggregated individual acts of this kind confirmed and consolidated the system; indeed, in a sense they *were* the system.[1]

Against such a regime the normal methods of political struggle—the formation of oppositional parties and the drawing up of alternative programmes—were impracticable or futile. Social interest groups had no identity separate from the nomenklatura hierarchy, so there was no question of their formulating their distinct interests, let alone of forming associations in order to defend them. That constituted the strength of the system.

Its weakness was the brittleness of the structure of simulated assent. A paradoxical fruit of the ascendancy of ideology was that it conferred high status on people whose profession was ideas—that is, those who were the most thoroughly integrated into the system but who were also the most likely to be aware of the emptiness of its public charade. It was, then, among intellectuals and professional people that the first stages of self-detachment from the system took place. Once enough of them had become convinced that the emperor was not only scantily clad but was also failing to deliver the goods—in the form of food, housing, basic services, even (the regime's great speciality) armaments— then the whole integument of deceit suddenly looked remarkably flimsy. This is what happened in much of Eastern Europe in the autumn of 1989.

What intellectuals did publicly has been characterised by Solzhenitsyn and Havel as 'living in the lie'. What they did privately, among close friends and trusted colleagues, might be quite different, as we shall see. The problem was to find a way of transferring honesty from their private to their public lives.

Strangely enough, it may be that in that sense the first germ of civil society was contained in the Stalin Constitution of 1936. Its guarantees of a full range of civil freedoms, though totally ignored in Stalin's lifetime and largely so for long after his death, nevertheless remained on paper. The first person to attempt to turn them to good use was Aleksandr Esenin-Vol'pin, in 1962, at the time of the trial of young poets for unauthorised readings of their works on Maiakovskii Square. Initially the idea of calling on the Soviet authorities to observe their own laws occasioned only dismissive mirth among his friends, but gradually it dawned on them that in the era of 'socialist legality', when, for their own reasons, the authorities were no longer prepared to apply indiscriminate terror, the tactic did make a certain sense. Most important of all, from the existential point of view, it offered a way of no longer 'living in the lie'. As Vladimir Bukovskii later observed: 'The inspiration of this idea was that it enabled us to eliminate the split in our personalities by shattering the internal excuses with which we justified our complicity in all the crimes. It presupposed a small core of freedom in each individual, his "subjective sense of law".'[2]

No less important was the fact that the Soviet Union had ratified the 1948 United Nations Declaration on Human Rights. Later, in 1975, the human rights clauses of the agreements on European Security and Cooperation drawn up at Helsinki gave a new impetus to the human rights movement inside the USSR. Helsinki watch groups were set up in a number of Union republics. The Soviet Union's acknowledgement of a complex of international juridical obligations, no matter how purely symbolic at first, aided the process of the formation of a civic consciousness inside the country, especially since foreign radio stations, broadcasting in Russian, spread information about these obligations and about the Soviet authorities' violations of them. Furthermore, inside the Soviet Union itself, teaching about 'socialist legality' in schools and colleges, and among the general public by the Znanie society, disseminated elementary knowledge about legal concepts. In short, for the second time in Russian history (the first was during the period 1905–17), the elements of a legal culture were being inculcated in the population, and especially among professional people.

The results manifested themselves first of all in literature, perhaps because, more even than other intellectuals, the best writers had inherited from the past a strong sense of dignity and independence even in the face of overwhelming state power. Literary journals such as *Novyi mir* took the leading role in revealing unpleasant truths about the Stalinist past, as well as in raising questions about present official policies, especially in the economic field: not a task that would normally be incumbent on a literary periodical. Alongside the officially permitted culture the new semi-tolerated samizdat emerged in the early 1960s. The authorities' first attempts to stamp out samizdat, in the wave of Ukrainian repressions of 1965, and in the arrest of Siniavskii and Daniel' in the same year, marked the beginning of the human rights movement. Viacheslav Chornovil in Kiev and Aleksandr Ginsburg in Moscow collected documents on the violations of legality committed by the authorities, and sent them to the Soviet procuracy; the materials also reached foreign journalists and were partially rebroadcast to the Soviet public from foreign radio stations.[3]

This was the first stage of the process which led to the creation of the *Khronika tekushchikh sobytii* (*Chronicle of Current Events*), a samizdat journal which for fifteen years recorded and made known the Soviet authorities' violations of their own laws in the area of civil rights. Its front cover always displayed Article 19 of the UN Declaration on Human Rights, and its materials were presented without editorial comment, so that it could not be accused of any kind of political affiliation.[4] This was the pure legality Esenin-Vol'pin had preached.

But of course it had political implications. The *Chronicle* was the only coordinating organ (and that in the loosest sense) of a number of movements of 'dissent' which by the early 1970s were, in a muffled form, articulating the grievances of a wide variety of discontented religious and ethnic groups in the population. Here the intellectuals were beginning to locate a potential mass following, though they were in no position to mobilise it until the party leadership began seriously to pursue glasnost' and 'democratisation'.

'Dissent', then, represented all that it was possible to achieve in the narrow framework of the Brezhnev regime. It was a vital breakthrough by comparison with the past. Yet it had drawbacks as the basis for a civil society. Its activists were usually isolated from the mass of the population whose concerns they were or claimed to be articulating, and indeed they were sometimes viewed askance by their colleagues for 'rocking the boat' and attracting persecution where otherwise the authorities turned a blind eye. Their network of contacts was inevitably restricted by the primitive and laborious technology of samizdat, even if the results of their activities were more widely known, thanks to foreign radio stations. Above all, the tangible political rewards of their activities were minimal: there seemed to be little practical that dissenters could accomplish beyond the repeated assertion of principle in the wilderness. This was discouraging in itself, and also sometimes caused trivial disagreements within the movements to escalate into bitter disputes fuelled by personal antipathies.

For all that, the contribution of the human rights movement to the later emergence of independent political associations was vital. With the widespread freeing of political prisoners, beginning with the release of Andrei Sakharov from administrative exile in December 1986, former human rights activists returned to the scene, some of them ready to resume their work, first of all to obtain the release of their less fortunate colleagues, then in the name of political freedoms generally. In Armenia and Georgia in May–June 1987, committees were formed for the release of named political prisoners, and both were led by prominent Helsinki watch group figures of the 1970s: the Armenian group's chairman was Robert Nazarian, while both Zviad Gamsakhurdia and Merab Kostava were members of the Georgian one.[5] Somewhat later the Ukrainian Helsinki Group announced that it was resuming its existence, including its surviving members Viacheslav Chornovil and Mikhail Horyn', within the framework of the Ukrainian Culturological Club, which from August 1987 began organising public meetings on ecology, culture, historical monuments and the 'blank spots' of recent history. They sponsored, for example, a memorial gathering for Vasyl' Stus, one of the leading 1960s generation poets, who died in a labour camp in 1985, and evenings of testimony and discussion on the famine of 1932–4. The evocation of Helsinki in their name was important not only because it provided a link with the past, but also because it plugged the new movement into an international diplomatic and juridical process.[6]

Together the three Helsinki groups formed an International Committee for the Defence of Political Prisoners, which issued its first statement on 14 January 1988. This noted that most of those still 'inside' were participants of national liberation movements, and adumbrated a whole programme of ethnic rights, much of which was soon to become the working fare of the Popular Fronts: the right to an official language, to education, publication and the conduct of public business in it, the right of each republic to plan its economy in accordance with its own needs and to avoid environmental degradation.[7]

The first national liberation movement to hold mass demonstrations was that of the Crimean Tatars. Deported from their homeland by Stalin in 1944, and resettled in various parts of Central Asia, they had begun as early as 1956 to address loyal petitions to the government asking to be allowed to return. During the 1960s and 1970s they were able to collect hundreds of thousands of signatures for such petitions, and also occasionally held mass meetings, invariably broken up by the police. This unusual tenacity in such a difficult period was undoubtedly due to the fact that they were the largest deported people not permitted to return home in the late 1950s: they thus had one simple overwhelming grievance on which all were agreed.[8]

During the summer of 1987 their Initiative Group held meetings with the Presidium of the USSR Supreme Soviet in Moscow. Frustrated by the outcome, they began to hold regular meetings in Izmailovsky Park, and then finally, on 25 July, a demonstration on Red Square, where some 500 Tatars paraded with banners, chanting 'Homeland! Homeland!' and 'Gorbachev! Gorbachev!'. The police tried to ease them off the square without using force, since foreign correspondents were present, but failed, and the demonstration continued till the following afternoon, when those remaining were induced to disperse by the promise of a meeting with Gromyko (then President of the USSR). They gained nothing but vague promises from that meeting, and subsequently members of the Initiative Group and other participants were arrested, put on planes and sent back to Tashkent, where they were warned they might be charged with 'group activities disturbing public order'. In spite of that, they subsequently organised a number of other demonstrations in Central Asian towns.[9]

Like the Crimean Tatars, the Jews had kept their ethnic awareness alive during the 1970s by political campaigns. In their case, since they had no Soviet homeland and felt that Jewish national life was impossible in the USSR, they focused on the right to emigrate. They held occasional small-scale demonstrations of 'refuseniks' (those refused an exit visa), which were invariably broken up by the police.[10] From 1987 the emphasis of Jewish political activity changed. Refusenik demonstrations continued,[11] but as the number of exit permits increased emigration ceased to be the single dominant issue; instead, the development of Jewish culture within the USSR, and the protection of Jews from *Pamiat'* and other anti-Semitic movements, now publicly active, came to the fore.[12] The change of mood was marked by a demonstration at Vostriakova cemetery on 26 April 1987 to commemorate the Jews murdered in the Holocaust.[13] The first Jewish Cultural Society was set up in Moscow in May 1988, and it was soon followed by others, in Kiev and L'viv (where their initiative was explicitly supported by Ukrainian activists), in Vil'nius, Riga, Tallinn and Minsk. Their aim was to commemorate the Jewish past, to spread knowledge of Yiddish and Hebrew (the latter hitherto forbidden in the USSR), to perform Jewish plays, music and dance, and generally to bring Jews together in celebration of their diverse and ancient culture. A first all-Union congress of these cultural associations was held in Moscow in March 1989.[14]

In Moscow the Press Club Glasnost' (not to be confused with the unofficial journal of the same name) was the first organisation to espouse publicly the cause of human rights. Set up in July 1987, its initiators contained a number of former human rights activists and editors of samizdat journals: Larisa Bogoraz, Sergei Kovalev, Reshat Dzhemilev, Aleksandr Ogorodnikov, Iosif Begun, Viktor Brailovskii, Sergei Grigor'iants and Lev Timofeev.[15] In December it organised an international human rights seminar, the first time such an event had ever been held on Soviet soil. The attitude of the authorities towards this unprecedented gathering was ambivalent: they did not prevent it meeting altogether, but obstructed the journeys of many of the participants, both from abroad and from inside the Soviet Union, and blocked the hire of any premises large enough to accommodate the whole event. As a result, no plenary sessions could be held, and the occasion was reduced to its various sections meeting separately in private apartments scattered all over Moscow. In spite of the difficulties, about 400 Soviet citizens took part, together with about thirty from abroad, including representatives of the International Helsinki Federation.[16] The occasion was significant in that it made possible the resumption of human and organisational links broken off in the 1970s, as well as the creation of new ones.

The heritage of the former human rights movement was also revived in the new unofficial journals which now started appearing to provide an information and communications base for the emerging political movements. The journal *Ekspress-khronika*, for example, launched in August 1987 by Aleksandr Podrabinek, was consciously modelled on the *Khronika tekushchikh sobytii*. It aimed to get its information to readers much faster by appearing weekly but, like its model, it recorded baldly and without editorial comment violations of human rights within the Soviet Union. Podrabinek had had experience of this kind of work, having in the 1970s edited an information bulletin on psychiatric abuse, and published a book on the subject, for which in 1978 he was charged with slandering the Soviet state and sentenced to five years' exile.[17] Now his latest journal rapidly built up a network of informants around the country, relying partly on older communications links, partly on the new ones now being created. Its editors would meet every Saturday morning to sift the items of information they had received during the week. On Saturday afternoons the typists would get to work, usually carrying on far into the night, at this stage without benefit of word-processing technology. Then on Sunday morning, *Ekspress-khronika* would be sold on Gogol Boulevard in the centre of Moscow, along with a gradually growing gaggle of other unofficial publications, whose editors would come along to meet each other and to distribute their wares under the watchful eye of the militia. By April 1988, 200 copies of *Ekspress-khronika* were being typed out and dispatched to fifty-three towns, in eleven of which they would be retyped and distributed further. Taking part in such a venture could be dangerous: Podrabinek was frequently followed and more than once attacked in the street in circumstances which the police subsequently refused to investigate.[18]

Another former political prisoner, Sergei Grigor'iants, started a journal at about the same time. In March 1983 he had been arrested and sentenced to ten years for editing a human rights periodical called simply *Bulletin V* (short for *vesti* or 'news'). This had appeared roughly twice a month from 1980 to 1983 to supplement the information given in the increasingly sporadic *Khronika tekushchikh sobytii* or to speed up its dissemination. *Bulletin V* had only a very limited circulation and was not known at the time outside the Soviet Union. But it did fulfil its function of keeping informational channels and personal connections open, and Grigor'iants was able to use some of them again after his release in 1987.[19]

The title of his new journal, *Glasnost'*, made adroit use of Gorbachev's own catchword. Grigor'iants conceived *Glasnost'* not only as a bearer of information about the human rights movement, but also as a forum for new political movements to announce their existence and make their aims known, and also for them to expound and discuss their ideas about what was wrong with the Soviet Union and how it might be changed. Within a few months, *Glasnost'* enjoyed such a high reputation that Grigor'iants was able to attract senior members of the official intelligentsia (hitherto cautious about involvement in informal politics) to write for it. Registration of it was, however, refused on the grounds that there was a paper shortage and already quite enough newspapers and journals. Moreover, on 9 May 1988, the police arrested Grigor'iants at his out-of-town dacha, and confiscated all his equipment, including a recently acquired computer. He was released a few days later, but the equipment was not returned.[20]

A third journal which began to appear shortly afterwards (December 1987) was *Referendum*, whose editor, Lev Timofeev, had been arrested in 1985 for circulating in samizdat and publishing abroad his books, which gave a frank picture and a sociological analysis of the state of the Soviet countryside. The journal reflected the thoughtful and scholarly nature of its editor: it was a purveyor of opinion and discussion, allowing its authors space to expound and develop their ideas, and to contest those of their opponents.[21]

Another strand of social protest, quite distinct from the human rights movement, though parallel with it, was the burgeoning youth movement. During the 1960s the situation of young people in Soviet society had begun to change, in paradoxical fashion. Up to that time they had always been in the thick of events, in demand for the urgent tasks of war and peace; often they had been able to win high promotion on the basis of minimal education. Now their lives had become materially more comfortable, and they were no longer threatened by war, revolution or social upheaval; they were also better educated and more sophisticated, with a wider range of interests. By comparison with the past, however, society could no longer offer them an obvious role. Their sometimes impressive qualifications were often not matched by the work they could find, and their promotion was typically blocked by much less able nomenklatura appointees from the past. These changes generated a deep conflict of generations, awaking in the young (and not so young) a sense of alienation and of belonging to a limbo called 'youth', which often considerably outlasted the maximum Komsomol age of 28.

In these dispiriting circumstances, an autonomous youth culture began to form in the 1960s and 1970s, and made its influence felt beyond what one would conventionally term 'youth'. In a sense it was an intense expression of the outlook of a society infantilised by its own rulers. The origins of this culture can be traced back to the 20th Party Congress, with its questioning of the Stalinist past, and to the International Youth Festival of 1957, when young Soviet citizens were able to communicate with their foreign contemporaries for the first time for more than a generation. Its early beginnings were in the Komsomol volunteer brigades and 'communards' of the Khrushchev period.[22] But quite soon, especially under western influences, it became independent of the official Soviet youth movement. In the words of a Soviet sociologist, young people were seeking 'self-fulfilment and sociability, the feeling of belonging to one's age-group, to one's town, district, courtyard, school, social stratum, that is, the sense of having one's own circle which is associated with the word "we".[23]

Some young people found the focus of their sociability in supporting sports teams, forming fan clubs which would accompany their heroes, wear their colours and emblems, and sometimes get into fights with their rivals.[24] Others were attracted by rock music (the universal symbol of youth culture), becoming rockers, punks, metallists or breakers according to inclination and circumstance. Some became religious seekers, of Christian or non-Christian persuasion. Some experimented with drugs and with other means of exploring one's social and personal identity.[25] Yet others stood out against the general westernising trend, reaffirming traditional proletarian values in a coarse and sometimes violent form: such were the *Liubery*, militant suburbanites from near Moscow, who would dress in slim-cut jeans and highly coloured shirts, and go into the city in bands, to cut off long hair, tear off jewellery, or even beat up young people of stylish or western appearance.[26] Already here some of the characteristic features of 'informality' can be discerned: the absence of any legal status, the introversion, the search for alternative life-styles, the intense personal relations. Such groups did not struggle against the existing social and political system, but ignored or passively resisted it, while carving out for themselves little niches within it.

Where they formulated a philosophy of life, they did so in reaction against what they saw as the artificial and insincere adult world. The hippies of the so-called 'Older Generation', which appeared in the late 1960s, took as their basic principle that 'in a world deprived of freedom, one can acquire it only in one's own soul'. They conducted the search by means of Yoga, Buddhism, and various forms of mysticism, sometimes accompanied by the use of drugs.[27] The 'people of the System', who came somewhat later, preached a gospel of the reconciliation of all people by the force of universal love: 'The hippy ideal is a society of equality and brotherhood, where there will be no distinction between nations, and where love will be the basic factor in the relationships between people.'[28]

These ideals led naturally on to pacificism and to concern for the urban and natural environment. The 'people of the system' rejected nuclear deterrence and urged increasing contact between ordinary people of east and west, with freedom of travel to make that possible. They also condemned the Afghan war, which they considered made 'moral cripples' out of those who had to fight in it and threatened to revive the fascist mentality. On the environment, the group 'Free Initiative', which grew out of the 'System', proclaimed: 'We want harmony with Nature, not the raping of it for the satisfaction of unnatural needs ... In harmony with nature we will resurrect the gods, who have died of cancer or suffocated in the fumes of factories.'[29]

By the mid-1980s, as a result of continual friction with society and police, some of the hippies had become politicised, and were forging links between groups in different towns, even bringing out manifestos and journals, and organising Union-wide assemblies (in Tallinn, where the authorities were more tolerant than elsewhere).[30]

The hippies' worries about the military and ecological threat were widely shared in society, and not only among young people. They had formed a major part of Andrei Sakharov's argument in his memorandum of 1968, and had been much discussed among scholars in private and semi-public seminars. Together with the protection of historical monuments, these themes became the principal arenas on which, after 1985, it proved possible to begin challenging official policies and to form a more broad-based political movement. Even before the advent of glasnost' some young people, impatient with the sluggishness of officially approved organisations like VOOPIK, had on occasions formed informal detachments for the defence of specific monuments or natural sites.[31] Now it became possible to communicate with a wider public and mobilise them for action.

One of the first examples of such action came in the autumn of 1986, when the Mossovet decided to demolish the seventeenth-century mansion of the merchant Shcherbakov to make way for a motorway. An action group of students and schoolchildren, led by Kirill Parfenov, occupied the building for two months, while Parfenov himself appeared on a popular television programme to explain the need to protect the capital city's historical heritage.[32]

In Leningrad a similar proposal, to demolish the hotel Angleterre, provoked a number of disparate informal groups to get together and agitate publicly. Leningrad had long possessed a 'second culture', centred around the Klub-81, which had several years earlier concluded an informal agreement with the authorities that they would be allowed to hold unofficial poetry readings and bring out a samizdat journal, provided they did not attempt foreign publication.[33] Klub-81 and its associates linked up with several ecological and preservation societies led by *Spasenie*, which in the previous year had organised a successful campaign to save the house of the poet Del'vig on Vladimir Square. Together they set up a picket outside the hotel and started collecting signatures from passers-by for a petition to the city soviet.

They failed to save the hotel. The soviet moved in its demolition workers suddenly one morning when the pickets were absent.[34] But this failure had a positive effect: it provoked the protesters into a realisation of their need to work more closely together, and to be more systematic in their appeals to the public. In other words, what had happened was a course of political education for them: a question of environmental protection had also become a question of human rights, and one to be pursued by political means.

The informal groups established an umbrella organisation, the Cultural Democratic Movement, or Epicentre, and stationed an information kiosk on the square in front of St Isaac's Cathedral, to hand out leaflets and answer questions. Epicentre started to issue a journal, *Merkurii*, with the watchword 'Claws and teeth for public opinion!', reflecting the lessons learned. It continued its self-politicisation by nominating a candidate, Alexei Kovalev, for the forthcoming local Soviet elections. The authorities, however, refused to register him, and indeed barred him from a graduate course he wished to begin.[35]

Some Russians drew very different conclusions from the progressive degradation of the natural and historical environment. The organisation *Pamiat'* was founded in the late 1970s or early 1980s as a literary and historical society attached to the Ministry of the Aviation Industry: its members carried out voluntary restoration work at weekends. By 1985 some at least of its leaders had decided that the fundamental reason for the disastrous environmental situation, as well as for Russia's other afflictions, lay with an international conspiracy of freemasons and Zionists aiming to undermine Russia, and working through Jewish leaders of the Soviet Communist Party as well as through the imperialists. Those who thought this way even dug up the notorious Okhrana forgery, *The Protocols of the Elders of Zion*, as evidence for their view. Thereafter *Pamiat'* became radically opposed to the emerging liberal and reformed socialist currents in society. During May 1987 it organised a number of demonstrations in Moscow, which assembled some hundreds of people, and one of which was received by El'tsin, then the first secretary of the city's party committee.[36]

Ecological concerns drew ordinary citizens into the first examples of mass political agitation in a number of republican and provincial towns during 1986–7, encouraged perhaps by the success of scientists and writers in having the planned diversion of northern rivers called off in the summer of 1986. In Latvia in the autumn of 1986 a public petition attracted 30,000 signatures in a call to abandon plans for a hydroelectric power station on the Daugava River, which would have drowned a good deal of arable land and several villages. The republican authorities supported the protest, and Gosplan revoked the scheme.[37]

In Yerevan 2,000 people demonstrated on 17 October 1987 to protest against existing chemical plants and also against plans to build a nuclear power station. They listened to speeches by the writer Sil'va Kaputikian and the journalist Zorii Balaian, both of whom enjoyed popularity among Armenians, before parading with banners reading 'Save Armenia from chemical and radioactive genocide!'. A total of 1,500 signatures were collected for a petition to the Supreme Soviet of the USSR.[38] This was the beginning of a movement which led later to much stormier assertions of Armenian national feeling over Nagornyi Karabakh.

In Ufa in November more than 2,000 people gathered one Sunday on the appeal of an 'initiative group' to protest against the proposal to build a polycarbon factory in a city already suffering severely from polluted air. They marched down Oktober Prospekt carrying banners reading 'Clean air for Ufa!' to the City Ispolkom building, where members of the initiative group were invited in for consultations. As a result the City Soviet decided to appeal to the USSR Council of Ministers to relocate the planned factory outside the city, an appeal which was later upheld by a special commission dispatched from Moscow.[39]

At about the same time, another concern of youth culture, international peace, was making itself felt. The 'Group for establishing trust between the USSR and the USA' had a comparatively long history: it was set up in 1982. It grew out of an unofficial seminar, Peace and Social Research, which at that time was being held at Dolgoprudnoe, just outside Moscow, and attracted scholars from a number of disciplines as well as people from the hippy movement concerned about the seemingly unstoppable drift towards nuclear war between the superpowers. In 1982 some of the seminar's members became dissatisfied with the academic nature of their deliberations, and decided to 'go public' in an attempt to undertake more practical and fruitful work. Having formed the Trust Group, they invited Soviet and western journalists to a press conference—the Soviet ones did not come—at which they launched an 'Appeal to the Governments and the Public of the USSR and the USA'. Renouncing criticism of any particular government, they called upon members of the public in all countries to draw up proposals for keeping the peace and to meet in order to discuss them and decide on ways of putting pressure on their governments to implement them. They called this process 'four-sided dialogue'.[40]

At a time when the last Helsinki watch groups were being disbanded under pressure of official persecution, to announce publicly the formation of an independent movement with political aims seemed the height of folly. Yet in fact the initiators of the Trust Group had chosen their moment and their methods well. The Soviet government was putting forward nuclear disarmament proposals which were being rebuffed by western governments, but finding quite a positive response in western public opinion; it was accordingly reluctant to be seen suppressing a home-grown public movement making similar proposals.

The Trust Group continued the tactics of earlier human rights activists in cultivating contact with western journalists, and particularly with their sympathisers in the western peace movements; but they also opened up contacts among the Soviet public on a much broader scale than their predecessors. This is probably where they assimilated the legacy of the unofficial youth culture.[41] They staged an exhibition of children's paintings on peace, and also of photographs of the consequences of the Hiroshima bomb. In the summer of 1984 they stood on the Arbat collecting signatures for a petition urging Chernenko and Reagan (then going through a period of glacial non-contact) to hold a summit meeting: passers-by proved less timid than feared and, though surprised by an initiative which had no official backing, about 300 gave their signatures in the two hours which elapsed before the police woke up to the fact that the petition was unauthorised. In 1986, the Trust Group handed out leaflets in Gor'kii Park, providing facts about the Chernobyl' nuclear explosion and passing on recommendations about precautions to be taken; in this way they carried out a public service which the government had neglected on a matter which caused most people deep and legitimate worries.[42]

The Trust Group established links with the former human rights movement through the seminar *Demokratiia i gumanizm*, set up in the spring of 1987.[43] This had originated in the kitchen-table discussions which were the natural habitat of the 1970s dissenters. With the return of political prisoners from labour camps, and with the activation of political life during the winter of 1986–7, these discussions took on a more purposeful character. Participants undertook specific tasks, studying and reporting on particular problems of the Soviet Union's politics, culture and history. It became a systematic seminar, and adopted its new title in the spring of 1987, setting itself to elaborate practical proposals for the democratisation of the USSR.[44]

It took its stand on the idea, often reiterated by Andrei Sakharov, that world peace could not be secured as long as one of the two superpowers withheld basic freedoms from its own citizens. The proclaimed aim of the seminar, then, was to study ways of promoting the democratisation of the Soviet Union. It assumed a campaigning stance from the start, envisaging democratisation not in the sense understood by the Communist Party, but in a return to the liberal-democratic ideals of the February revolution. Its manifesto called for a thorough investigation of the country's recent past; the 'de-ideologisation' of the Soviet constitution, education system and culture; the abolition of the 'political' articles of the Criminal Code, and the release of all political prisoners; the abolition of the death penalty; the abolition of censorship and the publication of all the best samizdat. One way or another, the Soviet state subsequently fulfilled most of these demands, but in 1987 they still sounded utopian, even provocative. The group helped to organise a number of public demonstrations, some of them broken up by the police, and the following year played the leading role in establishing the first self-proclaimed opposition political party since 1921, the Democratic Union.[45]

In addition to the human rights movement and the youth movement, a third stream was also preparing, if in more urbane and cautious style, to make its contribution to the swelling flow of informal politics. In universities and academic institutes, groups of scholars had been studying subjects not at all envisaged in the Marxist–Leninist world outlook. Some had been investigating the history, folklore, religion and culture of their peoples, reassembling the fragments of a lost world. Much of their work was officially sanctioned, but some of it was conducted in private or informal seminars. They were restoring the disrupted memory of whole nations, and their labours, once their fruits became widely known, did much to underpin the ethnic revival which burst to the forefront of politics during and after 1988, bringing to prominence such unlikely figures as the musicologist Vytautas Landsbergis in Lithuania, the orientalist Levon Ter-Petrosian in Armenia, and the literary scholar Zviad Gamsakhurdia in Georgia.

More modestly, other scholars had been cultivating among themselves awareness of a world beyond the Soviet frontiers, of political, economic, legal, philosophical and religious alternatives to the society in which they lived. Some of their work later bore fruit in the post-1985 reform process, beginning with the theoretical study of market economics in Novosibirsk, which generated the Zaslavskaia memorandum of 1983. Social science and humani-

ties faculties and institutes, which had long been centres of discreetly culti-
vated non-conformism, gave high intellectual status to the search for
post-totalitarian structures.

It was from this milieu that proposals began to come forth concerning not
just single issues but the whole range of politics. On the whole, however,
leading scholars were reluctant to jeopardise their establishment status by
becoming involved in unauthorised political activities. The most they were
prepared to do was to extend discreet protection to younger colleagues who
were ready to take more risks.

It was in this fashion that the Klub Perestroika emerged from an ongoing
seminar at the Central Economic-Mathematical Institute in Moscow. During
the early months of 1987 this seminar had been bringing together young
economists, jurists, sociologists, political scientists and others, most of them in
their late 20s and 30s, initially to discuss the drafting of a new enterprise law
(eventually promulgated in July). The discussions at it were expert, yet also
wide-ranging and spontaneous: question and answer soon outgrew the original
theme of the seminars, raising problems which affected the whole of Soviet
society, and stimulating in many participants the aspiration to move beyond
discussions and do something practical. Specialist sections were formed to give
shape to these aspirations: one, for example, to discuss models of socialism,
another for 'self-administration', another for 'citizens' diplomacy'. One, called
Memorial, set itself to solicit support for the idea of a memorial centre
dedicated to Stalin's victims.[46]

As the debates broadened and drew in more young scholars, Klub
Perestroika faced a problem which was to become paradigmatic for all informal
movements over the next few years. Growing numbers and looseness of
membership criteria raised the questions: should we not have a tighter
organisational structure if we are to achieve anything? Should we not have a
definite political programme? What should our relationships be with the
Institute which shelters us and, beyond that, with the authorities in general?

A political kernel was emerging around four members in particular: Andrei
Fadin, Boris Kagarlitskii, Pavel Kudiukin and Gleb Pavlovskii. Fadin,
Kudiukin and Kagarlitskii had been arrested in 1982 for editing an unofficial
journal propagating unorthodox socialist ideas. The main point of their argu-
ments was the same now as it had been then: that a fundamental restructuring
of Soviet society was needed to revive local self-administration through
genuinely elected soviets and workers' committees, guided and helped where
necessary by a 'new socialist' party of trained intellectuals. Ideas which had
been considered criminal in 1982 were accepted in 1987 in one of the most
prestigious institutes as a basis for action.[47]

This programme not only posited 'socialism' as an acceptable ideal, but also
implied cooperation with reformist elements in the party-state apparatus as a
way of bringing it about. Not everyone in Klub Perestroika accepted either the
ideal or the means. In November 1987 a debate was held, explicitly on the
'socialist choice', and as a result of it the club split into two groups. Those who

wanted to include the word 'socialism' in their programme and were prepared to work with the authorities called themselves Democratic Perestroika and continued to hold meetings at the Institute. Those who rejected the 's-word' and identified the apparat unequivocally as the enemy, who must be confronted, renamed themselves Perestroika-88 and had to look for other premises.[48]

Before this split took place, Klub Perestroika had already made the first moves to coordinate its efforts with those of other informal political clubs in organising an 'informational meeting-dialogue' of informal political associations. One of those it associated with was the Club for Social Initiatives, which had originated in a youth discussion group, *Nash Arbat*, held regularly from the spring of 1986 in the *krasnyi ugolok* of a block of flats in central Moscow. Its members had decided to move beyond discussion and become an enabling group to help people with practical proposals for social work to get them realised. Among the early activities they helped launch were a theatre studio, a computer club, and a construction brigade to build a home for the deaf and dumb in Zagorsk.[49]

The club's constitution talked of 'involving broad strata of the population in the process of self-government'. As with the ecological initiative groups of the same period, only on an even wider front, the Club for Social Initiatives was trying to convert ideas into action and also to fill some of the glaring gaps in the social provision afforded by the Soviet state. In this endeavour it was encouraged by the Committee for Social Initiatives of the Soviet Sociological Association, which provided it with premises more appropriate to its ambitions than the *krasnyi ugolok*. This élite patronage was crucial to its survival. The Club was also involved to some extent in defending human rights: in May 1987 it investigated an incident when the police beat up some hippies on the Gogol' Boulevard. The documents it laid before the procuracy provided enough evidence for an acquittal of the hippies.[50]

Another partner in the organisation of the 'meeting-dialogue' was the 'historical-political club' *Obshchina*, the first roots of which went as far back as 1982, when a student discussion circle in the History Faculty of Moscow University began to study the Marxist–Leninist heritage and its application to the contemporary Soviet Union. The circle was still going in the winter of 1986–7, when dissatisfaction among the students with the University's Komsomol organisation came to a head. The circle produced a set of recommendations which would have turned the all-Union Komsomol into a federation of self-governing youth organisations, whose delegates would be subject to recall at any moment. This was both a reassertion of the principle underlying the workers' soviets of 1905 and a return to the ideas of Bakunin, Kropotkin and Proudhon on the optimum structure of society. To underline their debt to the *narodniki* the circle renamed itself *Obshchina*: a reference to the traditional village commune which was finally destroyed by Stalin. The recommendations were spurned by the Komsomol, but they provided the keynote for *Obshchina* as a political club, and later on for the Confederation of

Anarcho-Syndicalist (KAS) of which it became the leading member. Its aim was to reactivate soviet democracy through the peaceful undermining of the party-state apparatus and its replacement by a network of democratically elected soviets, while the economy would be run by self-governing workers' councils within each enterprise.[51]

Another organisation involved in the early stages of the organisation of the 'meeting-dialogue' was the All-Union Socio-Political Correspondence Club. This originated from a letter written in the autumn of 1986 by Aleksandr Sukharev, a young scholar from Orenburg, to *Komsomol'skaia pravda* about social problems in the Soviet Union. The editors passed on to him several hundred letters which they received in reply: as a result, an extensive correspondence came into existence on the theoretical problems of socialism. In May 1987 some forty of these correspondents met in Moscow, gave their association its name and charter, and decided that they would organise a conference of independent socialist clubs later that summer. For reasons which are not clear, the Club for Social Initiatives regarded this group as a rival rather than a potential partner, and in the end the Correspondence Club held its own conference at the same time as the Moscow one, but in Taganrog, with about a hundred delegates representing fifty or so towns. The Club remained organisationally sickly, but its network of correspondents helped later to fill the membership lists, especially in provincial towns, of FSOK and KAS.[52]

The 'meeting-dialogue', when it finally took place in Moscow on 20–3 August 1987, was a major turning-point, for it brought together individuals and groups from diverse backgrounds and geographical origins and it established a communications network. It also began the process of differentiation among the 'informals', laying down the main political tendencies and thus preparing the way for later parties. It was held in the House of Culture 'Innovator' with the permission of the party committee of Moscow's Brezhnev raion (soon after renamed Novye Cheremushki). One can only speculate as to the reason why this permission was granted: but some party officials wanted to encourage and maintain links with informal groups of a socialist orientation supporting perestroika from below, and this approach may well have been encouraged by El'tsin, who was head of the Moscow party organisation at the time. At any rate, two conditions were imposed on the organisers of the conference: that all participants should be oriented towards socialism, and that foreign correspondents should not be told of the conference before it was over.[53]

Some fifty-two groups were represented. Apart from *Obshchina*, the Club for Social Initiatives and the Klub Perestroika, there were the Trust Group and the seminars *Demokratiia i gumanizm* and *Druzhba i dialog*, the Leningrad ecological and cultural groups allied in Epicentre, the hippy association 'the System', some romantic socialist groups like the *Kommunary*, the Che Guevara Brigade and the Farabundo Marti Brigade.[54]

In spite of the diversity of the participants, everyone agreed on certain negative statements: no to violence and the propaganda of violence; no to racial and national discrimination; no to any pretension to a monopoly on the truth.

Everyone also rejected the Russian chauvinism and anti-Semitism of *Pamiat'*. But that was as far as the unanimity went.[55] Hitherto protest had of itself been a sufficient qualification: to declare openly for radical reform of the system had been enough to distinguish the 'goodies' from the 'baddies'. Now the question arose: what kind of reform and with what ultimate aim in view? It turned out that not everyone shared the commitment to some kind of socialism which had animated the conveners of the meeting. The seminar *Demokratiia i gumanizm*, and in particular its most flamboyant member, Valeriia Novodvorskaia, attracted a good deal of criticism, and there was even a proposal (rejected by the majority) that they be excluded from the conference. Their total rejection of the Soviet experience and of any kind of socialism, their call for a return to the principles of the liberal-democratic February revolution, met with a good deal of support from the floor, but not from the organisers. There was talk of the authorities closing the meeting, since anti-socialist ideas were being expressed.[56]

In the end, the participants decided to accept the fact that there was an unbridgeable division of opinion. Nine clubs agreed to ally themselves as the Federation of Socialist Clubs (FSOK), which envisaged a fairly tight organisation making an explicit commitment to socialism, acknowledging the 'constitutional role of the Communist Party', and declaring a readiness to support its 'healthy and progressive elements' in 'the course towards developing socialism and democracy which was proclaimed at the 27th Party Congress'. FSOK reaffirmed the notion of the 'withering away of the state' and added: 'we see the formation of independent social groups and associations, and an increase in their influence, as one way of developing a self-managed society and eliminating administrative and bureaucratic structures.'

The other clubs, who remained outside FSOK, envisaged a looser, more non-committal alliance, for mutual information and support, and were disinclined to compromise with the Communist Party. They called themselves the Social Initiatives Circle (KOI) and claimed their ideal to be 'the renewal of social practice in the spirit of the ideals of socialism, democracy, humanism and progress'.[57] In practice, KOI was so loosely organised that it was stillborn, but FSOK played a leading role in the later move to Popular Fronts, as we shall see below.

One Leningrad delegate exclaimed hopefully, 'This is the start of perestroika's "going to the people".'[58] This was over-optimistic as yet, but it is true that out of the working sections of the 'meeting-dialogue' came discrete initiative groups (some of them started initially by Klub Perestroika) which planted the roots of later single-issue movements. The most important offspring was *Memorial* (see below), but it was not the only one. *Obshchestvennoe samoupravlenie* (Social Self-Government) began to hold seminars to train workers to exercise effectively the new powers envisaged for their representatives in the new enterprise law: their proposed system for electing councils of workers' collectives was tried out at two Moscow factories and three publishing houses.[59] *Sotsial'nyi mir* (Social Peace) began to conduct public workshops on conflict resolution and the maintenance of social peace. *Grazhdanskoe dostoinstvo* (Civic Dignity) was formed to advise and aid people whose legal rights had been violated by the authorities. *Miloserdie* (Charity) undertook to provide counselling and practical help for the old, sick, handicapped, poverty-stricken or lonely.[60]

The most important of the working sections of the 'meeting-dialogue' was *Memorial*, which had its origins in Klub Perestroika. Conference delegates from Klub Perestroika started to collect signatures calling for a thorough examination of the illegal repressions of the past and the erection of a memorial to Stalin's victims. The campaign continued in the streets through the autumn and winter of 1987–8 and attracted sporadic police harassment. Along with Perestroika-88, Democracy and Humanism and the Trust Group, *Memorial* organised a demonstration in memory of Stalin's victims, despite an official ban, on October Square in Moscow on 6 March 1988: many of the participants were detained, but speedily released. By the time Gorbachev lent the idea of a memorial official legitimacy at the 19th Party Conference in June 1988, some 30,000 signatures had been collected.[61]

At this stage the organisers took to the streets again, in provincial towns as well as major cities, this time to find out who the public thought should head an organisation dedicated to erecting a memorial. This was an important new development, for it was the first time for nearly seventy years that the Soviet peoples had been invited to take a genuine vote, even in so rudimentary a form, on personalities or issues. This particular 'election' was of course both eccentric and makeshift, but it did constitute a crude indicator of the moral standing of public figures, at least among the urban population. Significantly, nearly all those who stood highest were either scholars or creative artists. They included Sakharov and Solzhenitsyn, the writers Ales' Adamovich, Vasil' Bykau, Evgenii Evtushenko, Grigorii Baklanov, Lev Razgon, Bulat Okudzhava, Mikhail Shatrov and Anatolii Rybakov, the literary scholars Dmitrii Likhachev and Iurii Kariakin, the actor Mikhail Ul'ianov, the historians Iurii Afanas'ev and Roi Medvedev, the new-style journal editor Vitalii Korotich, and—the only politician—Boris El'tsin. Amongst the organisations which declared themselves sponsors of *Memorial* were a number of creative unions (writers, theatre workers, cinematographers, designers, architects, artists), as well as the weekly journals *Literaturnaia gazeta* and *Ogonek*.[62]

During the signature campaign and the vote for public figures, *Memorial* began to build up an impressive organisation. By January 1989, when its founding congress was held, it had 180 or so branches (103 of which were represented at it), with perhaps 20,000 active members.[63] At this stage the significance of *Memorial* as a formative influence on public attitudes and as a nursery for future political movements can scarcely be overstated. It lent the name of prestigious establishment figures to demands and ideas which until very recently had been officially condemned as subversive and which had brought down persecution on those who professed them. It offered constructive engagement and therefore catharsis for the very powerful feelings of

Russians (mainly, since other peoples had other channels) about the unfinished business of their recent past. Its programme of action embraced a whole variety of concerns, which were well articulated by Iurii Afanas'ev at its founding conference:

The most important task of *Memorial* is to restore to this country its past. But the past is alive in the present. Therefore *Memorial* is a political movement, in so far as today has not yet settled accounts with yesterday.

Our problem is the human being in history. But for us history is not just politics projected into the past, for man's historical habitat is culture. Therefore *Memorial* is also a cultural movement.

By talking about terror and lawlessness, we help to form a notion of legality in the public mind. Therefore *Memorial* is also a movement concerned with the rule of law (*pravovoe dvizhenie*).[64]

Memorial was endeavouring to reconstitute the historical, cultural and legal consciousness of the Soviet peoples, and above all of the Russians. In November 1988 it held a 'week of conscience' in a number of towns. In Moscow a 'wall of memory' was erected, where thousands of photographs of the repressed were exhibited. People came to it to seek out relatives they had lost, and to leave forlorn notes of the kind 'Does anyone know my father?' In front of a huge map of the USSR marked with the 'islands' of the Gulag Archipelago was a convict's wheelbarrow in which visitors could place their donations towards a memorial to the victims.[65]

Memorial thus undertook a very ambitious and all-embracing formative role. In most of the non-Russian republics Popular Fronts had already taken up the challenge (often growing out of movements like *Memorial*, for example, the Ukrainian Culturological Club, *Martirologiia* in Belorussia, and the Heritage Society in Estonia). In Russia, however, no single movement had shown itself equal to the task, for the enemy could not be identified as a simple ethnic target: the oppressors and murderers of Russians had usually been Russians, which much complicated the emotional equation. (Those who persuaded themselves otherwise belonged well outside *Memorial* in the political spectrum, close to the organisation which appropriated to itself an analogous name in Slavonic clothing: *Pamiat'*.) In that sense *Memorial*, at least for a time, came close to fulfilling the role of a Russian Popular Front: it drew prestigious intellectuals and cultural figures for the first time into openly sponsoring and even leading 'informals' and it accustomed broad ranks of the urban population to confrontation with the party-state apparatus over fundamental issues of civic consciousness.

However, although it did play a political role in putting forward and agitating for candidates in the elections of 1989–90, *Memorial* never claimed for itself the status of an oppositional party. Instead, since early 1989, with the growth of electoral alliances and other political movements, it has devoted itself more especially to its historical and juridical functions: investigating the past, assembling archival materials, preparing plans for a memorial complex which will contain libraries, archives and exhibitions. It has also been working to prevent the creation of 'memory holes' in the present, sending observers to tense regions, such as Baku and the Armenian–Azerbaijani border, where human rights violations are occurring today.[66]

The role of actual political opposition, then, has fallen to other movements. By early 1988 the 'new socialists' of FSOK looked like the most energetically purposeful of these. But there was another, forthrightly non-socialist alternative.

Rejecting what they considered FSOK's compromise with the party-state apparatus, *Demokratiia i gumanizm* left the 'meeting-dialogue' of August 1987 determined to proceed instead by confrontation, forming what they styled an 'opposition party'. Their main partners in this enterprise were the Trust Group (E. Debrianskaia), the juridical commission of Perestroika-88 (V. Kuzin, Iu. Skubko) and the Society of Young Marxists (A. Griaznov).[67] What united this assortment of *neformaly* was not any particular political tendency (there were both liberals and socialists among them), but rather the determination not to cooperate with the communist party or to compromise with the existing system.

The founding conference of the Democratic Union was held in May 1988, and was attended by some 150 delegates from fourteen cities. They were harassed by the police, and the dacha where they were intending to hold their final session was raided, so that the organisational and programmatic arrangements were not entirely clear.[68] There were also disagreements among the participants about whether they envisaged an actual party or merely an alliance of informal groups. The statutes finally issued after its second congress in January 1989 described the Democratic Union as being 'a political party in opposition to the totalitarian structure of the USSR, aiming to bring about its non-violent transformation and the construction of a law-governed state on the principles of humanism, democracy and pluralism'. Being a party of 'the transitional period between totalitarianism and democracy and bringing together people of a variety of democratic convictions', it announced that it had a 'fractional structure and is built on the confederative principle'. Among the fractions which could be identified were Social Democratic, Liberal Democratic, Christian Democrat and Euro-Communist.[69]

In practice, though, the Democratic Union usually described itself as a party, even if one drawing on a wide variety of political outlooks: what united them all was forthright opposition to totalitarianism. During the summer and autumn of 1988 it demonstrated this opposition by a number of demonstrations, notably the one on Pushkin Square in Moscow on 21 August, held to commemorate the twentieth anniversary of the invasion of Czechoslovakia. The police broke it up, arresting one hundred or so demonstrators, forty of whom were given short jail sentences. Soldiers beat some of them up in a police station with the apparent connivance of the authorities.[70]

The Democratic Union's strategy was to refuse to be drawn into the soviets or to cooperate with the party-state apparatus, in order to preserve moral and political purity. It adopted instead a course of non-violent civil disobedience and of campaigning in the streets—'political theatre', as Valeriia Novodvorskaia calls it—seeking gradually to build up parallel alternative institutions of a civil society, until it became possible to convene a Constituent Assembly and establish a fully democratic parliamentary system.[71] There was a daunting moral purity about this, but also a certain sterility. The strategy meant boycotting soviet elections, through participation in which other informal groups were able to extend their public appeal and make a real input into the political system. As a result, though the Democratic Union proved a fertile source of ideas, vitality and campaigning devices, it seemed more a fringe group of martyrs than a real opposition, a little like the Old Believers in Tsarist Russia, and it continually lost individuals and groups to other movements.

FSOK and the other wing to emerge from the 'meeting-dialogue' of August 1987 took the opposite course, risking corruption and compromise in the interests of engaging directly with the political system. The dangers of this approach were shown in January 1988, when FSOK tried to work together with the Komsomol in convening another conference of informal groups. This was in line with the current Komsomol strategy of working with informal groups of socialist persuasion in order to gradually assimilate and take them over. The Komsomol attempted to screen those admitted to the conference. FSOK resisted this political pressure, and as a result the meeting degenerated into a parade of mutual accusations, continued in a bitter attack on FSOK in *Komsomol'skaia pravda*.[72]

During the winter of 1987–8, FSOK's strategy took the form of encouraging the activities of the working groups which had come out of the 'meeting-dialogue'. It also sponsored a discussion in March of the new law on voluntary associations being drawn up inside the apparatus, and began the work of preparing an alternative, more liberal draft.[73]

The announcement of the impending 19th Party Conference gave them the opportunity to attempt a direct input to the centre of power. By this time events elsewhere in the Soviet Union had suggested the possibilities of action based on mass support. In Armenia, from February 1988, a so-called Karabakh Committee had proved able to mobilise hundreds of thousands of people to protest over the continued inclusion of Nagornyi Karabakh, an autonomous region inhabited mainly by Armenians, in the Azerbaijani SSR. This Committee was composed largely of writers, journalists and scholars, as well as by officials and state employees acting in a private capacity. It had its branches in enterprises, offices and educational establishments—just like the Communist Party, and in effect in rivalry to it. So great was its influence that in February the Nagornyi Karabakh Regional Soviet requested to join Armenia, while in June the Armenian Supreme Soviet itself voted to incorporate Nagornyi Karabakh in the Armenian SSR, the first time any official Soviet state bodies had openly flouted party discipline.[74]

Similarly, from April 1988, in Estonia and Latvia, the formation of Popular Fronts had begun, bringing together members of the intelligentsia and reformist elements in the party-state apparatus, with a political programme which very soon attracted strong popular support (see below, Chapter 2).

These examples suggested that small coteries of intellectuals, if they could find the appropriate programme, could appeal to and mobilise broad masses of the population. The difficulty was to find the right programme, and here Russians were to experience much greater problems than Armenians and Estonians.

The grievances which sparked the creation of the first Russian Popular Fronts grew out of the elections to the 19th Party Conference. As it became clear that delegates from many cities and regions were being 'elected'— essentially appointed—in the time-honoured nomenklatura manner, public meetings began to be held demanding a more open and democratic procedure. Strictly speaking, this was a matter only for party members: in practice, non-party members took part as well, treating the Communist Party for what it really was, the centre of power, answerable to all citizens.

In Yaroslavi', for example, F. I. Loshchenkov, first secretary of the district party committee, had been chosen as conference delegate without any consultation with ordinary party members. He was unpopular because he had sanctioned the construction of a new chemical works in the town, and an initiative group decided to call a public meeting on the banks of the Volga on 8 June. This meeting attracted some 5,000 people, and even more signatures were gathered for a petition demanding Loshchenkov's recall and the holding of new elections. A week later the party committee replaced Loshchenkov with a more popularly acceptable delegate. Encouraged by this success, the initiative group began to hold regular public meetings to discuss problems, including food supplies, housing and labour conditions, and announced the formation of a Popular Front for the Support of Perestroika to keep up popular pressure on the politicians.[75]

In one or two other provincial towns similar successes were achieved. In Iuzhno-sakhalinsk hundreds of people poured out on to the streets to protest against the unopposed 'election' of the local party first secretary, Petr Tret'iakov, who was notorious for allocating housing to his friends and relatives, and for ensuring a high level of privilege to his officials. The crowds declared no confidence in the party leadership, and elected an alternative committee of eight to negotiate with them and choose more suitable representatives. After what a newspaper described as a 'tumultuous week', they brought about Tret'iakov's resignation. This local coup was explicitly approved by Gorbachev at a news conference. In Astrakhan' another party secretary was replaced in similar fashion. Demonstrations, apparently not marked by such success, were also held in Krasnoiarsk, Kuibyshev, Magadan, Omsk, Odessa and Sverdlovsk.[76]

In Moscow, too, political agitation began to transfer from the club and seminar room to the streets. But the first big demonstrations, on 25 June 1988, were marked by the divisions among the city's informal associations. Not one but two groups gathered at the classical venue, on Pushkin Square. At the centre of one was the Democratic Union, and of the other FSOK and the so-called 'initiative group for the establishment of the Moscow Popular Front'. They both soon attracted quite large crowds. The police, unaccustomed to dealing with unauthorised public gatherings of any kind, eventually moved in on the Democratic Union as the more odious of the two, and hustled its speakers away to their special buses, while onlookers booed them: 'We just wanted to hear what they have to say!' The Popular Front demonstration was then 'moved on', and escorted down Tverskoi Boulevard out of the police precinct.[77]

FSOK conceived the Popular Fronts as 'organisations which, unlike the Democratic Union, would not proclaim themselves an "opposition party"', but would nevertheless 'be capable of putting forward their own candidates at elections, of formulating alternative political and socio-economic proposals and of coordinating the activity of independent initiative groups in the localities'.[78]

Inside FSOK, however, two principal tendencies had by this time crystallised. One was *Obshchina*, with its anarcho-syndicalist outlook. The other was the 'Socialist Initiative' group (originally formed inside the Club for Social Initiatives), led by Boris Kagarlitskii and Mikhail Maliutin, which, while also favouring a renewal of self-governing workers' councils in the economy, tended more towards parliamentarism in its political programme than *Obshchina*, being prepared to draw on the Eurocommunist and even the Scandinavian Social Democratic traditions.[79] In temperament, too, there was a marked distinction between the two groups, *Obshchina* being romantic, rebellious, with something of the 'eternal opposition' about it, while 'Socialist Initiative' was hard-headed, calculating and concerned with power.[80] Personal clashes almost certainly widened the (at this stage rather insignificant) ideological divergences.

Working relationships between the two wings survived long enough to organise a petition campaign for more democratic elections, and to hold two public meetings, on 5 and 12 June 1988, to draw up a 'Public Mandate (*Obshchestvennyi nakaz*) to the 19th Party Conference'. This was far more radical than any document being placed before the party conference. It accused the conference of choosing its delegates by the traditional method, the 'self-cooptation of apparatchiks', and proposed instead democratic elections on the basis of platforms. The 'mandate' urged a radical reform of the entire political system, which would involve the removal of the Communist Party from all governmental functions and the genuine transfer of power to the soviets; the right of independent political associations to nominate candidates for public office and to have access to the media to propagate their political programmes; the introduction of workers' control in economic enterprises through democratically elected councils; freedom of the press and of associations and meetings; the foundation of a law-based state guaranteed by an independent Constitutional Court; humanisation of the criminal code and an end to the internal passport system; political and economic autonomy for the republics.[81]

Thereafter, in the Popular Front organising committee the familiar split re-emerged between those who wanted an explicit commitment to socialism, and those who simply envisaged a 'union of all democrats irrespective of ideological differences'. In this latter persuasion *Memorial*, *Grazhdanskoe dostoinstvo* and Perestroika-88 were joined by *Obshchina*, whether out of undoctrinaire democratic broad-mindedness, distaste for disciplined structures or from a desire to bid for the leadership of the Popular Front is not clear.[82] All three groups quit the organising committee, and in August *Obshchina* set up its own Alliance of Federalist-Socialists as an alternative to FSOK: this later on became the kernel of the Confederation of Anarcho-Syndicalists.[83]

Nevertheless, on 29 July 1988, twenty-five informal groups met in the information centre of Bauman raion, announced the foundation of the Moscow Popular Front and elected an 'information and coordination committee' to 'extend the maximum practical, informational, theoretical and coordinating assistance to activists of perestroika and participants in the spontaneous democratic movement in other regions of the country, and to support the creation of an All-Union Popular Front'.[84] Two days later, at a mass meeting which gathered about 1,000 people at the Olympic sports complex, the new Front proclaimed the need to ensure that the radical political reform foreshadowed at the 19th Party Conference was transformed into a reality by mass action from below. They welcomed the conference's call for a 'broad patriotic movement in support of perestroika', and claimed that the Popular Front, 'standing for the revolutionary renewal of socialism', should assume this role.[85]

It proved impossible, however, to set up an all-Union Popular Front. A conference was held in Leningrad in August to attempt to achieve it, but was unable to reach agreement on basic organisational principles. The Moscow Popular Front pressed for a tight organisational structure and a programmatic commitment to socialism. Most of the Leningrad groups (not yet reconstituted as a Popular Front), the Moscow dissenters and many of the provincial groups warned of the dangers of centralisation and bureaucratism, and rejected 'socialism' as an ideal, preferring to talk of 'general democratic principles'.[86] The organisation of the conference was confused, and in the end there was disagreement even about what had been agreed. As Kagarlitskii puts it:

The Leningrad conference had paradoxically repeated the situation at the Second Congress of the Russian Social Democratic and Labour Party (RSDLP)—the departure of a section of the delegates, the division into majority and minority, the dispute over who was the real victor . . . The difference was that this time the movement had no well-organised nucleus or unified press, such as *Iskra*, founded in exile, was in 1903, nor did it have a generally recognised ideological leader like Plekhanov.[87]

In the absence of a unifying ethnic motif, it proved impossible for Russians to create a single nation-wide movement. The Popular Fronts remained confined for the moment to a few organisations scattered here and there in Russian cities. The authorities' attitude towards even these fragmentary groups was ambivalent. On the one hand, the party leadership welcomed support for perestroika; on the other, they were anxious to prevent such support from bursting out in wild and unpredictable directions. In Moscow and some other cities the local soviets began from the summer of 1987 to place restrictions on public demonstrations, but did not always insist on them, lending an air of unpredictability to such occasions.[88] Finally on 28 July, the Presidium of the USSR Supreme Soviet issued a decree laying down a strict procedure to be followed for all public meetings and demonstrations: organisers must apply for permission to hold them at least ten days in advance, specifying precisely the aim, type and place and the number of those expected to take part. An event could be banned if it contravened the constitution (which appeared to exclude occasions organised by non-socialist associations) or if it threatened public order.[89]

The real importance of the embryonic Popular Fronts was that they showed that mobilising the public of large cities against the unreformed party-state apparatus was not hopeless (though it required, at least initially, the tolerance of part of that apparatus), and thereby shattered a taboo which had paralysed Soviet political life for nearly seventy years. The way was open for the electoral blocs of 1989–90 to initiate a process of real and fundamental political change.

However, the mould chosen by FSOK, and especially by *Sotsialisticheskaia initsiativa*, as the most energetic and best organised proponents of the Popular Front idea, was too narrow. 'Socialism' was not a word designed to appeal to most urban voters; at the very least it was divisive. All that most voters wanted was opposition to domination by a self-perpetuating nomenklatura élite: to seek agreement on anything more was to invite conflict. It was on that minimal basis that the following year the more successful Associations of Voters were set up. For the moment the exclusive loyalties and doctrinaire proclivities of *kruzhkovshchina* limited the success of the new movements.

Nevertheless, by the autumn of 1988 it had been shown that mass mobilisation against the party-state apparatus had a chance of success, and some of the country's leading intellectuals had been drawn into the struggle. For all their failings, the *neformaly* had that achievement to their credit.

Notes

1. Vaclav Havel, *The Power of the Powerless: Citizens Against the State in Central-Eastern Europe*, London, Hutchinson, 1985, pp. 27–8.
2. Vladimir Bukovskii, *To Build a Castle: My Life as a Dissenter*, London, André Deutsch, 1978, pp. 191–2.
3. Lyudmila Alexeyeva, *Soviet Dissent: Contemporary Movements for National, Religious and Human Rights*, Middletown, Connecticut, Wesleyan University Press, 1987, pp. 31–9, 274–82.
4. Mark Hopkins, *Russia's Underground Press: The Chronicle of Current Events*, New York, Praeger, 1983.

5. *Glasnost'*, nos. 2–4, June 1987, published as a supplement to *Russkaia mysl'*, 11 September 1987, p. 3.
6. Bohdan Nahaylo, 'Informal Ukrainian Culturological Club helps to break new ground for glasnost', *Radio Liberty Research Report*, 57/88, 8 February 1988; interview with Viacheslav Chornovil and Oles' Shevchenko, 25 April 1988.
7. *Materialy samizdata*, vypusk 13/88, 25 March 1988, AS 6172, pp. 5–10.
8. Alexeyeva, *Soviet Dissent*, Chapter 7.
9. *Vesti iz SSSR*, No. 14, item 4 (henceforth 14–4 etc.), 15/16–4, 1987; Edward J. Lazzerini, 'Crimean Tatars', in Graham Smith (ed.), *The Nationalities Question in the Soviet Union*, London, Longman, 1990, pp. 332–7.
10. Alexeyeva, *Soviet Dissent*, Chapter 10.
11. They were held weekly outside the Lenin Library in Moscow in the early months of 1988. I witnessed one myself on 21 April: the participants were peacefully marched off to waiting police buses and driven away.
12. Yoram Gorlizki, 'Jews', in Smith, *Nationalities*, pp. 339–59.
13. *Vesti iz SSSR*, 8–31, 1987.
14. L. Hirszowicz, 'Breaking the mould: the changing face of Jewish culture under Gorbachev', *Soviet Jewish Affairs*, vol. 18, no. 3, winter 1988, pp. 25–45; the associations which existed by the time of the first congress are listed in ibid, vol. 19, no. 2, summer/autumn 1989, pp. 51–3.
15. *Glasnost'*, nos. 2–4, June 1987, in *Russkaia mysl'*, 11 September 1987, p. 3; *Vesti iz SSSR*, 13–3, 1987.
16. *Vesti iz SSSR*, 23–3, 1987; *Ekspress-khronika*, no. 19, 13 December 1987, pp. 3–4, no. 20, 20 December 1987, p. 1.
17. Alexeyeva, *Soviet Dissent*, pp. 348–9.
18. Interview with Aleksandr Podrabinek, 18 April 1988; *Ekspress-khronika*, no. 15, 15 November 1987, p. 5, no. 14, 3 April 1988, p. 2.
19. Alexeyeva, *Soviet Dissent*, pp. 373–4; interview with Sergei Grigor'iants, 23 May 1991.
20. Interview with Sergei Grigor'iants, 23 May 1991; *Ekspress-khronika*, no. 20, 15 May 1988, p. 6.
21. For a sample of the journal, see issue no. 12 in *Materialy samizdata*, vypusk 37/88, 29 July 1988, AS 6262.
22. V. N. Shkurin, *Neformal'nye molodezhnye ob"edineniia*, Moscow, Ministerstvo kul'tury, 1990, p. 56.
23. ibid.
24. I. Iu. Sundiev, 'Neformal'nye molodezhnye ob"edineniia: opyt ekspozitsii', *Sotsiologicheskie issledovaniia*, No. 5, 1987, pp. 58–9.
25. I. Iu. Sundiev, 'Samodeiatel'nye ob"edineniia molodezhi', *Sotsiologicheskie issledovaniia*, No. 2, 1989, pp. 56–62; Jane Ellis, 'USSR: the Christian seminar', *Religion in Communist Lands*, no. 8, 1980, pp. 92ff.
26. Shkurin, *Neformal'nye*, pp. 66–7.
27. Sundiev, *Sotsiologicheskie issledovaniia*, No. 5, 1987, pp. 59–60.
28. 'Ideologiia sovetskikh khippi', *Strana i mir*, No. 6, 1987, p. 140; Shkurin, *Neformal'nye*, op. cit., pp. 98–100; *Neformaly: Civil Society in the USSR*, Helsinki Watch Report, February 1990, pp. 128–9.
29. 'Ideologiia sovetskikh khippi', pp. 140–3.
30. ibid., pp. 140–1.
31. Sundiev, *Sotsiologicheskie issledovaniia*, No. 5, 1987, p. 61.

32. S. N. Iushenkov (ed.), *Neformaly: sotsial'nye initsiativy*, Moscow, Moskovskii rabochii, 1990, p. 22; Boris Kagarlitsky, *The Thinking Reed: Intellectuals and the Soviet State from 1917 to the Present*, London, Verso, 1988, p. 334.
33. Alan Bookbinder *et al.*, *Comrades*, London, BBC Publications, 1985, pp. 159–60.
34. Iushenkov, *Neformaly*, pp. 22–3; V. N. Berezovskii and N. I. Krotov (eds), *Neformal'naia Rossiia*, Moscow, Molodaia Gvardiia, 1990, p. 370.
35. A. Ezhelyov, 'V odnoi lodke', *Izvestiia*, 1 August 1987; M. Nazarov, 'Na nicheinoi zemle perestroiki', *Russkaia mysl'*, 18 September 1987, p.5; *Vesti iz SSSR*, 10–13, 13–27 (1987).
36. Julia Wishnevsky, 'The origins of Pamyat', *Survey*, vol. 30, no. 3, October 1988, pp. 79–91.
37. N. R. Miuzneks, 'The Daugavpils hydro-station and glasnost in Latvia', *Journal of Baltic Studies*, vol. 18, no. 1, spring 1987, pp. 63–70.
38. *Vesti iz SSSR*, 19/20–5, 1987; *Ekspress-khronika*, no. 12, 25 October 1987, p. 1.
39. Zh. Mindubaev, 'Gorod pered litsom problemy', *Literaturnaia gazeta*, 9 December 1987, p. 10; Iu. Sivakov, 'Za chertoi miloserdiia', *Pravda*, 26 January 1988, p. 3.
40. *Amnesty*, no. 7, February/March 1984, p. 18; Ludmila Alekseeva, 'Obshchestvennye ob"edineniia v SSSR', *SSSR: vnutrennie protivorechiia*, no. 21, 1988, pp. 74–5.
41. From an early stage they were associated with the post-hippy group *Svobodnaia initsiativa*. See *Vesti iz SSSR*, 22/23–3 (1987).
42. Olga Medvedkov, 'The Moscow Trust Group: an uncontrolled grassroots movement in the Soviet Union', *Mershon Centre Quarterly Report* (Ohio State University), vol. 12, no. 4, spring 1988.
43. *Vesti iz SSSR*, 7–27 (1987).
44. ibid.; interview with Eduard Molchanov, editor of *Svobodnoe slovo*, 11 June 1991.
45. *Vesti iz SSSR*, 11/12–15; 17/18–42; 19/20–42, 1987.
46. *Glasnost'*, no. 1, in *Russkaia mysl'*, 17 July 1987, p. 6; *Materialy samizdata*, AS 6015, pp. 39–45; V. Kardanovskii, 'Klub Perestroika: opyt pervykh mesiatsev raboty', *Otkrytaia zona*, vypusk 2, November 1987, pp. 4–10.
47. Liudmila Alekseeva, 'Novye partii v SSSR?', *SSSR: vnutrennie protivorechiia*, no. 20, 1987, pp. 35–44.
48. *Glasnost'*, op. cit.; P. Kudiukin, 'Uroki odnogo krizisa', *Otkrytaia zona*, vypusk 3, January 1988, pp. 77–84; Igor' Chubais, 'The democratic opposition: an insider's view', *Report on the USSR*, 3 May 1991, pp. 4–6. The Klub Perestroika contained many individuals who were later prominent in independent political movements and/or journals. They included Oleg Rumiantsev, Pavel Kudiukin and Leonid Volkov of the Social Democratic Party; Viktor Zolotarev of the Constitutional Democratic Party; Viktor Kuzin of the Democratic Union; Andrei Fadin, political commentator of *Kommersant*; Igor' Chubais of the Democratic Platform; Viacheslav Igrunov of the Moscow Bureau of Information Exchange; Iurii Samodurov of *Memorial*; and Sergei Stankevich, deputy mayor of Moscow.
49. Interviews with Grigorii Pel'man, 18 April and 5 May 1988; Nick Lampert, 'Russia's new democrats: the club movement and perestroika', *Detente*, nos. 9–10, 1987, p. 10.
50. Grigorii Pel'man, 'Neformal'nye kluby Moskvy', *Forum*, no. 20, 1989, pp. 108–10; Viacheslav Igrunov, 'O neformal'nykh politicheskikh klubakh Moskvy', *Problemy vostochnoi Evropy*, nos. 27–8, 1989, p. 63; V. N. Shkurin, *Neformal'nye*, pp. 199–20.

51. Berezovskii and Krotov (eds), *Neformal' naia Rossiia*, p. 260; A. Shubin, 'Politika i pedagogika: ot "obshchiny" k konfederatsii anarkho-sindikalistov', in Iushenkov, *Neformaly*, op. cit., pp. 101–6; interview with Andrei Isaev, 20 September 1990.
52. Berezovskii and Krotov (eds), *Neformal' naia Rossiia*, pp. 239–41; Igrunov, 'O neformal' nykh', op. cit., pp. 69–71; I. Sundiev, 'Nashestvie marsiian', in Iushenkov, *Neformaly*, op. cit., p. 19.
53. Alekseeva, 'Novye partii', p. 52.
54. ibid., pp. 45–6.
55. V. Iakovlev, 'Proschanie s Bazarovym', *Ogonek*, no. 36, 1987, p. 4.
56. Alekseeva, 'Novye partii', p. 56.
57. *Guardian*, 12 September 1987; Iakovlev, 'Proshchanie', p. 5; Pel'man, 'Neformal'nye', pp. 110–12; 'Dokumenty pervoi informatsionnoi vstrechi-dialoga', *Otkrytaia zona*, vypusk 1, October 1987, pp. 2–19.
58. Gleb Pavlovskii, 'Khoziaeva vozvrashchaiutsia', *Kul' turno-prosvetitel' naia rabota*, 11/87, p. 22.
59. *Nyeformaly: Civil Society in the USSR*, Helsinki Watch Report, February 1990, op. cit., p. 60.
60. Pel'man, 'Neformal'nye', pp. 111–12; Iakovlev, 'Proshchanie', p. 5; *Nyeformaly*, Helsinki Watch Report, op. cit., p. 25; *Materialy samizdata*, vypusk 9/88, 22 February 1988, AS 6154.
61. Berezovskii and Krotov (eds), *Neformal' naia Rossiia*, pp. 282–5; *Vesti iz SSSR*, 21–38 (1987); 5/6–4 (1988); interview with Arsenii Roginskii, 16 April 1991.
62. Berezovskii and Krotov (eds), *Neformal' naia Rossiia*, p. 283; Julia Wishnevsky, 'Conflict between state and *Memorial* society', *Report on the USSR*, 20 January 1989, pp. 8–9.
63. Interview with Arsenii Roginskii, 16 April 1991.
64. A. V. Gromov and O. S. Kuzin, *Neformaly: kto est' kto?* Moscow, Mysl', 1990, p. 107.
65. Soviet television report of 27 November 1988, in *Summary of World Broadcasts*, SU/0331, 10 December 1988, B/5; *Guardian*, 22 November 1988; *Moskovskie novosti*, no. 48, 1988, pp. 8–9.
66. Interviews with Dmitrii Leonov, 16 September 1990, and Arsenii Roginskii, 16 April 1991.
67. Berezovskii & Krotov (eds), *Neformal' naia Rossiia*, p. 250.
68. It belonged to Sergei Grigor'iants: see above, p. 7.
69. *Guardian*, 9 May 1988; *Partiia demokraticheskogo soiuza: vtoroi s" ezd: dokumenty*, Riga-Moscow, 1989, p. 6; Jonathan Aves, 'The Democratic Union: a Soviet opposition party?', *Slovo*, vol. 1, no. 2, November 1988, pp. 93–4.
70. Aves, 'Democratic Union', p. 94.
71. Interview with Eduard Molchanov, 11 June 1991.
72. V. Gubenko and N. Pisarev, 'Samozvantsy i "samodel'shchiki"', *Komsomol'skaia pravda*, 31 January 1988; V. Gurbolikov, 'Itogi ianvarskoi vstrechi', *Obshchina*, no. 4, 1988, pp. 2–5.
73. *Nyeformaly*, Helsinki Watch Report, pp. 60–1.
74. *Survey of World Broadcasts*, SU/0210, 22 July 1988, B/16–17; Angus Roxburgh, *The Second Russian Revolution: The Struggle for Power in the Kremlin*, London, BBC Books, 1991, pp. 81–2, 108.
75. *Ogonek*, no. 34, 20 August 1988, pp. 25–7; Berezovskii and Krotov (eds), *Neformal' naia Rossiia*, pp. 223–4.
76. Roxburgh, *Second Russian Revolution*, pp. 92–3; Boris Kagarlitsky, *Farewell*

Perestroika: A Soviet Chronicle, London, Verso, 1990. pp. 8–9; *Vesti iz SSSR*, 10–22, 10–23, 10–29, 11–27, 12–17, 12–20, 12–32, 12–38, 1988.

77. Roxburgh, *Second Russian Revolution*, pp. 93–5; Kagarlitsky, *Farewell*, op. cit., pp. 12–18.

78. Kagarlitsky, *Farewell*, p. 7.

79. Boris Kagarlitsky, *The Dialectic of Change*, London, Verso, 1990, pp. 327–33.

80. I formed this impression in two interviews, with Boris Kagarlitsky on 15 April 1988, and with Andrei Isaev on 20 September 1990.

81. *Vesti iz SSSR*, 11–16, 1988; interview with Boris Kagarlitskii in *Labour Focus on Eastern Europe*, vol. 10, no. 3, January 1989, p. 4; *Otkrytaia zona*, vypusk 7, August 1988, pp. 67–72.

82. Kagarlitskii naturally suspects the latter: *Farewell*, pp. 9–10.

83. Berezovskii and Krotov (eds), *Neformal'naia Rossiia*, p. 261; E. Dergunov, 'Moskovskii narodnyi front', *Otkrytaia zona*, vypusk 7, August 1988, pp. 84–5.

84. 'Rezoliutsiia soveshchaniia samodeiatel'nykh ob"edinenii Moskvy – uchastnikov dvizheniia Narodnogo Fronta', *Otkrytaia zona*, vypusk 7, August 1988, p. 88.

85. 'Rezoliutsiia mitinga Moskovskogo Narodnogo Fronta', *Otkrytaia zona*, vypusk 7, August 1988, p. 89.

86. Kagarlitsky, *Farewell*, pp. 31–2.

87. Kagarlitsky, *Farewell*, p. 34.

88. *Vesti iz SSSR*, 15/16–20, 1987.

89. *Vesti iz SSSR*, 14–16, 1988.

2 The evolution of independent political movements after 1988

Jonathan Aves

This chapter identifies some of the broad chronological and organisational patterns that emerged in the development of independent political organisations after the summer of 1988. This period saw the vindication of the Popular Front strategy over that of the radical anti-communist groups in the republican elections of early 1990. In the second half of 1989 and the first half of 1990 the new political movements were on the crest of a wave as hundreds of thousands of people flocked to the banners of the popular fronts and even where they did not gain direct access to the levers of power they, nonetheless, forced important figures in the Communist Party to respond to their agenda of radical democratisation and republican sovereignty and independence. After the republican elections the independent political movements entered on a much more difficult period as they sought to come to terms with their success and find new organisational forms to consolidate their popular support. This led to a proliferation of political parties few of which had any significant popular support or a distinctive programme. Most of the material covered in this chapter is taken from the republics not dealt with in separate chapters and those chapters should be consulted for detailed accounts of the development of independent political organisations in the Russian Federation, Estonia and Georgia.

In the summer of 1988 independent political groups began to develop new forms of organisation and activity that greatly increased their impact on the Soviet public. Firstly, the success of the single-issue campaigns and the growing public interest in politics persuaded many leading political, academic and cultural figures to start taking a more active role in shaping the new political agenda. From this alliance of figures already prominent under the Soviet regime and new, young activists who had begun their careers in the political clubs and some ex-dissident figures arose that new form of political organisation characteristic to the perestroika period, the Popular Front.

Secondly, some of the activists from the single-issue campaigns, the new political clubs and particularly from the revived human rights groups set up radical political parties which rejected all forms of compromise with Soviet institutions and put forward maximalist programmes (in the case of the non-Russian republics, independence from the Soviet Union) which amounted to a dismantling of the Soviet system. Activists who had suffered repression for their political activity in the pre-perestroika period were much more prominent in the radical organisations than in the popular fronts. These radical organisations, in most cases, faded fairly quickly from political prominence. They could not compete with the Popular Fronts in terms of access to decision-makers in the Communist Party structures and the media and in terms of their political and organisational experience, but they did play a crucial role in setting the political agenda.

One of the first of the radical political parties to appear was the Armenian Movement for National Self-Determination (AMNSD) which was formed in the autumn of 1987 with Paruir Hairikian as its leader, along with other ex-dissidents such as Mekhak Gabrielian and Movses Gorgisian.[1] In September Hairikian organised a demonstration to protest against pollution in Yerevan. A month later the first demonstrations took place in Yerevan on the Nagornyi Karabakh issue.[2] Hairikian was arrested in March 1988, after the campaign for unification with Nagornyi Karabakh began to threaten the Communist Party's grip on power, and was expelled from the Soviet Union in July. He was allowed to return to Armenia in 1990. The AMNSD was estimated to have only 500 members in the summer of 1990 but it was able to make a considerable public impact with its unambiguous calls for Armenian independence.[3] It stood out from other Armenian political groups in declaring that independence was the necessary precondition for securing the return of Nagornyi Karabakh. At this stage all the other main Armenian political organisations hoped that Moscow would take their side in the dispute with Azerbaijan. Similar radical parties were formed in Georgia, the Georgian National Independence Party and the Georgian National Democratic Party, at the end of 1988. These parties soon came to play a much greater role in the life of that republic than the AMNSD played in Armenia.

In the spring and summer of 1988 radical political parties were established in the Russian Federation and Lithuania. The Democratic Union, 'a political organisation of opposition to totalitarianism' formed in May 1988 by activists from the Democracy and Humanism Seminar in Moscow and from other clubs in the Russian Federation, went on to receive a high level of publicity in the official media.[4] The Lithuanian Liberty League, which had originally been founded in 1978 to work for independence and was re-formed in the spring of 1988, was another organisation frequently highlighted in the media. Its representatives gave a cautious welcome to Sajudis publicly but, in practice, disdained any compromise with Soviet structures. In February 1989 its leader Antanas Terleckas told a British correspondent that the elections to the Congress of People's Deputies were 'a joke, we're an occupied country'.[5] In many cases these radical parties played an important unintentional role that was almost more important than their intended role in encouraging the development of more moderate groups, as their activities were highlighted in the 'conservative' press as a warning of the dangers of democratisation. For their part reformist commentators in the official media also played up their importance in order to force the authorities to make concessions.

The national independence parties in Estonia and Latvia arose out of the Group to Publish the Molotov-Ribbentrop Pact and Helsinki-86 respectively.

By openly insisting on independence and the need to reduce the size of the Russian-speaking population in Estonia and Latvia, both these parties constituted persistent rivals to the more moderate Popular Fronts. The Estonian National Independence Party was founded at the beginning of 1988. In the summer an analogous organisation, the Latvian Movement for National Independence, first declared its existence in the neighbouring republic. It first made the headlines with a demonstration in August to mark the anniversary of the Molotov-Ribbentrop Pact. It went on to hold its founding congress in February 1989 and by mid-1990 it claimed to have at least 8,000 members. It called for the voluntary emigration of a large part of the Russian-speaking population.

Despite its radical stance on ethnic issues and on cooperation with the communist authorities the Latvian Movement for National Independence (LMNI) worked quite closely with the Popular Front and had an overlapping membership. In contrast to the Popular Front, however, almost all its members were ethnic Latvians and practically none of them were members of the Communist Party. Its leader was Eduards Berklavs who had been a leading member of the Latvian Communist Party until he was purged in 1959 for 'bourgeois nationalism'. He was expelled from the Party in 1968. Soon after its founding congress, in March 1989, the Latvian Supreme Soviet declared the LMNI an 'anti-constitutional organisation'. But only two months later, the proceedings of its second congress were broadcast on Latvian radio.[6] The national independence parties, together with activists from the single-issue campaigns and, in particular, the re-formed Helsinki groups (which themselves had helped give birth to the national independence parties) were important for the role that they played in the congress movements which began to gain momentum in the summer of 1989.

As organisations these radical parties tended to be small and closely knit, better able to mount attention-grabbing stunts than to put forward coherent programmes of reform. As the policy of democratisation widened the possibilities for genuine participation in political decision-making their limitations became more glaring. Moreover, they drew their activists chiefly from the ranks of ex-dissidents and people who had 'dropped out' of Soviet society. Their uncompromising stance towards the Soviet regime reflected this and while their radicalism did attract some young people into their ranks they frightened off many more people who discreetly supported their aims.

From the summer of 1988 Popular Fronts began to appear in the Baltic republics and the model then spread to the remaining Soviet republics till they became almost ubiquitous. The Popular Fronts were based on a compromise. Few people were in any real doubt that their true aims included the breaking of the political monopoly of the CPSU and, in the non-Russian republics, the attainment of much greater autonomy and even independence. For this reason they were able to build up mass support amongst the population as organisations that were genuinely responsive to nationalist aspirations. At the same time the

Popular Fronts made a number of formal compromises that meant that they enjoyed a high degree of toleration from the authorities. Initially they all declared that they were 'in support of perestroika', they recognised 'the leading role of the Communist Party', and they avoided open demands for independence.

Whilst these compromises often led to a degree of scepticism amongst the population about the motives of Popular Front leaders, it also meant that they were able to attract into their ranks many leading figures from the political, cultural and academic life of their respective republics without them compromising their Communist Party membership. The Popular Fronts were able to secure registration with the authorities, hold mass rallies, which ordinary citizens could attend without fear of arrest, publish newspapers and gain a high degree of publicity in the official media. These factors gave the Popular Fronts a decisive advantage over their rivals in the radical political parties. Furthermore, the figures from the media, academic and cultural worlds, particularly the republican writers' unions and republican academies of sciences, who flocked to the ranks of the Popular Fronts had unrivalled access to all sorts of informal networks of contacts within the political leaderships of the republics, experience of administration and organisational work in the Communist Party, Komsomol and so on, and, in the case of writers in particular, an easy familiarity with the rhetoric of nationalism.

The Popular Fronts usually adopted a decentralised form of organisation without a central membership.[7] Primary organisations were formed both in geographical localities and frequently in places of work. The latter were useful for fund-raising; works collectives often voted large donations from their enter-prise's or institute's budget.[8] There were both collective (i.e. clubs, movements and societies) and individual members. Consistent with their declared support for perestroika, the Popular Fronts frequently adopted the tactic of using official campaigns, such as that against Stalinism, as a basis on which to make much broader demands for observance of civil rights and economic reform, especially republic economic sovereignty. In this way the Popular Fronts soon developed into genuinely mass organisations with hundreds of thousands of active sup-porters.

The first of the Baltic Popular Fronts to hold its founding congress was the Estonian but the other two republics were not far behind. From early summer of 1988 various appeals were issued in Latvia calling for the establishment of a Popular Front. They came from leading figures in the official cultural and media organisations and also from ex-dissident nationalists in the Helsinki-86 group. The founding congress of the Latvian Popular Front was held at the beginning of October and a ruling council of thirty members was elected, headed by a young journalist Dainis Ivans who had first made his name in the campaign against the Daugava dam project. Amongst the delegates at the congress were both signifi-cant numbers of Communist Party members and members of the LMNI. Considering the demographic situation in the republic, where ethnic Latvians made up barely 50 per cent of the population by the end of the 1980s, it is not surprising that the programme agreed at the Congress contained strong demands on the national question. It demanded that legislation should be enacted to guarantee for Latvians 'a constant and irreducible majority of places' in the republic's councils; it called for Latvian to be made the state language and for curbs on the immigration of Russians.[9]

On the whole, however, the tone of the programme agreed at the founding congress was conciliatory, referring to the decisions of the 19th Party Conference, 'socialist pluralism' and 'the Leninist principles of socialism' in its preamble and general principles. The congress heard demands for independence and official recognition that Latvia was incorporated into the Soviet Union 'by means of force and without the Latvian people expressing their opinion' but settled for a plan to secure the republic greater autonomy, with economic independence on the line of the IME plan drawn up in Estonia in 1987.[10] The leadership of the Popular Front was largely dominated by moderates who had good links with reformist elements in the Communist Party but it continually had to manoeuvre so as not to lose the initiative to the radicals in the LMNI. Thus as early as May 1989 the board of the Popular Front stated its readiness to consider openly declaring that its goal was full independence for Latvia.[11] Like other Popular Fronts the Latvian Popular Front took advantage of its relationship with the authorities to put out substantial, professionally produced newspapers. The main newspaper of the Latvian Popular Front, *Atmoda*, which was published in both Latvian and Russian, had a print run of 30,000 by May 1989 and had become a well-known newspaper far beyond the boundaries of Latvia.[12]

In May 1988 an initiative group for the Lithuanian Popular Front, widely known simply as Sajudis (Movement), with thirty-six members was set up. Amongst its leading figures were Romualdas Ozolas, Vytautas Landsbergis, a musicologist, and Zigmas Vaisvila, a leading figure in the republic's new Green movement. Over the summer a network of organisations was established all over the republic. It held a mass meeting of 100,000 people to send off the Lithuanian delegates to the 19th Party Conference in July. The movement's founding congress took place in Vilnius in mid-October 1988. At the congress there were a number of calls for Sajudis to declare that it was openly in favour of independence. Rolandas Paulaskas from Kaunas argued that if the article stating that Lithuania was part of the Soviet Union remained in the programme then this would imply recognition of the legality of the occupation of 1940.[13] This was exactly the argumentation used by the radicals who joined the National Independence parties in Latvia, Georgia and Estonia against the whole Popular Front strategy but in Lithuania the radicals almost all stayed under the organisational umbrella of the Popular Front. Nonetheless it took an appeal both by Cardinal Sladkevicius and Algirdas Brazauskas, who had been appointed first secretary of the Lithuanian Communist Party only a few days previously, to persuade the congress to stay within the bounds of what was acceptable. Brazausakas told the congress that 'We must learn to wait.'[14] The delegates elected Landsbergis as chair and a literary translator Virgilijus Čepaitis as 'responsible secretary' of the Popular Front. By 1989 Sajudis had full-time paid officials in every electoral district in the republic and in 1991 its central offices employed fifteen full-time officials. It was supported by Lithuanian emigrés organisations.[15]

As in Latvia and Estonia, the differences between those members of Sajudis who believed that the organisation should make an immediate open declaration that it aimed at independence and those who believed in a more step-by-step approach was reflected in the make-up of the movement's ruling body. The radicals, such as Vytautas Landsbergis, generally came from Kaunas, the old capital, where the political atmosphere had been more relaxed and nationalist sentiment was more openly expressed, and the moderates, such as Kazimiera Prunskiene, tended to come from Vilnius and have good links with reformist elements in the Communist Party. Unlike in Latvia and Estonia, however, the political line of Sajudis was generally determined by radicals in the leadership. The strength of the radicals within Sajudis undermined the potential constituency of groups like the Liberty League and made the idea of a citizens' congress redundant in Lithuania.

At the end of October 1988 the 'public discussion' of amendments to the Soviet Constitution began. Amongst the proposed changes was the removal of the formal right of republics to secede from the Union. This and other changes provoked a fierce response from the Baltic republics and Georgia. On 8 November representatives from all three Baltic popular fronts met and decided to organize a petition against the amendments and soon hundreds of thousands of signatures had been collected. Even the dispatch of Politburo members from Moscow to the Baltic could not stem the popular mood and the proposed changes were eventually considerably watered down by the Supreme Soviet in Moscow giving the Popular Fronts their first major victory. In the meantime the nationalist movements had gained new momentum. On 11 November, independence day, the hitherto banned Latvian national flag was raised on Riga castle.[16] On 18 November Lithuania followed suit and hoisted its flag over the republican Supreme Soviet, although an attempt to follow the Estonian example and declare sovereignty was rejected by Brazauskas.[17]

The elections to the Congress of People's Deputies in Moscow on 26 March 1989 demonstrated the power of the Baltic Popular Fronts. The 'pre-election meetings', which effectively prevented the registration of independent candidates in most parts of the Soviet Union, were practically ignored in the Baltic republics. In Latvia the Popular Front did not put up its own candidates but gave its endorsement to candidates of whom it approved. Ivans was elected and the great majority of successful candidates had received the endorsement of the Popular Front. A leading figure in the Latvian Movement for National Independence was only narrowly beaten by the republican first secretary and the communist prime minister was defeated by a Popular Front member.[18] The results in Lithuania were even more spectacular because Sajudis had been able to register with the authorities. It was able to put up its own candidates, including twenty-five members of its thirty-five-member ruling council. Sajudis candidates won in thirty-one out of the thirty-nine electoral districts and

Brazauskas and his deputy only secured election because Sajudis withdrew its candidates in their constituencies. Calls to boycott the voting by the Lithuanian Liberty League, the Democratic Party, the Helsinki Group and the Lithuanian Christian Democratic Party failed to affect the result.[19] In December 1989 a Baltic Parliamentary Group was formed in the Congress of People's Deputies in Moscow with nearly half of the deputies from Estonia and Latvia and nearly three-quarters of those from Lithuania.[20]

As a result of the overwhelming public support for the nationalist movements, the political atmosphere in the three Baltic republics changed dramatically in 1989. In particular the media began to publish large amounts of material about the inter-war independent republics in a re-discovery of history which fatally undermined any legitimacy that Soviet rule retained. Lithuania and Latvia followed Estonia and declared sovereignty. At its 2nd Congress in October 1989 the Latvian Popular Front voted to declare that its aim was to prepare for the transition to full independence, and the Lithuanian Supreme Soviet voted at the beginning of December to delete article 6, which enshrined the Communist Party's leading role, from the republic's constitution. The registration of political parties began at the end of December.[21] The readiness of the Baltic Communist Party leaderships to cooperate with the nationalist movements, and the good connections of the Popular Front leaderships with them, was under-lined when Edgar Savisaar, the leader of the Estonian Popular Front, and Kazimiera Prunskiene, a leading member of the Sajudis, were offered jobs in the communist governments in 1989. (In December 1989 Prunskiene was elected to the politburo of the Lithuanian Communist Party which was preparing to split formally with the CPSU.) Both Savisaar and Prunskiene became prime ministers in the Popular Front governments that were elected in their respective republics the following spring.

One of the first achievements of the popular movements that sprang up in all the republics was the approval of language laws which made the language of the eponymous national group in the republic the 'state language'. These language laws sparked off much of the ethnic strife that afflicted various parts of the Soviet Union from 1988. In the Baltic republics the electoral laws proposed for the elections to the republican supreme soviets, scheduled for early 1990, were also a bone of contention because they excluded a large proportion of the Russian-speaking population. The issue was particularly acute because of the large numbers of Soviet servicemen stationed in the republics and because of the large-scale immigration of Russians, particularly into Estonia and Latvia, since the establishment of Soviet rule.

The Baltic language and election laws provoked a response from the mainly Russian-speaking minorities. In November 1988 a movement called Unity was set up in Lithuania, with A. P. Gel'bak as leader, to organise non-Lithuanians against the growing influence of Sajudis.[22] On 15 February 1989 it organised strikes in more than sixty Vilnius enterprises against the republican language law.[23] Lithuania is the most ethnically homogeneous of the three Baltic republics with around 80 per cent of the population being ethnically Lithuanian. This was, no doubt, one reason why Unity failed to develop into a real force in Lithuanian politics. However, as in all the republics it soon became clear that 'conservative' elements in the CPSU were manipulating the organisations claiming to represent the Russian-speaking population which tended to discredit them even with their chosen constituency. Like other 'interfronty', Unity originally proclaimed that it was 'in support of perestroika' but growing political polarisation soon marginalised the small, genuinely reformist elements within it. As in Latvia the main focus of opposition to the nationalist movement was transferred to the section of the Communist Party which remained loyal to Moscow.[24] In the Vilnius region, where there was a large Polish minority,[25] a movement in favour of autonomy and establishing a Polish university sprang up, and increasingly came into conflict with Lithuanian aspirations.

The political scene in Latvia was potentially much more explosive because of the delicate ethnic balance. In October 1988 a committee was set up to organise the founding congress of an International Front of the Working People of Latvia (Interfront). The congress was held at the beginning of January 1989, attended by nearly 600 delegates nearly all of whom were Russian-speaking. Of the delegates, 81 per cent were Russian and only 4 per cent Latvian. All those present were agreed that it was vital to maintain the integrity of the Soviet Union and that the CPSU should retain its leading role in the life of the country but two trends soon appeared within the Interfront leadership. One group, represented by Anatolii Belaichuk and T. Zhdanok held to the idea of a 'socialist perestroika' whilst the other trend was represented by A. Alekseev and Igor Lopatin who were determined to resist the Latvian nationalist movement by playing on the fears of the Russian-speaking minority. The position of the former group was rapidly undermined. They hoped that some sort of coexistence could be agreed with the Popular Front but the Popular Front regarded the Interfront as a tool of the Communist Party and kept up a uniformly hostile stance.

More important than its failure to develop a relationship with the Popular Front was the steady decline of the Interfront's standing in its chosen constituency, the Russian-speaking population, through 1989–90. It was unable to organise strikes on anything like the scale that occurred in Estonia or even Lithuania and the Latvian Interfront was unable to have any appreciable effect on the elections to the republican Supreme Soviet in March 1990.[26] After its second congress in June 1989 the Interfront became 'a phantom organisation' as internal divisions meant that its Council 'in practice ceased its activity'.[27] In January 1990 an attempt was made to emulate the Estonian United Council of Labour Collectives (OSTK) which had successfully initiated strikes by the Russian-speaking population in that republic in July and August 1989. The Latvian OSTK failed to achieve anything like the strength of its Estonian progenitor, and resistance to the Latvian nationalist movement more and more fell into the hands of the 'conservative' wing of the Latvian Communist Party.

Over 1989–91 the Baltic Popular Fronts were remarkably successful in defusing the potential resistance amongst the Russian-speaking population in their republics to independence. They enjoyed some advantages over other republics: the Baltic minorities did not have the political autonomy granted to minorities in other republics, and the continued refusal of many western states to recognise their incorporation into the Soviet Union gave the claims of the nationalist movements greater force. Nonetheless, the Baltic nationalist movements displayed enough flexibility to win over part of the Russian-speaking population in their republics. For example, on the eve of the strikes called by the Interfront in Latvia in the spring of 1989, the Latvian Supreme Soviet moderated the proposed language law. Furthermore, through their links with the democratic movement in the Russian Federation the Baltic Popular Fronts were able to marginalise those movements which sought to mobilise the Russian-speaking population against them. In this way they were able to attract small numbers of active supporters from the Russian-speaking community into their ranks and secure the neutrality of most of the rest. This was demonstrated most graphically in the support of a sizeable section of the Baltic Russian-speaking population for independence in the referendums conducted in all three republics in early 1991.

In the other republics of the Soviet Union the local Communist Parties were much less willing to make any sort of compromise with the burgeoning popular movements. Popular Fronts were established in most of the Soviet republics but although, like the Baltic Popular Fronts, they were able to mobilise mass support they were unable to achieve the same sort of dramatic electoral breakthrough in the 1990 republican elections. None of them was formed soon enough to make a real impact on the 1989 elections to the Congress of People's Deputies. They did, however, frequently mobilise large numbers of people to the slogans of sovereignty and democracy.

The key republic for the future cohesion of the Soviet Union in terms of scale of territory, size of population and contribution to the Soviet economy was Ukraine. The local Communist Party leadership remained under the control of 'conservatives' epitomised by the elderly first secretary Volodymyr Shcherbits'kyi long after Gorbachev had replaced his 'conservative' colleagues as first secretaries of the Baltic Communist Parties in the summer of 1988. Ukraine was also divided between a nationalist west and a russified east and even after the replacement of Shcherbits'kyi the Ukrainian Communist Party enjoyed considerable success in obstructing the development of a Popular Front.

The first moves to establish a popular front in Ukraine were made in the summer of 1988, in the western part of the republic, by groups associated with the Helsinki Union. These efforts came to nothing because of harassment by the authorities, and leading members of the Writers' Union in Kiev, such as Ivan Drach, Dmytro Pavlychko, Oles' Honchar' and Volodymyr Yavorivs'kyi, decided to take the initiative to overcome the embargo being placed on information about the Popular Front in the official media. On 16 February 1989 the newspaper of the Writers' Union published the draft programme of a Popular Front which rapidly became known as Rukh (Movement) after a threat to send it to a sympathetic Moscow journal.[28] Over the summer a network of groups was set up across the republic despite constant attacks in the official media. The founding congress was eventually held on 8–9 September 1989 in Kiev a year after the founding congresses of the Baltic Popular Fronts. There were over 1,100 delegates of whom 944 were ethnic Ukrainians. They included nine deputies to the Congress of People's Deputies in Moscow and 228 members of the Communist Party. Like most of the Popular Fronts, Rukh's membership was drawn principally from the intelligentsia and 800 of the delegates at its founding congress had completed some form of higher education.[29]

The congress confirmed Drach as leader and elected a People's Deputy Serhiy Koneyev as his first deputy. Yavorivs'kyi and Volodymyr Chernyak were elected deputy chairs and Mykhailo Horyn of the Helsinki Union was made chair of the secretariat symbolising an alliance between the moderate Kiev writers and the radical L'viv ex-dissidents. The congress was addressed by Adam Michnik, a prominent member of Solidarność, offering not only the possibility of a new, more friendly relationship between Ukraine and Poland but also the example of a nationalist movement with a strong base amongst industrial workers. The intervening politicisation of Soviet society, prompted by the debates of the Congress of People's Deputies in Moscow, had made its mark. The congress voted to remove the words expressing its support for the 'leading role' of the CPSU from the draft programme.[30] However, there was little in the approved programme which pointed to a fundamental break with the Soviet system. It stipulated that 'Rukh supported the principles of radical social renewal as proclaimed by the 27th Congress of the CPSU'. In economic policy its insistence that 'the right to choose forms of ownership and management should belong exclusively to the Ukrainian SSR' and its rejection of 'both an uncontrolled free market and a bureaucratic anti-market' indicated that its main concern was to establish control at the republican level rather than to force through a programme of radical marketisation.[31] Calls were made by individual delegates for independence but afterwards a leading member of Rukh could still say that 'I don't think that at present it is even possible to speak about independence for Ukraine . . .'[32]

In recognition of the new political situation in the republic Shcherbits'kyi was finally replaced as republican first secretary at the end of September by Volodymyr Ivashko. The Popular Front moved rapidly to dampen potential problems in the east of the republic and the Crimea. In the summer of 1989 the political life of the east had been transformed by the workers' committees established by the miners in the course of their strikes. At first the miners were very wary of Rukh because of its support for Ukrainian to be declared the state language and the waving of the previously banned Ukrainian national flag at its founding congress which raised fears of an upsurge of chauvinistic nationalism. But their representatives attended Rukh's founding congress where they were won over to at least a position of benevolent neutrality as far as republican sovereignty was concerned. The position of the Crimea within Ukraine was anomalous in that it had been transferred from the Russian Federation only in 1954 and the bulk of its population was Russian-speaking. Here Rukh took up the cause of the Crimean Tatars who had been expelled from their homeland by Stalin and had fought a prolonged campaign to return. By associating itself with this classic dissident concern Rukh occupied the moral high ground and undermined any potential support from the Russian democratic movement for the Russian-speaking population of the Crimea.

There was a similar situation in the neighbouring republic of Belorussia where the Communist Party was under the leadership of Nikolai Sliunkov. Initial moves towards setting up a Popular Front were made in Belorussia in 1988 but there was not a readily identifiable base for it like L'viv had been for Rukh. Furthermore, the local Communist Party leadership made it clear that they were willing to use force to prevent the organisation from developing. Later in the Congress of People's Deputies the reference of the liberal Belorussian writer Ales' Adamovich to the republic as the Soviet Union's 'Vendée', the reactionary, monarchist region of France during the French Revolution, became a widely used term to describe the Belorussian political atmosphere.

The discovery of mass graves of victims of Stalin's terror at Kuropaty, just outside Minsk, in early 1988 provided the pretext for independent organisations to emerge. In March the formation of a Belorussian equivalent to Memorial, Martyrolog, was announced by a local historian and archaeologist who had taken the initiative in publicising the Kuropaty graves, Zianon Paz'niak. Mass demonstrations by the graves could not be openly suppressed by the Belorussian authorities because of the Moscow-directed campaign against Stalinism. This chink in the armour of the Belorussian Communist Party allowed unofficial activists to begin preparing for the setting up of a Popular Front. On 19 October at the founding conference of Martyrolog a Popular Front Organizing Committee was set up headed by the journalist V. Iakavenka.[33] Other organisations with more overtly nationalist aims were already active, such as the informal youth group Talaka. At the end of October 1988 a mass meeting held just outside Minsk, sponsored by Martyrolog, to condemn Stalinism and to discuss the establishment of a Popular Front was broken up by special forces, some of whom used CS gas, in what many Belorussian political activists later interpreted as a rehearsal for the Tbilisi massacre of April 1989. In February 1989 a rally with 40,000 participants, many waving the banned Belorussian national flag, was allowed in Minsk[34] but the authorities consistently prevented the Popular Front from holding its founding congress.

Eventually, the Popular Front was able to hold its founding congress in Vilnius, at the invitation of Sajudis, in June 1989.[35] There was less controversy about the aims of the Belorussian Popular Front than about those of the Baltic Popular Fronts, which centred on demands for measures to encourage the Belorussian language and to promote the economic self-sufficiency of the republic. Zianon Paz'niak was elected chair, with Iu. Khadyka and M. Tkachou as his deputies, and amongst the board members were the prominent writer

Vasil' Bykau and the Congress of People's Deputies deputy and economist Aliaksandr Zhurauliou.

In Moldova [Moldavia] as well the Communist Party was under the control of a 'conservative' leadership in the person of Semen Grossu, who had been appointed by Brezhnev, until the end of 1989. In early 1988 the Alexei Mateevici Literary and Musical Club, led by a physicist, Anatol Selaru, and two journalists Ion Cataveica and Dinu Mihail,[36] had been set up ostensibly to promote the use of the Romanian[37] language in the republic and, in particular, secure the return of the Latin script. By the summer of 1988 the organisation was holding mass rallies in the capital Kishinev and at the beginning of 1989 the local Communist Party agreed to draw up a language law.[38] With a number of other groups, such as the Democratic Movement in Support of Perestroika, it was one of the main forces behind the Moldovan Popular Front which was established in May 1989. It held its founding congress in August 1989 and elected Ion Hadisca as leader.

The development of the Moldovan Popular Front led to a reaction amongst the Russian-speaking population in that republic analogous to that which had occurred in the Baltic republics. In July 1989 an organisation called Unity held its founding congress in the Moldovan capital, Kishinev, with the aim of defending the interests of the Russian-speaking population of the republic. At the end of August the Moldovan Supreme Soviet, under pressure from gigantic rallies organised by the Popular Front, approved a law making Romanian the 'state language' of the republic. The Russian-speaking population responded immediately with mass strikes organised by a United Council of Labour Collectives (OSTK). In the south of the republic the Christian Turkic Gagauz minority formed an organisation, Khalky, to struggle for the granting of autonomy.

In Transcaucasia the local Communist Party leaderships were even more uncompromising and attempts were made, with greater or lesser degrees of success, to suppress the mass nationalist movements that emerged in all three republics at the end of 1988 forcibly. In January 1988 a Karabakh Committee was set up in Yerevan to support the campaign of the Armenian enclave in Azerbaijan to join the Armenian republic. The main initiators were men such as Vano Siradegian and Levon Ter-Potresian, who had been active in an unofficial campaign in the late 1960s to have a monument erected to the victims of the Armenian genocide in Turkey at the beginning of the century. However, the organisation also appealed to people outside unofficial nationalist circles and its membership included leading cultural figures and younger activists such as Ashot Manucharian. Attracted by the fiery oratory of Igor Muradian demonstrations called by the Committee brought hundreds of thousands of Armenians on to the streets.

There was a lull in activity at the end of February after the Supreme Soviet in Moscow discussed the issue but it flared up with a new intensity at the end of May after the Azeris who had participated in the killing of Armenians in Sumgait were given lenient sentences. The Karabakh Committee soon developed into something resembling an alternative government. Its demands included the right to open Armenian consulates in countries with large Armenian populations, the creation of an Armenian-speaking army detachment to serve on home soil, freedom to fly the pre-Soviet tricolour and the power of veto over all-Union projects built in the republic.[39] Although two independent deputies, including Ashot Manucharian, were able to secure election to the Armenian Supreme Soviet in by-elections in the spring of 1988, the communist regime tried to mark out boundaries for legitimate political activity when it arrested Hairikian of the AHNSO and expelled him from the Soviet Union in July. The Karabakh Committee was banned at the same time but this move had little effect on its activity which had begun to include the organisation of strikes and the sponsorship of paramilitary formations. The government's authority was steadily being eroded by the popular movement and, taking advantage of the disastrous earthquake, it arrested the leaders of the Karabakh Committee in December 1988 and January 1989.

The campaign by the nascent Armenian nationalist movement for the union of Nagornyi Karabakh with Armenia provoked a response in Azerbaijan. During 1988 tension between the two peoples frequently became violent, most horrifyingly in the massacre of Armenians in Sumgait in February 1988, and an outflow of the minority population from both republics began. In November 1988 massive crowds began to collect in Lenin Square in the centre of Baku, the capital of Azerbaijan. Many of the demonstrators were workers who had gone onto the streets partly because of the grim social and ecological consequences of the local petro-chemical industry. The most prominent orator was a 26-year-old factory worker Nemet Panakhov but there was little doubt that the main concern of the crowds was to pressurise the Communist Party to resist the Armenian claims on Nagornyi Karabakh more effectively. Portraits of the Ayatollah Khomeini were raised by some of the demonstrators although Panakhov condemned this.[40] The authorities attempted to intimidate the emerging nationalist movement and a state of emergency was imposed. Panakhov was arrested in early December. These actions did not dampen down the popular mood and an article in *Pravda* 'painted a picture of nationalist sentiment raging in every sector of society from factories on strike to the Azerbaijani Academy of Sciences'.[41]

In early 1989 the Azerbaijani Popular Front was formed uniting activists who had come to prominence during the demonstrations of the winter with figures from the intelligentsia. Abulfaz Aliev was appointed the leader with Etibar Mamedov, Leila Iunusova, Iu. Samedoglu and I. Kambarov amongst the other leading members of the board. The Popular Front programme was remarkable for the absence of references to the decisions of the Communist Party or even perestroika. The programme asserted the rights of Azerbaijanis as 'the dominant ethnic group in the republic' and called for 'the restoration of the ethnic unity of Azerbaijanis living on both sides of the [Soviet–Iranian] border'. Nonetheless, the programme was a moderate document. It stressed that the aim of the Popular Front was 'to build a just society of free citizens in Azerbaijan'. It called for 'decisive steps towards the development of understanding and cooperation with Islam' but not for Islam to play any dominant social or political role. Reflecting the widespread perception that Moscow had exploited Azerbaijani oil without contributing anything back, the programme called for much greater economic independence and on the political level called for the establishment of sovereignty rather than independence.[42] The organisation rapidly established a network of local groups across the republic each of which enjoyed a high degree of autonomy.[43] By August 1989 the Popular Front claimed 30,000 'active members'.[44]

Resentment in Azerbaijan continued to grow after the December demonstrations, fostered by the decision to transfer control of Nagornyi Karabakh to Moscow and the growing number of refugees. In the summer of 1989 the Popular Front helped organise a new round of strikes culminating in an economic blockade of Nagornyi Karabakh and Armenia, which depended on Azerbaijan for supplies from the rest of the Soviet Union, in protest against continuing Armenian pressure over the Nagornyi Karabakh issue. The new level of tension forced the government to enter into negotiations with the Popular Front at the end of September. Abulfaz Aliev addressed the Azerbaijani Supreme Soviet and, after prolonged discussions, called off the blockade on 5 October. On 6 October the government granted the Popular Front official registration.[45]

If Popular Fronts were able to establish themselves in most of the European republics of the Soviet Union, independent political activists in the Soviet Central Asian republics faced a whole complex of obstacles that often proved insurmountable. In addition to local Communist Party leaderships infamous for their 'conservatism', the particular position of the urbanised intelligentsia in Central Asia, russified and isolated from the bulk of the indigenous population who lived in rural areas, deprived the Popular Fronts of a ready-made social base. Realising their weak position, independent political organisations made more moderate demands than their Baltic models. Thus the leaders of Birlik, the Uzbek Popular Front, opposed independence for their republic right up to the eve of the August 1991 coup attempt.[46] Local 'conservative' Communist Party leaderships used outbreaks of inter-ethnic conflict, most notably in pogroms against Meskhetian Turks[47] in the Fergana Valley region of Uzbekistan in June 1989, which led to around 100 deaths, and the fighting between Uzbeks and Kirgiz in the Osh region of Kirgizia (Kirgizstan) in June 1990, when over 200 people were killed as a pretext to suppress independent political activity.[48]

In Kazakhstan groups campaigning on ecological issues, such as the Nevada-Semipalatinsk group, founded in February 1989, which opposed the nuclear tests carried out in the republic, were encouraged by the authorities but this was unusual. Nevada-Semipalatinsk was founded on the initiative of Olzhas Suleimenov, head of the Kazakhstan writers' union.[49] Similar groups in Uzbekistan which campaigned to publicise the desperate state of the Aral Sea were tolerated by the authorities. The atmosphere was such that groups with wider interests, such as Popular Fronts, were unable to function. However, a number of small groups did establish themselves.

In 1989 Nursultan Nazarbaev, an ethnic Kazakh, was appointed first secretary of the Kazakhstan Communist Party, replacing Gennadii Kolbin, an ethnic Russian, whose appointment in December 1986 had provoked riots in the republican capital Alma-Ata. Nazarbaev soon began to pursue a policy of asserting republican sovereignty, making moderate concessions to Kazakh nationalism, particularly on the language issue, and technocratic economic reform with remarkable success. In Tajikistan a similar strategy by the republican first secretary Kakhar Makhkamov to promote economic reform whilst keeping democratic and nationalist demands in check came to grief at the beginning of 1990. The local Communist Party leadership had ensured that various attempts to form independent political organisations in the republic from the end of 1988 had been stymied. Then in February 1990 demonstrations began in the capital Dushanbe after rumours had circulated that refugees from Armenia were being given preference for housing. Informal groups gave the demonstrations a more coherent set of demands focusing on implementation of the language law and the raising of Tajik claims on Bukhara and Samarkand in Uzbekistan. The leading role in forming a committee led by Buri Karimov, a republican Gosplan official, to negotiate with the government was taken by a nationalist group formed in the autumn of 1989, Rastokhez (Renaissance). After an initial failure of nerve by the authorities and an offer by Makhkamov to resign, Internal Ministry troops brought in from Moscow broke up the demonstration leaving twenty-two dead. Subsequently, Makhkamov began to pursue a more consistently 'conservative' line. The United States and Afghan Mujaheddin were alleged by Soviet officials to be stirring up unrest and opposition leaders were subjected to harassment.[50]

In Kyrgyzstan [Kirgizia] appalling economic and social conditions combined with a particularly inept local 'conservative' Communist Party leadership conspired to give victory to independent political organisations. At the end of 1990 informal organisations, most notably Ashar (Living Space), had become involved in organising Kirgiz who were squatting on land in the capital Frunze (subsequently renamed Bishkek). By the end of 1989 the organisation had 7,000 members. At the end of January and early February 1990 there were disturbances in Frunze in which Ashar played a leading role. In the elections to the republican Supreme Soviet in March 1990 only one opposition candidate, Qazat Akhmatov, the leader of the Kyrgyzstan Democratic Movement, an umbrella organisation of which Ashar was a member, was elected. In an interview a leader of the Democratic Movement denied that it was a narrow nationalist organisation. Attention then switched to the Osh region in the north of the republic, where most of the Uzbek minority population lived. Rural organisations sprang up to promote Uzbek and Kirgiz rights in the region, including one called Osh Aymaghi (Osh Region) which the local 'conservative' leadership used to play on Kirgiz nationalist feeling.[51] The violence that broke out in the region in June 1990 backfired on the local Communist Party leadership and when the republican Supreme Soviet met in October, partly under pressure from a hunger strike organised by the Kyrgyzstan Democratic Movement, the deputies failed to elect the republican first secretary Absamat

Masaliev[52] as president and instead appointed a liberal academic Askar Akaev to the post. Akaev identified himself with the aims of the Democratic Movement and persuaded the hunger strikers to end their protest.[53]

In Uzbekistan, the most populous of the five Central Asian republics, a 'working group' of eighteen Uzbek intellectuals gathered to begin organising a popular front, Birlik (Unity), in November 1988. In May 1989, 300 delegates from all over the republic met and elected a mathematician, Abdurrahim Pulatov, as leader. During the following year the group organised a number of protests against cotton monoculture in the republic and the drying-up of the Aral Sea. Taking advantage of its weakness the local Communist Party leadership, headed by Islam Karimov, was able to split Birlik by a number of concessions, including a law making Uzbek the state language of the republic and declaring sovereignty. As a result a group led by the poet Mohammed Salek broke with Birlik and formed Erk (Freedom). This group was then registered by the authorities and Salek was elected to the republican Supreme Soviet in February.[54]

In September 1989 a group of intellectuals in the republic of Turkmenistan (Turkmenia) gathered and set up a Popular Front, Agzybirlik (Unity). They drew up a draft programme of concerns including the state of the environment, the status of the Turkmen language, and the shortage of consumer goods. The authorities refused to register Agzybirlik until October 1989 and then in January 1990 they banned it. The organisation defied the ban and held a founding conference in February at which it adopted a programme similar to that of Birlik. The government replied with a law declaring Turkmen the state language and arranging the arrest of one of the Popular Front's leaders on what were widely regarded as trumped-up charges.[55]

By the middle of 1990 independent political movements had appeared in all the Central Asian republics but only in Kirgizstan had they been able to achieve a direct role in government. Elsewhere, communist officials remained in control. Despite the organisational weakness of the new movements and their apparent limited social appeal, they did force local leaders to broaden their base by adopting language laws, asserting republican sovereignty and, most notably in the case of Kazakhstan, promoting economic reform.

1989 was a year of real hope as the proceedings of the Congress of People's Deputies in Moscow were broadcast live throughout the Soviet Union raising expectations and constantly pushing the boundaries of what was politically acceptable forward. In the Congress radical deputies were seen openly challenging the country's political leadership. The formation of the Inter-Regional Group of Deputies in July 1989 not only consolidated their political victories and gave the new democratic politicians a power base; it also provided an organisational focus for building popular support outside the Congress and, perhaps most importantly, a network of contacts between reform-minded politicians in the different republics which proved very useful when, for example, the Balts sought support for their independence campaigns in 1990.

The basis for the formation of the Inter-Regional Group of Deputies lay in the campaign which had been conducted in Moscow to secure the election of opposition candidates, most notably Andrei Sakharov and Boris El'tsin. Before the Congress of People's Deputies convened, deputies from Moscow met together to formulate demands for the forthcoming session, including the live broadcasting of proceedings and the setting up of investigative commissions into the Molotov–Ribbentrop Pact, the Tbilisi killings and the Gdlian and Ivanov affair.[56] On the third day of the session Gavriil Popov, a radical economist from Moscow formally called on deputies to join an Inter-Regional Group. Boris El'tsin told Moscow Radio that the new faction 'leans on the radical left strata of the public ... which considers that the process of restructuring should be carried out more decisively and consistently'. By the end of the first session over 250 deputies had joined up. On 31 July five co-chairs were elected, Boris El'tsin, Gavriil Popov, Iurii Afanas'ev, Viktor Palm (from Estonia) and Andrei Sakharov.[57]

The Inter-Regional Group was unable to achieve a major impact on legislation. By the time of the second session of the Congress of People's Deputies in December 1989 frustration had got to the point where Sakharov drew up an appeal calling for a 'two-hour political strike' to protest against the slow pace of change. The number of deputies in the group gradually declined from a peak of around 360 in December 1989 to 255 by December 1990.[58] However the indirect impact of the Inter-Regional Group, particularly on Russian politics, was crucial in at least two respects. Firstly, it was able to set the political agenda between spring of 1989 and 1990 constantly pushing the boundaries of debate forward and politicising the population. Secondly, members of the Inter-Regional Group were instrumental in setting up Democratic Russia and provided a ready-made source of reliable people for El'tsin when he set up the Russian government in the summer of 1990.

Surprisingly, 'conservative' forces were slower in trying to organise on an inter-republican basis. At the beginning of September 1989 representatives of the Interfronty and the United Workers' Fronts from six republics met in the Urals city of Sverdlovsk and set up a United Workers' Front of the USSR. This initiative was not particularly fruitful but the formation of the Soiuz (Union) group in the Congress of People's Deputies was a serious attempt to provide the 'conservatives' with an organizational base. The example of the Inter-Regional Group had prompted 'conservative' deputies in the Congress of People's Deputies to try and emulate it. In October 1990, as Gorbachev began his shift to the 'right', the Soiuz group held its founding congress. It differed from the Inter-Regional Group in that it attempted to organise outside the Congress from the start. So the founding congress was attended by 354 deputies from all levels, including 175 from the Congress of People's Deputies and twenty-six from republican supreme soviets. Deputies representing the Russian-speaking population in the non-Russian republics were particularly prominent. The chair of the new organisation was Iurii Blokhin, who had helped organise the strike movement amongst the Russian-speaking population in Moldova. Other leading members were Evgenii Kogan, who had tried to rally support for the Russian-speaking strikers in Estonia, and Anatolii Chekoev, a delegate from South Ossetia in Georgia. Perhaps the best-known member was Viktor Alksnis, an ethnic Latvian army colonel, whom the democrats quickly dubbed the 'black colonel'. The main preoccupation of the organisation was the need to hold the Soviet Union together. The presence of Anatolii Lukianov, the chair of the Congress of People's Deputies, and Rafik Nishanov, the chair of the Council of Nationalities, at the founding congress left little doubt but that the new organisation had supporters at the very top of the Soviet political apparatus.[59]

Towards the end of 1989 there were a number of attempts by democratic activists to establish organisations that united independent political organisations across republican boundaries. The most serious of these bodies was the Inter-Regional Association of Democratic Organisations and Movements which was widely known by the acronym MADO. The founding conference of MADO was held in the Urals town of Cheliabinsk at the end of October. Although the initiative in setting up MADO had come from the Leningrad Popular Front, it was joined by seventy organisations from eight republics, including both the Azerbaijani Popular Front and the Armenian Pan-National Movement (see below). The conference expressed general support for the Inter-Regional Group and approved a programme of democratic and market reforms which stressed the 'priority of human rights and universal values over any social and national interests'. Subsequent conferences were held in Tallinn and Vilnius at the beginning of 1990.[60]

Moves to set up a union-wide organisation of social democrats had begun in the autumn of 1989 and an organisational committee was set up. In Tallinn, between 13 and 14 January 1990, the founding congress of the Social-Democratic Association was held; 170 delegates, including ten Congress of People's Deputies, representing seventy organisations were present.[61] There were also about twenty foreign observers. However, the union-wide organisation was rapidly overshadowed by organisations based on the union republics. Of the three co-chairs of the Association one was an Estonian, but of the fifteen members of the Executive Committee only one, Leila Iunusova of the Azerbaijani Social-Democratic Group, was not from the Russian Federation.[62]

There is no better example than the Baltic republics for the way in which the Congress of People's Deputies radicalised the political life of the Soviet Union. Its decision to publish the secret protocols of the Molotov–Ribbentrop Pact and declare them illegal in December 1989 legitimised the calls for independence which, until then, had been kept off the mainstream political agenda. In early 1989 those nationalists in Estonia and Latvia who had refused to work with the Popular Fronts, mainly in the national independence parties, announced that they would begin registering the citizens of the inter-war independent republics and their descendants in preparation for elections to citizens' congresses that would proclaim the resumption of independent statehood.

The decision to initiate a Latvian congress movement with the formation of a coordinating committee in April 1989 followed the example set by Estonia and drew its activists from analogous groupings, with the main initiative being taken by the Latvian Movement for National Independence, plus support from sections of Helsinki-86, the environmental movement and some fledgeling political parties, such as the Latvian Social Democratic Workers' Party. A network of Citizens' Committees spread over the republic and the registration of citizens began in June. Elections to the Latvian Citizens' Congress took place in April 1990 when over 700,000 registered citizens voted, with approximately 30,000 Russian-speaking residents who had declared their intention to become Latvian citizens. The first meeting of the Congress took place at the beginning of May when Aigars Jirgens was elected chair and a standing committee elected.

The Latvian Congress, like the Estonian Congress, although it enjoyed a considerable reservoir of support amongst the ethnically Latvian population, was unable to play a constructive political role at this stage. Its public prominence was further diminished because, unlike those in Estonia, the elections to the Latvian Congress were held after those to the Supreme Soviet. The Baltic congresses provided an example to other republics, most notably Georgia, and they even had a muted resonance in Ukraine where some small groupings, such as the Ukrainian National Democratic Party, began registering citizens in the summer of 1990. Despite playing second fiddle to the supreme soviets the congresses in Latvia and Estonia did force the Popular Fronts to adopt more and more overtly nationalist positions in order not to be outflanked. At its second congress in October 1989 the Latvian Popular Front now noted in the introduction to its programme that 'Latvia's social and political life has radically altered. A real possibility to struggle for the independence of Latvia by non-violent means has appeared'.[63]

For most of the new political movements the elections to the republican supreme soviets scheduled for March 1990 were their first main test. The elections to the Congress of People's Deputies in March 1989 had provided ample evidence of popular discontent with the CPSU and in some cases voters' clubs had been able to channel it against the apparat. By the end of 1989, in many republics, there were republic-wide organisations prepared to profit from the deep-seated disaffection. Although in the Baltic republics Georgia and Armenia the new movements achieved a decisive breakthrough, the final picture elsewhere was more fluid as the local Communist Parties managed to retain the allegiance of a majority of deputies.

In Lithuania Sajudis did not face the challenge of a congress movement but pro-independence sentiment was overwhelming. In December 1989 the Lithuanian Communist Party, at its extraordinary 20th Congress declared itself 'independent' of the CPSU in the teeth of sustained opposition from

Moscow and despite a visit by Gorbachev in person in January.[64] Elections to the Lithuanian Supreme Soviet were held at the end of February 1990. Not surprisingly, they were a resounding success for Sajudis with ninety-nine out of the 133 deputies in the parliament being elected on its platform.[65] The leader of Sajudis, Landsbergis, was elected chair of the new Supreme Council[66] and the deputy leader, Prunskiene, appointed prime minister, with Brazauskas and Ozolas as her deputies. At a meeting of Sajudis deputies on 8 March the decision was made to vote for independence.[67] Concerned that new procedures due to come into Soviet law in mid-March 1990 would drag out the procedure for acquiring independence by insisting on referendums and extended transition periods (in January Landsbergis had called the proposal a 'cheap lie')[68], the Supreme Soviet proclaimed the restoration of Lithuanian independence on 11 March. On 10 March Gorbachev telegrammed Landsbergis with the text of a resolution passed by the Congress of People's Deputies annulling the declaration of independence.[69] A war of nerves began as Moscow became anxious to prevent the secession of further republics. In the middle of April an economic blockade was imposed on Lithuania which, despite the help of Latvia, Estonia and Leningrad, began to have a serious effect on life in the republic. Prunskiene, the prime minister, proposed that Lithuania announce a moratorium on its declaration of independence in order to get the blockade lifted. After a show of resistance by Landsbergis, the Lithuanian Supreme Council passed a resolution following up Prunskiene's proposal at the end of June. However, negotiations with Moscow failed to make progress and resentment against the moratorium grew.

The Latvian Popular Front enjoyed victory in elections to the republican Supreme Soviet on a comparable scale, receiving 131 out of the 201 seats available. This was despite the much larger Russian-speaking population than in Lithuania, indicating that many of them must have voted for pro-independence candidates. The deputies elected two reformist communists, Anatolijs Gorbunovs and Ivars Godmanis, as chair of the Supreme Council and prime minister respectively. On 4 May 1990 the Latvian Supreme Council made a declaration of independence similar to that made by Estonia. Both Latvia and Estonia had clearly been intimidated by the sanctions imposed by Moscow on Lithuania after its full declaration of independence since both their declarations allowed for a transition period of unspecified length until the *de facto* establishment of independence.[70]

In Ukraine, Belorussia and Moldova the obstruction of the local Communist Parties which had delayed the formation of Popular Fronts and then restricted their development prevented the new movements achieving decisive victories in the republican elections in early 1990. In Moldova tension continued to rise as the increasingly assertive Popular Front clashed with the local 'conservative' communist leadership. At the Revolution Day parade through Kishinev on 7 November 1989 a counter-demonstration organised by the Popular Front ended with Communist Party buildings in the capital being attacked. Ten days later Grossu retired as first secretary and was replaced by Piotr Luchinskii (an ethnic Moldovan, despite his name), who was a flexible reformer. The elections to the republican Supreme Soviet at the end of February 1990 gave the Popular Front enough leverage to force the Communist Party leadership to accept Mircea Snegur, a Communist Party member sympathetic to the Popular Front, as chair of the Supreme Soviet. With the fall of Nicolae Ceauşescu at the end of December there was a rapid growth of links with Romania and unification seemed an increasingly likely prospect.

By the beginning of 1990 Rukh was already a substantial organisation with a network of branches across Ukraine and with many tens of thousands of members including prominent figures from the cultural and academic worlds. In January it organised a human chain from L'viv to Kiev to commemorate the 1918 declaration of Ukrainian independence. Official harassment continued. In the run-up to the republican elections rumours, which the opposition believed emanated from the KGB, were spread that pogroms against Jews were about to begin. The Communist Party refused to register Rukh until February 1990, which meant that it was unable to register its own candidates for the Supreme Soviet elections. Consequently, Rukh candidates stood formally as the candidates of already registered unofficial groups, such as Green World and the Taras Shevchenko Language Society, but united in a Democratic Bloc. Democratic Bloc candidates stood in 129 constituencies, with independents supported by the Bloc in another seventy-two, out of the total of 450 in the republic.

As a result of the elections the Democratic Bloc could count on the votes of 170 deputies in the new Supreme Soviet whilst the Communist Party could count on 280. Highlighting the underlying divisions in Ukraine, Rukh candidates did significantly better in the west of the republic. The organisation took control of the L'viv regional soviet and Viacheslav Chornovil, a founder member of the Helsinki Union and a leading member of Rukh was elected chair. Recognition of the real strength of the Rukh agenda was underlined when the new Supreme Soviet voted with only four votes against to declare sovereignty.

In Belorussia the Popular Front could achieve only meagre results because of the repressive regime imposed by the local Communist Party. Out of the 360 seats in the new Supreme Soviet it only gained twenty-seven. However, a Democratic Club of Deputies founded by the Popular Front deputies was soon joined by large numbers of reformist communists so that by July nearly a third of the deputies in the Supreme Soviet were members. One of the Club's leaders was a deputy chair of the Supreme Soviet, Stanislau Shushkevich.[71]

The authority of the Azerbaijani Popular Front had continued to grow after its registration and at the end of October 1989 it reimposed its blockade on Armenia and Nagornyi Karabakh. Differences in the leadership of the Popular Front began to grow. A Social Democratic Group emerged which regarded Panakhov and his supporters as potentially authoritarian populists. At the end of October Leila Iunusova, a member of the Popular Front's board and a supporter of the Social Democratic fraction, complained that the democratic elements were in danger from 'the new powerful force of the "lumpen" who have felt their strength in the course of mass rallies and strikes and have become aware of their new power, become certain of its "indestructibility" and the possibility of solving all problems by force'.[72] By contrast, an Azerbaijani National Independence Party, led by Etibar Mamedov, was founded campaigning for a complete break with the Soviet past.

The authority of the Azerbaijani Communist Party began to collapse. At the end of December 1989 'angry crowds' took over the southern town of Dzhalilabad and at the beginning of January 1990 the Popular Front overthrew the Communist Party in the nearby town of Lenkoran. Then after an appeal by Panakhov in Baku the Soviet border with Iran was breached in the Azerbaijani autonomous region of Nakhichevan.[73] In mid-January Azeri refugees from Armenia began to hunt down the remaining Armenians in Baku but the Soviet Army waited for a week before intervening on the night of 19–20 January and occupying the city with great loss of life. Martial law was declared and many leading figures in the Popular Front were arrested and elections to the republican Supreme Soviet were postponed to September when only a few opposition deputies from Baku were able to secure election.

In Armenia, after prolonged pressure, the leaders of the Karabakh Committee were released in the summer of 1989. Some of these activists were instrumental in setting up a new organisation, the Armenian Pan-National Movement which was registered by the government at the end of June with Levon Ter-Potresian as leader. The Pan-National Movement was designed to act as an umbrella group for the large number of independent organisations that had proliferated in the republic. Many of them supported the new movement, with the notable exception of the Armenian Movement for Self-Determination, and it was also supported by important parties in the Armenian diaspora, the Dashnak Party and the Democratic Liberal Party (Ramkavar). It also had the support of some elements in the Communist Party and the Movement's first congress, held in November, was addressed by its first secretary, Suren Harutiunian who had been appointed in May 1988. Over 50 per cent of the delegates, one-third of whom were members of the Communist Party, were in favour of full independence for Armenia.[74] Elections to the Armenian Supreme Soviet were eventually held in May 1990. Although there was a very low turn-out, only 46 per cent, they gave the Pan-National Movement over half the places and Ter-Potresian was elected chair. Another former Karabakh Committee member, Vazygen Manukian, was appointed prime minister. Hairikian also secured election from prison. The oldest Armenian political organisation, the Dashnaktsutiun (Federation of Armenian Revolutionaries), which had been founded at the end of the nineteenth century, gained ten deputies.[75] Ter-Potresian quickly showed himself to be one of the most astute politicians to arise out of the independent political movements by his deft solution of a crisis brought on by an ultimatum from Moscow to disband paramilitary groups.

The elections to the republican supreme soviets in 1990 marked a watershed

in the development of independent political organisations. The most important change was the confirmation of a shift away from the Soviet Union towards
the republics as the arena for the new politics as a consequence of the greatly
increased authority of the republican supreme soviets elected on a more
democratic franchise. Even attempts to coordinate between independent
political organisations in the republics became moribund. The third MADO
conference, due in March–April 1990, never took place.[76] A further attempt to
revive inter-republican cooperation in early 1991, the Democratic Congress,
failed to develop. The initiative in this case came from the Republican Party of
Russia, the Party of the Democratic Renaissance of Ukraine and the United
Democratic Party of Belorussia, which had all grown out of the Democratic
Platform (see below), in December 1990.[77] Representatives of forty-one
political movements and parties, including Democratic Russia, Sajudis, the
Belorussian Popular Front, Rukh and the Azerbaijani social democrats, met in
March 1991 and adopted a series of declarations setting out an alternative to
the draft Union Treaty that Gorbachev was proposing. Despite the violent
repression in Lithuania and Latvia in January 1991, which gave the need for
inter-republican cooperation a new urgency, the Congress's deliberations were
undermined by the demands of the Democratic Party of Russia for guarantees
for the Russian-speaking population in the non-Russian republics.[78]

The optimism of 1989 and the euphoria that followed the republican elections
in 1990 sparked off a new wave of organisational creativity. Many activists now
confidently believed that the Soviet republics were rapidly moving towards a
situation where genuine multi-party politics would be possible. The formation
of political parties was given a filip by the abolition of Article 6 of the Soviet
Constitution, which enshrined the 'leading role' of the CPSU in Soviet society,
in March 1990 and the passage of legislation by the republican supreme soviets
allowing for the registration of political parties. In contrast to the first wave of
political parties, the national independence parties and the Democratic Union,
with their dissident roots the second wave grew out of the divisions within the
CPSU in the first instance.

The polarisation of Soviet politics into 'conservatives', symbolised by Egor
Ligachev, and radical reformers, symbolised by Boris El'tsin, and the growing
tide of opinion in favour of a multi-party system gave rise to intense pressure
within the CPSU for the right to form factions, which had been banned since
1921. Despite this proscription, communist reformers had begun to establish
Party Clubs at the local level in 1986. In January 1990 the first All-Union
Conference of Party Clubs was held in Moscow, attended by 455 delegates
from 102 cities in thirteen republics and representing nearly 60,000 Communist Party members. The initiative in setting up the conference had come
from Moscow party club activists such as Igor Chubais, Vladimir Lysenko and
Sergei Stankevich. The conference declared the formation of a Democratic
Platform within the CPSU. The new organisation adopted a comprehensive
programme which included ensuring the transfer of power from party bodies to

the soviets, the repeal of Article 6 of the Soviet Constitution and the preparation of a law on political parties, the acceptance that universal values should
take precedence over class values, the acceptability of different forms of
property, the abolition of democratic centralism as the organising principle for
the CPSU, more freedom for the Communist Party press, the removal of
Communist Party bodies from the armed forces and KGB, full rights for
factions to be formed within the CPSU, and greater rights for the party rank-
and-file against officials. Taken together this implied not a return to Leninism,
as Gorbachev advocated, but a decisive break with Marxism-Leninism. The
Democratic Platform was transformed from a grass-roots ginger group to a
potential, national force when a whole series of prominent reformist People's
Deputies, such as Iurii Afanas'ev, Boris El'tsin, Gavriil Popov, Telman Gdlian
and Nikolai Travkin announced their support.[79]

The Democratic Platform was the most important organisation to announce
its formation as a faction within the CPSU but it was not the only one. The
organisation Unity for Leninism and Communist Ideals, established by Nina
Andreeva in 1989, had small groups of supporters all over the Soviet Union. A
more serious rival to the Democratic Platform was the Marxist Platform within
the CPSU, founded by Aleksandr Buzgalin and Aleksei Prigarin, which also
grew out of Moscow party clubs. A draft programme was published in March
1990 and its first conference was held in April. The organisation was equally
hostile to the 'bourgeois liberals' who wanted to introduce a market economy
and the 'conservative-bureaucratic' tendency which was attempting to hold up
perestroika in its own interests. Instead, supporters of the Marxist Platform
emphasised a vaguely conceived popular self-management making them close
ideological allies of Boris Kagarlitskii's Socialist Party.[80]

The strains that the fast-moving political situation placed on all political
organisations closely associated with the Communist Party, particularly if they
hoped to organise on an All-Union level, showed at the second conference of
the Democratic Platform in June. Travkin had already departed to form the
Democratic Party of Russia and most of the other most prominent deputies
who had been willing to associate with the organisation a few months previously failed to participate actively. A poll carried out in May showed that 49
per cent of the population considered that the CPSU had lost control of events.
Viacheslav Shostakovskii, the rector of the Higher Party School in Moscow
and a supporter of the Democratic Platform, appealed to delegates to avoid
confrontation with the CPSU and remain members in order to fight the 'conservatives' and to obtain a share of the CPSU's vast assets which included
buildings, newspapers, as well as large sums of money. However, it was already
clear that the Platform would not gain a fair representation at the 28th Party
Congress, due in July, and delegates decided that their aim was to form a
political party outside the CPSU. At the congress in July most of the leading
figures in the Platform announced that they were leaving the party and went on
to form political parties at the republican level.[81]

One of the largest political parties to arise in the Russian Federation was the

Republican Party which grew out of the Democratic Platform. Similar parties with a large initial membership were founded in Ukraine and Belorussia. The Party for the Democratic Renaissance of Ukraine was formed at a congress at the beginning of December 1989 in Kiev attended by 320 delegates. Disputes broke out about how far the new party should disown its communist roots with the anti-communist line propounded by V. Khmel'ko, V. Filenko and others victorious. Although the new party claimed more than twenty deputies in the republican Supreme Soviet it failed to grow.[82] In Belorussia supporters of the Democratic Platform founded the United Democratic Party in the autumn of 1990.

The schizophrenia resulting from the rightwards drift in the Soviet political spectrum affected those parties which developed out of the Democratic Platform particularly severely. In terms of potential membership these parties appeared to face a brighter future than most but they soon became embroiled in wrangling between 'social democratic' and 'anti-communist' wings, the latter anxious to distance themselves as far as possible from their communist past.

The summer of 1991 saw the final attempt to create a new political movement by reformers within the CPSU. Although Gorbachev had swung back to 'the left' with the 'nine-plus-one' agreement in April, the reformers were increasingly isolated in the party. At the end of June, Eduard Shevardnadze, Aleksandr Iakovlev, Anatolii Sobchak and Gavriil Popov agreed to form the Movement for Democratic Reforms. The initiative was welcomed by Gorbachev and some commentators interpreted the new organisation as an attempt to provide him with a political base for the elections to the Soviet presidency due in 1992 according to the draft Union Treaty.

The Movement was originally conceived of as working within the CPSU but Shevardnadze and Iakovlev were soon forced to resign their Party membership.[83] Whilst members of the Movement seemed, for a while after the August coup, to have occupied many of the leading positions in the Soviet state, its late formation meant that it had already been overtaken by other democratic movements and, even more seriously, its declared aim of acting as an All-Union organisation was an obvious miscalculation. Six months after the formation of the Movement, the state in which it intended to operate, the Soviet Union, had been dissolved.

Although the national independence parties established in 1988 were still active they appeared to be increasingly marginalised by the end of 1990. Where they had organised congresses they did at least have a tribune from which to propound their views but they were not able to make a practical contribution towards the attaining of independence. From the summer of 1989, activists from the Popular Fronts began to establish new political parties. In contrast to the simple, uncompromisingly anti-communist and nationalist programmes of the ex-dissident activists who usually dominated the radical political parties, these Popular Front activists, buoyed up by their optimism about the possibility of a smooth advance towards a multi-party system, consciously borrowed western models. As a result a profusion of social democratic, green, Christian democratic, liberal and peasant parties were set up in all the European republics of the Soviet Union in 1989–90. Although they were all founded with great high hopes few managed to make any impact on the public.

In view of the prominence of environmental movements in the early stages of democratisation it is not surprising that many activists moved rapidly to set up green parties. At the beginning of July 1989 a session of the embryonic Lithuanian Green Movement decided to set up a political party. In the February 1990 elections to the republican Supreme Soviet three members of the Lithuanian Green Party were elected, including its leader Zigmas Vaisvila.

Like other green parties the potential of the Lithuanian Green Party was undermined by the 'rightwards' drift in the political spectrum experienced in all of the Soviet republics. The party was slow to develop as an organisation and it held its founding congress only in mid-June 1990.[84] In the Lithuanian Supreme Council Vaisvila became one of the leading proponents of the establishment of a Lithuanian defence force, which did not sit easily with the anti-militarist ethos of the European environmental movement which had provided the model for the Lithuanian Green Party.

In April 1990 the leader of the Ukrainian Ecological Association Green World, Iurii Shcherbak, announced the formation of a Ukrainian Green Party which held its founding congress in September. The party's programme formally stated that it regarded itself as part of the world-wide green movement and as an anti-militarist organisation. Later it joined the Democratic Bloc and supported student protests against the Ukrainian prime minister in October. However, the Green Party clearly intended to place itself on the moderate wing of the Ukrainian political spectrum. It defined itself as a 'left-centre' organisation ready to carry out 'constructive cooperation with all constructive and democratic forces in Ukraine' and stood for a 'commonwealth of sovereign states' and a 'federal Ukraine'.[85]

Not surprisingly, at first, the most popular labels amongst those setting up political parties were associated with the 'left' of the traditional western European political spectrum. This reflected both a still genuine belief in the virtues of socialism and the influence of official propaganda about the virtues of the 'social market' in Germany and the 'Swedish model'. Social democratic parties were established in practically all the European republics of the Soviet Union, including many of the autonomous republics of the Russian Federation, and in some of the Central Asian republics as well. The 'left-wing' parties shared the same problems as the other putative political parties but some affected them particularly severely, leading to early mortal splits. Firstly, their 'leftist' orientation made it particularly tricky for them to define their relationship with the local Communist Party, for example, both the Latvian and Lithuanian Social Democratic Parties were subject to splits over their relationship with the local Communist Parties.

A declaration calling for the re-establishment of the Lithuanian Social

Democratic Party was published by a group including three prominent members of Sajudis, Kazimieas Antanavicius, A. Sakalas and Kazimieas Uoka, in May 1989. The party held its 14th Conference, numbered from the last pre-Soviet conference, in December. Antanavicius, a leading academic economist, was elected leader. At the same time the Latvian Social Democratic Workers' Party held its 20th Congress in Riga, electing Valdis Shteins as its leader. The Latvian Social Democratic Workers' Party split almost as soon as it had been refounded. The Riga branch, which had half of the party's membership, broke away to form the Latvian Social Democratic Party. The new party advocated a more moderate approach both to Communist Party members and to attaining independence. It accused the parent party of not differentiating between rank-and-file Communist Party members and those who had committed 'amoral acts' in deciding who was eligible for membership. It also criticized the parent party's decision to give support to the congress movement as well as to parti-cipate in the elections to the Supreme Soviet. As a result of these conflicts and the failure of both parties to attract leading figures from the reformist wing of the Communist Party or the Popular Front into their ranks, neither managed to make a significant impact on Latvian public opinion.

Conflict in the Lithuanian Social Democratic Party arose in the summer of 1991 over the decision by Antanavicius to participate in the Lithuanian Future Forum.[86] The majority of the Social Democratic Party members opposed this action because of the predominant role of the Democratic Labour Party (former Communist Party) in the Forum. In August Antanavicius was replaced as leader by A. Sakalas. Although Antanavicius did not join the Sajudis Centre Fraction in the Supreme Council like the other Social Democrat deputies he did not move to set up a break-away organisation and, by the end of 1991, was moving towards a reconciliation with his social democratic colleagues.[87]

The Ukrainian United Social Democratic Party (a party of the same name had existed in the western Ukraine before the imposition of Soviet rule) split at its founding congress in May 1990. Fifty-eight out of the eighty-six delegates refused to accept the draft programme prepared by the leadership because it called for 'the building of democratic socialism' in Ukraine and envisaged Ukraine remaining part of a Soviet confederation. The leadership went ahead and founded the Ukrainian United Social Democratic Party with Aleksandr Nizhnik as its leader. The party claimed to set up a network of organisations across the republic with 'more than a thousand members' and although it had a couple of deputies in the Kiev city soviet it did not gain representation at the republican level. The dissident majority at the May congress founded the Ukrainian Social Democratic Party with a rival organisation. Despite having two deputies in the republican Supreme Soviet the party failed to secure official registration because its membership, estimated at 1,300 in early 1991, was below the number (3,000) required. The differences that emerged at the founding congress did not prevent both parties joining the Democratic Bloc.[88]

The 'left-wing' parties were affected more than most by the growing polarisa-tion of Soviet politics and the increasing popularity of overtly anti-communist slogans. Intellectually, socialist and even social democratic ideas steadily lost ground as 'neo-conservatism', with its advocacy of an unfettered market economy and 'small government' proved more and more compelling to activists in the new political movements. 'Liberal' wings emerged in many of the social democratic parties whilst many of the new liberal parties advocated the ideas of the Chicago School rather than the 'social liberalism' associated with many European liberal parties.

Almost all the new political parties, in what could be construed as a throwback to a crude form of Marxism, were anxious to identify their 'social base'. Many social democrats began by identifying industrial workers as their constituency but few actual workers were recruited. This problem was given an extra dimension by the fact that in the Baltic republics the workers were overwhelmingly Russian-speaking. This was one of the reasons for the split in the Latvian social democratic movement. More and more social democratic parties spoke of the intelligentsia and the 'middle strata' (*srednie sloi*) as their base. Apart from an ideological drift to the right and the unattractiveness of the very idea of political parties to social groups outside the intelligentsia, the obvious financial attraction of seeking support amongst the emerging groups of new entrepreneurs gave an extra impulse to 'right-wing' parties.

One of the most common 'right-wing' trends in the emerging political spectrum which specifically referred to western European models was that of Christian democracy. The situation in the Russian Federation was complicated by the formation of two significant organisations claiming the mantle of Russian Christian democracy, the Christian Democratic Union, led by the ex-dissident Aleksandr Ogorodnikov, which held its founding conference in the beginning of August 1989, and the Christian Democratic Movement, led by Viktor Aksiuchits and Gleb Iakunin, which held its founding conference in April 1990.[89]

Christian democratic groups sprang up in practically every republic, in Protestant Estonia and Latvia as well as Orthodox Georgia and Ukraine. Historically, however, Christian democracy has usually been a feature of Catholic countries. Therefore it was not surprising that a relatively strong Christian democratic organisation, the Christian Democratic Union,[90] should have been established in Lithuania, a predominantly Catholic country where a Christian Democratic Party had existed in the pre-Soviet period. By a strange quirk, though, the Lithuanian party's strength also proved its downfall. Four of its leading members were eventually appointed ministers (such as the foreign minister Algirdas Saudargas) in the republican government, upon which they resigned their party positions, thus depriving the party of its best-known members. Such an attitude was widespread in all the republics and was reflected in El'tsin's resignation from the CPSU after his appointment as chair of the Russian Supreme Soviet in the summer of 1990. It stemmed from a desire not to repeat the Communist experience but of combining state and party positions had the unintended effect of holding back the development of new political parties.

An attempt to establish a democratic Islamic party met uniform attempts at repression from the republican leaderships in Central Asia. In June 1990 the

Islamic Party—Renaissance was set up to promote the rights of Muslims all over the Soviet Union. Although the initiative originally emanated from the north Caucasus in the autumn of 1990 there was an attempt to set up branches of the organisation in Central Asia. The founding conference of the Tajik branch was banned by the republican government but even so 300 delegates turned up. In January 1991, 400 delegates turned up to a similar conference in Uzbekistan, including Pulatov the leader of Birlik, but the police arrested a number of the participants and in February the Uzbek Supreme Soviet banned the organisation. Secular democratic parties were, however, successfully established in Tajikistan, the Democratic Party of Tajikistan, and the Azat party in Kazakhstan.

In practice, 'right-wing' parties were little more successful in establishing organisations and distinctive identities than 'left-wing' parties. Social base and ideology were relatively unimportant factors in determining the success of political parties. The main reason for the insignificance of the political parties established in 1989–90 stemmed from the fact that they had mechanistically adopted models from western Europe before there was any real political demand for them. Until the summer of 1991 none of the republics was independent and there was a real possibility of a communist restoration. The predicament of the new political parties was epitomised by a statement made by the joint leaders of the Latvian Green Party at the time of its founding congress in 1990. They stated that they had 'no disagreements' with the Popular Front and that 'an independent Latvia is a prerequisite for the solution of its ecological problems'.[91] In these circumstances an intelligent Latvian might well have asked what point there was in having a separate Green Party. Nonetheless, five members of the Party did find their way into the republic's supreme command.

On the other hand, where new political parties were able to attract well-known figures either from the reformist wing of the local Communist Party or Popular Front they were able to establish some sort of independent organisation and identity. The Lithuanian Social Democratic Party was able to secure significant representation in the Lithuanian Supreme Council and the participation of well-known figures such as Sakalas and Antanavicius ensured it a high profile. So, at the end of 1991, there was still a good chance that the Lithuanian Social Democratic Party might establish itself as a permanent feature in the political life of the republic. Similarly, the Ukrainian Green Party gained considerably from the fact that Shcherbak was already a well-known figure in the republic before the party was established.

To an extent, the chances of a political party could be improved if it could claim to be continuing the traditions of a pre-Soviet party. The continued existence of the parties in émigré communities could be helpful in terms of financial and organisational support as well as international contacts. This was the case with some of the Baltic parties, even if friction between émigrés and home-grown activists did sometimes hinder cooperation. In Armenia, the Dashnaktsutiun, which had governed Armenia between 1918 and 1920, was able to re-establish itself as a serious force opposing the Pan-National Movement-dominated government. Significantly, though, it was to the much richer (but historically less important) émigré Democratic Liberal Party that Ter-Potresian turned for endorsement in his presidential election campaign. The attempts to re-establish the Georgian Social Democratic Party, which had ruled the country between 1918 and 1921, despite its continued existence in exile, and the Mussavat Party, which had ruled Azerbaijan between 1918 and 1920, were much less successful.

By the middle of 1991 it was clear that the tendency to create political parties, whilst it had created a plethora of new organisations, had not made an appreciable impact on public opinion, and far from increasing participation had probably served to dissipate the strength of the broader movements. When the 'conservatives' attempted to take central control in January–February and August 1991 it was in a half-hearted fashion but popular resistance and, significantly popular resistance mobilised by the broad movements and Popular Fronts rather than political parties, was an important factor in obstructing the attempt to restore the 'old centre'.

In many republics the independent political movements had made the major contribution towards abolishing the political monopoly of the Communist Party and, in some, they had taken over the reins of government themselves but they all found it difficult to maintain the political momentum of the heady days of 1988–9. Even where they did not face the responsibility of power themselves they still faced the problem that their agenda of democratic and economic reform and, crucially, republican sovereignty and nationalism was being adopted by the Communist Party organisations that had been their main opponents. Facing an inevitable falling-off in popular enthusiasm the new political organisations deployed a range of strategies to try to retain and build on the support that they had mobilised in 1988–9.

The least successful of the new organisations were those which had been associated with 'conservative' elements in the CPSU. The various United Workers' Fronts quickly faded from the scene. The demise of 'conservative' organisations which sought to represent the interest of the Russian-speaking populations in the Baltic republics was particularly surprising in view of the stringent conditions for citizenship which the local nationalist movements were advocating. In early 1991 shadowy National Salvation Committees were set up in Lithuania and Latvia. It was significant that their members were chiefly drawn from the local 'conservative' Communist Parties and representatives of the Soviet military rather than the organisations that had attempted to mobilise the Russian-speaking population in 1989–90. The Equal Rights fraction which united many deputies representing the Russian-speaking population in the Latvian Supreme Council dissociated itself from the National Salvation Committee. In Moldova, the organisations representing the Russian-speaking population were more successful and declared the establishment of a Transdnestrian Republic in the summer of 1991.

The Popular Fronts were divided over how to adapt to the role of governing party or the wholesale adaptation of their programmes by their Communist opponents. There were a number of moves to define their ideology and forms of organisation more tightly and create still broad but specifically populist anti-communist movements, and even a tendency to transform the Popular Fronts into political parties. In April 1990 the 2nd Sajudis Congress dropped the words 'in support of perestroika' from its title and confirmed that its primary goal was 'the affirmation of an independent, democratic Lithuanian state'. Unlike some of the other Popular Fronts in 1990, and reflecting the popularity of Brazauskas, Sajudis did not take measures to exclude Communist Party members from its organisation or to declare itself ideologically hostile to it.[92] Landsbergis stepped down as leader as it was felt that the combination of leadership of the ruling 'party' with the chairmanship of the Supreme Soviet was too reminiscent of the position of Communist Party leaders. He also attempted to create a more disciplined base for his government in the Supreme Council by transforming the Popular Front into a political party but the delegates rejected the idea.

In October an important section of the radical wing of Sajudis, headed by Čepaitis,[93] formed an Independence Party which adopted a radical anti-communist programme, explicitly excluding ex-communists from its ranks which led many commentators in the republic to accuse it of intolerance. The new party rapidly acquired a strong base in the republic's soviets. In the Supreme Council the Sajudis fraction split into a radical nationalist United Fraction, which gave consistent support to Landsbergis, and a smaller, moderate Centre Fraction. At the beginning of January 1991 the radicals in the Independence Party, the Christian Democratic Union and the Sajudis United Fraction took advantage of the unpopularity of the government's decision to raise prices to force Prunskiene to resign. Prunskiene became one of the leading figures in the Lithuanian Future Forum which was launched in April 1991. The Forum criticised the Landsbergis government for pursuing a policy of confrontation with Moscow and called for a 'step-by-step' approach to attaining independence. Although the Forum was launched as a second Sajudis it was organisationally dominated by, and many of its leading figures came from, the Democratic Labour Party, the former Lithuanian Communist Party, which led to strong attacks from supporters of the government. At the other end of the political spectrum the Tautinikai (Nationalist) Party which had supported Smetona, the inter-war dictator, was revived and was supported by a significant group of deputies in the Supreme Soviet. The new party set itself the aim of protecting the interests of ethnic Lithuanians in the republic and refused to accept non-Lithuanians as members.[94]

The idea of creating political parties propagating broad anti-communist and nationalist programmes on the basis of a strong popular front weakened Rukh in Ukraine without leading to the establishment of successful new organisations. The radicalisation of Rukh which had already been apparent in 1989 continued to make itself felt in 1990. In the summer leading figures of Rukh began to propose that Ukraine should set up its own army. This was prompted by the popular resentment against sending Ukrainian conscripts to serve in Transcaucasia and Central Asia, but the fact that the idea could even be raised showed how far the political situation had changed.

Tension between the Rukh leaders drawn from Kiev and those drawn from the western regions of the republic took on an organisational form.[95] At a conference of the Ukrainian Helsinki Union in March 1990 some participants spoke in favour of setting up a political party. In April 1990 the founding congress of the Ukrainian Republican Party was held attended by 495 delegates. Levko Luk'ianenko was elected chair of the party with Stepan Khmara and Grigorii Grebeniuk his deputies. The Republican Party adopted an ideology of 'anti-communism' with its radicalism strengthened by a high proportion of ex-dissidents amongst its members. At its founding conference almost half the delegates were former political prisoners. The new party rapidly became a serious political force in the western Ukraine.[96] The 'Kiev wing' of Rukh, led by Pavlychko and Drach, announced in March 1990 the formation of the Ukrainian Democratic Party. It held its founding congress in December 1990, attracting a similar size of membership as the Republican Party but with a high proportion of ex-Communists.[97]

Rukh held its second congress in October 1990. The congress voted to remove the words 'in support of perestroika' from its name and confirm that its aim was now to achieve independence for the republic. It declared that it was in opposition to the CPSU and that membership of a political party or organisation whose leadership was situated outside the borders of Ukraine (i.e. the CPSU) was not compatible with membership of Rukh. On the second day of the congress delegates left the hall to demonstrate against a visit by the Moscow Orthodox Patriarch to Kiev.[98] Deprived of a fair representation in the Supreme Soviet by the machinations of the Communist Party, the nationalist movement became more bold in its actions. In October demonstrations and hunger strikes led by new students' organisations against the conscription of Ukrainian young men to serve in the Soviet Army outside the republic forced the resignation of the prime minister Vitalii Masol. They also forced the Supreme Soviet to postpone a decision on whether to sign the new Union Treaty that Gorbachev was proposing.

In reality, however, Rukh was losing the political initiative. Leonid Kravchuk, a former ideology secretary of the Central Committee of the Ukrainian Communist Party, who had been appointed chair of the republican Supreme Soviet in July 1990, was able to appeal successfully to Ukrainian nationalist sentiment whilst still presenting himself as a guarantee against nationalist excesses to the non-Ukrainian population. The communist fraction in the republican Supreme Soviet initiated a declaration of sovereignty in July, and in March 1991 Kravchuk cleverly out-manoeuvred Rukh's opposition to the referendum on the Union, proposed by Gorbachev, by inserting a second question asking voters if they would approve a new union if it was based on the principles enunciated in the declaration of sovereignty. Ukrainians voted in large numbers to stay within Gorbachev's 'renewed union' and by a larger margin to uphold the declaration of sovereignty, leaving Rukh on the sidelines.

The unimaginative 'conservatism' of the Belorussian leadership led to an explosion of popular anger in April 1991. On 3 April, in the wake of price rises on 2 April, workers in a number of the main enterprises in Minsk stopped work and gathered in the town centre. A strike committee was formed led by activists with close links to the Popular Front and political demands, including most crucially a call for new elections to the republican Supreme Soviet, were drawn up. The strike movement spread to other enterprises in the republic. After promises of negotiations the strikes were called off on 11 April; these negotiations broke down, however, on 23 April, and strikers began a blockade of the Orsha railway junction which was vital for Soviet trade with the west. Finally, when the situation appeared to be getting out of control, the action was called off. The Belorussian strikes were an impressive display of workers' power but the government refused to concede to their political demands and in the wake of the strikes began to harass activists.

The August coup came too unexpectedly and crumbled too quickly for independent political movements to be able to organise opposition to the State Committee for the State of Emergency except where they dominated republican governments. They did issue appeals for resistance and joined with those republican leaders and Supreme Soviets which opposed the coup. In Lithuania Sajudis called for demonstrations and strikes if attempts were made to overthrow the government and, at the other end of the country, the Kyrgyzstan Democratic Movement helped Akaev defeat a local attempt to impose a state of emergency. In Moldova the Popular Front helped mobilise massive crowds to support Mircea Snegur against the coup. In Uzbekistan the leader of Birlik, Pulatov, was detained for a day. In Azerbaijan Popular Front supporters demonstrating against president Mutalibov, who had openly supported the coup, were arrested.[99] It was also important for the failure of the coup that its leaders did not mobilise any popular support. The failure of the coup leaders to establish firm links with Russian nationalist groups, the Soiuz group of deputies and, perhaps, 'conservative' labour organisations demonstrated how ill-equipped many old-style Communist Party politicians were to cope with the new politics.

The main consequence of the failure of the coup was a speeding up of the disintegration of the Soviet Union into nation states based on the republics. So whilst it did not give the new political movements a chance to show the real strength of their appeal, it did confirm the irresistibility of their political agenda. Those republican leaders who had prevaricated at the beginning of the coup or even supported the imposition of a state of emergency moved quickly to try and insure themselves against accusations from the opposition movements in the Supreme Soviets and outside them. The Ukrainian Supreme Soviet declared independence on 24 August after the opposition bloc had criticised Leonid Kravchuk's actions during the coup. In Belorussia the Communist Party fraction in the Supreme Soviet actually initiated a proposal that the republic should declare independence, which was approved on 25 August. In the Central Asian republics, Communist Parties swiftly declared their independence from the

CPSU and renamed themselves. The Uzbek Communist Party became the People's Democratic Party, for example. At the end of August Makhkamov resigned as first secretary of the Tajik Communist Party, which temporarily renamed itself the Tajik Socialist Party shortly afterwards. At the beginning of September a 'conservative' hard-liner, Rakhman Nabiev, tried to seize power but was forced to back down after demonstrations by the Islamic and democratic opposition.[100]

In the Baltic republics the aftermath of the coup and international recognition of independence saw a renewed upsurge of nationalist feeling, particularly in Estonia and Latvia where the Russian-speaking population was an important political factor and the need for laws on citizenship to be approved became more and more urgent. In Estonia a new council was created with equal representation from the Supreme Soviet and the Congress Movement to draw up a new draft constitution. In Latvia the leadership of the Popular Front advocated the application of more strict criteria for citizenship than the government which contained many prominent Front members and the Popular Front fraction in the Supreme Council. The leadership of the Popular Front argued that the final decision on the law on citizenship should only be taken after a referendum amongst citizens of the inter-war republic and their descendants. The Citizens' Congress went even further and disputed the right of the republican Supreme Council to make any decision on the matter at all and was supported in this by the Latvian Movement for National Independence. By the end of 1991 the Popular Front was on the verge of fragmentation.[101]

Whilst the defeat of the coup led to a reactivation of radical nationalist forces in the Baltic republics in Ukraine and Moldova, it was figures who had not been directly associated with the nationalist movements that benefited from the new situation. At the beginning of December 1991 Ukrainians went to the polls to vote on whether to approve the independence declaration of 24 August and elect a president. More than 80 per cent of Ukrainians voted to approve independence and elected Leonid Kravchuk as president by a 60 per cent vote so avoiding a second round, defeating Viacheslav Chornovil, the official Rukh candidate, and Levko Luk'ianenko from the Republican Party. Kravchuk's defence of republican sovereignty and internal divisions left Rukh unable to exert much influence on the government. In Moldova rising inter-ethnic tension provided the background to the presidential elections held at the beginning of December. The Russian-speaking population in the Transdnestr region and the Gagauz minority voted in referendums for secession from Moldova. Relations between the Popular Front and Mircea Snegur, the chair of the republican Supreme Soviet had gradually deteriorated since the beginning of the year as Snegur had opposed the Front's support for a rapid move towards union with Romania and, instead, proposed a longer transition period in which Moldova would be an independent state. The Popular Front decided to boycott the presidential elections and Snegur was elected unopposed.[102]

Independent political movements had been at the centre of the process which had led to the disintegration of the Soviet Union. In a number of instances they participated directly in government or had mobilised popular support which had forced concessions from the authorities. In many more instances they had forced elements in the republican Communist Parties to adopt their agenda. In the face of a fracturing communist apparat, the independent political movements were unable to consolidate themselves organisationally and hence began to splinter and lose their ability to mobilise the population. As a result, the old structures of power and authority fell apart and political instability threatened as different elements in the old élites and the new political forces jockeyed for position.

Notes

1. See *Vesti iz SSSR*, No. 27, 1987.
2. Christopher J. Walker, *Armenia: the Survival of a Nation* (second edition), London, 1990 (hereafter Walker, *Armenia*), p. 393.
3. *Russkaia mysl'*, 7 September 1990.
4. Jonathan Aves, 'The Democratic Union: a soviet opposition party?' *Slovo*, November 1988, p. 94.
5. *Summary of World Broadcasts*, 28 October 1988; *Independent*, 8 February 1989.
6. *Grazhdanskie dvizheniia v Latvii 1989*, Moscow, 1990, pp. 30–4; *Radio Free Europe Research*, 13 July 1988, pp. 27–9.
7. See: *The Popular Movement of Ukraine for Restructuring. Rukh. Program and Charter*, Kiev, 1989, p. 41; *Narodnyi front Latvii. Programma. Ustav*, Riga, 1988, pp. 23–5; *Osnovnye dokumenty vtorogo s" ezda saiudisa*, Vilnius, 1990, pp. 25–6.
8. Interview with Andrius Kubilius, Sajudis executive secretary, conducted by the author, 24 September 1991.
9. *Narodnyi front Latvii. Programma. Ustav*, pp. 9–10.
10. *Narodnyi front Latvii. Programma. Ustav*, pp. 3–4, 15–17.
11. *Grazhdanskie dvizheniia v Latvii 1989*, p. 28.
12. *Grazhdanskie dvizheniia v Latvii 1989*, Moscow, 1990, pp. 22–5. By the end of the year the Latvian version had a print-run of 100,000 and the Russian version of 65,000. *Report on the USSR*, 13 October 1989, p. 25.
13. *Summary of World Broadcasts*, 29 October 1988.
14. *Independent*, 24 October 1988.
15. Interview with Andrius Kubilius, Sajudis executive secretary, 24 September 1991, conducted by the author.
16. *Radio Free Europe Research*, 22 November 1988.
17. *Independent*, 19 November 1988.
18. *Report on the USSR*, 28 April 1989, p. 17.
19. *Report on the USSR*, 14 April 1989, pp. 29–30.
20. *Report on the USSR*, 1 December 1989, p. 19.
21. *Independent*, 9 October 1989, 10 October 1989, 8 December 1989, and *Guardian*, 8 December 1989, 29 December 1989.
22. *Stroitel' naia gazeta*, 2 December 1988.
23. *Vesti iz SSSR*, 15 November 1988; 28 February 1989.
24. In Lithuania this was a small rump that was derisively known as 'the midnight party' because it was hurriedly formed at the beginning of 1990. In Latvia pro-Moscow

elements were more significant in the local Communist Party and there was not such a determined move to set up an independent Communist Party as in Lithuania.

25. Vilnius had been part of Poland until 1940.
26. *Spravochnik politicheskikh i obshchestvennikh organizatsii Latvii*, Moscow, 1990; *Report on the USSR*, 20 October 1989.
27. *Spravochnik politicheskikh i obshchestvennikh organizatsii Latvii*, 1991.
28. *Guardian*, 10 May 1989.
29. *The Popular Movement of Ukraine for Restructuring. Rukh. Program and Charter*, Kiev, 1989, p. 4.
30. Keith Sword (ed.), *Times Guide to Eastern Europe*, London, Times Books, 1991, p. 242.
31. *The Popular Movement of Ukraine for Restructuring*, Kiev, 1989, pp. 11, 20–1.
32. *Report on the USSR*, 13 October 1989.
33. *Russkaia mysl'*, 7 September 1990.
34. *Krasnaia zvezda*, 22 February 1989.
35. A meeting of Belorussian youth groups had also been forced to take place in Vilnius in early January. *Independent*, 18 January 1989.
36. *Survey of World Broadcasts*, 27 August 1988; *Report on the USSR*, 25 August 1989; the Club was named after a 19th-century Romanian priest who helped spread the use of the Romanian language.
37. The Moldavian 'language' was simply Romanian written in Cyrillic as Stalin had ordered after the republic had been annexed in 1940.
38. *Independent*, 21 January 1989, and *Guardian*, 2 February 1989.
39. Walker, *Armenia*, p. 404.
40. *Izvestiia*, 28 November 1988; *Independent*, 3 December 1988.
41. *Guardian*, 27 December 1988.
42. *Central Asia and Caucasus Chronicle*, August 1989, pp. 7–10.
43. Leila Iunusova, '*Konets leninskogo perioda (Azerbaijan v avguste-sentiabre 1989 g)*', unpublished paper, October 1989, p. 10.
44. *Guardian*, 15 August 1989.
45. Iunusova, '*Konets leninskogo perioda*', op. cit. pp. 9–11.
46. *Report on the USSR*, no. 32, 1991, p. 25.
47. They had been deported from Georgia to Central Asia in 1944.
48. See, for example, Gorbachev's remark that Islamic fundamentalists were involved in the Fergana disturbances. *Guardian* 14 June 1989. Such allegations were used to discredit informal political organisations and provide an excuse for their suppression.
49. *Report on the USSR*, 26 January 1990.
50. *Report on the USSR*, 23 February 1990, 4 January 1991; *Daily Telegraph*, 20 February 1990.
51. *Komsomolets Kirgizii*, 14 February 1990; *Eastern Europe Newsletter*, 25 June 1990; *Rabochaia tribuna*, 19 July 1990; *Sovetskaia Kirgiziia*, 19 September 1990 (quoted in *Summary of World Broadcasts*, 6 November 1990).
52. Masaliev was a well-known supporter of the politburo's arch-conservative Egor Ligachev.
53. *Report on the USSR*, 30 November 1990.
54. *Central Asian and Caucasus Chronicle*, December/March 1990, p. 4.
55. *Report on the USSR*, 4 January 1991.
56. Two state prosecutors investigating corruption in the Central Asian republics who

had alleged that the network reached up to the highest reaches of the CPSU in Moscow. Subsequently, attempts had been made to remove them from their work and suggest that they had broken the law in carrying out their investigations.

57. *Summary of World Broadcasts*, 1 August 1989 and *Ogonek*, no. 32, 1990, pp. 7–8.
58. ibid. pp. 8–9.
59. *Narodnyi deputat*, no. 9, 1991.
60. V.N. Berezovskii, N.I. Krotov and V.V. Cherviakov, *Rossiia. Partii. Assotsiatsii. Soiuzy, Kluby, Spravochnik.*, vol. 1, no. 1, Moscow, 1991, pp. 60–1.
61. Including Iurii Afanas'ev, who gave a keynote speech.
62. *Informatsionnyi biulleten' Sotsial-demokraticheskoi assotsiatsii*, no. 19; *Esdek*, no. 4, 1990, p. 8.
63. *Grazhdanskie dvizheniia v Latvii 1989*, p. 84.
64. One year later a second extraordinary congress announced the renaming of the party as the Democratic Labour Party.
65. *Russkaia mysl'*, 7 September 1990; *Times Guide*, p. 224, claims 88 out of 141.
66. From now on the Supreme Soviets of the Baltic Republics will be called Supreme Councils as they renamed themselves.
67. *Independent*, 9 March 1990.
68. *Independent*, 13 January 1990.
69. *Guardian*, 17 March 1990.
70. *Russkaia mysl'*, 11 May 1990.
71. *Report on the USSR*, 10 July 1990.
72. Iunusova, *Konets leninskogo perioda*, op. cit. p. 11.
73. *Sunday Times*, 31 December 1989; *Eastern Europe Newsletter*, 5 February 1990; *Summary of World Broadcasts*, 4 January 1990, 5 January 1990.
74. *Krasnaia zvezda*, 14 November 1989.
75. *Kommersant*, no. 20, 1990.
76. *Rossiia. Partii. Assotsiatsii. Soiuzy. Kluby. Spravochnik.*, vol. 1, no. 1, Moscow, 1991, p. 61.
77. *Kommunist Ukrainy*, no. 5, 1991, p. 111; see below.
78. *Rossiia. Partii. Assotsiatsii. Soiuzy. Kluby. Spravochnik.*, vol. 1, no. 2, Moscow, 1991, p. 280.
79. *Argumenty i fakty*, no. 7, 1990; *Rossiia. Partii. Assotsiatsii. Soiuzy. Kluby. Spravochnik.*, vol. 1, no. 1, Moscow, 1991, pp. 242–3.
80. *Rossiia. Partii. Assotsiatsii. Soiuzy. Kluby. Spravochnik.*, vol. 1, no. 2, Moscow, 1991, pp. 281–3; *Moskovskaia pravda*, 31 March 1990.
81. *Ogonek*, no. 25, 1990, p. 1; *Rossiia. Partii. Assotsiatsii. Soiuzy. Kluby. Spravochnik.*, vol. 1, no. 1, Moscow, 1991, pp. 243–4; *Izvestiia*, 18 June 1990.
82. *Kommunist Ukrainy*, no. 5, 1991, pp. 110–12.
83. *Report on the USSR*, 12 July 1991; *Times*, 29 June 1991, 2 July 1991, 3 July 1991; *Guardian*, 4 July 1991.
84. *Izvestiia TsK KPSS*, 1991, no. 3, p. 97; *Russkaia mysl'*, 7 September 1990.
85. *Kommunist Ukrainy*, no. 5, 1991, pp. 93–4.
86. See below.
87. Interview with Dobilus Kirvelis, conducted by the author, 24 September 1991.
88. *Kommunist Ukrainy*, no. 5, 1991, pp. 46–62.
89. *Khristiansko-Demokraticheskii Soiuz Rossii*, London, 1990, p. 5, and *Rossiiskoe Khristianskoe Demokraticheskoe Dvizhenie. Sbornik materialov*, Moscow, 1990, p. 3.
90. A Christian Democratic Party had been set up by the ex-dissident Viktoras Petkus

in 1988. It took the radical line of opposing participation in Soviet structures and remained very small. The two organisations were hardly divided ideologically, both advocated a firmly nationalist line, but attempts to unite them were not successful.

91. *Spravochnik politicheskikh i obshchestvennykh organizatsii Latvii.*

92. *Osnovnye dokumenty vtorogo s"ezda saiudisa*, p. 20; the analogous words in the programme agreed at the 1st Congress had been 'the restructuring of socialist society which has been started by the CPSU on the basis of democracy and humanism', *Summary of World Broadcasts*, 11 November 1988.

93. Čepaitis was disgraced in early 1992 when it was revealed that he had collaborated with the KGB earlier in his career.

94. Interview with Smetona, conducted by the author, 23 September 1991.

95. *Sovetskaia kul' tura*, 10 November 1990.

96. *Kommunist Ukrainy*, no. 5, 1991, p. 37.

97. *Kommunist Ukrainy*, no. 5, 1991, pp. 120–2.

98. *Ukrainian Review*, winter 1990, pp. 74–7.

99. *Report on the USSR*, 6 September 1991.

100. Nabiev subsequently won presidential elections held at the end of November against an opposition candidate, Davlat Khudonazarov, who was supported by opposition Islamic and democratic organisations.

101. *Report on the USSR*, 22 November 1991.

102. *Independent*, 3 December 1991; *Guardian*, 7 December 1991.

3 The rebirth of politics in Russia*
Peter J. S. Duncan

The aim of this chapter is to describe the activity of political associations, movements, parties, electoral blocs and alliances in Russia (i.e. the RSFSR) from late 1988 to the end of 1991. The principal focus will be on movements which sought to operate throughout Russia, and on groups in Moscow, since the capital proved to be the seeding-ground for many of the groups which spread through the country. The national movements of the Tatars and other minorities inside Russia will not be covered in detail. Leningrad/St Petersburg will be considered in Chapter 4. It will be seen how local associations developed nation-wide links, and how electoral blocs and, less successfully, nation-wide Russian parties developed. It will be argued that most of the Russian democrats wished to reform the USSR as a whole, and not to destroy the federation as such, as was the ultimate result. The attempted coup of August 1991 was defeated mainly within Russia. The victory of democracy was largely due to the changes in political consciousness among the civilian population and the armed forces, the MVD and the KGB, effected by the new movements and their spokespersons, taking advantage of the conditions of glasnost introduced by Gorbachev over the previous few years.

The main questions to be considered will be why no mass Russian Popular Front appeared, bringing together all those opposed to the communist regime; and the related but distinct question as to why no strong parties appeared which were able to be taken seriously as rivals to the CPSU, in the period of perestroika. In view of the fact that the independent movements interacted with the people more during elections than at other times, particular attention will be paid to these periods.

Elections to the USSR Congress of People's Deputies

The decision of the Communist Party leadership, headed by Gorbachev, to create a new-style parliament with competitive elections opened up an unprecedented opportunity for the new groups to test the popularity of their ideas with the mass of the population. Gorbachev spoke of restoring the soviets

* I should like to thank Robert Service, Martin McCauley and Tim Spence for their prompt reading of a draft of this chapter.

to becoming the dominant political organs of the state, as Lenin had argued in 1917. 'The Soviet state is based upon the idea of full power of the soviets within their territory, each soviet acting as a constituent part of the supreme power.' The new Congress of People's Deputies (CPD) would 'ensure against abuses of power in the upper echelons of the state structure'. The General Secretary did not speak of abuse of power by the Communist Party; his line was that only the CPSU, which had initiated perestroika, could unify the diverse interests in the country. At the same time the CPD should represent 'All social strata and shades of public opinion . . . The most distinctive feature of the new election law is that it envisages multicandidate elections in constituencies returning one deputy each'.[1] The CPD would elect a new Supreme Soviet which would be a full-time parliament.

The first round of the elections to the CPD were fixed for 26 March 1989, but the campaign began four months earlier, on 1 December 1988. In the RSFSR, the democratic associations included *Memorial*, the Popular Fronts such as those in Moscow and Iaroslavl', electoral blocs such as Elections-89 in Leningrad and many smaller groups. They lacked a coordinating centre analogous to the Baltic Popular Fronts. Ranged against them was the great bulk of the Communist Party and state apparatus, already suspicious of Gorbachev's moves towards democracy, and the small but vocal Russian chauvinist groups such as *Pamiat'*. Most of the Democratic Union boycotted the elections.

The democrats did not stand on a level playing field. The electoral law allocated 750 seats in the CPD—one-third of the total—to public organisations, such as the CPSU, the trade unions and the Komsomol. These seats were frequently filled by the decision of the leaders of these bodies without discussion. The other 1,500 were divided between 750 territorial constituencies of equal population size and 750 national-territorial constituencies designed to give greater representation to the smaller Union republics and to the 'autonomous' republics and regions. At every stage of the nominations and election procedure for these 1,500 seats the apparatus had opportunities to block undesirable candidates. Nominations could be made by work collectives, approved public organisations and residents' meetings. Unregistered, informal associations did not have the right to make nominations. The traditional inertia of the population helped the apparatus to manipulate work-place meetings. The radical weekly *Moscow News* helped the democrats to fight this by reporting a case where the apparatus candidate was opposed at a work-place meeting in the Oktiabr'skii electoral district of Moscow.[2]

The same newspaper publicised cases of abuses by the authorities of the rules concerning residents' nominating meetings. The group wishing to nominate an opposition candidate might find that the room allocated by the authorities was too small to hold the required minimum of 500 residents. Alternatively, the room might be filled by residents called out by the authorities and supporters of the group which had called the meeting might be denied entry—a phenomenon reported in Iaroslavl', Saratov, Novosibirsk, Tuimazy (Bashkiria) and Stavropol.[3] Most importantly, in every constituency a pre-election meeting had the right to vet the list of nominated candidates and only those which it approved appeared on the ballot.[4] In 384 constituencies—over a quarter—only one candidate was registered.[5] The degree to which the apparatus sought to manipulate the process varied widely from place to place, and even between different constituencies of Moscow.

Just after the start of the campaign, confusion was created by a body proclaiming itself to be the much-desired Russian (*Rossiiskii*) Popular Front (RPF). Following a conference on 15 December 1988, the RPF demanded that local Popular Fronts subordinate themselves to it. This was the work of Valerii Skurlatov, who had not previously taken part in the Popular Front movement. While a functionary in the Moscow Komsomol in 1965, he had achieved notoriety with a bloodthirsty and chauvinistic manifesto called 'A Code of Morals'. It advocated corporal punishment in schools and for Russian women who gave themselves to foreigners. Two decades later, Skurlatov and his RPF maintained a Russian nationalist ideology but now argued unequivocally for private enterprise, the import of foreign capital and a staged shift towards a free market. According to Skurlatov, the RPF was established in direct imitation of the Baltic Popular Fronts. The TASS news agency and then the conservative *Sovetskaia Rossiia* gave wide publicity to the RPF, at a time when the democratic Popular Fronts were being ignored by all but some local media. Skurlatov's activities disrupted the work of the democrats and allowed the apparatus to denigrate the Popular Front movement.[6]

In autumn 1988 the Moscow Popular Front (MPF), lacking a central leadership, had chosen a Coordinating Council to prepare a founding conference of the Front. Whereas the Organising Committee represented the different groups within the Front, the Coordinating Council was chosen on a personal basis. All eight active members, including Boris Kagarlitskii, Sergei Stankevich, Mikhail Maliutin and Aleksandr Fedorovskii, were members of socialist groups, and four belonged to the CPSU. Skurlatov's initiative attracted some elements within the MPF, and by February 1989 divisions within the Organising Committee paralysed it. This led to a conference of the MPF on 2–3 March, in which the Coordinating Council sought approval from the movement for a draft programme, emphasising the importance of the socialist tradition. Moving the draft, Kagarlitskii argued that the MPF should shift from demanding a faster pace for perestroika to a greater concern with the final goal. He wanted more attention to be given to social problems, including the preservation of social guarantees. While arguing for a multi-party system, Kagarlitskii saw the main problem not in the number of parties but 'in the lack of viable democratic institutions'. The main opposition to the Coordinating Council came from Evgenii Dergunov, whose speech echoed Skurlatov's position and warned of the need not to underestimate Russian patriotism. With the support of a speech by Stankevich, however, the Coordinating Council won the approval of the conference for its own socialist position.[7]

The activists and leaders of the MPF were mainly in their twenties and early thirties; many of the delegates to the conferences were new to any sort of political activity. At the other generational end of the democratic camp, leaders of the older intellectual élite organised a discussion group, the Moscow Tribune. The first meeting on 4 February 1989 elected a bureau including Andrei Sakharov, the space scientist Roal'd Sagdeev, the historians Iurii Afanas'ev, Leonid Batkin and Mikhail Gefter, and the writers Ales' Adamovich and Iurii Kariakin. The group planned to draw on the resources of the Academy of Sciences in analysing problems, and Afanas'ev admitted that it would remain 'an "élitist" association, admitting new members by careful selection'. Its importance was that it brought respected members of the intellectual establishment into alliance with the informals.[8]

At the same time, activists of informal groups who were also members of the CPSU began to raise the demand for free debate within the party itself. In spring 1988, they had established in Moscow the Inter-Club Party Group (*Mezhklubnaia partiinaia gruppa*). This included Maliutin and Stankevich from the MPF and Igor' Chubais from Klub Perestroika. Prior to the 19th Party Conference the group circulated proposals to democratise the party and helped Afanas'ev to be elected a delegate against stiff apparatus opposition. Chubais has argued that the group represented the first faction in the CPSU since 1921 (although this overlooks the opposition platforms of the mid-1920s). In February 1989 the group, together with Democratic Perestroika, organised a discussion at the Central Mathematical Economics Institute on whether free debate should be allowed within the party. A report to the meeting not only called for a multi-party system but also said that a split in the ruling party would be the easiest way to achieve this.[9]

In Moscow and the other large cities of Russia, the informal groups campaigned for their candidates with meetings, leaflets, rallies where possible, posters and even stickers on trains on the Metro. Initially, they were confronted with apathy on the part of the voters. People did not expect any improvement in the political system to come from the communists. The All-Union Centre for the Study of Public Opinion, polling in twenty-five large towns throughout the USSR, found in December that less than half the population even knew about the change in the Constitution. In January very few people thought that real changes were occurring, but in February with the completion of the nomination process respondents began to understand that something unusual was in the wind. At the beginning of March over 80 per cent knew that a real change in the electoral process was under way. In the last week before the elections the level of activity in the large towns increased substantially. Asked at this time whether the new system would allow better candidates to emerge, 48 per cent said yes, 12 per cent said no, and 39 per cent did not know.[10]

How were the democratic movements outside Moscow faring, and how did they succeed in the elections? In Leningrad the movement 'For a Popular Front' led an electoral bloc, 'Elections-89'. They were more effective than the democrats anywhere else in Russia, and the following chapter examines the particular factors operating in the second capital in more detail. The Iaroslavl' Popular Front had succeeded in establishing groups in the main industrial factories of the city in autumn 1988. It campaigned successfully for special food shops for pregnant women and mothers, and for more food for children in hospital. It organised monthly meetings at the Political Education House and established a stall on Marx Square.[11] In the town of Andropov in Iaroslav oblast', an 'Initiative Group to Support Perestroika (Popular Front)' was formed in December. In February 1989 it organised an election meeting to prepare 'mandates' for the deputies. It collected signatures in the streets protesting against the building of a nuclear power station and against the pollution of the Volga and calling for the restoration of the name Rybinsk to the town (this was done in April) and for the election of the Iaroslavl' Popular Front candidate Igor' Shamshev.[12] The Iaroslavl' Popular Front itself at first supported only Shamshev (a senior lecturer at the Iaroslavl' State University who belonged to the Organising Committee of the Popular Front), but then also gave support to two other candidates. All three candidates were elected ultimately. Shamshev, however, was excluded from the first round of voting by the apparatus, but allowed to stand in the second round since the first round was indecisive.[13]

In Petrozavodsk the Popular Front of Karelia (an autonomous republic within the RSFSR) appeared in November 1988 and organised meetings on questions of ecology and the economic independence and sovereignty of Karelia. It succeeded in having one of its leaders, S. V. Belozertsov, elected to the CPD.[14] In Iuzhno-Sakhalinsk in the Far East, the Democratic Movement for Perestroika had been formed in June 1988 and already could claim the enforced retirement of the Sakhalin obkom first secretary, Petr Tret'iakov. By the end of the year the movement had split between supporters of the Democratic Union and a more moderate group. This did not prevent the success of the candidate it supported for the CPD, the journalist V. V. Guliia, who defeated the new obkom first secretary.[15] In Novosibirsk the Democratic Movement, based on the Siberian division of the Academy of Sciences, supported two candidates, both of whom were successful.[16]

The other major focus of democratic activity was the Urals. In Boris El'tsin's home base of Sverdlovsk, the informal groups successfully supported the loader (and former judge) Leonid Kudrin.[17] Also elected was Gennadii Burbulis, deputy director of the Institute for Improving Qualifications of the USSR Ministry of Non-Ferrous Metallurgy. He had become well known in Sverdlovsk for his outspoken contributions to the Discussion Tribune organised by the gorkom. The Kuibyshev Popular Front did not succeed in getting any of its own candidates on the ballot paper, but instead supported A. A. Sokolov, the editor of *Volzhskii komsomolets*, and I. V. Sorokin of the transport police. Two big meetings were organised, one of which attracted 3,000 people. Both candidates were successful, defeating the commander of the Volga Military District and the obkom first secretary.[18] The 'Popular Front for Revolutionary Perestroika in Cheliabinsk', based on a wide spectrum of local organisations, succeeded in the election of one of its supporters, while two others were excluded by the electoral commissions.[19]

In Moscow, the intellectual élite was galvanised into action by the refusal of the Presidium of the Academy of Sciences of the USSR to nominate radicals to the Academy's delegation to the CPD. Sakharov (with the support of sixty institutes), Sagdeev, the literary historian Dmitrii Likhachev and the economists Gavriil Popov and Nikolai Shmelev had been nominated by more institutes than any candidates approved by the Presidium. On 2 February 1,000 scholars gathered at the Presidium building to protest against the decision.[20] Sakharov insisted on standing as a deputy from the Academy in order to defeat the Presidium, although he received nominations from several territorial and national-territorial constituencies.[21] A revolt at the Academy plenum encouraged by coverage in *Moscow News*[22] led to the rejection of many of the candidates favoured by the Presidium. All the radicals listed were elected (except for Popov, who was elected by the Union of Scientific and Technical Societies) as well as the classical literature specialist Sergei Averintsev.

The extreme Russian chauvinists put up a number of candidates and organised meetings. In Moscow the Komsomol neo-Stalinist monthly *Molodaia gvardiia*, the Moscow Writers' Union journal *Moskva* and the literary journal *Roman-gazeta* organised a meeting on 23 January 1989, where the speakers venomously attacked the leading reformers. Anti-Semitic slogans and *Pamiat'* banners decorated the hall.[23] The chauvinists' main impact, however, was in the violent disruption of meetings called by the democrats. By this time *Pamiat'* had split into factions. It was the one headed by Igor' Sychev that broke up a residents' meeting held to nominate Vitalii Korotich, the editor of *Ogonek*, in Moscow's Dzerzhinskii constituency on 9 January. According to Kagarlitskii, the MPF had offered to canvass support in the district and provide stewards for the meeting, but Korotich had refused the offer, considering the Popular Front to be too radical. Without the assistance of the MPF, the meeting failed to attract the necessary 500 people. Suddenly *Pamiat'* supporters took over the hall, and Korotich was saved by Fedorovskii of the Popular Front from being beaten up. Maliutin and Fedorovskii later sent a letter to *Ogonek* stating the MPF view of the need to organise against *Pamiat'*, but it was published only after the removal of all references to the Popular Front. Kagarlitskii sees *Ogonek*'s lack of support for the MPF as exemplifying the Moscow intellectual élite's fear of creating a mass organisation.[24] It is interesting that *Moscow News*, likewise, gave hardly any coverage to the MPF as such during the election campaign (although the Iaroslavl' Popular Front was mentioned several times). Both journals may have been treading a thin line between publicising the programmes of individual democratic candidates and avoiding giving offence to the conservatives, who were mobilising against organisations opposing the CPSU.

The most important contest in the country turned out to be in the national-territorial constituency of Moscow, which covered the whole city. Although nominated in his political base in Sverdlovsk (where he had risen to the post of

First Secretary of the party obkom) and in Berezniki (Perm oblast', also in the Urals) where he had grown up, Boris El'tsin decided to stand in the capital. While serving as first secretary of the Moscow gorkom of the CPSU from 1985 to 1987, this career party apparatchik had earned great popularity among the citizens for his stand against privilege and corruption. His attack on Egor Ligachev, the CPSU Central Committee secretary responsible for ideology, for holding up perestroika, delivered to the Central Committee in October 1987, and his spectacular resignation from the Politburo, had earned him no less hatred among the party cadres. Gorbachev and his two most senior radical allies, Foreign Minister Eduard Shevardnadze and Central Committee Secretary Aleksandr Iakovlev, had all fiercely denounced El'tsin at the Central Committee. El'tsin had been later called from a hospital bed to face the Moscow gorkom where he was humiliated and sacked. El'tsin was gambling on his popularity among the voters now overcoming the tricks of the apparatus.[25] He had not been completely expelled from the party élite; he remained a member of the Central Committee, and deputy chairperson of the USSR State Committee for Construction (Gosstroi) with the rank of a minister. El'tsin stood on the basis of the official programme adopted for the elections by the CPSU Central Committee, and emphasised his support for Gorbachev as head of the Supreme Soviet. While campaigning against the secret privileges of the nomenklatura, he expressed opposition to a transition to capitalism and to the secession of the Baltic States.[26]

It should be said at this point that the Moscow intellectual élite seem to have been rather wary of El'tsin. They were unsure whether his open attack in October 1987 had been wise; it seemed to have weakened Gorbachev at the time, and forced him towards the conservatives. As Moscow first secretary he had not appeared particularly sympathetic to democratic associations. At the same time, some intellectuals were unhappy with his populism; his attack on the privileges of the élite seemed to verge on demagogy. As late as November 1988 he had told a Komsomol school that 'as regards an ideal of a political leader, I cannot imagine a higher ideal than Lenin'.[27] This could not endear him to the western-oriented intellectuals. For the mass of the population, however, the contest was between a heroic defender of their interests and the director of the ZiL car Factory, Evgenii Brakov, an establishment figure with a lacklustre style. The party apparatus saw defeat looming ahead of them. A Central Committee plenum, held on 15–16 March, decided to establish a commission to investigate El'tsin's actions. This could have been the first step to expelling him from the Central Committee or even from the party. The conservative press campaigned against him, depicting him as a demagogue. But these attacks on El'tsin only strengthened his image among the masses as a fighter on their behalf whom the authorities wished to victimise. Three mass demonstrations and meetings were organised in defence of El'tsin in Moscow: the first by Skurlatov's RPF on 19 March, and the other two by the MPF on 22 and 25 March. The latter, at the Luzhniki stadium, on the eve of the elections, attracted 35,000 people.[28]

It seems to have been the attack on El'tsin which concretised the alliance between the former Moscow party chief and the MPF. Before then, El'tsin does not seem to have been close to the informals; his campaign manager was Lev Sukhanov, his assistant at Gosstroi.[29] In the Moscow territorial constituencies the MPF got four candidates nominated, of whom only one, Stankevich, the young researcher on American constitutional history, made it to the ballot paper, in Cheremushki constituency.[30] In the Oktiabr'skii constituency, the Society of Invalids nominated Il'ia Zaslavskii, who received the backing of the MPF and, a few months later, was to become one of its leaders. His campaign was boosted by two special articles in *Moscow News*.[31] El'tsin's alliance with the MPF was to benefit both sides. Stankevich organised a telegram of protest from radical Moscow candidates about the Central Committee attack on El'tsin. Zaslavskii and Arkadii Murashev, who was also close to the MPF, signed the telegram, as did Oleg Bogomolov, the director of the Institute of the Economics of the World Socialist System, Tel'man Gdlian, the prosecutor in the Uzbekistan corruption case, Iurii Chernichenko, the radical specialist on agriculture, and seven other candidates.

In the election, those candidates who signed the telegram did on average significantly better than those who did not. Zaslavskii won outright in the first round on 26 March with 55 per cent, and Bogomolov also won outright in the Sevastopol electoral district. Gdlian, well known for his public fight against high-level corruption, won the highest proportion of the vote of any candidate in the Moscow territorial constituencies, with 86.8 per cent in the Tushino constituency, which included the radical suburban town of Zelenograd.[32] El'tsin himself won a tremendous victory, with 90 per cent of the votes cast; 5.3 million people had voted for him.

Those signatories who made it through to the second round of voting on 9 April were rewarded with a telegram of thanks and support from El'tsin. These candidates gave the maximum publicity to this association with the popular hero. In the Gagarin constituency, both participants in the second round had signed the telegram: Chernichenko came out on top. It is possible to speak of the 'El'tsin effect', with candidates capitalising on their real or supposed connection with him. An exception was the second round in the Voroshilov constituency, where the dissident Marxist historian Roi Medvedev, who had by then been readmitted to the CPSU, defeated a signatory to the telegram. Medvedev's candidacy had been backed by *Moscow News*.[33]

A particularly interesting contest was in the Cheremushki electoral district. In the first round, Stankevich received 49 per cent and the runner-up was the radical environmentalist, Mikhail Lemeshev, with 32 per cent of the votes. One might have expected that Stankevich's position was unchallengeable. Lemeshev had not signed, or had not been asked to sign, the telegram about El'tsin. On the second round ballot MPF supporters backing Stankevich found themselves confronted by *Pamiat'* enthusiasts supporting Lemeshev. Prominent writers of Russian nationalist views such as Vladimir Soloukhin, Valentin Rasputin and Vasilii Belov and the artist Il'ia Glazunov appeared on his behalf. While Stankevich's campaign emphasised the question of democratisation and power, as well as his role as initiator of the El'tsin telegram, some of Lemeshev's supporters used anti-Semitic slogans against their opponent. A banner at a Lemeshev meeting read 'Jews—vote for Stankevich!' Lemeshev's campaign linked Stankevich with the nomenklatura, describing him as a lecturer in scientific communism who led a group attached to the local raikom of the CPSU which sought to influence independent movements from within. (This was presumably a reference to the Inter-Club Party Group.) In the second round of the election on 9 April, Stankevich defeated Lemeshev by a small majority.[34] Stankevich was the only actual member of the MPF to become a USSR people's deputy; Zaslavskii and Murashev joined after being elected. Stankevich himself attributed his victory largely to the efforts of the MPF.[35]

Pamiat' also intervened in the Kuntsevo constituency of Moscow, backing the Hero of the Soviet Union and former POW of the Afghan war, Col. Aleksandr Rutskoi. The colonel attacked the democratic groups for their abuse of public officials and the army, and denounced the new cooperative firms as 'legalised speculation'. According to Kagarlitskii, he was supported by a reactionary spectrum ranging from Stalinists to monarchists, whose slogans recalled 'fascist propaganda clichés'. Rutskoi came top in the first round, but without winning an outright majority. The MPF and other democrats united around Vladimir Logunov, the reformist deputy editor of *Moskovskaia pravda*, who had come second, in order to stop Rutskoi. Logunov won on the second round.[36] Even outside Moscow, conservative Russian nationalists generally failed to be elected. Those who made it to the Congress did so through the public organisations: Vasilii Belov via the CPSU, Valentin Rasputin and Viktor Astaf'ev via the Union of Writers. Iurii Bondarev, a leader of the RSFSR Union of Writers, stood in Volgograd with a proposal to restore the name of Stalingrad to the city, and lost.[37]

The real losers of the campaign in the RSFSR, however, were the apparatchiks of the CPSU and of the state administration. It had not only been claimed for decades in the Soviet Union, but believed by many in the west that the party had won acceptance from the Russian population. The extraordinary results of the first competitive elections in the USSR astonished and for a while paralysed the losers themselves. Around thirty obkom first secretaries were defeated in a nation-wide vote of no confidence in the party which had brought the country to perestroika. The defeat was worst in Leningrad, where key party and soviet figures were rejected by the voters, including the obkom first secretary and candidate Politburo member Iurii Solov'ev. Nikolai Ivanov, Gdlian's colleague in the Uzbek corruption investigation, won the Leningrad national-territorial seat. The role of the independent movements, not only in Moscow and Leningrad but in most of the major Russian cities, was decisive in securing the election of deputies who articulated a positive democratic alternative to communist officialdom.

From Popular Fronts to Democratic Russia

This section will show how the local democratic associations developed their ideas between spring 1989 and spring 1990, and how they tried with difficulty to create a Russia-wide organisation. This was a time of rapid change not only in the USSR itself, but also in Central and Eastern Europe, where the collapse in late 1989 of the communist regimes imposed by the Soviet Union had a radicalising effect on the Russian democrats and led them to question more openly the 'socialist choice' which the country had supposedly taken in October 1917.

After the elections to the USSR Congress of People's Deputies, the attention of the Popular Fronts and other democratic groups in Russia continued to be concentrated mainly on events at the all-Union level. In April 1989, Moscow Tribune organised a meeting with elected people's deputies. It was attended by Sakharov, Afanas'ev, Popov, Murashev and Iurii Kariakin from Moscow, Marju Lauristin from Estonia and Eldar Shengelaia from Georgia, among others. The meeting discussed increasing the importance of the role of the Congress, and ensuring that the debates be given full publicity.[38]

The victories in the elections did not lead to a hiatus in grass-roots activity. On 20–1 May the MPF held its founding conference. In a replay of an old debate, a 'democratic' faction demanded the removal of references to socialism from the constitution, but was rebuffed. The conference adopted a charter and a resolution entitled 'On democratic socialism'. This defined socialism primarily in terms of political rights, together with workers' participation in management and social security. The charter called for the abolition of Article 6 and for the CPSU to have equal rights with other parties. On the nationality question, it wanted a new Union Treaty allowing secession and equal rights for all the peoples of the USSR, but at the same time called for the use of the Russian language throughout the Soviet Union for communication between nationalities. Stankevich topped the poll for the Coordinating Council.[39] On 21 May, 100,000 people attended a rally organised by Moscow Tribune and chaired by Popov. The speakers included a full line-up of the democratic wing of Soviet politics, including El'tsin, Sakharov, Gdlian, Zaslavskii, the MPF, the Democratic Union and the Confederation of Anarcho-Syndicalists. Part of the crowd began to shout 'El'tsin for President'—a demand far from the intentions of most of the leaders, who saw no alternative to Gorbachev's leadership.[40]

Despite being armed with a new constitution, the MPF seems to have gone into some decline shortly after its official foundation. The failure of the Popular Fronts across Russia to link up with the miners' strikes of summer 1989 and the greater political freedom persuaded Kagarlitskii and other socialists within the MPF to move towards establishing an independent socialist party. They had already established a 'Committee of New Socialists'.[41] The MPF now had to compete with newly formed associations of voters in the raiony of Moscow. These represented a wider democratic base than either the 'socialism' of the Popular Front or the confrontationalist approach of the Democratic Union. The Constitution of the 'Club of Voters of the Tagan'ka Raion of Moscow', for example, adopted at the founding conference in July 1989, set out its purposes in broad terms.

The aims of the activity of the Club are the raising of the political culture and civic activity of the electors, the defence of their rights, the securing of the organisational basis of their participation, with full rights, in the formation and activity of the soviets of people's deputies, true pluralism.[42]

Even before the opening of the CPD, the 'Moscow group' of deputies formed an identifiable core of radical opinion. They not only demanded a faster pace of change towards democracy but also criticised Gorbachev for reactionary measures, such as restrictions on demonstrations and the law against the 'discrediting' of state functionaries. Two events sharpened the fears of the radicals about the possible consequences of a conservative restoration: the killings of Georgian nationalists in Tbilisi on 9 April, and the massacre in June of protesters on Tienanmen Square in Beijing on the orders of conservative Chinese communists. The Tbilisi killings had also helped to raise the sympathy of the Russian democrats for the aspirations of the deputies from the Baltic Popular Fronts for self-determination, while the continuing conflict between Armenia and Azerbaijan over Nagornyi Karabakh and ethnic clashes in Central Asia forced the nationality question towards the top of the political agenda. The dominance of Moscow in the democratic Inter-Regional Group of Deputies was illustrated by the fact that four of the five co-chairpersons—El'tsin, Sakharov, Popov and Afanas'ev—lived in or represented Moscow (with the fifth, Palm, coming from Estonia). Additionally the secretary of the group was Murashev.

The crisis in the CPSU after the elections, with regional party leaders and even the prime minister, Nikolai Ryzhkov, openly or implicitly blaming Gorbachev, allowed the Inter-Regional Group to have an influence beyond the size of its membership. In May–June 1989, as the whole country listened to the Congress debates on radio and television, it was not only the outlying republics that were waking up but Russian society itself that was undergoing a profound rebirth. The miners' strikes highlighted not only the crisis in the economy but also the desire of many ordinary people to fight for change.

While in most cases recognising the right of the Baltic States to independence, the Russian democrats saw the main area of struggle at the all-Union level. They wanted to democratise the USSR, not to destroy it. At the same time, the inevitable result of the growing nationalism of the non-Russians was an increase in the national consciousness of the Russians themselves. One way in which this was expressed was the belief that, under the Soviet system, the Russians were subsidising the ungrateful non-Russians. At the Congress, the conservative Russian nationalist writer Valentin Rasputin suggested sarcastically to the Baltic and Georgian nationalists that the non-Russian republics might be better off if the RSFSR were to withdraw from the Soviet Union.[43]

For the democrats, it was essential that this arising national consciousness should be channelled into the direction of support for democracy and not into a conservative-imperial direction which might lead to a restoration of communist power.

Skurlatov's Russian Popular Front could not help to form a democratic national consciousness because it was itself tainted with imperialism. During and after the elections it attracted a certain following in Moscow for its support of El'tsin and of Gdlian and Ivanov. A conference it held in April 1989 attracted delegates from small groups from forty cities across Russia. The following month a 'patriotic-democratic fraction' led by Evgenii Dergunov split away, accusing Skurlatov of a 'bourgeois-western deviation' and creating the Moscow Popular-Patriotic Front. Democratic groups also left the RPF and tried to create a Popular Front of the RSFSR.[44] A meeting of delegates from nearly fifty cities, held in Iaroslavl' in the early summer, failed to establish an organisation, mainly because of disagreements over whether the movement should be primarily democratic or focus on Russian ethnic demands.[45]

The founding congress of the Popular Front of the RSFSR was finally held, also in Iaroslavl', on 21–2 October 1989. Among those taking part were the Popular Fronts of Iaroslavl', Leningrad, Moscow, Karelia and Tataria, Dergunov's group and Vladimir Osipov's Christian Patriotic Union. There were 116 delegates from forty-one areas, claiming to represent between 10,000 and 16,000 people. Skurlatov attended but the RPF did not enter the new organisation. The holding of the congress was facilitated by three members of the Inter-Regional Group, Igor' Shamshev from Iaroslavl' and two social democrats, Aleksandr Obolenskii and Sergei Belozertsev. The congress adopted a constitution and elected a fifteen-person Coordinating Council, including Gennadii Bogomolov of the Leningrad Popular Front, Andrei Babushkin of the MPF and Osipov; a five-person Control Commission; and five co-chairpersons, including Bogomolov.

The rules defined the Popular Front as 'a confederation of mass public-political organisations, uniting the democratic movements of the republic'. The programme called for people's power, a law-governed state, democratic freedoms and a mixed economy. There was no commitment to socialism. The programme demanded greater rights for the RSFSR: 'the establishment of the political, territorial and cultural sovereignty of the republic, the restoration to the Russian Federation of full statehood, the securing of equal rights for all nationalities living in the republic'. While the liberal-democratic current was dominant, socialist and nationalist tendencies were also present. It was notable that none of the people's deputies who organised the meeting entered the leading bodies. The organisation proved, however, not to have much of a future: the Coordinating Council met on 12 November to discuss tactics for the Russian elections, but subsequent meetings were inquorate.[46]

The Popular Front of the RSFSR had to contend with competition from two similar attempts to create networks of democratic activists which also took place in October 1989: the Inter-Regional Association of Democratic

Organisations (MADO) and the All-Union Association of Voters (VAI). Since both of these tried to operate on the Union level, they do not properly belong in this chapter. The VAI seems to have disappeared after its foundation,[47] although its newspaper *Khronika* continued to appear at least until summer 1990. The meeting of MADO in Cheliabinsk on 28–9 October (see Chapter 2) was addressed by Afanas'ev, and among those elected to the Organising Committee were Marina Sal'e from the Leningrad Popular Front and Oleg Rumiantsev from Democratic Perestroika.[48] None of these three bodies—the Popular Front, MADO or VAI—became well known to the electors, however.

Of greater significance was the Inter-Regional Association of Voters, which grew out of the Moscow Association of Voters (both, rather confusingly, known in Russian as MOI). The Moscow Association of Voters had been formed in June 1989, mainly out of the raion-level voters' associations such as that in the Taganka raion referred to earlier. MPF activists played a major role in its formation, and *Memorial* a smaller one. A fifteen-member Coordinating Council included Vladimir Bokser and O. Orlov representing the MPF, Lev Ponomarev of *Memorial* and Lev Shemaev and Aleksandr Muzykantskii, who were both close to El'tsin. The Moscow Association began regular publication of a newspaper, *Golos izbiratelei*, in September 1989. The Association was oriented towards the Inter-Regional Group. An All-Union Conference of Voters' Movements which it hosted in Moscow on 2–3 December, with 300 people from eight republics, was addressed by Sakharov, Afanas'ev and Zaslavskii. Most importantly, MOI played the major grass-roots role in establishing two electoral blocs for the Russian elections of March 1990: Elections-90 for the Moscow City Soviet (Mossovet) and Democratic Russia for the Russian Congress of People's Deputies. Moreover (to anticipate), after the elections, MOI played an important part in establishing the grass-roots Democratic Russia movement.[49]

It should perhaps be emphasised that the majority of the Russians who were active in the democratic movement at this stage had no desire to dispense with the USSR. The forthcoming contests for the Russian Congress and the local soviets were seen as part of the struggle for the democratic transformation of the Union as a whole. El'tsin, Afanas'ev, Popov, Nikolai Travkin and others who led the Democratic Russia movement were also at the same time key figures in the Democratic Platform within the CPSU and in the Inter-Regional Group of Deputies. At this time the fight at the all-Union level seemed the decisive one. Sakharov, who unlike most of the leading radicals was not a member of the CPSU, proposed in his draft constitution for the country to drop the word 'socialist' from the title. But even he still retained the word 'Union' in what he called the 'Union of Soviet Republics of Europe and Asia'.[50]

The establishment of an all-Russian electoral bloc originated in initiatives taken by the Confederation of Anarcho-Syndicalists and Democratic Perestroika in August 1989, and by the Moscow Association of Voters in September. MADO's support in October was also important. Other organisations involved by the time of the founding conference on 20–1 January 1990 were the Moscow Party Club, the MPF, Moscow Tribune, Memorial, the Social-Democratic Association, the Union of Constitutional Democrats, the democratic writers' association *Aprel'*, the socialist trade union Sotsprof and the Popular Front of the RSFSR. (By this time the anarcho-syndicalists had dropped out and the Moscow Association of Voters had left the committee after accusations that it was trying to act as leader.) The bloc underwent two name changes, going from 'Elections-90' through 'Democratic Bloc' to 'Democratic Russia'. The programme was signed by over fifty organisations from sixteen towns (not a great number of local groups, a fact which reflected the dominance of Moscow-based organisations).[51]

The conference called on all candidates to the all-Russian and local elections who were sympathetic to the programme to unite in the bloc. The signatories of the programme expressed their orientation towards the documents of the Inter-Regional Group and towards the decree on power and draft constitution prepared by Sakharov just before his death the previous month. They expressed support for the course of perestroika begun in 1985, but warned that 'conservative elements of the apparatus who preach equality in poverty and stir up zoological chauvinism are quickly organising and now coming out in a single front'.

The basic principles of political reform were

the state for the people, and not the people for the state, the priority of the interests of the individual over the interests of the state . . . The first Congress of People's Deputies of the RSFSR must do what has still not been achieved at the all-Union level—take upon itself the whole totality of state power in the RSFSR.

The programme called for a new constitution, corresponding to the UN Declaration of Human Rights, the ending of the monopoly of the CPSU, the ending of party control in the economy and society, and the ending of its activity in the army, the security organs and the diplomatic service. Citizens of Russia should be given the right to organise politically, to freedom of speech, freedom of the press, and freedom of conscience. The KGB should be brought under the control of elected bodies.

The economic programme called for a market with state-controlled levers of economic control as the basic regulator of the economy, the economic independence of enterprises, an anti-monopoly policy, the juridical equality of all forms of property, and mechanisms of ecological security and social defence. The creation of the market sector was to be accompanied by measures to ease the effects of the transition on the standard of living, especially of the weaker layers. These measures included a guaranteed minimum wage, linked to the price index, the temporary freezing of prices, the linking of pensions to wages and prices, and an employment and retraining service. Help should be given to people wishing to lease or own land for agriculture. All this would be financed by a sharp reduction in military expenditure and the ending of privileges for the nomenklatura.

The economic programme avoided calling for an end to socialism in so many words; the 'platitude' of the 'socialism or capitalism' dichotomy, said the programme, did not help answer the question of what sort of economy was needed. This ambiguity probably reflected divergent views about whether an open break with 'socialism' should be demanded. It seems clear, however, that what the majority sought was a capitalist economy of the West European social-democratic type. It was undoubtedly not only frustration with the half-hearted economic reform proposals of the Union government but also the collapse of the communist regimes of Central and Eastern Europe towards the end of 1989 that propelled the democratic movement in the direction of capitalism.

On the nationality question, the programme made an appeal to ethnic Russians.

The national feelings of the Russian [*russkii*] people, which has created a great culture of world significance, have been infringed together with the other peoples of the Russian Federation. It has been outraged by its identification with the totalitarian regime.

The Congress would need to

declare and legally define the sovereignty of the Russian Federation. According to a new Union Treaty, which must be drafted and concluded in a very short time, the Union should receive only those rights which are voluntarily transferred to it by the republics.

Union laws would require the approval of the republics. Within the Russian Federation, 'the sovereignty, territorial and national-cultural autonomy of the peoples of Russia' would be promoted, with the aim of 'the renaissance of all the peoples of Russia'. The programme was published in *Ogonek* and thus acquired a potential readership of millions.[52]

Indeed, the voters were so keen to acquire information about the changes in Soviet life that the journals which made the most of glasnost had a readership of many millions. The weekly newspaper *Argumenty i fakty* had a circulation of 33 million and a readership probably several times this. Travkin told *Argumenty i fakty* that the number of candidates for the Congress and soviets who had joined the electoral bloc had increased from 170 at the January conference to over 5,000 by 20 February.[53] While members of the Inter-Regional Group like Travkin played an important part in building Democratic Russia across the republic, the local formation of electoral blocs was undertaken by the existing grass-roots organisations. In Moscow MOI helped create 'Elections-90', in Leningrad the Leningrad Popular Front formed 'Democratic Elections-90', and in Sverdlovsk the democrats created 'Democratic Elections'. Similar blocs were particularly active in Novosibirsk, Tomsk, Vologda, Khabarovsk and Irkutsk. In the latter two cases, the informal movements created a joint bloc with Communist Party officials.[54] The Leningrad bloc succeeded in putting up candidates in nearly every seat on the Leningrad City Soviet, while the

Moscow bloc contested 422 out of 498 on Mossovet.[55] The Democratic Union continued to boycott elections, with the exception of its social-democratic faction, which worked within the democratic blocs.

The activity of Democratic Russia interacted with developments within the CPSU. The Inter-Club Party Group mentioned above became in April 1989 the Moscow Party Club 'Communists for Perestroika'. This worked, together with branches throughout the USSR, to bring about a split in the CPSU. The claim of one of its co-chairpersons, Igor' Chubais, that by December 1989 it was, together with *Memorial* and the Inter-Regional Group, one of the three 'most authoritative democratic' organisations in Moscow should be treated with caution; MOI and the MPF seem to have had more authority among the activists and the voters. But the Moscow Party Club was clearly influential in the establishment of the 'Democratic Platform within the CPSU' (see Chapter 2). The first conference of the Democratic Platform took place on 20–1 January 1990, coincidentally the same time as the Democratic Russia meeting. The Coordinating Council of Democratic Platform included El'tsin, Afanas'ev and Popov.[56] On 3 March 1990 *Pravda* published the programme of the Democratic Platform as part of the discussion leading up to the 28th Party Congress scheduled to begin in June. This made demands akin to those of Democratic Russia (but without specifically Russian features): the abolition of Article 6 of the USSR Constitution, the transformation of the CPSU into a social-democratic party competing with other parties (in itself a call for a split), and a mixed economy. All of these demands would have meant fundamental change not only in the Communist Party but also in the Soviet Union as a whole.

By then the debate had moved to the streets. Calls for democratising the Communist Party and the state played a central role in the democrats' campaign for the Russian elections. On 4 February huge demonstrations in support of a multi-party democracy were held in Moscow and other Russian cities ahead of a special plenum of the Central Committee. According to the police, 200,000 marched in Moscow alone; the organisers claimed 300,000. It was probably the largest independent demonstration since October 1917. A wide spectrum of democratic groups organised it: the Inter-Regional Group, the Moscow Association of Voters, *Memorial*, the Democratic Union, the MPF and Democratic Platform. The demand to abolish Article 6 was supplemented by the call for the resignation of the senior conservative Politburo member, Egor Ligachev, and of the Defence Minister, Dmitrii Iazov. With slogans such as '72 years on the road to nowhere', '*Pamiat'* is fascism' and 'Who are you with, Mikhail Sergeevich?', the marchers filled the Manege Square and listened to El'tsin, Popov, Travkin and others.[57] The references to *Pamiat'* were brought on by rumours of pogroms and fears that agents of *Pamiat'* might attack the marchers. On 18 January, a meeting of the association of democratic writers, *Aprel'*, at the Central House of Writers had been violently disrupted by thugs from one of the *Pamiat'* groups, the Union for National Proportional Representation '*Pamiat''*. Its leader, Konstantin Smirnov-Ostashvili, had been escorted out of the building by the police and allowed to go free. On the Manege, *Pamiat'* did not dare to show its face.

Under pressure from the democrats, and increasingly frustrated by the resistance of the Politburo to his reforms, Gorbachev persuaded the Central Committee Plenum to agree to the abolition of Article 6, thereby ending the leading role and monopoly of the CPSU, and to the introduction of a presidency. More demonstrations were held on 25 February, preceding the Supreme Soviet meeting held to discuss the new Gorbachev line. In Moscow 100,000 people attended; Popov blamed the lower turnout on a campaign by the official media about the danger of violence, but it may have been simply that people were exhausted. El'tsin addressed a crowd of 10,000 in Sverdlovsk, where he was standing for the Russian Congress.[58] The slogans at these demonstrations seem to have been more specifically directed against the party as such.[59] The USSR Congress of People's Deputies finally amended the Constitution, ending the party's monopoly and creating an executive presidency, on 14 March, in between the two rounds of voting in Russia.

The Russian nationalist alternative

In the Russian elections, the democrats were opposed not only by the apparatus but also by the forces of an imperialistic, conservative Russian nationalism. The 'Bloc of Public-Patriotic Movements of Russia' was an umbrella for an interlocking network of creative unions, cultural organisations and informal associations. It enjoyed the support of the General Staff of the Armed Forces, part of the upper echelons of the hierarchy of the Russian Orthodox Church and the more conservative part of the CPSU apparatus. At the centre of this network was the Union of Writers of the RSFSR, and the editorial board of its monthly journal *Nash sovremennik*.

A word should be said here about the Union of Writers. In the Baltic States and Ukraine, the writers' organisations had taken an important role in the Popular Front movement, but the Russian Union of Writers was at the ideological centre of opposition to perestroika. It is important to note that the Russian body was specifically created in 1957 as a conservative counterweight to the more liberal Moscow writers and to the Union of Writers of the USSR, and had continued to occupy a conservative position ever since. Equally relevant is that the form of the Soviet structures encouraged the republican writers' unions to think in ethno-cultural terms, to pose as the defenders of their national cultures. Gorbachev's attempted introduction of western political and economic models was seen as a threat by the Russian Writers' Union, whereas glasnost in the republics allowed the unions to champion national independence. The nationalism of the non-Russians fed the nationalism of the Russians. The conservative Russian nationalists considered their motherland to be the whole of the USSR—anywhere that Russians lived. They feared—correctly as it turned out—that the tolerance of ethnic separatism and of democratic politicking would lead to the breakup of the state. This made them into tactical allies of conservative communists who despised the religious orientation and peasant nostalgia displayed by many of the leading Russian nationalist writers, and led them even to see the CPSU as the guarantor of the Russian state.

Already in November 1988, members of the *Nash sovremennik* editorial board, including Sergei Vikulov, Viktor Astaf'ev, Vasilii Belov, Iurii Bondarev, Stanislav Kuniaev and Valentin Rasputin, together with Vadim Kozhinov (who joined the editorial board later) and Anatolii Ivanov, editor-in-chief of *Molodaia gvardiia*, established the Fellowship of Russian Artists (*Tovarishchestvo russkikh khudozhnikov*). This association declared the aim of opposing separatist groups in the Soviet Union and preventing the disintegration of the state in Russia itself. Its 'Appeal' blamed the communist system for the growth of separatism and for what it considered the moral decline of the Russian people.

The command methods used by the leadership in the sphere of nationality relations has led to a situation in which it has become common to identify the will of the administrative-bureaucratic apparatus with the views of the Russian people, whereas it is precisely Russia that is in the most critical position, close to collapse. And the collapse of Russia will inevitably lead to the loss of the unity of the political and state system of the whole country.[60]

The Fellowship of Russian Artists took the initiative in the formation of another organisation, the Association 'United Council of Russia "Popular Accord"'. Also represented at the founding congress of the latter in Moscow on 9 September 1989 was the All-Russian Cultural Foundation, the Leningrad and Moscow branches of the United Workers' Front (*OFT*), the Moscow, Leningrad and Tiumen (Western Siberia) *Otechestvo* (Fatherland) societies, the Union of Patriotic Organisations of the Urals and Siberia, the Union for the Spiritual Rebirth of the Fatherland, and the Internationalist Fronts from the Baltic and Moldavia.[61]

The All-Russian Cultural Foundation was an official body. The United Workers' Front grew out of an attempt by the party apparatus, originally in Leningrad, to capitalise on the fears of workers about the economic and social consequences of perestroika (see Leningrad chapter). The *Otechestvo* societies were informal Russian nationalist associations which were generally not as violently anti-Semitic as *Pamiat'*. The Moscow *Otechestvo* had been founded by the journals *Moskva*, *Nash sovremennik* and *Molodaia gvardiia*, and the Moscow City branch of the All-Russian Society for the Preservation of Historical and Cultural Monuments. Its aim was patriotic and internationalist education, especially military patriotic education, and it enjoyed military support. Its first conference was on 20 May 1989, and its council elected the historian Apollon Kuz'min chairperson and Aleksandr Rutskoi assistant chairperson.[62] The Union of Patriotic Organisations of the Urals and Siberia was a confederation of local societies, formed on 25 June 1988 in Cheliabinsk. It included *Vernost'*

(Loyalty) from Irkutsk, *Otechestvo* from Sverdlovsk and Tiumen, *Vstrechnoe dvizhenie* (Counter Movement) from Magnitogorsk, *Rodina* (Motherland) from Cheliabinsk, *Otchizna* (also Fatherland) from Zlatoust and the Novosibirsk *Pamiat'*.[63] The Union for the Spiritual Rebirth of the Fatherland was founded in Moscow on 16–17 March 1989 with the support of the Sovetskaia Rossiia publishing house, the Moscow City branch of the All-Russian Society for the Preservation of Monuments, the journal *Molodaia gvardiia* and the members of the Union of Patriotic Organisations of the Urals and Siberia. Its leader was Mikhail Antonov, a leading nationalist writer on economic policy. It maintained that there was no alternative to 'socialism'. At the same time it reportedly had an unwritten rule that only Orthodox Christian believers were admitted as members.[64]

All these organisations formed the United Council of Russia. The Congress in September 1989 elected Vitalii Skripko as chairperson and Eduard Volodin and Sergei Lykoshin as vice-chairpersons. It included Kuniaev, Antonov and the writer Aleksandr Prokhanov, known as the 'nightingale of the General Staff' for his militarist and chauvinist prose, on the Coordinating Council. Boris Gun'ko, a leading member of the Moscow 'Edinstvo' and United Workers' Front organisations, was responsible for links with the working class. The appeal by the congress emphasised the unity of the USSR, socialism and the strengthening of the Army.[65]

The 'Bloc of Public-Patriotic Movements of Russia' was formed by the United Council of Russia (itself an umbrella group), the Fellowship of Russian Artists, the United Workers' Front of Russia, the All-Russian Society for the Preservation of Monuments, the Union for the Spiritual Rebirth of the Fatherland, the 'Russia' Club of USSR People's Deputies and Voters, the Public Committee to Save the Volga, the 'Unity' Association of Lovers of Russian Literature and Art, the All-Russian Cultural Foundation, the Russian Section of the International Foundation for Slavonic Languages and Slavonic Cultures, the Russian Republic Voluntary Society of Book Lovers, and the Foundation for the Restoration of the Church of Christ the Saviour. This list of twelve organisations which signed the bloc's programme may seem impressive, but in several cases the same people and groups were appearing under different labels. As may be clear from the previous section, this was also the case in the democratic camp.

The electoral programme of the bloc, 'For a policy of Popular Accord and Russian Rebirth', was published in *Literaturnaia Rossiia*, the weekly of the Writers' Union of the RSFSR, at the end of 1989. It was a manifesto on which conservative or neo-Stalinist communists and conservative Russian nationalists were prepared to compromise. Like the democrats, it emphasised the sovereignty of the RSFSR, but unlike them it defended socialism and the territorial integrity of the USSR. The programme accused the CPSU of 'making concessions step by step to the bloc of separatists and "Left radicals"' who were allegedly preparing the 'dismemberment' of the Union. It attacked the mafias and politicians who supposedly wanted to turn Russia into a mere supplier of raw materials to the west. Demanding the creation of Russian institutions which had previously been subsumed in all-Union bodies, such as a Russian Academy of Sciences and a Russian broadcasting service, it gave top priority to the creation of a Russian Communist Party within the CPSU. This was a key demand of conservative apparatchiki at the time, who wished to build a conservative Communist Party structure in Russia as a platform from which to attack Gorbachev.

While promising to develop the autonomy of the peoples of the RSFSR, the programme nevertheless spoke of a 'single and indivisible Soviet Russia'. The attitude to the other Soviet republics was cautious: Russia should cease to subsidise them, and should defend the civil rights of emigrants from Russia living in the republics. The Soviet capital should be moved from Moscow, to allow the city to resume its historical role as the political and spiritual centre for Russians. Russia had to remain a great world power. The Russian Orthodox Church and other religions should be allowed to play a full role in developing 'patriotic consciousness'. As with the democrats, the tone throughout was one of crisis and of the resurrection of Russia. Although Russian nationalists are sometimes accused of anti-Semitism, there was no statement in the programme to which that epithet could reasonably be fixed.[66]

The apocalyptic state of mind of the imperial nationalists was revealed by an article by Prokhanov. Published in *Literaturnaia Rossiia* one week after the programme of the patriotic bloc, it warned of the impending dissolution of the Soviet Union. Prokhanov predicted that this would lead to a civil war and the invasion of the country by the rest of the world to prevent nuclear catastrophe. Germany would be reunited and would dominate Europe.[67]

The Russian elections, March 1990

The elections of March 1990 in the RSFSR were conducted much more fairly than the all-Union elections of the previous year. There were no pre-election meetings to screen undesirable candidates. No seats were reserved for public organisations. At stake was control of the new Congress of People's Deputies of the RSFSR, which would elect a Supreme Soviet (to be a standing parliament like the USSR Supreme Soviet); and the Supreme Soviets of the Autonomous Republics inside the RSFSR, and the regional, city and local soviets of the republic.

Control over the media naturally gave the party apparatus an advantage, but the death knell had sounded over its monopoly of power and it fought the elections in a state of demoralisation. In Tomsk, Barnaul and Volgograd the party leaders had been removed from power by the pressure of informal associations. Nevertheless, the apparatus was sufficiently well organised to learn lessons from the 1989 elections. First secretaries of regional party committees and other senior officials took care to stand in rural constituencies where there was little democratic activity. In the major cities, however, the apparatus was sometimes slow to mobilise behind specific candidates. In Moscow, in cases where several party members were standing for the same seat the raikom did not necessarily give backing to any one of them. Only on 3 March—the day before the first round of voting—did the Moscow party newspapers produce a programme and partial slate for the Moscow seats in the Russian Congress and for the Moscow City Soviet (Mossovet). A problem for the apparatus was that their candidates were used to winning elections only when they were unopposed, when they could close their eyes to the over-crowded housing and the pollution and proclaim the bright future.

The democrats, however, like the communists, were not sufficiently organised to avoid putting up more than one candidate for the same seat, or to ensure that every seat had a democratic candidate. The MPF produced a manual for democratic candidates in Moscow, written by Stankevich and Mikhail Shneider. It told them how to exploit the grievances of the voters, to urge collective action as a means to solving them and to make specific proposals about the renewal of the city. The democrats used academic institutes where they were employed as bases from which to nominate candidates in all parts of the city, since unregistered, informal associations did not have the right to nominate.

The posters, leaflets and megaphones which helped the democrats in 1989 again made their appearance. Candidates were able to state their political allegiance by reference to organisations in which they were active. For example, Pavel Kudiukin, standing in the Sevastopol raion of Moscow for the Russian Congress, mentioned in a leaflet his participation in *Memorial*, the Social-Democratic Association, Moscow Tribune and Democratic Pere-stroika. The literature did not, however, advertise the adherence of candidates to Democratic Russia (which was not a registered organisation and had been formed only after the close of nominations), but an issue of the independent newspaper *Pozitsiia*, published by the 'Commonwealth' Foundation, listed the democratic candidates for Mossovet. The newspaper *Moskovskii komsomolets* was prevented from publishing such a list. The Russian nationalist bloc's list of sixty-one candidates standing for Moscow seats in the Russian Congress was published by *Literaturnaia Rossiia* on 23 February. Only one (Tamara Pona-mareva) was clearly linked with *Pamiat'*. The same newspaper on 2 March published a list of 151 candidates for Mossovet.[68]

The democratic blocs did best in Leningrad and Moscow; the capitals were more radical than the rest of the country. It is noteworthy that this phenomenon was reproduced in most other countries of Central and Eastern Europe which enjoyed their first free elections over the next two years. Prague, Budapest, Warsaw, Tirana and Bucharest showed a more pronounced anti-communism than the norm in their country. Both in Russia and elsewhere, this reflected the fact that the population of the capitals had more contact with the west, more access to information and were better educated than their fellow citizens. Above all, the over-representation of the intelligentsia in the capitals (especially with the presence of the academies of science and the literary élite) provided the social basis for a cadre of leaders and activists for humanitarian and democratic organisations. In the other republics of the USSR, the phenomenon was not so consistent, because of the disproportionate presence in the capitals of an immigrant population which was resistant to political change.

In Leningrad, they won twenty-five out of thirty-three seats in the Russian Congress and 80 per cent of the seats in the City Soviet. In Moscow Democratic Russia won fifty-seven of the sixty-five seats in the Congress and 281 of the 463 seats (filled at the end of the second round of voting) on Mossovet. In Sverdlovsk, Democratic Choice had endorsed seven of the nine successful Congress deputies, including El'tsin, and eighty of the 194 victorious candidates in the City Soviet. Members of democratic electoral blocs took control of city soviets in some major oblast' centres, and became influential in a number of oblast' soviets such as Sakhalin, where the Democratic Movement for Perestroika in Iuzhno-Sakhalinsk was still strong and had helped to initiate the Sakhalin Popular Front. Democratic Russia could claim the allegiance of 370 out of 1,061 deputies to the Russian Congress. This meant that they would be dependent on the sympathy of most of an estimated 250 waverers to win a majority.[69]

Many leading democrats were elected. On the other hand, the supporters of the Russian nationalist bloc did badly, with many well-known figures suffering defeat. Of the sixty-one candidates standing for Moscow seats to the Russian Congress, none won on the first round of the elections but sixteen reached the second round. These included the artist Il'ia Glazunov, the editor-in-chief of *Nash sovremennik* Kuniaev and the editor-in-chief of *Literaturnaia Rossiia* Ernst Safonov. None of these three was elected, and the bloc won only two seats. Nikolai Doroshenko, the editor-in-chief of the anti-Semitic newspaper of the Union of Writers' Moscow organisation, *Moskovskii literator*, was defeated by a Jewish radical, Anatolii Shabad.[70] It seems that the appeal to chauvinism was unpopular; the Russian nationalists had discredited themselves by coming too close to the party apparatus, and, lacking traditional levers of patronage, they did even worse than the apparatchiki themselves. CPSU members accounted for 86.3 per cent of the deputies to the Congress, but this represented a broad spectrum of opinion. Only twenty-five of the seventy-seven regional first secretaries dared to stand, and of these twenty were elected.[71]

The dramatic democratic victories in the two Russian capitals tended to obscure the fact that the apparatus continued to dominate most of the oblast' soviets and the Autonomous Republics, and held nearly half the seats in the Russian Congress itself.

The democrats in office

The period from the democrats' electoral victories in March 1990 to the attempted coup in August 1991 highlighted the divisions among the democrats and their failure to create coherent parties which could guarantee legislative majorities to reformist executives. The wrangles in the Moscow and Leningrad city soviets between democrats lacking party discipline prefigured the disagreements between the Russian leaders after the collapse of the USSR.

The alignment of forces on the Moscow City Soviet, prior to its first session, was 281 from Democratic Russia; ninety-four from the 'Moscow' bloc, which reflected the views of the Moscow City Party Committee (gorkom); thirty-five in the bloc of 'independents'; ten Russian nationalists in the 'Otechestvo' bloc, which represented the Bloc of Public-Patriotic Movements; and forty-three undeclared.[72] Around nine-tenths of the deputies were new. The newspaper of the Moscow *Memorial* group declared: 'Mossovet is "taken" without a single shot!' But a correspondent pointed out the wide ideological differences within the Democratic Russia bloc of Mossovet deputies, ranging from the communist chairperson of the Bauman raion ispolkom Nikolai Gonchar, socialists such as Kagarlitskii and 'populists' such as Vladimir Bokser, to liberals such as Aleksandr Lukin as well as anarchists and Christian democrats.[73]

On 20 April 1990 by a substantial majority Mossovet elected Gavriil Popov, the Moscow University Professor of Economics, to be its chairperson and Sergei Stankevich to be his first deputy. The new leaders sought to take over the executive roles of both the Moscow City Soviet Executive Committee (ispolkom) and of the Moscow gorkom, in order to become the real controllers of the city. The party apparatus had already moved to undermine the position of the soviet, even before the election. The old city ispolkom transferred thirty-four buildings, built at least partly at the expense of the city, and the mass circulation newspaper *Vecherniaia Moskva* to the Moscow party gorkom. Gorbachev also intervened, hours before Popov's election, to issue a presidential decree removing the power to grant permission for demonstrations within Moscow's Garden Circle from Mossovet to the USSR Council of Ministers. It was a measure of the USSR's progress towards legality that that decree was later struck down as unconstitutional by the USSR Court of Constitutional Compliance. The soviet dealt with the need to establish its own means of propaganda by setting up the weekly mass-circulation newspaper *Kuranty* and the weekly magazine *Stolitsa*, by lending money to create a newspaper aimed at the intelligentsia, *Nezavisimaia gazeta*, and taking a part share in a new radio station.

Popov took a conciliatory attitude to those elements of the old soviet apparatus which were prepared to work with the democrats. He ensured the election of a former deputy chairperson of the old ispolkom, Iurii Luzhkov, to be the chairperson of the new ispolkom. This was recognition of the democrats' lack of administrative experience. Luzhkov, for his part, promised 'to realise the depoliticisation of the work of the ispolkom'.[74] Despite the vehement protests of the 'Moscow' bloc, the bust of Lenin was removed from the hall. When the Moscow Association of Voters wished to hold a pro-democracy demonstration on May Day, and the central government banned it,

Popov and Stankevich secured a compromise allowing the democrats to follow the official demonstration into Red Square. Traditionally, the May Day parade was intended as a demonstration of loyalty to the Communist Party leadership, but on this occasion the democrats heckled Gorbachev off the viewing stand on the Lenin Mausoleum.

The easiest changes to make in Moscow were the restoration of some of the pre-revolutionary names of streets and squares. Gor'kii Street became Tverskaia again, although Leninskii prospekt was left untouched (the memory of Lenin could not be treated so lightly).[75] Mossovet had little success in improving the housing and environment situation. Its most difficult problem proved to be the food supply. After the soviet banned people from outside Moscow from coming in to buy certain goods in the capital in order to maintain supplies for Moscow voters, the surrounding provinces that were still controlled by communists responded by cutting off food deliveries. Also rumours that the Ryzhkov government was about to free prices led to a rush on the shops. The result was that for much of Popov's first year supplies of food and consumer goods in Moscow fell dramatically. Whole shelves in some food shops were empty for long periods.

Popov had to contend not only with two other governments based in Moscow—the central and the Russian—but also with the soviets of thirty-three raions on the territory of the city, which had been elected at the same time as Mossovet. Some were controlled by communists and some by democrats. In the Oktiabr'skii raion, Il'ia Zaslavskii became chairperson of the soviet and proceeded to inaugurate a radical programme of privatisation. New democratic associations acquired their legal registration at the Oktiabr'skii raion. Whatever their colour, however, the raions defended their rights against Mossovet; one raion rejected a city decision to locate a bakery there, and the Krasnopresenskii raion declared its 'sovereignty'. In the wings, the party conservatives waited for the divisions between the levels of government and between the soviets and their executives to discredit the democrats and bring about the return of the old apparatus to office. Before 1990, the multiple levels of government had been a façade for the rule of the CPSU, but without communist dominance conflicts of interest would frustrate reform until new rules for political interaction were established.[76]

In Sverdlovsk, the democrats on the city soviet were outmanœuvred soon after the election. Iurii Novikov, the chairperson of the old soviet who had worked as second secretary of the gorkom while El'tsin was first secretary of the obkom, appealed to El'tsin to endorse him as candidate for the post of chairperson of the city ispolkom. El'tsin sent a telegram supporting Novikov and the latter was elected. After this, however, he broke with the democrats; there was not one on the ispolkom whom he proposed and who was elected. By April 1991, with the defection of eighteen deputies from the democratic camp, there were sixty-two active democrats left, thirty-five in the Sotrudnichestvo (Collaboration) bloc, which collaborated with the gorkom, and the remainder of the 194 deputies were a 'swamp' in between. On 1 April the democrats made one of a number of attempts to pass a no-confidence motion in Novikov. The voting was eighty-seven against him and seven for him with Sotrudnichestvo abstaining, but since the quorum was ninety-eight the decision could not be implemented.[77] The case is worth mentioning because the town was one of the most radical in Russia and the home base of El'tsin.

Elsewhere the democrats succeeded in gaining office but found themselves powerless against higher state authorities. For example, democrats won control of Riazan City Soviet but the Riazan oblast' remained in the hands of the conservatives. Officials from the oblast' and the obkom used their traditional patronage in the countryside to persuade a group of peasants to sign an ultimatum to the city, threatening to cut off food supplies.[78] An exception was Sakhalin, where the Democratic Elections bloc won control of the oblast' soviet and appointed a Moscow economics professor, Valentin Fedorov, as 'governor'. He sought to make the oblast' a free economic zone and begin the privatisation of trade.[79] (Later, he became a prominent opponent of any territorial concessions to Japan over the disputed Kurile Islands.) Democratic Russia also won majorities in the Far Eastern cities of Petropavlovsk-Kamchatskii and Iuzhno-Sakhalinsk and in Nizhnevartovsk in Tiumen oblast'.[80] In the latter, a Siberian oil town, the new democratic chairperson of the soviet, Stanislav Seleznev, later resigned for reasons that were unclear, and was replaced by the local communist first secretary.[81]

The Democratic Russia deputies to the Congress of People's Deputies of the RSFSR caucused on 14 April 1990. It was indicative of the priority given to all-Union matters that the private discussions of the delegates were less concerned with the Russian Congress than with the situation in the CPSU. *Pravda* on 11 April had published an 'Open letter' from the Central Committee, denouncing the Democratic Platform and suggesting that its supporters be removed from the party. Igor' Chubais was expelled from the party at this time. The deputies, not surprisingly, voted El'tsin as their candidate for the post of Chairperson of the RSFSR Supreme Soviet. Tat'iana Koriagina was the runner-up, while Travkin refused to stand.[82]

The Congress opened on 16 May. Gorbachev and the conservatives were agreed that the main task was to prevent El'tsin's election. They were unsure, however, who was best placed to stop it: the prime minister of the RSFSR, Aleksandr Vlasov, or the conservative first secretary of the Krasnodar Krai Party Committee, Ivan Polozkov, an outspoken opponent of the new cooperative enterprises. The democrats succeeded in reorganising the agenda of the Congress so that the discussion of Vlasov's report, as outgoing head of government, would precede the elections. This would allow them to criticise him and discredit his candidature. Vlasov's report in fact criticised the state of affairs in Russia in terms reminiscent of Democratic Russia, but since he had been in power he did not sound convincing. The CPSU Central Committee told him to withdraw his candidacy.

On 26 May the elections began; over two ballots El'tsin came ahead of Polozkov, but failed to gain the necessary 531 votes. The acting chairperson of the Congress then suggested that both El'tsin and Polozkov withdraw, but the Congress rejected this. El'tsin then promised to form the leading bodies of the republic, including the government, on a democratic and coalition basis—a conciliatory gesture that secured him victory on the next ballot. He won 535 votes against 467 for Vlasov (the Central Committee having changed its candidate).[83] Ruslan Khasbulatov, an economist of Chechen nationality, was elected his deputy, and Ivan Silaev, a deputy prime minister in the Soviet government, was elected prime minister. Both these appointments represented compromises between the democrats and the centre.

The Russian Congress did not end with these elections, but continued until 22 June. It adopted in principle a draft 'Decree on Power', which demanded an end to any interference by political parties—meaning the CPSU—in the running of state institutions, enterprises and the legal system, and preventing leaders of state bodies from simultaneously holding jobs in parties and public organisations. This would have made illegal the practice of first secretaries of regional and raion party committees chairing the corresponding soviets.[84] The most important act after the election of El'tsin was to pass a 'Declaration of State Sovereignty'. The Democratic Russia election platform had spoken of the need to establish the sovereignty of the RSFSR, and the conservatives (for other reasons) wished to strengthen Russian institutions.

The 'Declaration of State Sovereignty' adopted on 12 June expressed, in Soviet-type language, the sovereignty of the republic, and said that the bearer of sovereignty was its 'multinational people'. Breaking from Soviet tradition, however, it declared the 'superiority of the Constitution of the RSFSR and the laws of the RSFSR on the whole territory of the RSFSR', and that operation of the acts of the USSR which contradict the sovereign rights of the RSFSR 'is prevented by the Republic on its territory'. Disagreements between the centre and the republic would be settled according to the Union Treaty. In reality, the declaration marked a fundamental change in the relationship between the Union and the republics. It meant an end to the diktat of the centre which had lasted since the formation of the USSR in 1922, a diktat which was now challenged not only by the small Baltic republics but by Russia, with over half the Union's population and three-quarters of its territory. The declaration also granted political parties and social movements the rights to participate in political affairs. The declaration was carried by a huge majority, by 907 to thirteen.[85]

El'tsin had accepted two amendments in order to ensure this support. One was the provision that disagreements between the republic and the Union would be resolved according to the existing Union Treaty, which gave priority to Soviet law, and the other suspended activation of the declaration. Oleg Rumiantsev, by then leader of the Social-Democratic deputies, said that the amendments made the declaration 'an empty political declaration'. Sobchak, chairperson of the Leningrad Soviet, on the other hand, called it 'A huge step forward, a beautiful declaration'.[86]

The assertion of the superiority of Russian law over Soviet law was to inaugurate the 'war of laws'. This represented the struggle for supremacy between El'tsin and Gorbachev which was to continue right up until the resignation of Gorbachev as president and the dissolution of the USSR. The centre was already weakened by the victory of the Estonian and Latvian Popular Fronts in the republican elections and by Lithuania's declaration of independence, led by Sajudis. On 1 June, just after El'tsin's election, he met the Lithuanian leader, Vytautas Landsbergis. El'tsin made clear his support for Lithuania's independence and for direct trade between Russia and Lithuania, despite the blockade imposed by Gorbachev.[87] Gorbachev was coming under increased pressure from the newly formed Soiuz group in the USSR Supreme Soviet to keep the Union together. His preferred solution was to replace the USSR with a new union of sovereign states, not necessarily 'Soviet' or 'Socialist', in which power would be devolved to the republics except as far as foreign relations, defence and certain economic matters were concerned.[88] This solution was not in reality very different from that officially preferred by Democratic Russia. The Russian Congress went on to lay out principles for a new union treaty, making a detailed division of powers between the centre and the republics. The Union would keep defence, the KGB, communications and energy, while the RSFSR would have control over the Ministry of Internal Affairs (MVD), a Russian State Bank, a Russian KGB, and the bulk of the economy. Foreign affairs would be divided with the Union.[89]

The Russian declaration of sovereignty incited the 'parade of sovereignties' of the union republics, with the Ukrainian Supreme Soviet proclaiming its sovereignty on 16 July. The war of laws was not, however, to be confined to a struggle between the centre and the republics. Several autonomous republics in the Russian Federation, beginning with the Tatar ASSR, declared their own sovereignty and expressed their wish to become full members of the proposed new union, outside the RSFSR. El'tsin initially expressed support for these moves. He visited Kazan, the capital of Tatarstan (as the republic now wished to be called) and declared: 'A federal treaty will be concluded [between Russia and the autonomous republics], that is, Tataria will take the share of independence which it wants itself and will be able to realise.'[90] Tatar nationalist groups, such as the Tatar Public Centre (TOTs) formed in 1988, and the more extreme Ittifaq (Unity) formed in 1990, had called for autonomous republics to have the rights of union republics and for Kazan Tatar to be the official language of Tatarstan.[91] But they were not strong enough to have forced the declaration through the Tatarstan Supreme Soviet; rather it was the Communist Party which controlled the Supreme Soviet and was playing El'tsin at his own game. This allowed the local communists to pose as the defenders of the rights of the native Tatars. For the time being, however, El'tsin went along with the demands for sovereignty from regions within Russia, seeing them as strengthening his own position against the centre.

Before the end of the Russian Congress of People's Deputies, the founding congress began of the Communist Party of the RSFSR. This took place from

20 to 23 June 1990 and represented the fruition of the plans laid by conservative communists to undermine Gorbachev from within the party. Since the Leningrad party organisation played an important role in the creation of this body, its genesis will be considered in the chapter on Leningrad. For the first time, a party congress was upstaged by a state body, as Russians concentrated on the Congress of People's Deputies and ignored the communists, now increasingly marginalised. The Russian communists elected the conservative Ivan Polozkov as first secretary of their Central Committee. The atmosphere was hostile to Gorbachev for weakening the Union to the point of dissolution. It was Army General Al'bert Makashov, Commander of the Volga-Urals Military District, who attracted the most attention. He attacked the CPSU leadership and the Soviet government for allowing the armed forces to be weakened, for abandoning Eastern Europe and for allowing Germany to be united within NATO.[92] Within the Russian Congress, the conservative communists created the 'Communists of Russia' fraction to oppose Democratic Russia. The idea that the communists might be forced into opposition—in Russia, of all places—would have seemed unthinkable even six months before.

Building a democratic movement

Already some of the leaders of the Democratic Platform and Democratic Russia were leaving the Communist Party, in despair at the impossibility of reforming it, and without waiting for the 28th Congress of the CPSU. In March 1990 Afanas'ev had created a stir at the USSR CPD by denouncing Lenin for creating a system of 'mass violence and state terror'. On 19 April he resigned from the party, saying: 'To remain in the Communist Party now is equal to spreading illusions in society that it can reform its essence.'[93] Since he had spoken at the founding meeting of the Social-Democratic Association in January, there were hopes that he would join the Russian Social Democrats, but he preferred to remain outside parties and instead play the leading role in Democratic Russia. Several days later, the Democratic Platform group split. About half of the Coordinating Council voted for Travkin's proposal to leave the CPSU and establish a new anti-communist party.[94] In view of these disputes, El'tsin, Popov and Sobchak left the Coordinating Council of the Democratic Platform. Other leaders of the Democratic Platform, such as Viacheslav Shostakovskii and Vladimir Lysenko, who remained in the Communist Party, hoped that it would be possible to reunify with Travkin's group after the CPSU Congress, but this wish proved impossible to realise. On 26–7 May the Democratic Party of Russia (DPR) held its founding conference in Moscow (see p. 100). Travkin intended from the start to create a centralised, disciplined party, capable of beating the CPSU. In protest against the centralism of Travkin, the Leningrad section of the DPR split and established a separate Free Democratic Party of Russia (FDPR) led by Marina Sal'e and

Il'ia Konstantinov. As if things were not complicated enough, Arkadii Murashev and the world chess champion Garri Kasparov decided to remain in the DPR and create a 'fraction of free democrats'.

The 28th Congress of the CPSU in July 1990 represented an important stage in the reduction of the party's role in the political life of Russia. Gorbachev won not only his re-election and the dismissal of Ligachev but the consent of the delegates to a multi-party system. The party would continue to organise within the army, the KGB and the economy, but at least in theory other parties would now also have that right. Most importantly, El'tsin, Popov and Sobchak, the heads of the soviets of Russia, Moscow and Leningrad all left the party during the congress.

Without waiting for the decision of the Democratic Platform, El'tsin dramatically announced to the congress that in view of his responsibility to the people of Russia and the introduction of a multi-party system, he would be unable 'to fulfil only Communist Party decisions'.[95] Popov and Sobchak followed this with a joint declaration, saying that the party had shown its inability to reform society:

only democratically elected soviets can be the organisers of true perestroika . . . we have decided to leave the CPSU in order to facilitate the creation of a multi-party system and to have the chance of leading more effectively the soviets which we head. We call on the leaders of soviets of all levels not to enter any of the political parties.[96]

This was the real end of the 'leading role of the party' in Russia—the heads of key state institutions were no longer party members. Leaders of the Democratic Platform declared that the party had failed the people, and that therefore the Coordinating Council of Democratic Platform would become the organising committee of a new party. At the same time it would fight for a share of the assets of the CPSU, in proportion to the share of Democratic Platform in the membership of the party.[97]

The Russian government under Silaev had a technocratic colouring. Most of its members were members of the CPSU and apparently remained so until the August 1991 coup. Leaders of Democratic Russia and of the emerging parties did not join the government but instead turned to the committees of the new Russian Supreme Soviet. Travkin headed the Committee on the Affairs of Local Soviets (where, perhaps, he could extend his network of contacts). Fr. Viacheslav Polosin of the Russian Christian Democratic Movement headed the Committee on Freedom of Conscience, Rumiantsev became secretary of the Constitutional Commission, Lev Ponomarev headed the Committee for Liaison with Public Organisations and Sergei Kovalev, a former political prisoner, headed the Human Rights Committee. Of the 370 deputies who had been elected under the Democratic Russia colours, only 250 went into the parliamentary group of the same name.

While the process of splits in the Communist Party and the formation of new parties continued, most democrats saw a need to build at grass-roots level a broader movement. This would preserve unity across a considerable breadth of opinion, which had been achieved by the Democratic Russia bloc in the elections. A conference organised by the Moscow Association of Voters on 24 June 1990 established an organising committee, headed by Murashev, to hold a founding congress. An appeal by this committee made on 24 August asked democrats to leave the CPSU and unite in Democratic Russia. It called for coordinating councils to be formed in the regions of Russia to promote the formation of Democratic Russia committees at work-places and places of residence. In the autonomous republics of Russia, movements analogous to Democratic Russia could choose their own name. The appeal appeared in *Ogonek* in September.[98]

Also in September, a boost to the unity of the democrats was given by the signing of a joint declaration by the DPR, the Democratic Platform and the Social-Democratic Party of Russia (SDPR), expressing the intention to form a political coalition. The coalition would have the aims of supporting the economic programme of the Russian government, achieving the resignation of the Union government of Ryzhkov and supporting the creation of the Democratic Russia movement. The declaration did not call for the resignation of Gorbachev, who at that time together with El'tsin had established a commission under Stanislav Shatalin to devise a strategy for the shift to a market economy. The signatories established a joint commission and called on the supporters of the three groups in the soviets to form joint fractions.[99] A Moscow demonstration on 16 September, demanding the resignation of Ryzhkov's government, attracted 30,000 marchers.[100]

The founding congress of the Democratic Russia movement was held in the Rossiia Hotel in Moscow on 20–1 October 1990. There were 1,272 delegates, including 980 from the regions and 165 from societies, organisations and parties.[101] El'tsin was absent, recovering from a road accident. By then the political situation had changed. The Ryzhkov government, highly unpopular because of its policy of hefty price increases and its inability to reduce the shortages of food and consumer goods, had successfully prevented the adoption of the 500-day plan for the transition to the market proposed by Shatalin. Vladimir Kriuchkov, the KGB head, and Ryzhkov had persuaded Gorbachev that the Shatalin plan would devolve power to the republics and enterprises and make it impossible for the party and state apparatuses to hold the country together.

At the same time the central media were launching an attack on the democrats, accusing them of planning an illegal seizure of power. The tactic of the authorities was to give wide publicity to a document called 'Action Programme-90', which had been adopted by the Russian Democratic Forum on 31 July 1990. This body was dominated by Skurlatov's RPF, but it had some credibility because it grew out of MADO, and because the former political prisoner and leader of the Christian-Democratic Union of Russia, Aleksandr Ogorodnikov, was associated with it. The language of Action Programme-90 was far more strident than that of the mainstream democrats, calling for mass action, pickets and strikes to bring down the Union government and have the

USSR CPD dissolved. The Central Committee media presented the programme as that of the democrats as a whole, accusing the Russian democrats and Rukh in Ukraine of trying to destabilise the country. Leading democrats such as Lysenko and Galina Starovoitova suggested that Kriuchkov used Action Programme-90 to persuade Gorbachev not to cooperate with the democrats.[102]

Gorbachev's shift to the right led the Democratic Russia congress to call not merely for Ryzhkov's retirement but for that of the 'Gorbachev–Ryzhkov' government. It also called for direct elections for the new post of president of the RSFSR. If El'tsin were to be elected to this, it would considerably strengthen the legitimacy of his position *vis-à-vis* Gorbachev. The congress noted that members of the nomenklatura were seizing state and party property for themselves, on the pretext of privatisation. It demanded the nationalisation of CPSU property, and the creation of a 'social market economy by way of privatisation'. In the speeches, Popov called for a 'Left-centrist coalition', meaning one between Gorbachev and El'tsin. The alternative would be for Russia under El'tsin to leave the USSR, but that, said Popov, would lead the autonomous republics and other regions to leave Russia itself. Rumiantsev, on the other hand, said that a coalition with Gorbachev was not possible. The Soviet president had acquired exceptional powers in order to implement the transition to the market, but instead had supported Ryzhkov's conservative programme. The democrats should build links in the country. 'What shall all we democrats do if there is a state of emergency tomorrow?' 'What would happen if, say, Afanas'ev were arrested?' 'Who will go out on the street and protest? Who will strike? Who will "go on hunger strike from Nakhodka to Kaliningrad"? . . . we represent no one, no social forces.'[103] This was an important recognition of how fragile the position of the democrats was. Democratic Russia was the most important political group in the Russian Congress, but it lacked any control over the security forces. Some kind of backlash from the old apparatus seemed bound to come.

The atmosphere, it seems, was strained. Sergei Belozertsov accused Lev Ponomarev of having contacts with the Chairperson of the USSR Supreme Soviet, Anatolii Luk'ianov, and with the KGB. Elena Bonner, Sakharov's widow, came to defend him.[104] A more serious division was over Travkin's wish to make Democratic Russia a coalition of parties, with only collective and no individual membership. This view was rejected; membership was to be open to individuals and groups. After this, Travkin prevented the DPR from being a collective member, although individuals inside the DPR (such as Murashev) were active within Democratic Russia. Among the delegates, 16 per cent belonged to the DPR, 10 per cent to Democratic Platform, 8 per cent to the SDPR and 3 per cent were Christian Democrats.[105]

The constitution adopted at the congress emphasised that the movement was a coalition which did not seek to determine the tactics of its component parts. In between congresses the Council of Representatives from collective members and regional organisations would meet at least once every four months. This would elect working groups on particular problems and a Coordinating Council. [106] At the first meeting of the Council of Representatives, held on 8–9 December, sixteen working groups were created. Among them Bokser chaired the group on social policy, Zaslavskii was in charge of international links, Kudiukin headed the employment group and Chernichenko the land reform group. The sixteen chairpersons of the working groups were joined on the Coordinating Council by nine representatives of parties and organisations, and eight members elected on an individual basis. The representatives of the parties were Viktor Aksiuchits and Pavel Zhukov from the RCDM, Lysenko and S. I. Kulakov from the Republican Party of Russia (RPR), Rumiantsev from the SDPR, Ponomarev from the FDPR, Mikhail Astaf'ev from the Constitutional Democratic Party (People's Freedom), I. M. Surikov from the Party of Constitutional Democrats and A. A. Eksler from the Party of Free Labour. Afanas'ev, Murashev, Iakunin and Vera Kriger were among the individuals.

On 12 December the Coordinating Council met and elected six co-chairpersons: Afanas'ev, V. V. Dmitriev, Murashev, Ponomarev, Popov and Iakunin, with Bokser as responsible secretary.[107] The Coordinating Council was to be the general staff of the democratic movement. On 13 January nine more individuals joined, including Leonid Batkin, Iurii Boldyrev, Starovoitova, Gdlian, Kasparov and Obolenskii.[108] The movement published the newspaper, *Demokraticheskaia Rossiia*, which began life as the monthly of the DPR but in September 1990, with no. 3, became the organ of the movement. In March 1991 it became a weekly, edited by Iurii Burtin and Igor' Kliamkin. Finance of the movement was assisted by the Democratic Russia Foundation, headed by Afanas'ev.

The difficulty of the democrats was that they were much better at creating numerous new structures within the democratic movement than they were at taking control and making real decisions to improve people's lives. The clearest examples of this were the Moscow and Leningrad city soviets, where the democrats had clear majorities. On Mossovet, by October three factions had left the Democratic Russia bloc—the Liberal Group, the Democratic Platform and the Moscow Association of Voters. Democratic Russia itself had five factions (Greens, New Socialists, the pragmatists of 'Sodruzhestvo' [Commonwealth], DPR and Christian-Democratic groups). Naturally Popov wanted disciplined voting by Democratic Russia within Mossovet, but the factions within it opposed this.[109]

By late 1990 Popov in Moscow and Sobchak in Leningrad had become frustrated by endless wrangles between different democratic factions within the soviets, and between the soviets and their executive committees (*ispolkomy*). Both leaders came to believe in the need for a strong executive power, not limited by the politicking of the deputies, at local level, just as Gorbachev was trying to establish at the centre and as El'tsin was later to seek in Russia. In a wide-ranging article in *Ogonek*, Popov called for 'desovietisation'—a dramatic change from the position held by Democratic Russia in the March elections.

Popov called for the 'direct election of the leaders of executive power at all levels', president, 'governor' and mayor. The executive leader should have the decisive voice in administration, not the soviet. For Moscow, Popov proposed that the mayor should have the right to veto decisions of Mossovet, but the veto would be overridden by a two-thirds vote of all deputies.[110] Meanwhile the food supply in the two capitals deteriorated. From having been privileged towns, they were now less well supplied than the average provincial city. The democrats blamed this on sabotage by the Communist Party apparatus seeking to discredit the democrats. Stankevich reported that sugar deliveries from Ukraine to Moscow had been stopped, but attempts to stop the supply of fuel to Moscow had been thwarted by the democratic deputies of Nizhnevartovsk.[111]

Meanwhile, Gorbachev was shifting to the right. Having refused to ally with the democrats and introduce a rapid transition to the market, his priority now was to keep the Soviet Union together in its existing boundaries. In the USSR Supreme Soviet, the Soiuz deputies were making the running, enraged at the unification of Germany, the loss of Eastern Europe and the Lithuanian declaration of independence. For all this they blamed Gorbachev. His position was, in the long run, untenable; he was in alliance with people who hated him. Yet this situation was to last from October 1990 to March–April 1991. In December, under pressure from Soiuz, he sacked the liberal Communist Minister of Internal Affairs, Vadim Bakatin, and replaced him with the reactionary Boris Pugo. In December, Shevardnadze resigned as Minister of Foreign Affairs, warning of the danger of dictatorship. In January 1991 came the bloodshed in Vilnius and Riga as hardliners in the security forces sought to bring down the pro-independence governments of Lithuania and Latvia. Gorbachev proposed a moratorium on glasnost and his new head of broadcasting, Leonid Kravchenko, banned the news programmes 'Vzgliad' and 'TSN' which sought to report the Baltic events objectively.

Faced with the threat of a reactionary coup, Democratic Russia joined with other mass movements across the USSR to organise a body called the Democratic Congress (*Kongress*). The founding conference, held in Kharkiv on 26–7 January, brought together Rukh, Sajudis, the Belorussian Popular Front and other important groups. The DPR, SDPR, FDPR and the Union of Kuzbass Workers attended alongside Democratic Russia. According to the Democratic Russia Information Bulletin, it was the Russian delegation that produced the documents that were adopted by the Democratic Congress. As well as establishing a Consultative Council, the Congress condemned the crackdown in the Baltic and the decree by Pugo and Iazov setting up joint patrols between the MVD and the army. It demanded the retirement of Gorbachev, of the new Prime Minister Vladimir Pavlov (Ryzhkov had finally retired after a heart attack) and of Kriuchkov, Pugo, Iazov and Kravchenko. Turning to the referendum on the preservation of the USSR, proposed by Gorbachev and due on 17 March, the Congress demanded a 'No' vote. Instead it proposed the formation of a 'Commonwealth of Sovereign States', with the states having the right of free entry and exit.[112] Travkin attended the Democratic Congress but refused to sign the documents on behalf of the DPR, after the other groups refused to allow a clause which would have let Russia intervene to defend the rights of Russians living in other republics.

The new parties

The above discussion has emphasised the importance of Democratic Russia as a broad movement, but some words of explanation are now due concerning the new political parties which emerged in 1990 after the Communist Party's monopoly was abolished.[113] None of these parties acquired a mass following before the end of 1991, although some succeeded in creating a network through the major cities of the Russian Federation and in securing the allegiance of people's deputies of the USSR, RSFSR or local soviets.

The Democratic Party of Russia appeared at first to have the chance of becoming a serious opposition to the communists; for at least a year after its foundation in May 1990 it was the largest party in Russia, apart from the Communist Party, and it claimed 50,000 members. It was dominated by Nikolai Il'ich Travkin. With its membership of former active communists it was quite well represented in the soviets. The founding conference on 26–7 May 1990 was attended by representatives of ninety-nine towns and eighty-five regions of the RSFSR. The party declared its first aim as the 'creation of Russian statehood [*rossiiskaia gosudarstvennost'*] in the form of a Democratic Republic'. In other respects the programme was similar to that of Democratic Russia. It advocated 'the creation of a multi-party law-governed state with the separation of legislative, executive and judicial power' and decentralisation of the state. The economic section called for the destatification and demonopolisation of the economy, market relations, equal opportunities and the economic independence of the worker.[114]

Debates over the nature of the party and the role of Travkin bedevilled the new party. The Leningrad organising committee, before the conference, divided over the same question which had split the Bolsheviks and the Mensheviks in 1903—what should be the duties of a member of the party? As in 1903, the majority believed that a member should participate in the work of the party, not just sympathise.[115] This position was confirmed at the conference. The split between Travkin and the Leningraders was also mainly about organisation. Travkin and his allies insisted on one chairperson for the DPR (that is, Travkin), whereas the Leningrad delegation led by Marina Sal'e favoured a number of co-chairpersons. Protesting against what they understandably called the 'dictatorship' of Travkin's team, the whole Leningrad delegation walked out. When, under Sal'e's leadership, the Leningraders later formed the Free Democratic Party of Russia (see Leningrad chapter), the latter accused the DPR of 'neo-Bolshevism'.[116] The conference elected Travkin chairperson, with six deputies, including Burbulis (who later left, on the grounds of his own close relationship to El'tsin), Kasparov, Murashev and Khatsenkov.[117]

The DPR preserved itself, above all, owing to the undoubted charisma of Travkin. Indeed, the DPR was better known as 'Travkin's party'. A construction engineer who had headed a major construction combine and been made a Hero of Socialist Labour, Travkin is a lucid but soft-spoken man with a slightly elfish appearance. Already well known for his outspoken criticisms in the televised sessions of the USSR Congress of People's Deputies, he was given a thirty-minute television programme on 15 June to explain the views of his party.[118] The considerable wealth of Kasparov as world chess champion provided means for the party. Kasparov himself and Khatsenkov, as president and general director, respectively, of the Democratic Russia publishing firm were able, despite Travkin's displeasure, to move the newspaper *Demokraticheskaia Rossiia*, with its print-run of one million, from the DPR to the Democratic Russia movement. Most supporters of the broader movement saw the DPR as too sectarian a body; in place of the communism of the CPSU it offered a strident anti-communism, and emphasised the need for discipline.[119]

From November 1990 the DPR published its own newspaper, *Demokraticheskaia gazeta*. Travkin was sceptical of Democratic Russia; he had Khatsenkov excluded from the DPR for his excessive zeal for the broader movement. Murashev remained a deputy chairperson of the DPR until the first full congress of the party held on 1–2 December, but still played a leading role in Democratic Russia. He told *Moskovskaia pravda* (19 December 1990) of his disagreements with Travkin. The latter, he said, favoured a rather broad programme to attract different social strata but compensated for this by a 'strict discipline, close to democratic centralism'. Murashev and Kasparov, who had formed a liberal faction within the DPR, favoured a 'liberal-conservative' (i.e. Thatcherite or Reaganite) programme.[120] The two remained in the party until the second congress, held on 26–8 April 1991, when they left. Travkin himself saw a particular distinction between his party and other democrats in that he favoured building a party capable of defeating the communists in elections, whereas his opponents put more emphasis on extra-parliamentary activity such as strikes and demonstrations.[121]

The DPR was formed by leaders of Democratic Platform in Russia who left the CPSU before the party congress; the leaders of Democratic Platform who stayed in the party and left during or after the congress formed the Republican Party of the Russian Federation (RPR). This held its founding congress on 17–18 November 1990 in Moscow. The party claimed over 20,000 members and supporters from over fifty regions of Russia. Like the DPR, it had a representation in the soviets, including ten USSR, sixty RSFSR and fifty Mossovet people's deputies. It would be almost superfluous to state its aims; they hardly differed from those of Democratic Russia and the DPR, emphasising the need for democratisation, a market economy with privatisation, and Russian sovereignty (but not the 'statehood' beloved by the DPR). Unlike the DPR, it was committed to participate in Democratic Russia as a collective member.

Less inclined to militant anti-communism than the DPR, the RPR was the only party within Democratic Russia which was to join the Movement for Democratic Reforms, the body established by politicians close to Gorbachev in June 1991 on an all-Union basis.

The founding congress of the RPR confirmed the political 'coalition' with the DPR and SDPR. Indeed, 51 per cent of the delegates favoured ultimate fusion with the SDPR, and 22 per cent favoured it with the DPR. The congress established a commission to study the possibility of uniting with the SDPR, and recommended RPR members in the soviets to create joint fractions with the Social Democrats. The delegates elected a Coordinating Council, which elected three co-chairpersons—Lysenko (now an RSFSR people's deputy), Viacheslav Shostakovskii and Stepan Sulakshin, with Vladimir Filin as responsible secretary.[122] Chubais withdrew his candidacy as co-chairperson because he disagreed with the wish of the other three to promote cooperation with CPSU members. Moreover, while Sulakshin and Shostakovskii opposed unity with the Social Democrats, Chubais favoured it, and was included in the commission investigating unification. In January 1991, the Moscow branches of the RPR and SDPR formed a united organisation, and this pattern was repeated elsewhere.[123]

What, then, was the Social-Democratic Party of Russia? The core of the leadership—Oleg Rumiantsev, Leonid Volkov and Pavel Kudiukin—had been together in the Democratic Perestroika club. Rumiantsev and Volkov became prominent members of the Russian parliament. The founding congress was held in Moscow from 4 to 6 May 1990 (before the DPR or RPR), with 237 delegates, including fifty-two people's deputies of all levels, from ninety-four towns representing 4,000 members.[124] Although the founding conference of the Social-Democratic Association in January 1990, covering the whole USSR, had been held in Tallinn, it had attracted little attention from Estonian Social Democrats, who were primarily interested in their own republic. This, together with a similar preference from the Latvians and Georgians, encouraged the Social Democrats to work primarily on a republican basis, maintaining the SDA as a loose coordinating body.

Unlike the DPR and RPR, the SDPR was mainly composed of people who had not been in the Communist Party, and the average age was younger. While one member, S. S. Darasov, claimed the heritage of the (Menshevik) Russian Social Democrats, of Georgii Plekhanov, Iulii Martov and Vera Zasulich, Rumiantsev emphasised West European social-democratic values of freedom, justice and solidarity. These latter values dominated in the 'Declaration of Principles' adopted at the congress. This was drawn up by Rumiantsev, Volkov and Aleksandr Obolenskii (an engineer from Apatity who had stood against Gorbachev in the election for chairperson of the USSR Supreme Soviet in May 1989). A forty-person executive was elected, and a three-person presidium composed of Rumiantsev, Obolenskii and Kudiukin.[125] According to Volkov, the SDPR did not take too much from the Menshevik tradition: it was a democratic, not a revolutionary party. It had a socialist wing, oriented towards self-management socialism. The party took from Menshevism the opposition to Bolshevik adventurism, the humanitarian aspects of Menshevism, and a sense of the need for Russia to pass through a phase of normal market activity. This would be a long phase, said Volkov, because the market was necessary as a system of information transmission.[126]

The Social Democrats looked forward to forming a coalition government with parties such as the RPR, DPR, RCDM and the Constitutional Democrats. Obolenskii said that their particular concern, in the context of a shift to the market, would be 'social defence'.[127] Volkov, in a more detailed analysis for the party executive, argued that a 'new middle class' was emerging, made up of new entrepreneurs, professionals and skilled workers. The future would bring a struggle between this new middle class on the one hand, and the old nomenklatura on the other. The nomenklatura itself was split between those trying to restore their former political role, and those trying to seize state property in preparation for the transition to a market economy. The SDPR should help the new middle class to self-consciousness, and encourage the creation of the moral and legal prerequisites for entrepreneurship. (In fact, the SDPR received eight of the sixteen places on the Russian Supreme Soviet Constitutional Commission, and the adoption of a new Constitution by the Russian Federation was an issue of major concern to them.)[128] Volkov said that the party should struggle against both wings of the nomenklatura and help the workers defend their interests with independent trade unions. He attacked the new democratic leaderships of Russia, Moscow and Leningrad for being too willing to compromise with Gorbachevian 'centrists' and using 'authoritarian and apparatus methods' to get their way in the soviets.[129]

The second congress of the SDPR, held in Sverdlovsk from 25 to 28 October 1990, failed to approve a programme, but found time to attend a meeting organised by the Uralmash strike committee initiative group and to lay flowers in memory of the victims of the civil war on the site of the killing of the last tsar and his family.[130] Although it was favoured by such leaders as Rumiantsev, the merger with the RPR has not taken place, as much because of bureaucratic interests as because of any real political differences, but the two continued to cooperate in the soviets and in the Democratic Russia movement.

The only other party of significance formed in 1990 was the Russian Christian-Democratic Movement (RCDM), founded on 8–9 April. The organisers were a committee of three newly elected RSFSR people's deputies who supported Democratic Russia: Viktor Aksiuchits and two Russian Orthodox priests, Fr. Gleb Iakunin and Fr. Viacheslav Polosin. Aksiuchits was an Orthodox philosopher and a publisher of Christian literature. Together with Gleb Anishchenko, he edited the well-produced samizdat 'thick journal' *Vybor*. Iakunin was a dissident who had first spoken out in 1965 against state control of the church. He was sent to a labour camp in 1980 for his work on the Christian Committee for the Defence of Believers' Rights in the USSR. His suffering had not dampened his will to fight, and after his release he became a leading fighter for democracy in society as well as for religious freedom.

The founding meeting elected a fifteen-member 'Duma' (the old Russian word for parliament), including three co-chairpersons, Polosin, Aksiuchits and Anishchenko.[131] The programme of the movement proposed an 'All-Russian *Zemskii sobor* [Assembly of the Land] which will be called to re-establish the continuity of legal supreme power in Russia, which was interrupted by the revolutionary coup'.[132] It advocated a presidential republic for the transition period, while communist influence was removed. The economic section called for a 'social market economy', based on 'private property and Christian justice'.[133] The nationality problem could be solved only after the communists had lost power; peoples who then wished to secede should be allowed to do so only after a territorial plebiscite. The programme warned against the 'thoughtless, irresponsible splintering of the country'.[134] The movement differs from other democratic parties in its emphasis on Christianity (in reality, Orthodoxy) as providing the basis for Russia's revival. Aksiuchits cited Semen Frank, Sergei Bulgakov and Nikolai Berdiaev as among the Russian thinkers of the first half of the twentieth century whose works are now relevant.[135]

By February 1991 only three parties (other than the CPSU)—the DPR, SDPR and RCDM—had recruited the minimum 5,000 members required for registration.[136] Many other smaller parties appeared in the democratic camp during 1990; most cannot be discussed here. Boris Kagarlitskii and Mikhail Maliutin led the Socialist Party, which was founded on 21–4 June 1990 (although Maliutin later defected to the RPR). It defended an anti-Stalinist but socialist position; unlike the SDPR, it opposed privatisation and supported workers' control. Two groups claimed to defend the tradition of the largest liberal party before 1917, the Constitutional Democrats or Kadets: the Constitutional Democratic Party (People's Freedom), founded in September 1990, which Mikhail Astaf'ev came to head, and the smaller Union of Constitutional Democrats, formed in October 1989. Of the various Christian Democratic groups (other than the RCDM), Aleksandr Ogorodnikov's Christian-Democratic Union of Russia deserves further mention; it succeeded in gaining recognition from the Christian-Democratic International as its Russian section.[137] Igor' Korovikov's Party of Free Labour and Chernichenko's Peasant Party sought to encourage and represent the emerging urban and rural entrepreneurs.

On the other side of the fence, *Pamiat'* regrouped under Dmitrii Vasil'ev and launched a newspaper, also called *Pamiat'*, which was openly sold on the Moscow Metro. Nevertheless, neither it nor *Otechestvo* attracted mass support. More significant was the 'Liberal-Democratic Party of the Soviet Union', led by the demagogic lawyer Vladimir Zhirinovskii. This was launched in March 1990 with so much publicity that it was widely believed at the time to be a front for the KGB. On television Zhirinovskii summed up the party's programme as 'de-ideologisation'.[138] The party later helped to establish the Russian Democratic Forum (see p. 96) and evolved in an extreme imperialist-nationalist direction. Zhirinovskii was one of the leaders of the 'Centrist bloc', together with Skurlatov, Vladimir Voronin and Viktor Alksnis of Soiuz. This group was formed in June 1990 with the aim of supporting a crackdown on radical, especially separatist, movements. The fact that it was allowed to have meetings with Ryzhkov, Luk'ianov and Kriuchkov showed that it had backing in high places. Indeed, several leading members left Zhirinovskii's party and accused him of having links with the KGB.[139] Finally, while monarchist sentiment was by no means absent from the democratic camp, the specifically monarchist groups which appeared at this time were not sympathetic to the democrats. The most significant monarchist group was probably the Orthodox Constitutional-Monarchist Party of Russia, founded in May 1990 by Sergei Iurkov-Engel'gardt.[140]

Towards the coup

In March 1991 the newspaper *Demokraticheskaia Rossiia* conducted an analysis of the fractions in the RSFSR Congress. Among the democrats, the Democratic Russia fraction claiming 250 members was the largest. The Unified Fraction of Social Democrats and Republicans claimed fifty-six (deputies could belong to more than one fraction), the Workers' Union sixty-nine, the Left Radicals (who gave first priority to Gorbachev's resignation) fifty-three and the left-centrist group of Dmitrii Volkogonov around thirty. On the right were the Communists of Russia, which did not have a fixed membership, and the Russian nationalist Rossiia fraction led by Sergei Baburin, which claimed 160 deputies. In between was the Russian Union, for which Mikhail Astaf'ev was the rapporteur and which proclaimed its devotion to Christian-Democratic principles. It emphasised more strongly than any other group the benefits of preserving the political unity of at least some of the republics of the USSR in an 'indivisible single space'. All the fractions claimed to favour the market.[141] Outside the Congress, the Communist Party of the RSFSR was consolidating its links with nationalist organisations. On 26 February it held a 'Conference of Public-Political Associations and National-Patriotic Movements "For a Great, United Russia!"', with 500 representatives from ninety organisations seeking to create a broad anti-El'tsin coalition.[142]

On 17 March 1991, Gorbachev's referendum on the future of the USSR was held. In Russia, a victory for the Union on Gorbachev's terms was not in doubt. In order to undermine the increased prestige that such a victory would give Gorbachev, and to strengthen his own position, El'tsin succeeded in placing an additional question on the paper. This asked voters to support the establishment of a directly elected president of the Russian Federation (a post which he would be highly likely to win). Democratic Russia campaigned as a body for a 'No' to Gorbachev's Union and a 'Yes' to the elected presidency. El'tsin for tactical reasons avoided committing himself against the Union. On the Union referendum, 71 per cent of votes cast in Russia gave Gorbachev a 'Yes' (53.5 per cent of the whole population), while on the Russian presidency, 70 per cent gave El'tsin a 'Yes' (52.5 per cent of the whole population). Moscow and

Leningrad showed bare majorities of votes cast for the Union, while in El'tsin's base of Sverdlovsk only 34 per cent were for the Union but 90 per cent favoured the Russian presidency.[143] Thus El'tsin's strategy had paid off. In Moscow and Leningrad, Popov and Sobchak won local referendums on their proposals for a directly elected executive mayor.

The referendum took place against the background of a campaign by the conservative communists to remove El'tsin from the post of chairperson of the Supreme Soviet, and a strike wave in his support and against Gorbachev (see Chapter 5 on the Russian labour movement). El'tsin had spoken of the need for a war against the centre, and the communists planned a no-confidence motion at an emergency RSFSR Congress of People's Deputies. When the Congress opened, on 28 March, 100,000 demonstrators in Moscow, led by Democratic Russia, called for Gorbachev's resignation and supported El'tsin. They ignored the ban on the march, imposed by Gorbachev, who had ordered 50,000 MVD forces into the city, supposedly to defend the Kremlin and Red Square.

The Congress began by condemning the ban on the demonstration. This early victory for El'tsin came because of the defection of a group of communist deputies under the leadership of Col. Aleksandr Rutskoi, previously known as a Russian nationalist, to the El'tsin camp. The ineptitude of Gorbachev and the unpopularity of the Pavlov government, which was about to treble food and other prices, forced these communists to take account of the massive support for El'tsin in the referendum. On 2 April Rutskoi announced to the Congress the formation of a deputies' group, Communists for Democracy, composed of 179 CPSU members.[144] El'tsin's opponents abandoned their plans for a no-confidence motion, and on 4 April the Congress voted by 583 votes to 292 to give El'tsin emergency powers to deal with the economic situation. The power would continue until 12 June, when despite the opposition of the conservative Communists the Russian presidential elections would be held.[145]

Meanwhile, a wave of strikes appeared across the country, beginning with miners making economic demands (see Chapter 5). The attempt to remove El'tsin lent the strikes a more political character, with demands for the resignation of Gorbachev, and Democratic Russia organised some material help for the miners. The central government was unable to end the strike. The unpopularity of the Union government, the results of the referendum, the strike wave, and El'tsin's success at the Congress led Gorbachev to break with the right and form a new alliance with El'tsin and the leaders of eight other republics. Gorbachev himself cannot have been happy with the reactionary antics of the security forces at a time when he was still claiming within the country and in the west to be the instigator of democratic transformations. The result was the Novo-Ogarevo nine-plus-one agreement to produce a new Union Treaty, giving substantial powers to the republics and making membership of the USSR voluntary. Following this agreement, El'tsin was able to broker an end to the miners' strike.

The fear that some of the Russian democrats were forcing the pace of the dissolution of the old Union, without regard to the consequences, led three of the democratic parties to establish the 'Constructive-Democratic Bloc "Popular Accord" [*Narodnoe soglasie*]'. Travkin for the DPR, Aksiuchits for the RCDM and Astaf'ev for his Kadets signed a declaration on 19 April, agreeing to work together at elections, in the legislature and within Democratic Russia. The declaration began:

The catastrophic worsening of the situation in the country is conditioned on the one hand by the monopoly of the CPSU, preserving the totalitarian system, and on the other—the Left-radical spontaneity of disintegration ... We desire change in the political regime but not the destruction of statehood.

It called for the 'territorial integrity of the Russian Federation' and the 'transformation of the USSR into a new federal state'.[146]

The Russian presidential election was a relatively low-key affair. Democratic Russia was united behind El'tsin, who had chosen Rutskoi as his running-mate as vice-president. He won an outright victory with 57.3 per cent of the vote on the first ballot. Ryzhkov was the official candidate of the CP of the RSFSR; with his running-mate General Boris Gromov he came second, a long way behind with 16.9 per cent. Third was the Russian nationalist Zhirinovskii, fourth was Aman-Geldy Tuleev (chairperson of the Kemerovo oblast' soviet), fifth the hardline Colonel-General Al'bert Makashov, and sixth the Gorbachevian Vadim Bakatin. El'tsin did best in Sverdlovsk, winning 90 per cent of the vote, Moscow with 72 per cent and Leningrad with 67.5 per cent. Despite the fact that Mossovet had just passed a motion of no confidence in him, Popov was elected mayor in Moscow. Leningrad voted to make Sobchak mayor and to restore the name of St. Petersburg. Iurii Afanas'ev won a by-election to become a people's deputy of the RSFSR. Ominously, voter turnout fell below 50 per cent in Tatarstan, where the government was calling a boycott of the Russian election as part of its campaign for the status of a union republic; instead, most voters chose only a president for Tatarstan.[147]

On 20 July El'tsin banned communist and other party branches from ministries, local government agencies and factories within the jurisdiction of the RSFSR and threatened to ban party branches in the army and KGB as well.[148] This would have been a crushing blow at communist domination of society, had the coup not intervened.

At the same time Rutskoi, installed as vice-president, proceeded to plan his own grass-roots movement based on the Communists for Democracy fraction. The group would be called the Democratic Party of the Communists of Russia and would stay inside the CPSU for the time being.[149]

Strength in diversity?

At this point it is time to return to the questions posed at the beginning of this chapter: why was it that neither a mass Russian Popular Front nor strong parties which could seriously hope to challenge the CPSU appeared in Russia before the coup? The most successful movement—Democratic Russia—was an effective electoral bloc but did not achieve the level of support of the Baltic Popular Fronts or the mass activism of Rukh in Ukraine.

On the question of a Russian Popular Front, it is clear that in the Baltic republics, Moldavia and later in Ukraine, the principal political issue was the desire for greater autonomy or independence from the USSR. Until the formation of the Democratic Russia electoral bloc in January 1990, the question of greater rights for the RSFSR had hardly ever been posed by the Russian democrats; neither they nor the imperial nationalists seriously spoke of the total independence of Russia from the Soviet Union (Rasputin raised it in an ironical fashion at the first USSR CPD). In the absence of the overriding unifying factor of the desire for independence, there was a greater concern in Russia with ideological differences than in the non-Russian republics.

This is not quite the same point as Geoffrey Hosking has made in Chapter 1 on the beginnings of independent political activity (p. 18) about the absence of a single ethnic target. Rukh and the Latvian Popular Front mobilised ethnic Russians against the predominantly Russian centre, while the Russian democrats mobilised non-Russians (Sobchak, Khasbulatov, Popov, Bonner) against the centre. In other words the territorial or regional factor may have been as important as the ethnic.

One effect of the ideological differences was that the established cultural organisations which played a leading role in the formation of the Popular Fronts elsewhere were in Russia neutralised or in the conservative camp. In particular the Union of Writers, which in the non-Russian republics was in the forefront of the defence of the local language and culture, in the RSFSR was dominated by outspoken conservative nationalists. The democrats themselves were divided over the extent to which measures should be taken to secure the maintenance of a political Union of states, but these differences only became very important after the August coup.

Another factor militating against the formation of a Russian Popular Front was that much of the party-state apparatus was hostile to democratisation. Unlike the leaders who came to the fore in the Baltic CPs in 1988, but like the leaders of the Ukrainian, Belorussian, Kazakh and Central Asian CPs, the oblast' party leaders in the RSFSR and their friends in the central party apparatus opposed the establishment of a Russian Popular Front as a threat to the leading role of the CPSU.

A separate point is that many reformers in Russia were in the CPSU (as in the non-Russian republics) and were unwilling to break with Gorbachev, and not only stayed in the CPSU but avoided setting up organisations which appeared to be in confrontation with him. It was only at the end of June 1991 that Gorbachev appeared to approve an independent democratic movement, the Movement for Democratic Reforms—and that was intended to be established on an all-Union basis, not solely in Russia.

Finally, the sheer vastness of Russia made it harder to hold a nation-wide movement together under adverse conditions. The task was complicated by the widespread suspicion of Muscovite centralism.

Turning to the problem of the absence of strong political parties, it seems that the main reason lies within the CPSU itself. A good part of the progressive intelligentsia stood politically for much of this time between El'tsin and Gorbachev. In mid-September 1990 most ministers in the RSFSR government were still members of the CPSU (including Silaev); some of these and other leading figures such as Rutskoi and Khasbulatov remained in the party until the coup. Some ordinary members remained because of fears of victimisation at work; many remained because party membership was necessary at their place of work (such as the party press or the party apparatus itself) or because (even after the abolition of the leading role) CPSU membership continued to give access to points of influence. In the Russian CPD, deputies from the party apparatus usually supported 'Kommunisty Rossii', whereas secretaries of work-place branches usually supported Democratic Russia.[150]

Up to the time of the coup, it was widely expected that the CPSU would split and a mass democratic party would emerge. The desire to share in the breakup of the party's immense assets encouraged many democrats to wait for the split. In fact there was no big split on the scale envisaged; democratic leaders disagreed about the right time to break with the CPSU. Therefore they left at different times between May 1990 and August 1991, taking out tens of thousands of people with them and establishing parties of their own, especially Travkin's Democratic Party of Russia and Lysenko's Republican Party of the Russian Federation. Just before the coup, it seemed that Rutskoi's Democratic Party of Communists of Russia was in the best position to create a mass new Russian party. This was probably still the case after the coup, although by then the situation was transformed by the banning of the Communist Party in Russia.

Other factors which have prevented the appearance of democratic mass parties include the general discrediting among the population of the idea of a party, after seventy-four years of being ruled by one. Furthermore, the pre-revolutionary parties have all been discredited by Russian historical experience. The now-discredited Bolsheviks came to power because of the incompetence of the monarchists, Constitutional Democrats, Social Democrats (Mensheviks) and others. Most people look to strong personalities like El'tsin and Sobchak as good individuals. Since leaving the CPSU they have avoided entanglements with any of the parties, thereby freeing themselves from unwanted commitments and seeming to rise above the fray. Whereas El'tsin achieved fame as a victim of the nomenklatura, Sobchak and Travkin became known through their televised speeches at the first USSR CPD. As in the west, television has encouraged the personalisation of politics, but in Russia this has happened before parties have had a chance to engage the interest of the voters. Travkin was known as a personality rather than because he was leader of the DPR.

The voters did not see differences between the democratic parties: most wanted the rule of law, a multi-party democratic system, and the market, but this is what Gorbachev himself claimed to be offering from the summer of 1990. While the voters were not interested in the minutiae of differences between the parties and their splits and regroupings, they were much more enthusiastic about the democratic electoral blocs in the major cities and the Democratic Russia group. This last, which might have formed the nucleus of a new party, could not in fact be transformed into one, because of the proliferation of viewpoints within it. It was, rather, an umbrella for all democratic opposition, and was the nearest Russian equivalent to Civic Forum in Czechoslovakia and Solidarity in Poland (although it lacked the mass working-class membership of the latter).

The coup and after

With El'tsin openly moving against the structures of the Communist Party, and Gorbachev preparing to devolve considerable power to the republics, the right stepped up its preparations for the coup. Between April and July 1991 the *Soiuz* group of USSR people's deputies organised itself, with deputies from other levels, into a political party across the USSR. On 23 July 1991 *Sovetskaia Rossiia* published 'A Word to the People' [Slovo Narodu], the reactionary manifesto which called on the army to save the state. The writers Prokhanov, Bondarev, Rasputin and Volodin were joined by Deputy Minister of Defence Gen. Valentin Varennikov, Deputy Minister of Internal Affairs Gen. Boris Gromov, the leader of Soiuz, Iurii Blokhin, Vasilii Starodubtsev and Aleksandr Tiziakov. The last two men were later to join the plotters' Emergency Committee, and Varennikov was to play an important role in the coup.

On 19 August Kriuchkov, Pugo, Iazov, Pavlov, CPSU Central Committee secretary Oleg Baklanov, USSR vice-president Gennadii Ianaev, Starodubtsev and Tiziakov established a 'State Committee for the State of Emergency'. They had Gorbachev deposed and confined to his dacha and appointed Ianaev to replace him as USSR president. They sent tanks into the centre of Moscow and other major cities, took over central broadcasting and suspended the publication of all Moscow periodicals with the exception of nine reactionary and conservative newspapers. At the time of writing the full story behind the coup had still not been told, but it seems that the initiative was taken by the KGB leader Kriuchkov and that figures who had been or still were at the apex of the CPSU Central Committee organisation were involved.[151]

The response of thousands of Muscovites was to defend the centres of democratic power, the Mossovet building and above all the White House, the seat of the RSFSR Supreme Soviet. The usurpers had failed to cut off telephone links or to arrest El'tsin, who managed to get to the parliament building. The Russian president climbed on to a tank outside the White House which had been sent by the plotters but had been neutralised. He condemned the plotters, demanded the release of Gorbachev and his restoration to power, and called for strikes and other forms of resistance. The plotters allowed this to appear on Central Television. Journalists from the banned newspapers produced counter-propaganda and helped maintain links between the democratic leaders, the peoples of the USSR and the West. The coup collapsed on the third day.

The coup leaders hoped to prevent the signing of the new Union Treaty, due on 20 August, and to prevent the dissolution of the Union. Instead, their defeat meant the destruction of the communist system of power. The changes in society which had been introduced by Gorbachev and which had been promoted by the democratic organisations, even when Gorbachev had allied with reaction, prevented the fulfilment of the plotters' intentions. Even if Kriuchkov and the others had avoided some of their blunders and arrested El'tsin, popular support for him would have probably brought them down before long. As it was, the leaders of the coup had failed to prepare adequate political support; the *Soiuz* group does not seem to have been involved. Moreover, the plotters lacked the will to use massive force against the elected Russian parliament. Outside Moscow, sporadic strikes had already begun in response to El'tsin's public call for solidarity action, particularly in the Urals; in Leningrad, the coup was nullified almost at once by the actions of Sobchak and the soviet.

The defeat of the coup was above all the victory of El'tsin. Communist Party buildings were seized, and statues of communist leaders were torn down (although Lenin was allowed to remain in his Mausoleum for the time being). The Russian tricolour, already adopted by Democratic Russia for its lapel badges, flew unhindered. The Russian leaders secured the return of Gorbachev, but from 21 August until 25 December he was largely dependent on them. Within days of the coup Gorbachev and El'tsin suspended the activity of the CPSU, pending investigation of its role in the coup; on 6 November El'tsin by presidential decree banned it completely. To the consternation of the other republics, Russia tried to take over as many of the functions of the old centre as possible. Ukraine and the other republics joined in to seize what assets they could.

Over this period it became increasingly clear that, as the imperial nationalists had warned and some of the democrats had feared, the territorial integrity of the RSFSR had been maintained by the same forces which had kept the USSR together and now collapsed. Territories within Russia, especially the autonomous republics but also regions such as the Russian Far East, began to assert their independence more stridently. The communist élites of Tatarstan, Bashkortostan (formerly Bashkiria) and the Iakut-Sakha Republic (formerly Iakutia) sought to prolong their power by coopting nationalist sentiment. In October the National Congress of the Chechen People, led by General Jokhar Dudaev, seized power in Groznyi and declared the independence of the Chechen Republic. El'tsin's proposal to declare a state of emergency and send troops to crush the uprising was opposed by Democratic Russia and vetoed by the Russian Supreme Soviet.

The incident served to open a major split within Democratic Russia about how important it was to keep Russia, or even the Union, together. At the Second Congress of the Democratic Russia movement on 11–12 November, Afanas'ev condemned the 'imperialist' policy of the Russian government; on the other wing, the parties of 'Popular Accord' (DPR, RCDM and Kadets) left the movement, wishing to maintain the Union in some form.[152]

New parties were appearing, claiming to be the heirs of the banned CPSU. Rutskoi's party, now known as the People's Party 'Free Russia', had its founding congress on 26–7 October 1991. Its claim of 100,000 members would make it the largest of all the Russian parties. Rutskoi declared that it would support El'tsin's economic transformations. It was in some respects close to the Movement for Democratic Reforms, which retained the support of Aleksandr Iakovlev, Shevardnadze, Popov and Sobchak.[153] Part of the former Marxist Platform in the CPSU established the League of Communists in November.[154] Hard-line communists including Makashov established the Russian Communist Workers' Party at a founding congress on 23–4 November in Ekaterinburg, the former Sverdlovsk.[155] Communists from a broader spectrum of views established the Socialist Party of Working People, with seven co-chairpersons including Roi Medvedev. This had its first congress on 21–2 December, where it claimed 50,000 members.[156] Kagarlitskii's socialists and the Confederation of Anarcho-Syndicalists were meanwhile working with another part of the Marxist Platform and the Moscow 'official' (formerly communist-controlled) trade unions to create a Party of Labour, with an affiliated trade-union membership, like the British Labour Party. It had some strength on Mossovet. This party would oppose what they saw as enforced privatisation and the danger of a new totalitarianism.[157]

After the coup, El'tsin formed a new government, with himself as prime minister, Burbulis his first deputy, Egor' Gaidar deputy with responsibility for economics and Aleksandr Shokhin as deputy with responsibility for social affairs. Shokhin had entered the government as a representative of the SDPR. On 28 October El'tsin announced his programme of radical economic reforms to the Russian CPD, in front of a large statue of Lenin. The Congress gave him power to rule by decree, but added the proviso that the Supreme Soviet could annul a decree within a week of its promulgation.

Already in July he had appointed Stankevich State Counsellor with responsibility for liaising with public organisations, but now the need to convert the public support for himself into stable parliamentary support for his policies grew stronger. In November Democratic Russia and the democratic parties agreed, via Stankevich, to give parliamentary support to El'tsin in exchange for a say in government appointments, advance sight of proposed legislation and office premises. At the same time Democratic Russia decided to establish local committees to promote the reforms and prevent local officials from blocking them. This last did not meet the approval of the parties; it seemed to them that Democratic Russia might be in danger of being transformed into an apparatus in support of the government, a ruling party of a new type. Oleg Rumiantsev called the new bodies *revkomy*, likening them to Bolshevik revolutionary committees. In the first months the agreement between El'tsin and the democrats did not work to everyone's satisfaction, but El'tsin was able to rely on the democratic deputies for support for his economic programme.[158]

El'tsin himself came under attack from other democrats for what they saw as certain authoritarian measures. He appointed prefects in all the regions of Russia, effectively challenging the rights of the elected soviets; he postponed all elections for such posts and for the soviets, and any referendums until the end of 1992, fearing that the old nomenklatura would win in the localities; he merged the successor to the KGB with the MVD in a super-ministry, in a decree which was then annulled by the RSFSR Constitutional Court; his government appeared to be putting pressure on the media to relax their criticism of his policies; and even the banning of the CPSU was unpalatable to some liberals.[159]

The decision to dispense with the Soviet Union and create the Commonwealth of Independent States (CIS) came as a shock. Only days before signing the Minsk Declaration of 11 December, creating the Commonwealth, El'tsin had talked of the need to maintain the Union. Supporters of El'tsin saw the formation of the Commonwealth as an ingenious means of keeping Ukraine in some form of association with Russia, after Ukraine had voted decisively for independence. Others less charitably saw it as a way of deposing Gorbachev and concentrating power in his own hands. The democratic deputies largely welcomed the final abolition of the old Union, and the Russian Supreme Soviet gave its approval by a large majority to the Alma-Ata accords, whereby Russia and ten other republics confirmed their membership of the CIS. Nevertheless Travkin's RPR, Rutskoi and Sobchak joined Gorbachev in expressing the preference that the Union should have continued. With new political alignments emerging, it was not surprising that when the traditional right—Baburin, Alksnis and Volodin—established a 'Russian All-People's Union' (*Rossiiskii obshchenarodnyi soiuz*) on 21 December, representatives of the three parties of Popular Accord attended as observers.[160]

Gorbachev resigned as USSR president on 25 December. The hammer and sickle was lowered over the Kremlin and El'tsin moved into Gorbachev's office the following morning. On 26 December the Supreme Soviet renamed the RSFSR as the 'Russian Federation (Russia)', losing not only the epithets 'Soviet' and 'Socialist' but also 'Republic'. The USSR came to a legal end on 31 December 1991. This had not been the original aim of the Russian democrats, who had hoped to reform the Union rather than to destroy it. El'tsin now faced formidable problems: to find a new *modus vivendi* with the other former Soviet republics, to negotiate the dissolution of the Soviet Army, and to maintain the integrity of Russia. At the same time he was pursuing a tough policy of price rises and privatisation which his own vice-president, Rutskoi, was publicly opposing. New dangers would face the democrats, as the right-wing alliance of Russian imperialists and anti-Semites with frustrated ex-communists would try to mobilise opposition to El'tsin by attacking both his economic reforms aand his role in the collapse of the USSR. But the democrats had already achieved the destruction of communist rule far more quickly than anyone had considered possible.

Notes

Russia and the other larger republics of the former USSR are subdivided into a number of territorial units, involving a hierarchy of administrative levels. Among the levels are the *oblast'* (region or province), the *gorod* (city or town) and the *raion* (district). Until the attempted coup of August 1991, each territorial unit was ruled by the corresponding CPSU committee: the *obkom, gorkom* and *raikom* respectively.

1. M. S. Gorbachev, 'For full power to the Soviets, and the creation of a socialist state based on the rule of law', report to the USSR Supreme Soviet, 29 November 1988, *Moscow News*, no. 50, 11 December 1988.
2. A Chekavtsev, 'Waiting for further developments', *Moscow News*, no. 52, 25 December 1988.
3. 'The right to a seat', *Moscow News*, no. 6, 5 February 1989.
4. Journalists and members of democratic organisations contributed an analysis of the shortcomings in the electoral process: 'From real struggle to real elections', *Moscow News*, no. 11, 12 March 1989.
5. Dmitry Kazutin, 'Surprises of the political spring', *Moscow News*, no. 12, 19 March 1989.
6. Boris Kagarlitsky, *Farewell Perestroika: A Soviet Chronicle*, trans. Rick Simon, London, Verso, 1990, pp 102–3; Geoffrey Hosking's interview with Valerii Skurlatov, 1 July 1991; 'Kto sozdaet Rossiiskii narodnyi front?', *Khronograf* (Moscow samizdat), no. 23, 5 March 1989; V. N. Berezovskii, N. I. Krotov and V. V. Cherviakov, *Rossiia: partii, assotsiatsii, soiuzy, kluby. Spravochnik*, Moscow, RAU-Press, 1991, vol. 1, pt. 1, pp. 105–6.
7. Kagarlitsky, *Farewell Perestroika*, pp. 100–9.
8. Nina Belyayeva, 'Moscow Tribune', *Moscow News*, no. 7, 12 February 1989.
9. Igor' Chubais, 'The democratic opposition: an insider's view', *Report on the USSR*, vol. 3, no. 18, 3 May 1991, pp. 6–7.
10. Interview with Nikolai Popov, deputy director of the All-Union Centre for the Study of Public Opinion, Moscow, 19 April 1989.
11. Alexander Mineyev, 'Evolution of social awareness', *Moscow News*, no. 3, 15 January 1989.
12. Berezovskii, Krotov and Cherviakov, *Rossiia: partii*, vol. 1, pt. 2, p. 210.
13. ibid., pt. 1, pp. 135–6; 'The decisive day', *Moscow News*, no. 14, 2 April 1989.
14. *Rossiia: partii.*, vol. 1, pt. 1, pp. 136–7.
15. ibid., p. 132.
16. ibid., p. 131.
17. V. N. Berezovskii and N. I. Krotov (eds), *Neformal' naia Rossiia*, Moscow, Molodaia gvardiia, 1990, p. 197.
18. ibid., p. 143.
19. ibid., pp. 218–19.

20. Andrei Borodenkov, 'Our opinion was ignored', *Moscow News*, no. 7, 12 February 1989.
21. 'At the Academy or nowhere', *Moscow News*, no. 8, 19 February 1989.
22. ibid., Andrei Kuteinikov, 'How will the Academy vote?', *Moscow News*, no. 11, 12 March 1989.
23. Yevgeny Yevtushenko, 'False alarm', *Moscow News*, no. 6, 5 February 1989.
24. Kagarlitsky, *Farewell Perestroika*, pp. 95–6.
25. See Boris Yeltsin, *Against the Grain: An Autobiography*, trans. Michael Glenny, New York, Summit Books, 1990, pp. 39–42, 57–60, 83–5, for El'tsin's account of the nomination meetings.
26. John Morrison, *Boris Yeltsin: From Bolshevik to Democrat*, London, Penguin, 1991, p. 92; 'A minister or a people's deputy', *Moscow News*, no. 5, 29 January 1989.
27. *Leninets* (Bashkiria), 22 December 1988, translated in *Labour Focus on Eastern Europe*, no. 2, 1989, p. 29.
28. Kagarlitsky, *Farewell Perestroika*, pp. 117–20; Chubais, 'Democratic opposition', pp. 7–8, which claims the credit for the Moscow Inter-Club Party Group rather than the Popular Front.
29. Morrison, *Boris Yeltsin*, p. 89.
30. Kagarlitsky, *Farewell Perestroika*, p. 94.
31. Alexander Kabakov, 'One of 7,000,000', *Moscow News*, no. 5, 29 January 1989; idem., 'Those who enjoy our confidence', *Moscow News*, no. 11, 12 March 1989.
32. Brendan Kiernan and Joseph Aistrup, 'The 1989 elections to the Congress of People's Deputies in Moscow', *Soviet Studies*, vol. 43, no. 6, 1991, p. 1061.
33. Aleksei Flerovsky, 'Glasnost: no holds barred', *Moscow News*, no. 11, 12 March 1989. On the 'El'tsin effect', see Kiernan and Aistrup, '1989 elections', pp. 1051–3.
34. This is based on election material and conversations held in Moscow in April 1989. See also Kagarlitsky, *Farewell Perestroika*, p. 123.
35. Leonid Miloslavsky, 'Activist elected People's Deputy of the USSR', *Moscow News*, no. 22, 28 May 1989.
36. Douglas Smith, 'Moscow's "Otechestvo": a link between Russian nationalism and conservative opposition to reform', *Report on the USSR*, vol. 1, no. 30, 28 July 1989, p. 8.
37. Dawn Mann and Julia Wishnevsky, 'Composition of the Congress of People's Deputies', *Report on the USSR*, vol. 1, no. 18, 5 May 1989, pp. 1–6.
38. Nina Belyayeva, 'Gearing up for the Congress of People's Deputies', *Moscow News*, no. 18, 30 April 1989.
39. 'Khartiia Moskovskogo narodnogo fronta', undated typescript; Kagarlitsky, *Farewell Perestroika*, pp. 139–43.
40. Kagarlitsky, *Farewell Perestroika*, pp. 145–63; '100,000-strong rally', *Moscow News*, no. 22, 28 May 1989.
41. Kagarlitsky, *Farewell Perestroika*, pp. 188–90, 200.
42. 'Ustav Kluba izbiratelei Taganskogo raiona Moskvy', undated typescript.
43. Valentin Rasputin, 'Vystuplenie na S″ezde narodnykh deputatov SSSR', *Nash sovremennik*, no. 8, 1989, pp. 133–6.
44. *Rossiia: partii*, vol. 1, pt. 1, p. 105.
45. Alexander Mineyev and Iana Nikitina, 'Popular Front of Russia: let's wait until autumn', *Moscow News*, no. 29, 16 July 1989.
46. Vladimir Pribylovskii, 'Frontovaia Rossiia', *Panorama* (Moscow samizdat), no. 11,

November 1989; *Rossiia: partii*, vol. 1, pt. 1, p. 96 (including the constitution); 'Slovar' oppozitsii. Novye politicheskie partii i organizatsii Rossii', comp. Vladimir Pribylovskii, *Sostoianie strany*, no. 4/5, April 1991, pp. 21–2; 'Popular Front of the Russian Federation Created', *Moscow News*, no. 44, 29 October 1989.

47. *Rossiia: partii*, vol 1, pt. 1, pp. 39–40.

48. Galina Vokhmentseva, 'MADO', and Il' ia Kudriavtsev, 'Chto dal'she', *Panorama*, no. 11, November 1989; Gennady Zhavaronkov, 'Democracy's salad days', *Moscow News*, no. 47, 19 November 1989.

49. *Rossiia: partii*, vol. 1, pt. 1, p. 95; Andrei Vasilevskii, 'MOI', *Panorama*, no. 4, March 1990.

50. Edward Kline, 'Foreword', in Andrei D. Sakharov, *Moscow and Beyond: 1986 to 1989*, trans. Antonina Bouis, London, Hutchinson, 1990, p. xiii.

51. *Rossiia: partii*, vol. 1, pt. 1, pp. 92–3.

52. 'Sozdan izbiratel'nyi blok "Demokraticheskaia Rossiia"', *Ogonek*, no. 6, February 1990, pp. 17–18.

53. *Argumenty i fakty*, no. 8, 24 February–2 March 1990.

54. Vera Tolz, 'Informal political groups prepare for elections in RSFSR', *Report on the USSR*, vol. 2, no. 8, 23 February 1990, pp. 23–8; idem., 'A new approach to informal groups', *Report on the USSR*, vol. 2. no. 10, 9 March 1990, p. 2.

55. Tolz, 'Informal political groups', p. 25; Timothy J. Colton, 'The politics of democratisation: the Moscow election of 1990', *Soviet Economy*, vol. 6, no. 4, 1990, pp. 286, 324.

56. Chubais, 'Democratic opposition', pp. 7–12.

57. 'On the eve', *Moscow News*, no. 6, 11 February 1990; Mary Dejevsky, '300 000 join protest march in Moscow', *The Times*, 5 February 1990; Jonathan Steele, '200,000 march on Kremlin', *Guardian*, 5 February 1990.

58. John Rettie and Jonathan Steele, '100,000 march in Moscow', *Guardian*, 26 February 1990.

59. Mary Dejevsky in *The Times*, 26 February 1990; see also 'The hard parting with the past', *Moscow News*, no. 8–9, 4 March 1990.

60. Cited in John B. Dunlop, 'Two noteworthy Russian nationalist initiatives', *Report on the USSR*, vol. 1, no. 21, 26 May 1989.

61. 'Slovar' oppozitsii', p. 3.

62. Douglas Smith, 'Moscow's "Otechestvo"', pp. 6–9.

63. 'Slovar' oppozitsii', p. 45.

64. ibid., pp. 44–5; Douglas Smith, 'Formation of new Russian nationalist group announced', *Report on the USSR*, vol. 1, no. 27, 7 July 1989, pp. 5–8.

65. 'Slovar' oppozitsii', p. 3.

66. 'Za politiku Narodnogo Soglasiia i rossiiskogo vozrozhdeniia', *Literaturnaia Rossiia*, no. 52, 29 December 1989.

67. Aleksandr Prokhanov, 'Tragediia tsentralizma', *Literaturnaia Rossiia*, no. 1, 5 January 1990.

68. For a good description of the Moscow elections and the characteristics of the candidates, which this account draws from, see Colton, 'Politics of democratization', pp. 285–344.

69. 'So all power to the soviets?', *Moscow News*, no. 12, 25 March 1990; 'Parliamentary bloc', *Moscow News*, no. 14, 8 April 1990. For the Sverdlovsk figures I am grateful to Iurii Davydov, people's deputy of the Sverdlovsk City Soviet, interview 15 April 1991.

70. 'So all power to the soviets?'; Julia Wishnevsky, 'Patriots urge annulment of RSFSR elections', *Report on the USSR*, vol. 2, no. 14, 6 April 1990, p. 19; John B. Dunlop, 'Moscow voters reject conservative coalition', *Report on the USSR*, vol. 2, no. 16, 20 April 1990, pp. 15–17.

71. Dawn Mann, 'The RSFSR elections: the Congress of People's Deputies', *Report on the USSR*, vol. 2, no. 15, 13 April 1990, pp. 11–17.

72. 'Moscow Diary', *Moscow News*, no. 14, 8 April 1990.

73. V. Fadeev, 'Pirrova pobeda na vyborakh–90', *Svoboda. Gazeta press-tsentra 'Moskovskogo Memoriala'*, no. 2, April 1990.

74. 'Neskol'ko voprosov predsedateliu', *Argumenty i fakty*, no. 18, 5–11 November 1990.

75. 'Snova—Tverskaia!', *Izvestiia*, 29 July 1990.

76. Tatyana Tsyla, 'The sound and the fury', and Jenny Abdo, 'Popov's first year', in *Moscow Magazine*, no. 3 (11), March 1991; Timothy Frye, 'The Moscow City Soviet stakes its claim', *Report on the USSR*, vol. 2, no. 31, 3 August 1990, pp. 16–19.

77. Interview with Iurii Davydov.

78. Julia Wishnevsky, 'Fighter for reform triumphs in Ryazan', *Report on the USSR*, vol. 3, no. 39, 28 September 1990, pp. 10–12.

79. Vladimir Orlov, 'Governor in the dark', *Moscow News*, 29 December 1991–5 January 1992, no. 52.

80. 'Slovar' oppozitsii', p. 7.

81. Bridget Kendal, 'Letter from Russia', BBC Radio Four, 23 March 1991, 2245 GMT.

82. Dmitry Ostalsky, 'Before the Congress of the Russian Federation People's Deputies', *Moscow News*, no. 4, 22 April 1990; Igor Chubais, 'How I was expelled from the Party', ibid.

83. 'Vybor sdelan', *Argumenty i fakty*, no. 22, 2–8 June 1990. For El'tsin's final nomination speech of 28 May, see BBC *Summary of World Broadcasts*, SU/0778 B/1–4, 31 May 1990.

84. 'Dekret o vlasti', *Argumenty i fakty*, no. 25, 23–9 June 1990.

85. 'Deklaratsiia o gosudarstvennoi suverenitete Rossiiskoi Sovetskoi Federativnoi Sotsialisticheskoi Respubliki', *Argumenty i fakty*, no. 24, 16–22 June 1990.

86. Jonathan Steele and John Rettie, 'Russian Republic softens declaration of sovereignty', *Guardian*, 13 June 1990.

87. Richard Owen, 'Challenge for Gorbachov as Yeltsin talks to Lithuania', *The Times*, 2 June 1990.

88. Jonathan Steele, 'Gorbachev yields over sovereignty', *Guardian*, 14 June 1990.

89. 'O razgranichenii funktsii upravleniia organizatsiiami na territorii RSFSR', *Argumenty i fakty*, no. 26, 30 June–6 July 1990.

90. A. Uglanov, 'Poezdka B. El'tsina. Tatariia', ibid., no. 32, 11–17 August 1990.

91. On TOTs, see Uli Schamiloglu, 'The Tatar Public Center and current Tatar concerns', *Report on the USSR*, vol. 1, no. 51, 22 December 1989, pp. 11–15.

92. For the speech and the reaction, see Stephen Foye, 'Military hard-liner condemns "new thinking" in security policy', *Report on the USSR*, vol. 2, no. 28, 13 July 1990, pp. 4–6.

93. Reuter in Moscow, 'Radical leader quits party', *Guardian*, 20 April 1990.

94. Mary Dejevsky, 'Reformist split cools hope of Soviet party's renewal', *The Times*, 23 April 1990.

95. 'Yeltsin quits Communist Party', *Soviet News* (London), 18 July 1990, p. 240.
96. Gavriil Popov and Anatolii Sobchak, 'Zaiavlenie', *Smena* (Leningrad), 15 July 1990.
97. V. N. Lysenko *et al.*, 'K kommunistam i grazhdanam strany', *Smena*, 14 July 1990.
98. 'Obrashchenie orgkomiteta po sozdaniiu dvizheniia "Demokraticheskaia Rossiia"', *Ogonek*, no. 38, 1990 (September), p. 3.
99. 'Sovmestnoe zaiavlenie Demokraticheskoi partii Rossii, Demokraticheskoi platformy i Sotsial-demokraticheskoi partii Rossii', *Demokraticheskaia Rossiia*, no. 3, September 1990.
100. Reuter in Moscow, '30,000 urge Ryzhkov to quit', *Guardian*, 17 September 1990; 'Samoe glavnoe', *Argumenty i fakty*, no. 38, 22–8 September 1990.
101. 'Uchreditel'nyi s"ezd dvizheniia "Demokraticheskaia Rossiia"', *Russkaia mysl'*, no. 3851, 26 October 1990.
102. John B. Dunlop, 'The leadership of the centrist bloc', *Report on the USSR*, vol. 3, no. 6, 8 February 1991, p. 5; '*Pravda* on the activities of "Democratic" forces', *Soviet News*, 3 October 1990, p. 35; Scott Shane, *Baltimore Sun*, 21 October 1990; *Rossiia: partii*, vol. 1, pt. 1, pp. 104–5.
103. 'Uchreditel'nyi s"ezd dvizheniia "Demokraticheskaia Rossiia"', *Russkaia mysl'*, no. 3851, 26 October 1990; V. Naiman, 'Forum demokraticheskikh sil: budem probovat', poka ne poluchitsia mal'chik?', *Molodoi dal' nevostochnik*, 27 October 1990.
104. As previous note.
105. 'Itogi uchreditel'nogo s"ezda dvizheniia "Demokraticheskaia Rossiia"', *Demokraticheskaia Rossiia'*, no. 5, November 1990.
106. 'Ustav Dvizheniia "Demokraticheskaia Rossiia"', printed sheet.
107. *Dvizhenie 'Demokraticheskaia Rossiia'. Informatsionnyi biulleten'*, no. 1, January 1991.
108. 'Slovar' oppozitsii', p. 8.
109. Aleksandr Lukin and Valerii Fadeev, talk at School of Slavonic and East European Studies Soviet Press Study Group, 17 October 1990.
110. Gavriil Popov, 'Perspektivy i realii', *Ogonek*, no. 50, 1990 (December), pp. 6–8, no. 51, 1990 (December), pp. 5–8, esp. no. 51, pp 5–6.
111. 'Sindrom tsentra', *Argumenty i fakty*, no 38, 22–8 September 1990.
112. *Dvizhenie 'Demokraticheskaia Rossiia'. Informatsionnyi biulleten'*, no. 5, February 1991.
113. For early discussion of these groups and their leaders, see Vera Tolz, 'Leading members of sociopolitical movements in Moscow and Leningrad', *Report on the USSR*, vol. 2, no. 26, 29 June 1990, pp. 7–10; Aleksandr Meerovich, 'The emergence of Russian multiparty politics', ibid., no. 34, 24 August 1990, pp. 8–16.
114. *Demokraticheskaia Rossiia*, no. 1, July 1990, appendix.
115. Sergei Baluev, 'Partiia klassicheskogo tipa', *Smena*, 15 May 1990.
116. V. P. Davydov, 'Demokraticheskaia partiia Rossii', *Sotsial'no-politicheskie nauki*, no. 11, 1990 (November), pp. 66–74.
117. *Demokraticheskaia Rossiia*, no. 1, July 1990, appendix.
118. Elizabeth Teague, 'Soviet television features new political party', *Report on the USSR*, vol. 2, no. 26, 29 June 1990, pp. 4–5.
119. See, for example, Igor' Kharichev, member of the organising committee of Democratic Russia, 'Chto nas zhdet?', *Demokraticheskaia Rossiia*, no. 5, November 1990. Nikolai Travkin argued the case for discipline in his 'Otdadut li bol' sheviki vlast' sovetam?', ibid., no. 2, August 1990.

120. Reprinted in *Rossiia segodnia. Politicheskii portret v dokumentakh, 1985–1991*, ed. B. I. Koval', Moscow, Mezhdunarodnye otnosheniia, 1991, pp. 202–4. This book is a very useful collection of documents produced by the new movements.

121. Geoffrey Hosking's interview with Nikolai Travkin, 29 April 1991.

122. *Materialy Uchreditel' nogo s"ezda Respublikanskoi partii Rossiiskoi Federatsii. Sbornik No 1*; Igor' Iakovenko, 'Karlik ili velikan?' *Ogonek*, 1990, no. 52 (December), pp. 26–7.

123. Chubais, 'Democratic Opposition', pp. 14–15.

124. *Sotsium. Sotsial-demokraticheskoe izdanie*, no. 1, May 1990. For English translations of some Soviet views of the SDPR and other parties, see M. A. Babkina (ed.), *New Political Parties and Movements in the Soviet Union*, Commack, NY, Nova Science Publishers, 1991.

125. ibid.; *Rossiia: partii*, vol. 1, pt. 1, p. 113.

126. Interview with Leonid Volkov, Moscow, 16 April 1991.

127. Interview with A. Obolenskii, 'Sotsial-demokraty Rossii: partiia vybora', *Obshchestvennye nauki*, no. 6, 1990 (November–December), pp. 5–14, esp. p. 6.

128. Michael McFaul, 'The Social Democrats and the Republicans attempt to merge', *Report on the USSR*, vol. 3, no. 3, 18 January 1991, pp. 10–13.

129. Leonid Volkov, 'Situatsiia v strane', *Al'ternativa*, no. 3, September 1990. The last point was enlarged in A. Savel'ev, 'Mossovet: vzgliad iznutri', in ibid.

130. *Rossiia: partii*, vol. 1, pt. 2, pp. 333–4.

131. *Rossiiskoe Khristianskoe Demokraticheskoe Dvizhenie. Sbornik materialov*, Moscow, Duma Khristianskogo Demokraticheskogo Dvizheniia, 1990, pp. 3–6.

132. ibid., p. 38.

133. ibid., p. 44.

134. ibid., p. 49.

135. ibid., p 8. See also I. P. Vasil'eva, 'Rossiiskie khristianskie demokraty: Politicheskie vzgliady i idealy', *Sotsial'no-politicheskie nauki*, no. 7, 1991 (July), pp. 108–20.

136. Iu. Vorob'evskii, 'Professionaly chestoliubiia', *Sovetskaia Rossiia*, 15 February 1991.

137. *Khristiansko-demokraticheskii soiuz Rossii*, London, Overseas Publications Interchange, 1990.

138. For the TASS account, see V. Zen'kovich, 'Obrazovana novaia partiia', *Komsomol'skaia pravda*, 1 April 1990; also 'Liberalism: "A thing in itself"?', *Moscow News*, 6–13 May 1990, no. 17.

139. See John B. Dunlop, 'The leadership of the Centrist Bloc', *Report on the USSR*, vol. 3, no. 6, 8 February 1991, pp. 4–6.

140. *Argumenty i fakty*, no.16, 21–7 April 1990.

141. G. Koval'skaia and V. Nikitina, 'Chego nam zhdat' ot nikh', *Demokraticheskaia Rossiia*, no. 1 (7), 22 March 1991.

142. I. I. Antonovich, 'Patrioticheskie sily Rossii: vozmozhnost' ob"edineniia', *Izvestiia TsK KPSS*, no. 7, 1991 (July), pp. 67–9; *Rossiia segodnia*, pp. 316–18.

143. John Rettie, 'Referendum backs Union but gives boost to Yeltsin', *Guardian*, 22 March 1991; Associated Press, 19 March 1991.

144. I. Cherniak, 'Svoi sredi chuzhikh, chuzhoi sredi svoikh', *Komsomol'skaia pravda*, 6 April 1991.

145. I. Sichka and A. Pankratov, 'El'tsin idet va-bank', *Komsomol'skaia pravda*, 5 April 1991; also Sergei Parkhomenko, 'Rossiia poluchit Prezidenta v nachale leta', *Nezavisimaia gazeta*, 6 April 1991.

146. 'Deklaratsiia konstruktivno-demokraticheskogo bloka "Narodnoe soglasie"', *Demokraticheskaia gazeta*, no. 5 (8), n.d. but *c.* May 1991.

147. Jonathan Steele, 'Yeltsin races to victory in Russian poll', *Guardian*, 14 June 1991; John Rettie, 'Gorbachev hints at radical reform', ibid., 17 June 1991; Mary Dejevsky, 'Yeltsin races to poll triumph', *The Times*, 14 June 1991.

148. 'O prekrashchenii deiatel'nosti organizatsionnykh struktur politicheskikh partii i massovykh obshchestvennykh dvizhenii v gosudarstvennykh organakh, uchrezhdeniiakh i organizatsiiakh RSFSR', *Sovetskaia Rossiia*, 23 July 1991.

149. 'Partiia v partii', *Novoe vremia*, no. 30, 1991 (July), pp. 10–11.

150. L. Efimova, A. Sobianin and D. Iur'ev, 'Narod i nomenklatura—ediny?', *Argumenty i fakty*, 21–7 July 1990, no. 29.

151. On the events of the coup, see Martin Sixsmith, *Moscow Coup*, London, Simon and Schuster, 1991; Morrison, *Boris Yeltsin*, pp. 274–87; Mikhail Gorbachev, *The August Coup*, London, Harper Collins, 1991.

152. 'Vtoroi s"ezd Demokraticheskoi Rossii', *Russkaia mysl'*, no. 3904, 15 November 1991; Tatyana Yakhlakova, 'Democrats split over Yeltsin's state of emergency decree', *Moscow News*, no. 46, 17–24 November 1991.

153. Iulii Lebedev, 'Rutskoi posledoval sovety Meidzhora i Tetcher', *Nezavisimaia gazeta*, 29 October 1991; also, Vladimir Todres, 'Byvaet li Vitse-prezident bez partii?', ibid., 22 October 1991.

154. Marina Podzorova, 'Communism again—someday', *Moscow News*, no. 47, 24 November–1 December 1991.

155. S. Riabov, 'Reanimatsiia ili rozhdenie?', *Pravda*, 3 December 1991.

156. Roi Medvedev, 'Ne vopros taktiki, a priverzhennost' idealam opredeliaet tseli Sotsialisticheskoi partii trudiashchikhsia', *Pravda*, 17 December 1991.

157. Natal'ia Gorodetskaia, 'Tol'ko profsoiuzy mogut protivostoiat' novomu totalitarizmu', *Nezavisimaia gazeta*, 2 October 1991.

158. Vladimir Todres, 'Rossiiskii "Pakt Monkloa" pod ugrozoi', ibid., 3 December 1991; Iulii Lebedev, 'Novogodnii podarok rossiiskim partiiam', ibid., 4 January 1992. On the array of parties at the end of 1991, see 'The parties and Russian reform: who will act as a prop for the government?' *Moscow News*, no. 4, 26 January–2 February 1992.

159. Regular criticism of El'tsin appeared in *Moscow News* after the defeat of the coup. For a discussion of the issues, see Julia Wishnevsky, 'Russia: liberal media criticize Democrats in power', *RFE/RL Research Report*, vol. 1, no. 2, 10 January 1992, pp. 6–11.

160. Anna Kraevskaia, 'Gosudarstvenniki ob"edinilis' v bezbozhnom pereulke', *Nezavisimaia gazeta*, 24 December 1991; Tatyana Yakhlakova, 'Democratic Party of Russia wants to correct Democrats' mistakes', *Moscow News*, no. 50, 15–22 December 1991. On the dangers posed to democracy by the Russian nationalist right, see Vera Tolz and Elizabeth Teague, 'Is Russia likely to turn to authoritarian rule?' *RFE/RL Research Report*, vol. 1, no.4, 24 January 1992, pp. 1–8.

4 The return of St Petersburg
Peter J. S. Duncan

In March 1989, in the elections to the Congress of People's Deputies of the USSR, the CPSU apparatus suffered its most crushing blow in Leningrad. Five leading figures of the party and soviet bodies in the oblast' and the city were defeated. Among them was Iurii Solov'ev, the first secretary of the Leningrad obkom of the CPSU and a candidate member of the Politburo of the CPSU—the only member of the central leadership to be defeated. A year later, the democratic forces won control of the Leningrad City Soviet (Lensovet) with eighty per cent of the seats. In June 1991, the citizens voted to abandon the name 'Leningrad' and restore the original name of 'St Petersburg'. In August 1991, the actions of the elected leadership of the city prevented the entry of troops into Leningrad at the time of the coup. This short chapter investigates the reasons for the strength of the democrats in Leningrad, and some of the results of their victory.

St Petersburg was always more susceptible to western ideas than the rest of Russia. Peter the Great built the city and moved his capital there to provide a 'window on the west'. The very architecture of the city breathes western culture. In the nineteenth century, it was the centre of westernising thought in Russia. Throughout the twentieth century, it was the main centre of revolution and resistance to the existing powers. It was the site of the revolutions of 1905 and February and October 1917. Even after the Bolsheviks transferred the capital to Moscow, Petrograd continued to be a thorn in the flesh of the leaders. During the Civil War the Petrograd workers went on strike in protest at the famine. Under the control of the allies of Zinov'ev, the Leningrad party organisation was the last to hold out against Stalin in the mid-1920s, and in 1934 it was Sergei Kirov, the popular Leningrad party leader, who was the last man to pose a real threat to Stalin's position. Again in the late 1940s, the 'Leningrad case' reflected Stalin's fears about the challenge that might be posed from the city.[1]

The Leningrad party organisation was dominated by the military–industrial complex. As well as being the centre of the important Leningrad Military District, the headquarters of the Soviet Navy and the home of the Baltic fleet, the city boasted an economy which was dominated by the plants and research institutes of the defence industry. Leningrad obkom first secretaries at least since the Khrushchev era—Valerii Tolstikov, Grigoril Romanov, Lev Zaikov and Iurii Solov'ev himself—were identified with an approach to power which emphasised technocracy and especially discipline more than was normally the case in Moscow.[2] This reflected not only the habits of the military–industrial complex but also the need to keep under control the Leningrad cultural intelligentsia, which was more westward-looking than that in Moscow. The large number of institutions of higher education and of research institutes of the USSR Academy of Sciences (such as the Institute of Russian Literature) meant that the intelligentsia represented a relatively high proportion of society. But whereas in Moscow the years of *détente* in the 1970s caused an inflow of foreign correspondents and an increase in the level of permitted dissent, the atmosphere in Leningrad was much less tolerant, with the city polarised between the party and the military–industrial complex on one side and the western-oriented intelligentsia on the other.

The rise of the democrats in Leningrad

As Geoffrey Hosking has shown in the first chapter, the political impact of glasnost in Leningrad was first felt through the formation of environmentalist groups, particularly those concerned with the preservation of buildings. The Angleterre affair in 1987 saw open criticism in the media of the Lensovet ispolkom. In the same year the first openly political clubs of the Leningrad intelligentsia appeared, such as the *Memorial* society and the Perestroika club. These tended to be mostly made up of socialists, with some interest in self-management socialism, but were united by support for democracy and Gorbachev and by opposition to the conservative Leningrad obkom.

It was characteristic of the Leningrad atmosphere that the openly anti-perestroika manifesto, 'I Cannot Forsake My Principles', which appeared in *Sovetskaia Rossiia* on 13 March 1988, should have been written by a Leningrad communist. With her article, Nina Andreeva, a chemistry lecturer at the Leningrad Technological Institute, caused alarm among supporters of demo-cratisation throughout the USSR. Her complaint that perestroika was putting in doubt the achievements of socialism and causing ideological confusion among the young, published at the instigation of Egor Ligachev, went unanswered for three weeks, and many feared that this was the end of perestroika. It was equally characteristic of the Leningrad democrats that they should turn the conservatism of the Leningrad apparatus to their own advantage. On 6 April the Perestroika club had a discussion of the Andreeva letter, at which there was open criticism of the Leningrad party and demands for a mass movement to be created in support of perestroika. A few days later this discussion was shown on Leningrad television, where people sympathetic to democratisation had some influence. This gave publicity to the democrats and contributed to the gathering together of the clubs, first in the Union of Democratic Forces, then, under the influence of the Baltic Popular Fronts, in the Provisional Initiative Committee of the Leningrad Popular Front, and then, on 25 September 1988, in the group 'For a Popular Front'. This received a room and a phone from the Komsomol and had the chance to put its views across on television. The groups involved had had their first demonstration in the summer, in connection with the 19th Party Conference; by the end of 1988 they were organising regular meetings and claiming a membership of 200.[3]

At the same time, in summer 1988, in the Rumiantsev Gardens, *Pamiat'* were having meetings every week, denouncing the supposed Zionist–Masonic plot against Russia. Attempts by anti-fascists to stop them were blocked by the police, and it was said that the meetings were taking place with the approval of a raikom of the CPSU. In September, however, after the intervention of the Leningrad Procurator's Office, the meetings were banned on the grounds that they were propagating nationalism and mistrust towards Jews. The Vasileostrovskii (St Vasilii's Island) raion soviet ispolkom was blamed for allowing the meetings without investigating the aims of *Pamiat'*.[4] While *Pamiat'* itself was less active after this, a series of Russian nationalist groups in Leningrad appeared over the next years. In spring 1989 the *Patriot* society was registered by the Petrogradskii raion soviet ispolkom. Led by Aleksandr Romanenko, a veteran 'anti-Zionist', *Patriot* seems to have combined chauvinist ideas with conservative communist thinking.[5] Similar societies such as *Vitiaz'* (The Knight) and *Otchizna* (Fatherland), which both had a more pro-military profile, were an annoyance up to the time of the coup, apparently with support from conservatives in the CPSU and the Armed Forces.

In advance of the March 1989 elections to the Congress of People's Deputies of the USSR, the association 'For a Popular Front' created an electoral bloc called 'Elections-89'. This was organised on a constituency basis. As in Moscow, the conduct of the elections was inconsistent between constituencies. The democratic associations did not have the right to nominate candidates, but they could decide to support candidates nominated in the traditional ways. The main concern of the Leningrad party apparatus was to ensure that opposition was not allowed to their own key figures. Thus, in violation of Gorbachev's promise of competitive elections, the apparatus tried not only to prevent democratic candidates who had been nominated from appearing on the ballot papers (as also happened in Moscow) but to persuade the pre-election meetings to allow one-candidate elections. The atmosphere at these meetings could be very tense. When the apparatus argued that the Leningrad CPSU gorkom first secretary Anatolii Gerasimov should be the only candidate, a man who stood up and opposed this proposal collapsed on the platform and died. The meeting allowed Iurii Boldyrev, a democrat, to stand against Gerasimov, and in the election Boldyrev won easily.[6] In another constituency, a founder of the Perestroika club, Vladimir Ramm, tried to stand against Boris Gidaspov, a candidate favoured by the nomenklatura. Three policemen beat up his daughter. When he complained about this, he was accused of slander and sentenced to two years' compulsory labour (while being allowed to live at home).[7]

Anatolii Aleksandrovich Sobchak, born in 1937 in Chita in Siberia, was Professor of Law at Leningrad State University. Unusually for someone in such a responsible position, he had managed to be appointed to this post without joining the CPSU, and became a member only when perestroika was well under way. The Law Faculty and then the University nominated him for the Vasileostrovskii constituency. He survived the pre-electoral meeting and began an active campaign which was supported by democrats, colleagues and the University itself. His main opponent was a worker from the Baltic Ship-building Factory, which for years had had a monopoly on the seat. As well as the leaflets and posters used in Soviet cities for the first time in an election campaign, Sobchak claims to have made two innovations: he regularly harangued the rush-hour commuters at Vasileostrovskaia Metro station with a megaphone, holding mini-public meetings, and he had a debate with his opponent on television. On the second ballot Sobchak won with 76.5 per cent of the vote.[8]

In elections where only one candidate appeared on the ballot paper, the democrats campaigned with pickets and posters with the slogan 'One candidate—strike him out!' The law required a successful candidate to win a majority of votes, and the removal of the name would count as a vote against. At least five key figures in the Leningrad élite were defeated: the first and second secretaries of the Leningrad CPSU obkom, the first secretary of the gorkom, and the chairperson and first deputy chairperson of the city soviet. Three-quarters of the electorate voted. The obkom first secretary, Iurii Solov'ev, won 44 per cent of the vote, less than the required 50 per cent. Gidaspov was the only candidate supported by the apparatus to win his seat; and he was not a party or state official, but the director of the State Institute of Applied Chemistry and general director of the Tekhnokhim enterprise.

The defeated candidates of the apparatus refused to stand again in the reruns of the elections. Solov'ev told *Leningradskaia pravda* (31 March 1989) that those in a position of power were disadvantaged in the elections, in that they were blamed for the problems and, being realists, were unable to match the rash promises of their opponents.[9] He told a Leningrad joint meeting of the obkom and the gorkom that he 'should win back the people's confidence before there is any talk of a nomination.'[10] In the rerun for the national-territorial constituency, there were thirty-four candidates. The victor was the investigator in the Uzbek corruption scandal, Nikolai Ivanov, with more votes than the other thirty-three candidates put together. Interestingly, his candidature was opposed by the group 'For a Popular Front' because the Uzbek investigation had not followed all the legal procedures. Ivanov was seen as a populist figure, similar to the image of El'tsin who had won the equivalent seat in Moscow.

In spite of its defeat, the apparatus tried to carry on in the old way as much as possible. Smolny, the former girls' school which had become Lenin's head-quarters during the October Revolution, and since then the headquarters of the Leningrad party organisation, was the real seat of power in the city. Solov'ev called together to his Smolny office all the successful people's deputies from the region, to advise them how to behave at the Congress. Sobchak reports that he replied to Solov'ev, after the 'instructing', that 'deputies are elected by the people, and not by the obkom of the CPSU'.[11]

In order to create a counterweight to the democrats, the obkom created the United Workers' Front (OFT), which had its founding conference on 13 June. Nina Andreeva was guest of honour. This body was supposed to have 'the task of fighting at the grass-roots level for perestroika and the interests of the working people'.[12] In reality it sought to capitalise on the fears of workers about the consequences of perestroika: the dangers of inflation and the loss of job security. It was anti-market, pro-state farming, and tacitly Brezhnevite rather than Stalinist, and it showed particular concern for the position of Russians in the Baltic. It advocated the 'production principle' for soviet elections, whereby a number of the seats would be elected directly from labour collectives. This, it was thought, would make it easier for the work-place party organisations to control the electoral process. As Jonathan Aves shows below (pp. 145–6), the OFT grew from its Smolny-based origins to become a nation-wide body. It was dependent on the party apparatus, however, and never achieved significant influence on the workers.

A few days after the OFT, on 17–18 June, the Leningrad Popular Front (LPF) finally had its founding congress, organised by the 'Elections-89' electoral bloc. Over 600 delegates from over 100 organisations claimed to represent 6,000 members. The congress adopted a constitution and elected part of a Coordinating Council (the rest were to be chosen by constituent organisations). Those chosen included Marina Sal'e, a geologist, Sergei Andreev, a writer, former MVD captain Nikolai Arzhannikov, who had been sacked from his post for organising an unofficial meeting of police officers, and Petr Filippov, one of the founders of the Perestroika club. While the congress could not agree on a programme, they favoured the abolition of Article 6 of the USSR Constitution and the retirement of the party and state officials who had been defeated in the elections for the Congress of People's Deputies. Also, unlike the Moscow Popular Front, they were not committed to 'socialism' in any form.[13]

On 12 July, in the presence of Gorbachev, the Leningrad party obkom accepted the resignation of Solov'ev as first secretary and appointed Boris Gidaspov in his place. Sobchak reports that the democrats (many of whom remained in the party) welcomed Gidaspov's appointment, even though his appointment had been suggested by Solov'ev.[14] Gidaspov was a logical choice, since although a nomenklatura figure he had won the trust of the voters. At the obkom, he promised to work with the LPF. Gorbachev interrupted him and said 'with both fronts', that is, with the OFT as well. In November Anatolii Gerasimov resigned as first secretary of the party gorkom, and the gorkom was then united with the obkom under Gidaspov. Meanwhile, on 7 November, the LPF organised a demonstration on the anniversary of the October Revolution, separately from the official one. This was followed by a week of press attacks on the LPF, accusing it of links with the shadow economy and of having a secret plan to destroy socialism. By this time Gidaspov had shown himself to be on the side of the conservatives, supporting the OFT and attacking the LPF. On 22 November Gidaspov held a public meeting where the speakers attacked perestroika and supported the OFT. Placards in the hall demanded the removal of Gorbachev, Iakovlev and Shevardnadze from the Politburo.[15]

Two weeks later, on 6 December, the LPF held a meeting in defence of Gorbachev. This meeting played an important propaganda role for the LPF. It was shown several times on television. According to Leonid Kesel'man of the Leningrad Sociological Centre of the North-Western Division of the Soviet Sociological Association, before the meeting less than 50 per cent of the population knew what the LPF was. After the television screenings, 60 per cent said that they intended to vote for it.[16] Thus again it was the conservatism of the Leningrad apparatus which gave a boost to the democrats.

The Lensovet rejected by a large majority the 'production principle' for elections. The battlelines were now being drawn up for the elections to the Congress of People's Deputies of the RSFSR, to Lensovet and to the raion soviets of the city. The LPF helped to establish an electoral bloc, Democratic Elections-90. This also included *Memorial*, the Greens, the Union of Voters of Leningrad (around Nikolai Ivanov), Democratic Russia, the Consumers' Club and the trade union *Spravedlivost'* (Justice). On the other side were ranged the United Council of Russia, the Association of Voters of Leningrad, the 'Platform of the Central Committee of the CPSU', the 'Platform of the Leningrad Party Organisation', the OFT, and the nationalist *Rossy*.

The LPF itself was an amorphous organisation. In practice a member was somebody who thought that she or he was a member. There were no subscriptions, but lists were passed around at every meeting. The leaders and activists were mainly from the intelligentsia, over 45, particularly the 'people of the 1960s' who matured under Khrushchev. The LPF contained CPSU members, socialists, liberals, democrats, Christians, Marxists, and members of the Democratic Union. At the time of the elections three independent newspapers were organs of different trends within the LPF. *Nevskii kur'er*, run by Petr Filippov, Iurii Nesterov (who were both members of the CPSU) and Nikolai Kornev, favoured a moderate approach, parliamentary methods and cooperation with the authorities. *Nabat* was run by Marina Sal'e, who had left the CPSU, and Il'ia Konstantinov, and it was more radical, favouring mass meetings and being more inclined to confrontation. In between was Anatolii Golov's *Sever-Zapad*.

The raion organisations of the LPF decided which candidates to back for the RSFSR, Lensovet and raion soviet elections. Meetings were held weekly before the elections. Each candidate was invited to speak at the Coordinating Council of the raion; the latter would then decide whether or not to endorse the candidate. Many candidates declared their support for the LPF, sometimes three or four in the same electoral district. In some cases the LPF endorsed more than one candidate for the same election. Democratic Elections-90 adopted a similar process.[17]

The elections were carried out much more democratically than the year before. The party's leading role was on the way out, and it was abandoned officially throughout the country in the course of the election. Even Rostislav Evdokimov, known as a member of the stridently anti-communist, Frankfurt-based NTS, was allowed to stand, with the backing of Democratic Elections-90. The authorities tried to prevent voters from finding out who their candidates were and what they stood for. Things were complicated enough as it was; everyone could vote in four elections—territorial and national-territorial constituencies for the RSFSR Congress, and the Lensovet and the raion soviet. Typically people had to know twenty-five candidates. The authorities published the list of candidates two weeks before voters knew which electoral districts they were in. Two days before the first round, on 2 March 1990, the radical paper of the Leningrad Komsomol *Smena*, with a print-run of 200,000, published a list of candidates together with the organisations backing them. This was a considerable help to the democrats. The LPF reproduced this and it was stuck up at Metro stations. (The ballot paper contained no information about the affiliation of the candidates.)

The democrats campaigned on local issues of housing, the environment, the condition of the city and its neglected palaces, as well as on broad democratic issues. They were helped by the Leningrad Television programme, '600 Seconds'. The presenter, Aleksandr Nevzorov, regularly provided a series of items about crime and corruption in the city (apparently supplied with the help of the KGB), delivered with the speed of an automatic weapon. Just before the election, Nevzorov reported that the former party chief Solov'ev had been able to acquire a Mercedes on the cheap from the traffic inspectorate—a fact which received wide publicity and seemed to epitomise the corruption of the old élite. At the same time right-wing nationalists organised a series of 'Days of Russian Culture' before the elections, where anti-Semitic ideas were disseminated under the cover of the promotion of Russian culture. According to Anna Polianskaia, the Petersburg correspondent of the independent Moscow newspaper *Ekspress-khronika*, the meetings included appeals to beat up democrats. The ideologist of the Leningrad obkom, Iurii Denisov, praised the members of *Pamiat'* and *Otechestvo*.[18] Meanwhile, Arzhannikov, by now an LPF candidate for the RSFSR Congress, reported that he had discovered in the headquarters of the Frunze raikom of the CPSU piles of chauvinist leaflets in a photocopying room. The raikom responded that the leaflets had been gathered for analysis. For a week before the elections there was a very tense atmosphere in Leningrad, with rumours of an impending anti-Jewish pogrom and of weapons and gas being distributed by the army.

Participation in the elections was down on 1989. Of 3.7 million possible voters, 1.3 million abstained, 300,000 crossed out all the candidates and another 100,000 were invalid. Only 1.9 million participated. One million of these supported candidates backed by Democratic Elections-90 for the RSFSR Congress. In the final result, after the second round of voting on 18 March, twenty-five of the thirty-three successful RSSFSR candidates had been backed by Democratic Elections-90.[19] In Lensovet, the democrats won 65 per cent of the votes and 80 per cent of the seats. Of the 380 deputies, 240 had been endorsed by Democratic Elections-90, but several dozen more were sympathetic to the democrats. Around seventy supported the party apparatus; there were only five or six Russian nationalists elected, and no open members of *Pamiat'*. Although predictable, the overall result was an enormous defeat for the apparatus; it represented the end of their legal control of Leningrad. They had dominated the soviet since September 1917 and this had been the organ which had officially carried out the October Revolution. *Moscow News* spoke about a 'revolutionary situation' in Leningrad.[20] Of the raion soviets, nearly half remained under the control of the apparatus and only about four were won by the democrats; this reflected the fact that the party still found it easier than the democrats to field candidates, rather than any particular support for the apparatus at a local level.

The democrats in power

On Lensovet, CPSU members represented slightly over half the deputies, and the majority of these were with the democrats. Gidaspov called a meeting of party members elected to Lensovet and called on them to form a party group, the traditional means whereby the communists maintained control of the soviets. The deputies refused, on the grounds that they held different positions. Before the elections, Gidaspov had refused to have a Round Table meeting with the LPF on the grounds that they were 'different weight categories'. He used this boxing term to suggest that the CPSU and the LPF were comparable to heavyweight and lightweight players. After the elections, Gidaspov reverted to stressing the importance of dialogue. He invited the new leaders of the soviet, essentially the leaders of the LPF, to talk things over with him at Smolny. The democrats refused to go there, and insisted that Gidaspov come to meet them at the Mariinskii Palace, the headquarters of Lensovet. Gidaspov agreed and came to meet the Organising Committee of the soviet on 28 March. This unwieldy body had sixty-six members, headed by Sal'e and Aleksei Kovalev (the leader of the environmentalist group *Spasenie*). The subject was not yet the transfer of power in the city, but control of the media, with the soviet seeking to establish its own press centre.[21]

From then until the coup of August 1991, a power struggle was waged between Smolny and the soviet. At first the apparatus of the soviet, the ispolkom (executive committee) was dominated by the old nomenklatura, working for Smolny rather than the soviet. Indeed it quickly handed over some Leningrad palaces to the CPSU, before the democrats could stop this. The democrats were divided over the extent to which they should confront the apparatus, or cooperate with it in the way that Popov in Moscow was doing. There was no one of Popov's stature in Lensovet, and with the leaders of the different factions of the LPF constantly bickering and in the absence of party discipline it was clear that little could be achieved. It proved impossible even to elect a chairperson of Lensovet from among the deputies. *Moscow News* commented: 'The democrats appear to be unprepared to make use of their victory.'[22] Finally the factions agreed to ask Anatolii Sobchak to stand for election to Lensovet, promising to back him for the post of chairperson if he was elected.

Sobchak had achieved nation-wide fame as a USSR people's deputy over the previous year. As well as speaking in debates he had been a leading member of the commission established to investigate the killings in Tbilisi in April 1989, and he played a prominent role in the exposure of the affair of the cooperative ANT which was found to be illegally exporting tanks. He was very popular, especially with the intelligentsia. He had good relations with Gorbachev. Having won a by-election to the soviet, on 23 May he was elected its chairperson.

In his acceptance speech he referred to the problems faced by the city, including the ecological crisis brought on by the dam in the Gulf of Finland and the activity of the military–industrial complex. Among the chief tasks facing the city he mentioned first the need to create a multi-party system in Leningrad. He gave priority to housing, but also called for an end to the *propiska* system whereby the numbers living in the city were controlled. He called for a transition to a mixed economy, and here he highlighted the idea of making Leningrad a Free Economic Zone, a centre of tourism and the manufacture of consumer goods. In an interview he spoke of Leningrad having to enter a Baltic market. He expressed support for the Democratic Platform and democratic socialism, but talked of the need to work with Smolny.[23] Gidaspov, for his part, said that he had 'constructive, businesslike relations' with Sobchak.[24]

Immediately after his election, Sobchak told *Moscow News*: 'There will be no dual power. Even now we can speak about the Soviets' absolute power, even if it is seasoned with remnants of the past.'[25] A month later, however, he attacked the continuing party control over state bodies, even after the abolition of Article 6.

For a month already I have occupied the post of Chairman of the Leningrad City Soviet, but the daily reports on what is happening in the city are put on the table of Boris Gidaspov, First Secretary of the Leningrad Regional Party Committee. The heads of the administrative bodies do not consider it to be necessary to supply me, the Chairman of the Leningrad City Soviet, with corresponding information. I informed these comrades that the City Soviet has the authority to confirm them in their posts and, therefore, they need to make a choice about who governs them—the state or the CPSU.[26]

In this last sentence Sobchak showed the way in which the democrats might hope to exert their control—through the threat of sacking those members of the apparatus who refused to cooperate. In July Aleksandr Shchelkanov, a former naval captain, was elected as the new chairperson of the ispolkom.

As was shown in the previous chapters, the summer of 1990 was a time of major political development in the country as a whole, of splits in the CPSU and the formation of new parties. I have not often referred to opinion poll evidence on the level of support for different political trends in the country, because the way in which the questions are formed or the methodology used in these surveys does not always seem optimal. For what it is worth, however, I include the results of a telephone opinion poll taken in Leningrad at the end of May 1990. The distribution of support was as shown in Table 4.1. These figures suggest, first, the large number of people who were confused or indifferent; secondly, that over two-thirds of the remainder identified with the democratic forces, including the Democratic Platform and the Greens; and thirdly, that the conservatives and nationalists had minute support.

Table 4.1 *Results of a telephone opinion poll on political trends, Leningrad, May 1990*

CPSU on Central Committee Platform	11%
Democratic Platform in the CPSU	11%
New democratic movements and parties (LPF, social democrats Democratic Party, etc.)	23%
Russian CP (conservative communists)	0.3%
Nationalist-patriotic movements	0.3%
Greens	3%
None of the named political forces	5%
No definite position, don't know	45%

Survey by the Leningrad Sociological Centre of the North-Western Division of the Soviet Sociological Association, in 'Za kem poidut leningradtsy?' *Chas pik* (Leningrad), no. 16, 11 June 1990.

The Leningrad party apparatus did not confine itself to activities within the region but was actively involved in the campaign to create a Communist Party for the RSFSR, as a basis for resistance to Gorbachev. In September 1989 the OFT (itself a product of the Leningrad obkom) had promoted a meeting in Kuibyshev of Initiative Committees for the creation of a Russian Communist Party. In Leningrad in March 1990 was founded the 'Leningrad Initiative Committee for the Preparation of the Founding Congress of the RCP within the CPSU'.[27] A similar body was formed in Moscow. In Leningrad the first two stages of the 'Initiative Congress of the RCP within the CPSU' were held, on 21–2 April and 9–10 June, claiming to represent 1.5 million communists. The aim was to force a reluctant Gorbachev into allowing the CP of the RSFSR to be created 'from below', rather than called into existence by the centre or, worse, to be left without a structure and merely allowed to have conferences called by the Russian Bureau of the CPSU Central Committee. The aim was to convert the Russian Party Conference, due in June, into the Founding

Congress of the CP RSFSR, with its own Central Committee, Secretariat and Politburo. The slogan 'For the Rebirth of Russia' was combined with the defence of state property and the propagation of some sort of self-management. In an effort to avoid accusations of extremism, Nina Andreeva was condemned.

The Russian Party Conference, meeting on 20–3 June, duly transformed itself into the Founding Congress of the CP RSFSR, with Gidaspov playing a key role. At the 28th Congress of the CPSU which followed, Gidaspov was most unusually allowed to combine his Leningrad post with that of a secretary of the CPSU Central Committee. In spite of these victories, the Initiative movement did not disband, but was maintained in order to fight the increasing threats to socialism emanating from the central party leadership, which was now toying with the Shatalin plan. The third stage of the 'Initiative Congress of the RCP' was held in Leningrad on 20–1 October. Claiming to represent 2.5 million communists within the RSFSR, this congress proclaimed the Communist Initiative Movement.[28]

Meanwhile, at the 28th Party Congress, the split in the CPSU was confirmed. As discussed in the last chapter, Sobchak left the party, and Sal'e and the Leningrad delegation to the Democratic Party of Russia founding meeting formed the Free Democratic Party of Russia. Sal'e had earlier spoken of the need to create a Russian national party:

a new party of Russia, precisely of Russia, on the basis of a healthy national idea— national, but not nationalist ... It is impossible in any event to agree with the loss of national consciousness by the Russian [*russkim*] people, but I am sure that this loss has already happened.[29]

Between May and June the organising committees of the FDPR were built, under the leadership of Sal'e and Il'ia Konstantinov in Leningrad and Lev Ponomarev in Moscow. A special June 1990 issue of *Nabat*, which became the newspaper of the FDPR, carried the draft rules and programme of the party. In both of these (apart from the rejection of Travkin-style centralism) there was little to distinguish it from the larger democratic parties discussed in the previous chapter, or from the programme of Democratic Russia. The leaders' involvement in establishing the organisation of the Democratic Russia movement and Sal'e's involvement as an RSFSR people's deputy, and in particular in the acutely demoralising task of head of the Lensovet food commission probably held back the national development of the party.[30]

The process of party formation interacted with the developing factionalism of Lensovet. Towards the end of 1990, the journalist I. Katsman identified seven fractions on Lensovet. *Antikrizis'*, including Kovalev, 'Constructive Approach' led by Filippov (whose newspaper *Nevskii kur'er* was the largest informal paper in Leningrad), and the Inter-Professional Group worked together in a single, moderate-democratic bloc. The more radical democratic fraction was 'On the LPF Platform', headed by Sal'e. Katsman wrote that this fraction 'includes many ultra-radical ladies, and so is extremely aggressive'.

The moderate-conservative group 'Leningrad' worked with the 'Revival of Leningrad' fraction which was close to the Russian CP. There was also a Green fraction.[31]

Meanwhile, the situation in Leningrad deteriorated seriously. Throughout the country, shortages of food and other goods appeared, prices increased and services deteriorated. In Leningrad and Moscow the situation was worse than elsewhere. Rural party bosses tried to discredit the democrats by sabotaging food supplies. For their part the city did not take part in the traditional mobilisation of workers and students to help gather in the harvest of August 1990, seeing such methods as a legacy of the old regime. In December 1990 Lensovet began the rationing of many foods, going further than anywhere else in the country. This evoked memories of the wartime Siege of Leningrad.[32] On the positive side, Sobchak launched a world-wide campaign to raise funds to restore the city, establishing the International Foundation for the Salvation of Petersburg-Leningrad. This included a 24-hour telethon in January 1991, coinciding with the Orthodox Christmas.[33] Church buildings were to be restored and given to the churches; in a ceremony involving Patriarch Aleksii, Sobchak, El'tsin and Gidaspov, the Russian Orthodox Church was given back the right to hold services in St Isaac's Cathedral.

It is impossible here to discuss in any detail the issues involved or the shifting pattern of alliances. On 11 September 1990 the Coordinating Council of LPF declared its dissatisfaction with Sobchak, accusing him of undervaluing the deputies and creating his own apparatus. Many deputies felt that Sobchak was developing an authoritarian or even dictatorial style, behaving like a party first secretary. Conflict developed between Sobchak and his deputy, Rear-Admiral Viacheslav Shcherbakov, on the one hand, and the ispolkom head Shchelkanov on the other, with the LPF deputies supporting Shchelkanov. The soviet supported the idea of the Free Economic Zone as a means of attracting foreign capital, but criticised Sobchak's approach to it for giving too much control to Gorbachev. The radical deputies agreed with Sobchak about the need for privatisation, but criticised him for favouring a method of privatisation which they thought gave too much say to the factory managements and the military–industrial complex.[34] In general, the deputies accused Sobchak of working too closely with the old nomenklatura of the city, while Sobchak (like Popov in Moscow) was perhaps more concerned about getting his policies implemented than by the past positions of the people concerned.

Nevzorov's programme '600 Seconds' regularly attacked the soviet for its disunity and for the frequent foreign trips of the deputies. Towards the end of 1990 the soviet responded to such attacks by taking the unprecedented (and unenforceable) step of banning media criticism. In January 1991 the deputies and Sobchak were united in opposition to the killings by the security forces in Vilnius and Riga. Ever since March 1990 the democrats had opposed the centre's measures against the pro-independence government of Lithuania, and before this they had maintained links with the Baltic Popular Fronts. Opinion polls showed that most people in Leningrad believed that if the Baltic states voted in a referendum for independence, they should be allowed to secede from the Union without obstacles.[35] Nevzorov, however, portrayed the Vilnius and Riga killings as a myth; the Lithuanians had put corpses in front of the tanks, which supposedly were trying to restore order, and then claimed that the tanks had killed the civilians in cold blood. But the threat from the right did not encourage the democrats to unite; on 21 February 1991 Sobchak tried to sack Shchelkanov, but was blocked from doing so by the soviet.[36]

From Leningrad to St Petersburg

On 17 March 1991, as well as voting by a small majority for Gorbachev's renewed Union and by a big majority for El'tsin's proposals for a directly elected Russian president, the citizens of Leningrad voted for Sobchak's proposal for a directly elected executive mayor. On 12 June (the day also of the Russian presidential election) Sobchak was elected mayor with Shcherbakov his running-mate for vice-mayor. He secured 66 per cent of the vote, against the communist candidate, Iurii Sevenard, who gained 26 per cent. At the same time the voters approved, by 55 to 43 per cent a proposal (formulated by Kovalev) to restore to the city the name of St Petersburg.[37]

The return of 'St Petersburg' was a close result, and the outcome of the referendum was in doubt until the vote was counted. Many people who voted for El'tsin and Sobchak voted against the change. The democrats themselves had earlier been reluctant to raise the issue of renaming the city. In March 1990, they had considered the issue too divisive. Moreover, despite their hostility to the legacy of Lenin, the restoration of the imperial title was not universally supported by the democrats. Some feared its association with imperialism and Russian chauvinism. The right-wing, non-communist chauvinists favoured the change. Others thought that it was premature to restore the name to a city in such a decaying condition as Leningrad was at that time. The name Petrograd was unacceptable to most because of its association with war, revolution, civil war and famine.

Economic factors probably played a role. Sobchak seems to have become convinced that adherence to the name of Leningrad would frighten away foreign investors and impede the development of the Free Economic Zone. In the referendum he went out of his way to assure the voters that no criticism of Lenin's reputation was implied by the name change.[38] Rather it was a matter of reclaiming history, and regaining the city's position as a window on the west. The communists were uniformly hostile. Gorbachev spoke against it, and the USSR Supreme Soviet issued an appeal to Leningraders. 'How is it possible to strike out of the memory of our people the fact that precisely in your town the October Revolution began and the new Soviet state was born!'[39] A more powerful reason, in reality, for opposing the change was the memory of the Leningrad blockade during the Second World War. For most of those alive in the 1940s, the name of Leningrad was inextricably linked with the suffering and heroism of the city during the siege. The split in the vote was primarily generational, with those over 60 overwhelmingly pro-Leningrad, and those under 30 almost as strongly pro-St Petersburg. The central government refused to recognise the result of the referendum; the name of the city was a matter for the whole country. But their time was running out.

On 19 August, when Gorbachev was deposed in the attempted coup, the commander of the Leningrad Military District, Col.-Gen. Viktor Samsonov, went on Leningrad television. He declared a state of emergency in the city and announced that he was taking control. Sobchak flew back from Moscow to Leningrad (his safety secured by sympathetic members of the KGB) and went to meet Samsonov. Among those at the military headquarters were the heads of the KGB and of the MVD troops, and Gidaspov. According to Sobchak's own account, he persuaded Samsonov that there was no legal basis for sending troops into Leningrad, as had already been done in Moscow, Sverdlovsk and other cities, nor any need to do so. Samsonov said that he would try to avoid sending forces in, and later promised that troops would not come into the city. The coup had in effect been defeated in Leningrad, two days before Moscow.

Meanwhile, a meeting of Lensovet was convened by Aleksandr Beliaev, its new chairperson, and Leningraders flocked to the Mariinskii Palace to defend the elected organ of power. Sobchak went with Shcherbakov and Iurii Iarov, the chairperson of the Leningrad oblast' soviet, to the headquarters of Leningrad television, where they broadcast an appeal for resistance which was transmitted by satellite to other parts of Russia. A number of factories in the city went on strike. The following day a meeting of 200,000 people in Palace Square vowed resistance to the coup. Among the speakers was Academician Dmitrii Likhachev of the Institute of Russian Literature, the veteran defender of Russian culture and former camp inmate.[40]

After the coup collapsed, Leningrad was officially renamed St Petersburg. Smolny was seized and nationalised. Sobchak later moved into the office formerly occupied by Boris Gidaspov (a decision which strengthened some of the earlier criticism of him). The latter, with his party suspended and later banned, declared that it would be stupid to force it underground. He himself was devoting his time to finding work for unemployed party workers.[41] Nina Andreeva, on the basis of the *Edinstvo* group, founded the All-Union Communist Party (Bolsheviks), dedicated to the dictatorship of the proletariat.

Sobchak was criticised in the media for an order of 21 October subordinating the courts and defence lawyers to a department of his administration. (Furthermore, the title of the order retained the name Leningrad.)[42] On the anniversary of the October Revolution, which was no longer officially celebrated in Russia, St Petersburg instead celebrated its change of name. Sobchak invited Grand Duke Vladimir Kirillovich Romanov, the leading claimant to the tsarist throne, to participate in the festivities—another move which annoyed many democrats.

After the coup, Nevzorov's television programme had been taken off the air, but following accusations that Sobchak was imposing censorship the programme was restored in December. Nevzorov used his programme to promote the ideas of the chauvinist and neo-imperialist *Nashi* ('Ours') group, which was based in St Petersburg. The name *Nashi* had been the title of some programmes Nevzorov had made earlier in the year about the Baltic, and it referred to the Russians living outside the Russian Federation, whose rights were now sometimes being affected after the collapse of the USSR. *Nashi* included the former senior figures of *Soiuz*, Col. Viktor Alksnis and Col. Nikolai Petrushenko, Vladimir Zhirinovskii, the leader of the so-called Liberal-Democratic Party of the Soviet Union, the hardline General Albert Makashov and the editor of *Nash sovremennik*, Stanislav Kuniaev.[43] The hysteria emanating from Nevzorov was a grim warning to the democrats of what might be the consequences of their failure.

The collapse of the Union and the formation of the CIS was opposed by Sobchak, who considered the new Commonwealth structures inadequate to deal with differences between the new states. (Moreover, he clearly did not want those elements of the military—industrial complex who were nostalgic for the Union to line up with the extreme right). Like Popov, his sympathies were with the Movement for Democratic Reforms (favoured by Gorbachev). The major problems facing Sobchak's administration, however, were those of food supply, hyperinflation and poverty. His own popularity in the city fell significantly in the last months of 1991 although, like Gorbachev, he continued to be well liked abroad. With the price liberalisation of 2 January 1992, most Petersburgers were below the poverty line, and Sobchak attacked El'tsin's path to reform for impoverishing the people.

From the euphoria of March 1990 to the pessimism of the winter of 1991–2, when St Petersburg appeared dependent on food aid from the European Community, the city had undergone a change of identity much deeper than a mere change of name. Like the Bolsheviks before them, the Leningrad democrats had shown how much easier it was to destroy a repressive structure than to bring into being a new system, capable of feeding the people. It seemed unlikely that under the new conditions in Russia the former imperial capital would lose its reputation as a focus of resistance to central policy, or that it would be easy to reconcile the opposing interests and opinions within the city itself.

Notes

1. This oppositionist trend was pointed out to me by Ivan Titov in March 1990 when he was Responsible Secretary of the Leningrad Komsomol paper *Smena*. I am grateful to him for this and for other insights.
2. For the governing of Leningrad into the perestroika period, see Blair A. Ruble, *Leningrad: Shaping a Soviet City*, Berkeley, University of California Press, 1990. Like Moscow, the City of Leningrad has been under the direct subordination of the Russian government and independent of the Leningrad oblast'. Within the party, however, and unlike Moscow, the city organization was subordinate to the

Leningrad oblast' organisation. The key figure in Leningrad was, therefore, the obkom first secretary.

3. Much of the above draws from Andrei Alekseev, Vladimir Gel'man, Nikolai Kornev, Vladimir Kostiushev, Aleksandr Etkind, 'Obshchestvennye dvizheniia i stanovlenie novoi vlasti v Leningrade (1986–1991)', Leningrad, Institut Sotsiologii AN SSSR, Leningradskii filial, Sektor sotsiologii obshchesthennykh dvizhenii, 1991, See also *Obshchestvennye dvizheniia Leningrada. Informatsionnyi biulleten'*, Leningrad, Sovetskaia sotsiologicheskaia assotsiatsiia, Severo-Zapadnoe (Leningradskoe) otdelenie, Komissiia po izucheniiu obshchestvennykh dvizhenii, 1989; Elena Zdravomyslova, '"Neformaly" trebuiut . . .', *Leningradskaia panorama*, no. 8, 1989 (August).

4. 'Against national strife', *Moscow News*, no. 52, 25 December 1988.

5. Yuri Kupin, 'What is Patriot?', *Moscow News*, no. 22, 28 May 1989.

6. Anatolii Sobchak, *Khozhdenie vo vlast'. Rasskaz o rozhdenii parlamenta*, Moscow, Novosti, 1991, pp. 25–6.

7. ibid., pp. 145–6.

8. ibid., pp. 13–24.

9. Peter Lentini, 'Reforming the electoral system: the 1989 elections to the USSR Congress of People's Deputies', *Journal of Communist Studies*, vol. 7, no. 1, March 1991, pp. 69–94, at p. 89. This article is based particularly on Leningrad material.

10. Oleg Poptsov, 'A sense of where we are', *Moscow News*, no. 21, 21 May 1989.

11. Sobchak, *Khozhdenie*, pp. 144–5.

12. Sergei Nenashev, 'United Workers' Front', *Moscow News*, no. 26, 25 June 1989; LenTASS, 'Ob"edinennyi front trudiashchikhsia', *Leningradskaia pravda*, 14 June 1989.

13. Vladimir Pribylovskii, 'S"ezd LNF', *Atmoda* (Riga), 10 July 1989; Sergei Andreev, 'Chto takoe narodnyi front . . .', *Smena*, 16 June 1989; E. Alekseeva, 'Narodnyi front. Chto za pervym shagom?', *Smena*, 19 June 1989. For a more official view of the LPF, including extracts from the conference, and a comparison with the OFT, see A. V. Gromov, O. S. Kuzin, *Neformaly. Kto est' kto?*, Moscow, Mysl', 1990, pp. 196–225.

    For the relations between the LPF and the independent labour movement in Leningrad, see Chapter 5 by Jonathan Aves on the labour movement.

14. Sobchak, *Khozhdenie*, pp. 145–8.

15. ibid., pp. 149–52; Vera Tolz, *The USSR's Emerging Multiparty System* (The Washington Papers, 148), New York, Praèger, 1990, p. 64. Much of what appears here is based on my discussions in Leningrad, particularly with members of the LPF, in March 1990.

16. Interview with Kesel'man, 30 March 1990.

17. The list of candidates for the RSFSR Congress endorsed by the LPF appeared in *Nabat*, no. 3, February 1990. The Democratic Elections-90 list for the RSFSR and Lensovet appeared as a special issue of a voters' club newspaper called *Vybor*. The two lists for the RSFSR are similar but not identical.

18. Anna Polyanskaya, 'Red and brown: the communist fascist alliance today', reprinted in *Before August: The Soviet Union in 1991*, no. 1, published by *Ekspresskhronika*, Moscow, 1991.

19. Alekseev *et al.*, 'Obshchestvennye dvizheniia', pp. 23–4.

20. Yuri Kirillov and Yuri Kupin, 'Leningrad's new parliament', *Moscow News*, no. 15, 15 April 1990.

21. On Gidaspov, see Andrei Chernov, 'The last first secretary, or three myths about Boris Gidaspov', *Moscow News*, no. 25, 1–8 July 1990.

22. Andrei Chernov, 'Leningrad city soviet: a pitfall for democracy', *Moscow News*, no. 19, 20–7 May 1990.

23. 'Zdravstvuite, predsedatel'!', *Vechernii Leningrad*, 24 May 1990.

24. A. Afanas'ev, 'Dialog, a ne konfrontatsiia', ibid.

25. 'Anatoly Sobchak: "There won't be any dual power"', *Moscow News*, no. 22, 10–7 June 1990.

26. 'Anatoly Sobchak: who obeys whom?', *Moscow News*, no. 26, 8–15 July 1990, translation amended.

27. 'Za progressivnoe razvitie partii!', *Literaturnaia Rossiia*, no. 10, 9 March 1990.

28. V.N. Berezovskii, N.I. Krotov, V.V. Cherviakov, *Rossiia: partii, assotsiatsii, soiuzy, kluby. Spravochnik*, vol. 1, pt. 2, Moscow, RAU-Press, 1991, pp. 232–4; Evgenii Krasnikov, 'S″ezd RKP v Leningrade: kompromiss ili konfrontatsiia s TsK KPSS?', *Kommersant″*, no. 23, 1990.

29. 'Khochu sozdat' natsional' nuiu partiiu Rossii', *Leningradskii literator*, 10 January 1990.

30. 'Slovar' oppozitsii. Novye politicheskie partii i organizatsii Rossii', comp. Vladimir Pribylovskii, *Sostoianie strany*, no. 4/5, April 1991, p. 38.

31. I. Katsman, 'Karaul ne ustanet zhdat'', *Panorama* (Moscow), no. 13, December 1990; see also Valerii Barsukov, 'Vygodny li fraktsii?', *Smena*, 25 May 1990.

32. Peter Rutland, 'From *perestroika* to paralysis: the stalemate in Leningrad', *Report on the USSR*, vol. 3, no. 12, 22 March 1991, pp. 12–17.

33. Andrei Chernov, 'The return of St Petersburg', *Moscow News*, no. 1, 6–13 January 1991.

34. Interview with Petr Filippov, 'My pobedim Sobchaka', *Panorama*, no. 13, December 1990; V. N. Berezovskii, N. I. Krotov and V. V. Cherviakov, *Rossiia: partii, assotsiatsii, soiuzy. kluby*, 1991, vol. 1, pt. 2, p. 338.

35. For example, Leonid Kesel'man, 'Edina li nedelimaia?', *Chas pik*, no. 20, 9 July 1990.

36. Rutland, 'From *perestroika*', p. 13.

37. S. Sliusarenko, 'El'tsin, Sobchak, Sankt-Peterburg', *Vechernii Leningrad*, 14 June 1991. For the structure of Sobchak's administration, see 'Eto i est' meriia', *Vechernii Leningrad*, 3 August 1991.

38. Channel Four News, 7 June 1991, 1900 BST.

39. 'Zashchitim Leningrad', *Pravda*, 7 June 1991.

40. Anatoly Sobchak, 'Breakthrough', *Moscow News*, no. 34–5, 1–8 September 1991.

41. 'V lesa ia ne ukhodil . . .', *Pravda*, 11 September 1991.

42. Anna Polianskaia, 'Ia sam sebe Sud'ia, ili Predprinimateli v zone', *Russkaia mysl'*, no. 3906, 29 November 1991.

43. Vera Tolz and Elizabeth Teague, 'Is Russia likely to turn to authoritarian rule?', *RFE/RL Research Report*, vol. 1, no. 4, 24 January 1992, pp. 1–8.

5 The Russian labour movement, 1989–91: the mirage of a Russian Solidarność

Jonathan Aves

The new Russian labour movement has been the cause of more confusion and has confounded more expectations than any other aspect of the independent political movements that sprang up in the Soviet Union after 1987. Western observers and Soviet apparatchiks alike could only regard a workers' movement which appeared to react with equanimity to the restoration of capitalism with a sense of disbelief and scepticism. Many Soviet intellectuals were surprised that Russian workers could create any sort of movement at all. Once the phenomenon had established itself it neither turned out to be a Russian Solidarność nor a sectional trade-union movement with purely economic concerns. Not unsurprisingly the new Russian labour movement grew out of and reflected the specific political and social predicament of Russian workers at the end of the 1980s which was made up of, *inter alia*, disillusionment with socialism as an ideology reflecting the interests of the working class, the aftermath of authoritarian communism which had left little base on which to create independent organisations particularly in the provinces, and the unimportance of nationalism as an integrating ideology overarching social, economic and regional differences.

At the beginning of perestroika, despite the regime's promotion of social-democratic rhetoric and its lip-service to the idea of greater workers' self-management, manifested in the 1987 law on state enterprises,[1] most reformers regarded workers with suspicion if not hostility. When assessing the potential social sources of opposition to reform the sociologist Tat'iana Zaslavskaia, who had the ear of Mikhail Gorbachev, consigned most workers to the ranks of the 'conservative' opponents of perestroika.[2] Workers were seen as the main beneficiaries of what was known in the west as the Brezhnevite 'social contract' and in the Soviet Union as the 'you pretend to pay us, we pretend to work' syndrome. They were thought of as apathetic, apolitical and incapable of concerted political action.

Perhaps the confounding of this clearly exaggerated stereotype was bound to create the diametrically opposed but equally unrealistic expectation that the Russian workers' movement could be the basis of a new Russian democracy. From the summer of 1989 the evident hostility of workers to the old apparat gave many Russian liberals the hope that they could, in some way, make up for the lack of an overarching ideology, such as nationalism, in Russia which could unite the country against the old regime in the same way that Baltic workers had been mobilised behind the Popular Fronts and Polish workers behind Solidarność. Solidarność became the symbol of an intelligentsia/worker alliance that would make reform irreversible. In an early manifestation of this idea, in December 1989 a group of deputies in the Supreme Soviet, led by Andrei Sakharov and other members of the Inter-Regional Group, appealed to workers to call a two-hour 'warning strike' but the response was moderate. In November 1990 the reformist publicist Igor Kliamkin, in the course of a discussion of the ways in which the RSFSR Supreme Soviet might defend itself against the centre, called for the parliament to take the initiative in organising the dispersed mass of people who had supported it in elections 'into something like the Polish Solidarność'. He went on to suggest that the idea of political independence in Russia had usually had a social dimension and that the new Russian labour movement could take on a national colouring.[3] The hopes of Russian liberals were confirmed to the extent that workers rarely wavered in their hostility to the old regime and in their support for market reform but the organisational cohesion that was required for this to develop into a powerful movement continually eluded them.

Small, local workers' clubs and 'independent trade unions', which articulated basic desires for an amelioration of working conditions and political reform, appeared in many Russian cities after the beginning of perestroika. Workers' clubs fed on resentment against 'socialist competition', which was fertile soil for all kinds of management favouritism, and the victimisation of workers who stood up for their rights. In 1987 and 1988 there was a series of conflicts in the large Iaroslavl' Motor Works focusing on anger at the practice of demanding compulsory overtime on Saturdays, so-called 'Black Saturdays'. In the autumn of 1988 a Workers' Club was formed in the factory, on the initiative of the Iaroslavl' Popular Front, with the aim of 'ensuring real self-management by the workers' collective at the factory, genuine social justice, the breaking of the command-administrative system of management, the introduction, not just on paper, but in practice, of enterprise cost accounting, leasing and the encouragement of cooperatives in all ways'. A network of contacts with similar clubs in other cities, such as the Moscow Workers' Club founded in August 1987 by workers from the Proletarii industrial association, gradually evolved and a series of conferences of activists from these clubs followed, the last in July 1989, on the eve of the miners' strike.[4] One of the leading figures in the Workers' Club movement was Kazimieras Uoka, a tractor driver and founding member of the Lithuanian Popular Front, Sajudis, who established the Lithuanian Union of Workers in November 1988.

  To take another local example, in Leningrad independent labour organisations sprang up from an early stage, sometimes with close links to the city's different political groups. A group called Workers' Initiative was founded in October 1987 at the Red Star industrial association by the local Komsomol committee with the aim of representing workers' views to management. It sought to work through Komsomol and trade-union structures to improve working conditions and 'raise workers' political culture, actively participate in the process of democratisation of the life of society and is prepared to help carry out the policy of perestroika and glasnost'. In February 1988 the Club for the Democratization of Trade Unions was founded with the aim of making the official trade unions more responsive to the needs of workers.[5] It helped found an independent journal, *Rubikon*, which began to provide information about the labour scene in Leningrad from late 1988. The Democratic Union, formed in the summer of 1988, attempted to campaign actively amongst workers. A small Socialist Workers' Fraction was established in the Leningrad organisation in the autumn of 1988 some of whose members were also active in a Workers' Club which began issuing a journal in early 1989. Both the Democratic Union Socialist Workers' Fraction and the Workers' Club were active in the campaign to prevent representatives of the local communist apparat gaining election to the Congress of People's Deputies in March 1989.

In 1989 independent trade unions appeared in Leningrad. Vladimir Gomel'skii from the Club for the Democratization of Trade Unions and Vladimir Sytinskii,[6] a leader of the Workers' Club, helped found the trade union Spravedlivost (Justice) in April 1989. The union conducted agitation on social issues in Leningrad factories in the summer of 1989 and in the autumn collected money for the striking miners in Vorkuta. Spravedlivost called for wage rises, reductions in differentials, the abolition of socialist competition, the election of managers and other measures which would greatly restrict the arbitrary powers of management.[7] Whilst Spravedlivost broadly supported the Leningrad Popular Front another organisation, Nezavisimost (Independence), took a more uncompromising attitude. According to the theories of its founder L. Pavlov, it declared itself to be equally hostile to the apparat, which it regarded as a ruling class, and the liberal sponsors of perestroika which, it believed, was linked to a new form of exploitation of workers and was responsible for reducing workers' living standards. It refused to accept non-manual workers as members.[8]

In July 1989 a miners' strike broke out that spread to every major coalfield in the country which forced reformers and 'conservatives' at the national level to reassess their preconceptions about Russian workers for the first time. The strike began in mines at Mezhdurechensk in western Siberia on 10 July. It spread over the next few days to most of the other major pits in the Kuzbass coalfield. The strike reached the Vorkuta coalfield in the far north of the country, in the Komi Autonomous Republic, on 13 July, and the Donbass in the eastern Ukraine, still the most important coalfield in the Soviet Union in terms of production even if the seams were being rapidly exhausted and extraction was technically backward, on 15 July. At the height of the strike nearly half a million workers had stopped work.[9]

The strikers displayed an impressive level of organisation and discipline. Most of the strikes had a clear pattern. After walking out the miners would elect leaders, send out emissaries to neighbouring enterprises to inform the workers there of what was happening and try and persuade them to join the strike. Then they would parade to the main square of the local town, where the buildings housing the local soviet and Communist Party administration were situated, and commence a sit-down protest. Here a town strike committee would be elected to represent all the enterprises on strike in the town. The town strike committee then sent its representatives to the regional centre, in the case of Kuzbass, Prokop'evsk, and in the case of the Donbass, Donetsk, where a regional strike committee was formed. The strike committees would draw up lists of demands and conduct negotiations with the authorities.

Very soon the strike committees, like the soviets of 1905 and 1917, began taking on tasks that went far beyond merely organising industrial action. They ensured order in the mining settlements and formed pickets to enforce a ban on the sale of alcohol. The local population quickly began to see the strike committees as alternative organs of political power. The strike committee in the Kuzbass town of Kemerovo soon found itself besieged by petitioners who 'lined up all day for a stamp and a signature to enable them to get a bank loan; for advice about what to do when the person renting them a room wanted to terminate the lease; and to discuss a host of other everyday problems that fell far beyond the responsibilities the strike committee ever intended to under-take'.[10] At the same time the authority of the strike committees was not absolute. In the Kuzbass, at the beginning of the strike at least, the strike com-mittees did not have the right to make decisions, only to make proposals to gen-eral meetings of workers. In a number of cases strikers refused to cooperate with strike committee plans to carry out routine maintenance work in the pits.[11]

The demands advanced by the strikers were also notable for the absence of a backlash against perestroika; there were no calls for a return to the old order. There was only a faint echo of 'conservatism' in the early demand made by Donbass miners for the closure of cooperatives which they believed were making unfair profits.[12] Most of the miners' demands reflected the deteriora-tion in living conditions, particularly the worsening in supplies to the shops, that had taken place since the beginning of perestroika. Their economic demands were of two types. Firstly, they sought to improve pay, pensions and working conditions, including such things as pay for time taken to travel under-ground to the coal faces and the abolition of compulsory Sunday work. The second set of demands aimed to free the mines from the control of the central ministries and included such things as the right to sell coal produced over target at the discretion of the work collective and, most importantly, full economic independence for the mines from the dictates of Moscow.

The second set of demands, to the extent that they were directed, in the first instance, against the ministry bureaucrats who were widely perceived as the principal opponents of political and economic reform, enabled Gorbachev, after some initial hesitation, to react positively to the strikes. Addressing the Supreme Soviet on 19 July he implied that anti-socialist 'manipulators' were behind the workers' action but four days later, whilst criticising miners for using strikes to achieve their ends, he said 'workers are basically taking matters into their own hands and that . . . greatly inspires me'.[13] However, although the government did not respond to the strikes in the traditional way, there was no mass repression and there were no arrests, their first concession, the promise of large deliveries of extra consumer goods to the mining regions, did indicate that they thought that they would be able to buy off the strikers fairly easily.[14]

In fact the miners' deep suspicion of the government provided the basis for their future rapid politicisation. They refused to return to work until they had met with senior figures in the government. An initial agreement was signed in the Kuzbass by the coal minister Mikhail Shchadov but the return to work did not begin until negotiations had been concluded with Politburo member Nikolai Sliunkov. The government's concessions to the miners were far beyond what they were able to fulfil. The agreement signed by Sliunkov on 17–18 July in Prokop'evsk, for example, promised full cost-accounting status for mines in the Kuzbass, allowing Kuzbass enterprises, from 1 August 1989, to sell output produced beyond plan targets at market prices, large increases in pay for evening and night shifts, rises in wages and pensions in line with inflation, extra deliveries of foodstuffs and consumer goods, to ensure no loss of earnings as a result of strike action and no harassment of strike activists.[15] At the beginning of August the Council of Ministers in Moscow published Resolution 608 which summed up the measures which had been promised to the miners to improve their working and living conditions. The government's persistent failure to implement this resolution only served to fuel the miners' distrust of its intentions.

Although it began as a protest against economic conditions the strike movement became increasingly politicised. This process of politicisation stemmed from a deep-seated feeling amongst Russian workers that they were suffering from unjust treatment. At first the miners' demands reflected their grim living conditions, which even included a soap shortage, but they also focused on the system of privileges that oiled the cogs of the Soviet industrial enterprise. The strikers protested against the policy of singling some workers out for special treatment, the so-called 'model workers' (*shtatnie peredoviki*) and the colloquially named 'snowdrops' (*podsnezhniki*). In return for special treatment when housing or holidays were being distributed they acted as informers and defused resistance amongst workers to administration orders.[16] Miners expressed their alienation through a grim humour. Grafitti was painted on the walls of accommodation barracks in Novokuznetsk reading 'Welcome to the stone age!' and 'This is how Soviet miners live'. The legacy of the Communist Party, in the first instance, was suspicion of any involvement in politics. Even after the strike was over, miners in the Donbass were reluctant to admit that they had links with miners elsewhere in the country lest this be thought to constitute political organisation.[17] However, although attempts by activists in the democratic movement to forge links with the strikers took a while to bear fruit, hostility to adopting overtly political demands quickly passed.[18]

Tight ideological and coercive controls and the state's claim to act as the sole provider of all economic benefits meant that like all protest under authoritarian communist regimes the miners' strike movement naturally soon focused on the party/state itself as the main source of its problems. By August 1989 the demand of the Kuzbass strike committee for all the privileges enjoyed by officials to be abolished was linked with the demand for a new constitution in which the leading role of the CPSU would be removed.[19] At the local level the demand for new elections to Communist Party, trade-union and soviet bodies and, soon, the demand for the removal of party committees from enterprises led to 'the purging of a whole layer of the lower level Party, union and administrative bureaucracy, what was, in effect, the foundation of the silent opposition to perestroika'.[20]

Cautious strike leaders, particularly those with links with the old apparat, were replaced by more radical activists. Teimuraz Avaliani, who had been elected president of the Regional Council of the Union of Kuzbass Strike Committees in the summer of 1989, faded from the scene after he opposed political strikes in the autumn.[21] In the Donbass it was decided to move the coordinating council of the regional union of strike committees from Donetsk to Gorlovka because the city strike committee in Donetsk was reckoned to be 'weak and unambitious'. Subsequently, the committee split into 'economists' and 'politicals'. The latter quickly gained the upper hand. Amongst them was Iurii Boldyrev, who campaigned for the committees to pass resolutions in support of Telman Gdlian and Nikolai Ivanov, two state prosecutors who had been investigating high-level corruption, and for establishing links with the Inter-Regional Group of Deputies.[22] In 1990 the political scope of the strike leaders' demands evolved from changes in local party and soviet personnel to thoroughgoing democratic reform of the whole of society. The activities of the proliferating political organisations in Russia helped focus the political direction of the strike movement. In the summer of 1990 a struggle began between supporters of the Democratic Platform, a reform communist group, and supporters of Nikolai Travkin's militantly anti-communist Democratic Party of Russia, such as Viacheslav Golikov, the president of the Council of the Workers' Committees of the Kuzbass, for control of the Union of Kuzbass Working-People.[23]

The process of politicisation did not affect all groups of miners at the same rate. At the end of October 1989 miners in the Vorkuta coalfield, inside the Arctic Circle, went on strike again, this time with overtly political demands. Initially, the strikers called for independent labour organisations to be officially recognised and to protest against the law on labour disputes which had been passed by the Supreme Soviet in October banning strikes in vital industries. The repeal of Article 6 of the Constitution which guaranteed the party's leading role was also demanded. Within the coalfield some pits were clearly more militant than others. The Vorgashorskaia mine, the biggest in the region, remained out after the city strike committee ordered a return-to-work on 27 October and persuaded others to remain out as well.[24] Over the summer miners at this pit had become rapidly politicised and the Narodno-Trudovoi Soiuz, a radical democratic émigré organization, had managed to establish an active group of supporters.[25] In Vorkuta the Vorgashorskaia strike committee provided the basis for the creation of a trade union, the Democratic Workers' Movement, in the autumn of 1989. Sergei Kozlov was elected secretary of the Democratic Workers' Movement which was registered with the town soviet in the middle of December. In March 1990 ten members of the Democratic Workers' Movement were elected to the town soviet.[26] However, the strike failed to spread beyond Vorkuta. Miners in Donetsk voted not to support the action on 1 November because they were worried that their pits might be closed.[27] The Union of Kuzbass Working People threatened to strike only if the government refused to unfreeze the Vorkuta strike committee's bank account.[28]

In 1990 the politicisation of the strike movement intensified and affected new regions. After the First Congress of Miners met at the beginning of June 1990 delegates from the Donbass gathered in Gorlovka to discuss an appeal by miners at a pit in the Kuzbass for solidarity in their attempt to have the Communist Party cell in their pit disbanded. After heated debate it was decided to call a one-day general strike in the coal industry on 11 July to demand the 'depoliticisation' of the soviets, army and KGB and the resignation of the government. The call was rapidly supported throughout the Donbass, the Kuzbass and Vorkuta.[29] The government was clearly worried by the threat since it announced on 2 July that miners' holiday entitlement would be increased. On 11 July whilst many pits in the Donbass obeyed the strike call some voted to support the strike demands but did not stop work. In the Kuzbass about a third of the pits stopped work. In Vorkuta almost all the pits struck and a big demonstration was held in the town square. Some of the mines in the Karaganda coalfield in northern Kazakhstan condemned the strike.[30]

The one-day strike indicated that the miners' determination to confront the government, if necessary, in order to force thoroughgoing political and economic reform had reached a new pitch. One commentator, whilst admitting that the strike had been 'a disjointed affair', wrote that it 'showed that there are extensive contacts and a high degree of unity amongst miners throughout the Soviet Union'.[31] Furthermore, the workers' committees were gradually consolidating their position by gaining registration with the authorities, although it was a slow process and they were often still constrained. The Vorkuta strike committee, which had called an industrial action in November 1989 over the issue of registration, was only finally registered with the town's executive committee in September 1990. The workers' committee attached to the massive Donetskugol' industrial combine in the Donbass was registered with the town's executive committee in February 1990 but remained under its strict legal control.[32]

The miners' strikes of the summer of 1989 gave a further impetus to the attempts of political activists to establish links with workers. The hostility and suspicion that greeted the first unofficial activists who attempted to build contacts with the miners is reminiscent of the experience of the populist intellectuals who 'went to the people' in the 1870s. An activist from the Leningrad Popular Front, who arrived in Donetsk on 21 July just after the strikes had begun, knowing that the miners regarded the Popular Front as 'extremist', tried to pass himself off as a journalist of the unofficial press. Nonetheless, when he appeared in the town square, where the strikers were gathered, he was surrounded by a crowd shouting, 'Provocateur! Extremist!' He was eventually escorted away by the militia who advised him to leave the area as his safety could not be guaranteed.[33]

In June 1989 the founding meeting of the Union of Socialist Trade Unions (Sotsprof) was held in Moscow. From an early stage there were links between the union and Boris Kagarlitskii and the Club of Socialist Initiatives, on the basis of which the Socialist Party was founded in June 1990.[34] However, the links remained loose and the public pronouncements of Sotsprof activists eschewed socialist sloganising. In an interview, the leader of Sotsprof, S. V. Khramov, said that he disliked the term 'working class' because each group of workers had different interests. Sotsprof had no centralised system of membership but managed to establish groups of supporters in different regions of the Soviet Union although their numbers remained small.[35]

The Leningrad Popular Front attempted to sponsor the formation of a labour movement in the city in order to prevent popular discontent over the deteriorating economic situation from being exploited by 'conservative' forces. At its founding congress in June 1989 it created a Commission on Independent Trade Unions and subsequently it helped organise a city strike committee.[36] In the spring of 1990 it formed a committee to organise aid for strikers because of 'the tense political, economic and social situation'. Although it delegated members to work in enterprises most workers only turned for support after a strike had failed.[37] In a speech at the founding congress of the Confederation of Labour the president of the Leningrad Union of Workers' Committee, K. Boldovskii, stressed the need for the 'spontaneous' unrest likely to be provoked by the transition to a market economy to be channelled in order to prevent it becoming 'the soil for a provocation'. In a subsequent article he was quoted as saying that the Workers' Committee was discouraging individual strikes in order to channel discontent into a general political strike.[38]

These self-conscious efforts by democratic activists to channel workers' discontent and organise independent trade unions were almost uniformly limited in their success. If it was any consolation so were the efforts of the 'conservatives'. The official trade unions and 'conservative' elements in the Russian Communist Party made a sustained bid to establish a base amongst industrial workers by claiming that they would be the main losers from market reform. In July 1989 the founding congress of the United Front of Working People (OFT) took place in Leningrad under the protection of the new local first secretary Boris Gidaspov, who was making a name for himself as a critic of perestroika. The congress took place in the wake of the elections to the Congress of People's Deputies in March, when local Communist Party dignitaries had received a drubbing, and the founding congress of the Leningrad Popular

Front in June. The OFT–RSFSR held its first congress in Sverdlovsk in September 1989 and its second congress in Leningrad in January 1990.[39] Membership of the OFT was on a collective basis and consisted of the regional OFT organisations in Leningrad, Moscow and the Baltic interfronty.

In practice the OFT failed to bridge the credibility gap faced by all officially sponsored organisations and to establish real popular support. Its programme represented an intelligent attempt to capitalise on workers' concerns. Its aims included, *inter alia*, the struggle for greater participation by workers in management, the struggle with corruption, especially where it occurred in the new cooperatives and so-called 'socialist millionaires', the maintenance of free health care and frequent appeals to Soviet patriotism.[40] However, OFT not only demonstrated its dependency on the 'conservative' apparat by personal links and its opposition to market reform but also by its practical programme. From its inception the OFT persistently campaigned for soviet elections to be held according to constituencies based on place of work rather than place of residence. In the past this practice had given great scope to factory directors to pressurise workers to vote for officially approved candidates. So even if its agitation against market reform did sometimes find a resonance amongst ordinary workers its obvious aim of upholding the power of the 'conservative' apparat tended to discredit it.

The official trade unions, under the leadership of their central council (VTsSPS), were taken unawares by the miners' strikes in the summer of 1989 although the council had been attempting to coopt the new labour movement for some time. On 23 July at the height of the miners' strikes it had sponsored a meeting of 200 representatives of workers' clubs from around the country, in Moscow, which declared its support for the strikes in the coalfields.[41] The VTsSPS leadership had been playing lip-service to the slogan that defending the interests of working people should be its first priority for some time. However, the actions of the miners during their strikes and in the aftermath showed that most workers continued to regard the official trade unions as simply another part of the communist bureaucracy. In September a plenum of VTsSPS attempted to make a clean sweep and appointed a new president Gennadii Ianaev to signal its commitment to a new policy. One western specialist described Ianaev as 'street-wise'[42] and until the summer of 1990 the official trade unions pursued a vigorous campaign to improve its image with workers and mobilise them against reform.

In mid-March 1990 representatives of the official trade unions met in Moscow for the founding congress of the RSFSR trade unions. The congress set up a Federation of Independent Trade Unions of the RSFSR (FNPR) and stated that membership was open 'to all trade unions and professional bodies that accept the goals, tasks and principles of its work, which is directed at the consolidation of action in the defence of the lawful rights and general interests of working people'. The congress's declaration called for unity against regional and professional separatism which 'will sharply weaken the defensive potential of the trade unions in the face of the united bureaucracy, market economics with its intensive labour, and the assault on the social victories of working people'.[43]

At the end of May the presidium of the FNPR issued a declaration in which it announced its opposition to the government's plans for a transition to a market economy. It called for 'a round-table' discussion on reform and in the absence of specific alternative proposals placed its hopes on the establishment of RSFSR republican sovereignty.[44] When the founding congress of the FNPR resumed in September it was addressed by the 'conservative' leader of the newly formed Russian Communist Party, Ivan Polozkov, and the president of the OFT–RSFSR, Evgenii Khanin.[45]

Whether the FNPR attempt to attract mass support was ineffective because of its failure to offer an alternative economic programme or because of its lack of political credibility must remain an open question. However, it appeared at the end of 1990 that the efforts of 'conservative' forces to mobilise workers against reform had received a setback. In the summer of 1990, Ianaev was removed from his post and, at the end of October, he was replaced by Vladimir Shcherbakov.[46] In April 1990 Ianaev had made dire warnings of mass unemployment and mounting social tension to the VTsSPS plenum and called on the government to guarantee full employment. Shcherbakov, on the other hand, in his speech to the 19th VTsSPS Congress at the end of October, accepted the need for loss-making enterprises to be closed and emphasised the need for the government to make provision for the social and retraining needs of the unemployed. There were also organisational changes agreed that weakened the centralised union that Ianaev had canvassed.

At the end of 1990 a new economic phenonomen gave an impetus to activists who supported greater worker self-management. In September and December 1990 groups of activists from the Councils of Workers' Collectives, which had been established under the 1983 law on state enterprises, met in conferences in Moscow. The cause for this initiative came from the way in which, in a number of cases, state industries and enterprises were being turned into state corporations or firms with the bureaucrats receiving state assets as their private property. The main demand of the conferences of Councils of Workers' Collectives was that they should be given a greater say in deciding whether enterprises should be privatised in this manner. They also demanded that the Collective itself should have the right to become the owner of the enterprise if it so decided. The prospects of the new movement were limited because the Councils of Workers' Collectives were too often implicated in the old structures. Furthermore, the lead in the conferences of Councils of Workers' Collectives was taken by low-level managerial and technical staff who, it might logically be supposed, would most resent the new rights gained by the bureaucrats rather than rank-and-file workers.[47]

The strike committees and workers' committees which sprang up during the strikes in the summer of 1989 formed the organisational basis of a new labour movement. The strike committees were built up from below in each pit around figures who were already well known amongst the workers for their willingness to stand up to the authorities. Many of these rank-and-file activists were originally members of the CPSU. At the Vorgashorskaia mine in Vorkuta, for example, Sergei Kozlov, a CPSU member, was well known for his opposition to bribery. He had been circulating lists of grievances amongst the workers for a week before the strike and took the lead in organising the strike and the strike committee.[48] Like many such activists he soon left the CPSU.[49] Similarly, Iurii Boldyrev, who headed the Council of Donbass Strike Committees, was the Communist Party group organiser of his brigade. A campaign that he had led against favouritism and corruption had led to his expulsion from the CPSU (he was subsequently reinstated).[50] These activists formed a natural focus for the strikers and their existence explains the ability of the strike committee to appear from apparently nowhere. After the miners returned to work the strike committees reconstituted themselves on a permanent basis as workers' committees. Although the Kuzbass strike committees agreed with the authorities to disband themselves by 1 August, they decided to rename themselves workers' committees in order to oversee the implementation of Resolution 608 and to continue to defend the interests of workers in future.[51] Subsequently, activists from the workers' committees took the initiative in founding new labour organisations.

Some of the more politically active miners attempted to use the strike movement as a base on which to build organisations drawing in workers outside the mining industry. In mid-November 1989, 468 delegates, mostly representatives of strike committees, from sixteen towns in the Kuzbass region set up a Union of Kuzbass Working People. This union was attacked in the 'conservative' press for its advocacy of regional cost-accounting (in practice, regional economic autonomy), for the Kuzbass and for establishing an International Zone of Free Enterprise in the region. By mid-1990 the membership of the union was estimated at between 4,000 and 8,000.[52] The Union of Kuzbass Working People was one of the organisations which took the initiative in founding the Confederation of Labour which aimed to organise workers on a national basis.

The formation of the Confederation of Labour represented an ambitious attempt to unite labour organisations from across the Russian Federation and further. The Confederation was founded in Novokuznetsk between 30 April and 2 May 1990 at a congress of representatives of independent labour organisations attended by 330 delegates from forty-seven cities. Representatives of various opposition, democratic political groupings were also invited.[53] A declaration of 'fundamental principles' issued at the congress stated the following: 'The complexity and originality of the situation, the combination of political, social and economic tasks demands a search for new forms for the democratic movement of working people like that which the Polish workers made when they created "Solidarność".' The Confederation aimed to create a whole new structure of democratic government from below. It promised to struggle for democratic freedoms, labour free of bureaucratic shackles, for a just distribution of wages, real representation of workers in the organs of power and administration, for the economic autonomy of enterprises, and for 'the idea of developing regulated market relations in the working out of broad social programmes'.[54] The Confederation was formally supported by most of the existing independent labour organisations, including the first miners' congress in June 1990, but it was unable to act as an effective organisational focus and rapidly became moribund.[55]

The ambitions of the Union of Kuzbass workers and the Confederation of Labour were more political than economic and their links with workers in the enterprises rapidly attenuated. In the elections to the Kemerovo regional soviet, in the heart of the Kuzbass, in March 1990 the Union of Kuzbass Workers was unable to break the power of the local Communist Party apparat although a local strike leader, Viacheslav Golikov, was elected to the RSFSR Congress of People's Deputies. The formation of the Independent Miners' Union in the autumn of 1990 was the first time that a labour organisation was created successfully from the bottom up. The immediate catalyst for setting up a new national miners' union was disillusionment with the official union.

The official miners' union held its congress in Moscow in April 1990 but strike committee activists were only present by invitation. When they were refused recognition as delegates they walked out. The strike committee activists felt that unless they now organised their own union their authority would be undermined. The coordinating council of the Union of Donbass Strike Committees in the town of Gorlovka decided to convene the 1st Miners' Congress on 11 June in Donetsk, pre-empting an official congress scheduled for August.[56] The congress was hastily convened and the proceedings were sometimes badly prepared. The official union launched a propaganda campaign in its press against what they interpreted as an attempt to exclude engineering and technical personnel from the new union.[57] As a result delegates felt unable to choose between three alternative proposals for a new union and voted to leave the decision to a second congress which met at the end of October.[58] The growing links between the labour movement and the new democratic parties were signalled by the presence of Nikolai Travkin, the leader of the Democratic Party of Russia, who urged miners to leave the CPSU.[59]

The 2nd Miners' Congress, held at the end of October 1990, witnessed a struggle by the more politicised activists to mobilise a majority of delegates behind the idea of setting up an independent miners' union but the decision to set up an independent trade union was barely approved. In order to secure organisational help in calling the congress, activists had been forced to ask the Minister for the Mining Industry, Mikhail Shchadov, to join the organising committee. As a result a significant number of representatives of the official structures were present at both the miners' congresses which turned them into chaotic affairs. The opponents of the establishment of an independent union achieved a major victory when Shchadov was applauded by the Congress for promising to defend miners from any unemployment resulting from market reform. The decision to set up the union came on the last day of the congress when activists led a walk-out of 600 delegates to carry the vote. Even after the decision had been made to establish a new organisation the new union relied on the ministry to collect dues from workers. The new union was headed by its president Pavel Shushpanov[60] and vice-president Aleksandr Sergeev. Despite its weaknesses the Independent Miners' Union was the first Russian labour organisation created that could really pretend to coordinate strike action across the whole of the Russian Federation.

The 2nd Miners' Congress passed a resolution calling for the executive committee to begin negotiations with the government on securing a collective agreement for the industry. A draft agreement was drawn up by the union and submitted to the government in November. Nikolai Ryzhkov, the prime minister, accepted the justice of the miners' demands but refused to do anything about them.[61] The union extended the time-limit for a reply because of the appointment of Valentin Pavlov as prime minister in December. However, it rapidly became clear that the government was not really interested in negotiations with the union at all. At the beginning of January the leadership of the miners' union called a one-day strike to protest at the killing of thirteen demonstrators in Vilnius; it received little support.[62] Nonetheless, the increasingly 'conservative' nature of the government together with its ineffective economic policies, including a currency reform which made many Soviet citizens fear for their savings and rises in wholesale prices which had a particularly deleterious effect on mining enterprises, combined to create pressure both amongst union leaders and rank-and-file miners for a political strike. As Anatolii Malykhin, a member of the Independent Miners' Union told the RSFSR Supreme Soviet on 31 March, 'We struck in 1989 and put forward economic demands. For two years we have been made fools of in the offices of the ministries and it has become clear what the main reason for this is. Until the question of power is resolved there cannot be any economic changes'.[63]

On 1 March miners and workers in many enterprises in the Donbass struck after a strike call by the regional council of workers' committees with a series of economic demands, including a 250 per cent pay rise, addressed to the Ukrainian government.[64] On 4 March large numbers of miners in the Kuzbass walked out after the regional council of workers' committees had called for a political strike. Although both these strikes were envisaged as being only for one day, miners voted locally to continue their action and stoppages spread to other enterprises. On 7 March the Vorkuta miners came out. On 11 March the Kuzbass regional council of workers' committees called for an unlimited political strike against the government. By the middle of March up to fifty enterprises were on strike.[65] A week later an Inter-Regional Coordinating Council of Workers' (Strike) Committees, with ten to twelve members, was set up in Moscow with representatives of the regional councils and the Independent Miners' Union to organise the strike action. The list of demands drawn up by the Coordinating Council included the resignation of Gorbachev and his government, the dissolution of the Congress of People's Deputies and its replacement by a council representing the republics, the conclusion of a collective agreement for the industry with the ministry and improvements in pay and conditions.[66]

The determination of the miners clearly surprised the government and as the date, 2 April, fixed for rises in retail prices approached the government met at the end of March with representatives of the miners drawn mainly from pits which were not striking and made a whole series of economic concessions. These, not surprisingly, were rejected by the Coordinating Council. The price rises strengthened the determination of the miners and strike action began to spread to other industries, most notably to Minsk in Belorussia where workers held a mass demonstration in the city's main square on 3 April. Strikes also hit mines, engineering and metallurgical enterprises in the Urals and on 16 April thousands of factory workers in Ukraine began an indefinite strike.[67] On 24 April the Coordinating Council estimated that eighty enterprises were on strike in the Kuzbass, seventy-four in the Donbass, three in L'viv, twelve in Vorkuta, six in Sakhalin, one in Perm region, eight in Cheliabinsk, two in Severouralsk, four in Solegorsk and fifty-one across the whole of Belorussia.[68] Strike action only began to die down after El'tsin, on 23 April, signed the 'nine plus one' (Novo-Ogareevo) agreement with Gorbachev and leaders of eight of the other republics which effectively committed El'tsin to ending the strikes.

Links between the miners and Russian democratic activists had become much stronger since the 1989 strikes. Democratic Russia was at the forefront of organising financial and food aid to the miners who were not now receiving pay, as they had in 1989. Miners' leaders were frequently in contact with the Russian Federation government. El'tsin's decision to renew his alliance with Gorbachev caused anger amongst many miners but the conclusion of negotiations between representatives of the RSFSR government and miners' leaders, to transfer mines from Union jurisdiction to that of the RSFSR, led to the Vorkuta and Mezhdurechensk miners returning to work.[69] At the end of April El'tsin hurried to Novokuznetsk to convince sceptical miners that they should now return to work although none of their political demands had been met. On 1 May he signed an agreement in Novokuznetsk with the miners' leaders before a large crowd the terms of which transferred mines in the Russian Federation from the jurisdiction of the Union government to that of the Russian government. The miners were promised a large degree of control over the disposal of production from their enterprises and the final say in the form of any privatisation scheme for their industry. On 4 May Donbass miners returned to work. The suspicion of a sell-out in the Kuzbass was so great that miners there postponed their return to 10 May, after they had had the chance to inspect the transfer agreement.[70]

The miners' strike of March–April 1991[71] was arguably the most significant occasion on which mass popular action coordinated by independent political movements, in this case the Independent Miners' Union and the regional and enterprise workers' committees, changed the political fate not only of the

Russian Federation but of the Soviet Union as a whole. As a result of their action the bankruptcy of Gorbachev's alliance with the 'conservatives' was exposed and the creation of a new alliance between Gorbachev and the republics was brought about. The strike and its resolution also clearly demonstrated the political strength of El'tsin and his indispensability to the cause of reform in the Russian Federation and the Soviet Union.

Despite the determination of the miners there were clear weaknesses in the strike action. Firstly, the Coordinating Council was unable to do its job effectively and coordinate the strikes in such a way that it brought concerted pressure to bear on the government. The actual membership of the Independent Miners' Union remained small and it was unable to do anything more than advise the local strike committees what to do.[72] It was the regional councils which actually organised the strikes; so, for example, on 17 April it was the Kuzbass and Vorkuta Councils rather than the Coordinating Council that called for an all-out political strike. Secondly, strike action still did not spread outside the mining regions to any significant degree. The absence of any action at all by workers in such important political centres as Moscow or Leningrad was particularly noticeable, though by the summer of 1990 strike committees had been established in all of the latter's main enterprises.[73] Railway workers, and other communications workers, oil workers and other groups, crucial for the success of any general strike, stubbornly refused to stop work. Thirdly, the growing importance of the republics created new divisions amongst the miners; the Minsk strikers addressed their demands exclusively to the Belorussian government and the Donbass miners addressed their demands to both the republican and Union government. These weaknesses were to be shown up during the coup in August.

After their radicalism in the spring it was surprising that workers rallied to El'tsin's aid no more decisively than the rest of the population in August. In Moscow and St Petersburg where large numbers of demonstrators eventually gathered, most observers noted that there were few workers amongst those on the streets. On Monday 19 August El'tsin called for a general strike to protest against Gorbachev's illegal ouster. On Tuesday the strike call was supported by Anatolii Sobchak, the mayor of St Petersburg. It was reported that many enterprises in the 'second capital' were ready to stop work and Sobchak reported that twenty did so, including the giant Kirov works. The slow response of the miners might have owed something to disappointment at the conclusion of the March–April strikes. The Council of Kuzbass Workers' Committees called for an indefinite political strike and refused to recognise the legitimacy of the State Committee for the State of Emergency. In Vorkuta five out of thirteen pits stopped work and in Kuzbass twenty-six struck. There were strikes in the Kuzbass. In Ukraine Leonid Kravchuk, the republican president, called on workers not to strike and action in the Donbass was 'patchy'. In all about half the mines in the Soviet Union eventually stopped work, according to one source. The oil workers decided not to strike.[74]

As was noted at the beginning of the chapter, the new Russian labour move-ment has confounded everyone's expectations. It confounded expectations by its very existence and by the way that it became an important force for democratic and market reform. Even if it remained organisationally weak and ideologically unfocused this did not distinguish it greatly from other independent Russian movements and it was strong enough to exert a decisive influence on the course of Russian history on at least one occasion, in spring 1991. Its weakness and strengths reflected the particular legacy of communist authoritarianism and the predicament of Russian reform movements in general.

Radicals in the Supreme Soviet, not surprisingly, reacted particularly positively to the strike movement. Some democrats began to see in the embryonic labour movement not just an ally in the struggle against the old apparat but the basis of a broad mass movement for radical democratic reform. Inevitably the prospect of a Russian Solidarność arose to charm both the radical reformers and the new labour activists. The strikes of March–April 1991 were the nearest that the new Russian labour movement came to playing the role of a Russian Solidarność and it played a crucial role in breaking Gorbachev's half-hearted attempt to halt the process of reform and in putting the Soviet Union on the road to the August coup and its final break-up.

However, despite its consistently democratic orientation the new Russian labour movement failed to fulfil the hopes of the democratic theorisers. Regional differences prevented the evolution of an organisation which could mobilise workers from different industries across the whole of the Russian Federation. If anything, regional and sectoral differences became more important as the reform process proceeded as workers were divided by the break-up of the old union both politically and economically, and the limited introduction of market mechanisms highlighted basic differences of interest between miners in, say, the profitable Kuzbass and the nearly exhausted Donbass. The absence of an ideology, either in the form of western trade unionism or anti-capitalist socialism, that could effectively articulate the sectional interests of workers left them in an ambivalent relationship with the democrats. Their success in obtaining the promise of a decisive say in the form of privatisation to be applied to their industry indicated both their faith in radical economic reform and their suspicion of it. Once the democrats took power at the end of 1991 their disappointment at the absence of a Russian Solidarność probably began to ease.

Notes

1. Amongst other things this law gave the workers of an enterprise the right to elect their director.
2. Tat'iana Zaslavskaya, 'Friends or foes? Social forces working against perestroika', in A. Yakovlev (ed.), *Perestroika Annual*, vol. 1, 1988, pp. 256–60.

3. Igor Kliamkin, 'Oktiabr'skii Vybor Presidenta', *Ogonek*, no. 47, 1990, p. 7.
4. *Rossiia segodnia. Politicheskii portret v dokumentakh 1985-91*, Moscow, 1991, pp. 320-1, 339-40; see below.
5. *Vestnik Rabochego Kluba*, 1989, No. 2; *Rossiia segodnia. Politicheskii portret v dokumentakh 1985-91*, pp. 223-31.
6. Sytinskii had been arrested in the early 1980s for distributing literature from the dissident trade union SMOT.
7. *Rubikon*, no. 10, 1990.
8. *Russia and the World*, no. 17, 1990, p. 18; *Rubikon*, no. 10, 1990, pp. 8-13; *Uchreditel' noe Sobranie*, no. 3, 1989; *The Times*, 11 December 1989. For a detailed treatment of the Leningrad labour scene, see Anna A. Temkina, 'The workers' movement in Leningrad 1986-91', *Soviet Studies*, vol. 44, no. 2, 1992, pp. 209-36.
9. For an account of the Donbass strikes in English, see Theodore Friedgut and Lewis Siegelbaum, 'Perestroika from below: the Soviet miners' strike and the aftermath', *New Left Review*, no. 181, May/June 1990, pp. 5-32.
10. *Sotsiologicheskie issledovaniia*, no. 6, 1990, pp. 58-9; *New Left Review*, no. 181, p. 12.
11. *Uchreditel' noe Sobranie*, no. 3, 1989.
12. *Guardian*, 24 July 1989.
13. *Independent*, 20 July 1989, 24 July 1989.
14. Peter Rutland, 'Labor unrest and movements in 1989 and 1990', *Soviet Economy*, vol. 6, no. 3, 1990, p. 357.
15. *Rossiia segodnia. Politicheskii portret v dokumentakh 1985-91*, pp. 341-3.
16. *Sotsiologicheskie issledovaniia*, no. 6, 1990, p. 40; *New Left Review*, 181, p. 17; interview with Bakhtin and Dmitrienko conducted by the author.
17. *New Left Review*, 181, p. 9 n.
18. Miners in the small L'vov coalfield made political demands as early as 20 July. They demanded the bringing forward of municipal elections, the dismissal of local apparatchiks, including Volodymyr Shcherbit'skyi, the republican first secretary, and the establishment of a free trade union called Solidarność. *Guardian*, 24 July 1989.
19. *Sotsiologicheskie issledovaniia*, no. 6, 1990.
20. *New Left Review*, 181, p. 28; this process had begun before the strikes. In Vorkuta the minister for the coal industry, M. Shchadov, had been defeated in the elections to the Congress of People's Deputies in March 1989. There had been similar defeats for prominent members of the local apparat in the Kuzbass and only Shcherbit'skyi's 'brezhnevite' regime in the Ukraine prevented a similar outcome in the Donbass.
21. *Posev*, no. 3, 1990, pp. 68-9. Avaliani became an overnight hero when it was discovered that he had been dismissed from his job on trumped-up charges in 1980 for having written a letter calling on Brezhnev to resign and was elected to the Congress of People's Deputies by the Kuzbass in March 1989. He led the negotiations with N. Sliunkov, the Politburo member sent to meet the strikers in July. *Report on the USSR*, no. 32, 1989, p. 2. In the summer of 1990 he was expelled from the Union of Kuzbass Working People after defending the CPSU from attacks by the Democratic Party of Russia. *Nasha Gazeta*, no. 26, 1990.
22. *New Left Review*, 181, p. 29 and note.
23. *Nasha Gazeta*, no. 27, 1990.
24. *Summary of World Broadcasts*, SU/0600 B/2; *Independent*, 6 November 1989.

25. Teimuraz Avaliani's remarks to this effect in *Moscow News*, no. 32, 1989, were widely reported. See *Independent*, 3 August 1990, *New Left Review*, 181, p. 29.
26. Documents kindly supplied to the author by George Miller; *Moscow News*, no. 35, 1990.
27. *Moscow News*, no. 35, 1990; interview with Pavel Bakhtin and Iurii Dmitrienko; *New Left Review*, 181, p. 27.
28. *The Times*, 11 December 1989.
29. *Report on the USSR*, 27 July 1990, pp. 15–17; *Summary of World Broadcasts*, 30 June 1990. There are various versions about who first proposed the strike. One report states that a miner from Vorkuta put forward the idea for a strike on 1 July at the miners' congress. *Kommersant*, no. 23, 1990.
30. *Summary of World Broadcasts*, 12 July 1990.
31. *Report on the USSR*, 27 July 1990, p. 17.
32. *Rossiia segodnia. Politicheskii portret v dokumentakh 1985–91*, pp. 346–9.
33. *Rubikon*, no. 10, 1990, p. 31.
34. *Moscow News*, no. 25, 1989; *Moscow News*, 6 July 1990.
35. *Sotsiologicheskie issledovaniia*, no. 2, 1990, pp. 81–99.
36. *Feniks*, no. 6, 1989, p. 15.
37. *Rubikon*, no. 10, 1990, pp. 14–17. The Leningrad Popular Front has clearly had an uphill struggle convincing workers to support the democratic opposition. In the summer of 1990 local public transport workers threatened to strike in protest against the Leningrad Popular Front-dominated city soviet. *Personal observation of the author*.
38. *Posev*, no. 4, 1990, p. 18; *Smena*, 16 May 1990.
39. *Russkaia mysl'*, 7 September 1990; *Sibirskaia gazeta*, 22 January 1990.
40. *Rossiia segodnia. Politicheskii portret v dokumentakh 1985–91*, pp. 372–3.
41. *Literaturnaia Gazeta*, 19 July 1989; *Guardian*, 10 July 1989.
42. *Moscow News*, 27 July 1990, p. 16.
43. *Sovetskie Profsoiuzy*, nos. 9–10, 1990, pp. 5, 27.
44. *Trud*, 1 June 1990.
45. *Izvestiia*, 19 September 1990. (Thanks to Don Filtzer for this reference.)
46. In December 1990 he was appointed Soviet vice-president and was the formal leader of the coup attempt of August 1991.
47. I am obliged to Anna Temkina from the Institute of Sociology in Leningrad for this information.
48. Interview with Bakhtin and Dmitrienko.
49. Interview with Bakhtin and Dmitrienko.
50. *New Left Review*, 181, p. 17.
51. *Literaturnaia Gazeta*, 2 August 1989.
52. *Literaturnaia Rossiia*, no. 47, 1989; *Moscow News*, no. 35, 1990.
53. *Moscow News*, no. 35, 1990.
54. *Argumenty i fakty*, no. 22, 1990.
55. *Moscow News*, 27 July 1990, p. 17.
56. *Moscow News*, no. 24, 1990; *Trud*, 5 June 1990.
57. *Trud*, 5 June 1990.
58. *Moscow News*, 27 July 1990, p. 17; documents kindly supplied by Don Filtzer.
59. *Kommersant*, no. 23, 1990.
60. A Donbass miner who was born in 1946 and who had been elected to the regional strike committee in 1989.

61. Interview with Shushpanov conducted by the author, 12 April 1991.
62. A number of enterprises did strike elsewhere, especially in Leningrad. An interesting feeling of the mood amongst Kuzbass miners can be found in the reply of a member of the Novokuznetsk City Workers' Committee when asked why the strike to protest against the killings in Vilnius had not taken place, 'The strike will take place anyhow, but later and it will be much more terrifying. It will not just be a political action but a hunger riot'. *Argumenty i fakty*, no. 4, 1991.
63. *Argumenty i fakty*, no. 14, 1991.
64. *The Times*, 1 March 1991.
65. *Argumenty i fakty*, no. 11, 1991.
66. *Argumenty i fakty*, no. 14, 1991; interview with Eduard Ginsler (representative on the Coordinating Committee from Cheliabinsk) conducted by the author, 13 April 1991.
67. *The Times*, 17 April 1991.
68. *Argumenty i fakty*, no. 17, 1991.
69. *The Times*, 29 April 1991.
70. *Guardian*, 8 May 1991.
71. See Sarah Ashwin, 'The 1991 miners' strike: new departures in the independent workers' movement', *Report on the USSR*, no. 33, 1991, pp. 1–7.
72. Shushpanov estimated membership at only 3,500 in April 1991. Interviews with Shushpanov and Ginsler, conducted by the author, 12 April 1991 and 13 April 1991.
73. The passivity of the Moscow and Leningrad workers, compared to the miners, is surprising on first glance because of the highly politicised atmosphere in both cities but this probably stemmed from social factors. Miners lived in homogeneous, tightly knit communities whilst workers in Moscow and Leningrad were isolated in a much more heterogeneous population and were often recent immigrants to the cities, either the products of Technical Institutes (PTU) in provincial towns or imported workers, often from Central Asia (*limitchiki*).
74. *Guardian*, 20 August 1991, 21 August 1991; *Financial Times*, 21 August 1991.

6 The rise and fall of the Georgian nationalist movement, 1987–91

Jonathan Aves

By the end of 1991 Georgia faced complete political chaos. It is unlikely that it will be the only ex-Soviet republic to find itself in such a state but it was certainly the first to descend into anarchy. The scale of the difficulties that accompanied the transition from communist rule in Georgia were, perhaps, predictable but their character was less so. The multi-ethnic nature of the republic's population and the existence of three autonomous entities in such a small republic made a high level of inter-ethnic tension inevitable; and so it turned out. However, it was fighting between Georgians themselves which presented the most acute threat to the establishment of a new state.

It is easy to seek reasons for the fractiousness of the Georgian nationalist movement in generalisations about the Georgian national character and Georgian political culture but an account of Georgian politics after 1987 provides evidence that alternative courses were available at different moments. The particular outcomes that occurred were affected by traditional conceptions of what constituted legitimate political authority and even more crucially by the personalities of the key political actors but it was also determined by the nature of the existing republican élites and in the tactics adopted by the republican Communist Party in its attempt to deal with the new political organisations that emerged to articulate Georgian national aspirations.

When the policies of the Kremlin leadership began to indicate that there was scope for independent political organisations to emerge the Georgian political, intellectual and creative élites were particularly unsuited to accommodate themselves to the new situation. Nationalist sentiment was no less strong in Georgia than in the Baltic republics, west Ukraine and Moldavia. The independent Georgian Democratic Republic had been occupied by the Red Army in 1921 and although it had lasted barely three years the idea of independence had established itself in the popular consciousness. In contrast to other regions whose nationalist sentiment was strong, however, the Communist Party put down deep roots in Georgia. In the 1930s and 1940s Communist Party membership became indispensable for access to all important social and economic advancement in education, the economy and the cultural life of the country. By the 1980s the level of Communist Party membership in the republic was higher than anywhere else in the Soviet Union.[1] All-pervasive networks of patronage became the basis of rampant corruption which was, itself, a product of the cynicism engendered by Georgia's predicament.

Whatever its causes, the corrupt nature of the Georgian Communist Party rendered it particularly incapable of formulating a flexible political response to the high level of popular nationalist sentiment released in the republic after the initiation of the policy of democratization by Moscow. This was a decisive handicap for the new Georgian nationalist movement which began to emerge at the end of 1986 and had taken on a mass character by the autumn of 1988 because elsewhere it was the readiness of the republican Communist Party leaderships and of prominent figures from the cultural and academic institutions and the mass media (almost all Communist Party members) to respond to the agenda of nationalism and anti-apparat populism, particularly in the form of the Popular Fronts, that eased the whole transition away from control by the centre.

Nationalist sentiment had ensured that there was a persistent dissident movement in Georgia from the end of the 1960s and, in the absence of a decisive lead from established figures in cultural and academic life and Communist Party officials, dissidents achieved a much higher degree of political prominence in Georgia than in any of the other Soviet republics after 1986. Dissident-led independent political organisations lost out to élite-led groups in the other republics not only because the latter were able to secure concessions from the republican political leaderships and because they had much greater access to mass media but also because they were able to call on a relatively high level of political and organisational experience. Despite the moral authority of ex-dissidents in every other republic, members of the Communist Party and Komsomol activists were able to out-manœuvre their dissident rivals in the national independence parties and congress movements. The experience of dissident activity proved to be a poor preparation for more open politics. Inevitably it favoured stubbornness and an unwillingness to compromise. Understandably ex-dissidents were liable to suspect their collaborators of being *agents provocateurs* and to distrust every communist initiative as a mere smoke-screen behind which large-scale repressions were being prepared. All these phenomena were displayed in abundance by the new Georgian nationalist movement.

The first nationalist groupings to emerge in Georgia in 1987, the Helsinki Union and the Ilia Tchavtchavadze Society, were led by ex-dissidents. They called for human rights to be observed and for a revival of Georgian national life. Campaigns over environmental issues, such as the building of the Transcaucasian railway, and to protect national monuments, such as the Davitgareja monastery, had a wider resonance amongst students and received an airing in the official press. The local Communist Party leadership, under the first secretary Jumbar Patiashvili, moved swiftly to try and neutralise the burgeoning independent movement. In March 1988 it sponsored the foundation of the Rustaveli Society. The new organisation was supposed to promote

Georgian culture and language and although it rapidly claimed a large paper membership it was too obviously under communist control to develop into a broad popular movement.

At the end of 1988 the communist government published a draft law on the strengthening of the Georgian language as a panic reaction to the first mass demonstrations that had taken place in Tbilisi in November to protest at the changes to the Soviet Constitution being proposed in Moscow that would have removed the formal right of the republics to secede from the Union. Hundreds of thousands of people gathered first at the race course and then outside the building that housed the Supreme Soviet in the heart of the city. These demonstrations proved to be fertile recruiting grounds for a radical break-away group from the Ilia Tchavtchavadze Society, the Ilia Tchavtchavadze Society— Fourth Group, led by the ex-dissidents Zviad Gamsakhurdia, Merab Kostava, Giorgi Tchanturia and Irakli Tsereteli. These activists were united by their open demands for independence but there were hidden tensions. Apart from personality clashes there was a clear generational divide. Gamsakhurdia and Kostava had been the main figures in the Georgian Helsinki Watch Group of the 1970s whereas Tchanturia and Tsereteli had been arrested for their activity in student nationalist circles in the early 1980s.[2]

These divisions took on an institutional form. Gamsakhurdia established the Society of Saint Ilia the Righteous with Kostava. Tsereteli, who was a junior member of the society, formed the Georgian National Independence Party as his own power-base along with Irakli Batiashvili. Tchanturia, in his turn, founded the Georgian National Democratic Party. Gamsakhurdia seems to have envisaged the Society of Saint Ilia the Righteous as a broad movement, with an ostensible cultural and religious bent, and continued to organise his closest supporters in the Helsinki Union. All these radical groups were strongly in favour of independence. The National Independence Party even proposed that Georgia apply to join NATO. The National Democratic Party claimed the inheritance of a pre-Soviet party of the same name but was distinguished by its adherence to a philosophy of 'theo-democracy' by which the Georgian Orthodox Church would be given a decisive say in the political life of the republic.

The radicals' demonstrations forced the Georgian Supreme Soviet to protest against the proposed constitutional amendments and the concessions eventually made by the Supreme Soviet in Moscow gave their prestige a major boost. The radical surge continued into the new year. In March demonstrators gathered outside the building where the Rustaveli Society was holding its second congress. The grip of the local Communist Party leadership over the society was broken as Akaki Bakradze, a historian who had been sacked from his job in Tbilisi University in the early 1980s for the nationalist tone of his lectures, was elected leader.

Meanwhile, movements in the ethnic minority autonomies were beginning to develop independently of events in Tbilisi. By the beginning of 1989, 70 per cent of the population of the republic was ethnically Georgian. The biggest minorities were the Armenians, at around 8 per cent, who lived mainly in Tbilisi, the southern districts of Akalkalaki and Akalsikhe and Abkhazia, and the Russians, at around 6 per cent, who lived mainly in the cities of Tbilisi and Batumi and in Abkhazia.[3] However, it was the Abkhazians who lived in the north-west of the republic and one section of the Ossetian population who lived in the north of the republic who developed their own secessionist movements even though together they barely made up 5 per cent of its total population. In both these areas autonomous entities had been established under Soviet rule, the Abkhazian Autonomous Republic and the South Ossetian Autonomous Region, which gave a territorial coherence to their claims.

In June 1988 leading Abkhazian figures sent a letter to the 19th Party Conference in Moscow asking that the status of their region be raised to that of a full union republic. In November 1988 an initiative group, based in the Abkhazian writers' union, was formed to prepare for the formation of an Abkhazian Popular Front, Aidgylara (Popular Forum). In March 1989, 30,000 Abkhazians, including leading members of Aidgylara and of the regional committee of the Communist Party, met at the town of Lykhny, near Sukhumi the capital of Abkhazia, and approved a declaration, to be submitted to a forthcoming Central Committee Plenum on the nationalities question, calling on Moscow to recognise Abkhazia as a full union republic.[4]

The declaration was condemned by the Georgian Supreme Soviet and Georgian students at Sukhumi University, where Georgian political groups such as the Ilia Tchavtchavadze Society and the National Democratic Party had begun to organise, and they demanded that sanctions be imposed on Abkhazian officials who had participated in the Lykhny meeting. In Tbilisi, from the beginning of April, supporters of the National Independence Party and the National Democratic Party organised mass demonstrations in the middle of Tbilisi gradually changing the accent of the protest away from the Abkhazian issue to focus on demands for independence. These demonstrations ended in the massacre of 9 April.[5]

Events in Abkhazia moved to a bloody climax. The new Communist Party leadership, appointed in the wake of the Tbilisi massacre, in a blatant attempt to curry favour with the nationalist movement, gave into Georgian demands and agreed to the establishment of a branch of Tbilisi University in Sukhumi to serve the needs of Georgian students. The Abkhazians protested to Moscow and the Supreme Soviet condemned the Georgian decision as unconstitutional. Abkhazian students began to picket the building where Georgian students were being registered for the new university branch and serious fighting broke out on 15 July. Violence spread to the town of Ochamchira, to the south of Sukhumi, and arms were seized from militia stations. Georgians massed on the border of the autonomous republic but 3,000 Soviet Internal Ministry troops were ordered in on 17 July bringing an end to the violence.

Aidgylara held its founding conference in the same month and by early 1990 it was claiming 10,000 members. In the summer of 1989 it campaigned on behalf of Abkhazians who it believed were being unfairly persecuted for their participation in the fighting. Aidgylara was a moving force behind the establishment of the Assembly of Mountain Peoples which brought together Abkhazians and representatives of groups set up in the north Caucasian autonomous republics and regions in the Russian Federation. The first congress of the Assembly was held in Sukhumi in August 1989. There were some strains in the Abkhazian nationalist movement. 'Conservative' communists in the Abkhzian regional Communist Party organisation attempted to manipulate the movement for their own purposes linking anti-Georgian and anti-democratic rhetoric. At the end of 1989 there was a change in the leadership of Aidgylara when Aleksei Gogua, the chairman of the Abkhazian Writers' Union, was replaced by Sergei Shamba, a younger archaeologist.

The theme of the April demonstrations in Tbilisi broadened beyond the situation in Abkhazia to include demands for a restoration of Georgian sovereignty and the secession of the republic from the Soviet Union. A demonstration which had been held in February to mark the anniversary of the annexation of the Georgian republic in 1921 was confronted by 'a phalanx of security forces and armoured personnel carriers'; 150 people were arrested.[6] In early April the demonstrators were supported by workers who came out on strike in many of the republic's main enterprises.[7] On the evening of 7 April, Patiashvili telegrammed the Politburo in Moscow alleging that the situation was escalating out of control and requesting permission to arrest opposition leaders, to impose martial law and censorship. At meetings of the Politburo on 7 April, under the chairmanship of Egor Ligachev, and on 8 April, under the chairmanship of Viktor Chebrikov the head of the KGB, it was agreed to send units of the Soviet army to Tbilisi.[8]

At four o'clock in the morning of 9 April, troops of the Soviet army and Ministry of Internal Affairs moved against the demonstrators. An attempt was made to provoke the protesters and create the impression that they were attacking government buildings but when this failed the soldiers moved in and cleared them away killing twenty people with poison gas and sharpened trenching shovels. The brutal violence against peaceful protesters provoked outrage all over the Soviet Union.

The next day martial law was declared in the city and opposition leaders including Gamsakhurdia, Kostava, Tchanturia and Tsereteli were arrested. Opposition activists who were still at liberty presented eight demands to the government including the dismissal of the government and Communist Party leadership, the prosecution of those responsible for the massacre, and free elections.[9] A few days later Patiashvili was replaced as first secretary by Givi Gumbaridze and not long after sackings in the Abkhazian party and soviet leadership were also announced.[10] This was hardly likely to placate Georgian public opinion. Pro-independence feeling in the republic became much more overt. Although the death-toll in Abkhazia was greater, the tragedy of 9 April had a far greater symbolic effect for Georgians. Inevitably it strengthened the hands of the radicals who rejected any compromise with the Soviet authorities and any goal short of total independence.

The essence of Communist Party strategy did not change with the appointment of Gumbaridze as first secretary. The local leadership continued to try and placate nationalist demands but refused to let political power slip out of its hands. The impact of the 9 April massacre dealt the prospects of the Georgian Popular Front a mortal blow. An initiative committee to establish a Popular Front had been established in the summer of 1988 under the auspices of the Georgian Writers' Union. A new group was set up early in 1989 which included younger academics such as the historian Giorgi Zhorzholiani, the mathematician Guram Berishvili and the physicist Giorgi Tarkhan-Mouravi which submitted a draft programme to the original initiative group. However, the Popular Front was still not ready to hold its founding congress by the time that the Abkhazian situation began to absorb Georgian political attention in April and so a potential moderating force in events was absent.

Another reason why the Popular Front was so slow to take off in Georgia was an ill-conceived attempt to unite elements from the republican élites, younger activists and ex-dissidents. Gamsakhurdia, in particular, whilst opposing the idea of a Popular Front in principle, was involved in a great many of the practical discussions concerning its establishment. When the founding congress of the Popular Front was eventually held in July 1989 the unexpected presence of Gamsakhurdia with his supporters ensured that a philologist, Nodar Natadze, at that time considered close to Gamsakhurdia, was elected chairman in place of the film-maker Eldar Shengelaia. The organisation was also saddled with an over-large executive committee which prevented it working effectively. The stance and strategy of the local Communist Party, which refused to countenance concessions which would make a Popular Front viable, also hindered its development. Popular Fronts were based on a compromise according to which the Popular Front made formal statements of support for the official policies of perestroika and democratisation and avoided overt demands for independence and the overturning of communist rule. Furthermore, they maintained the fiction that they were 'social organisations' and not rival political organisations. In return they received considerable freedom to organise, obtain access to the official mass media and so on. In Georgia, the Communist Party demonstrated that it was not willing to cooperate with political organisations that were outside its direct control and that, if circumstances in Moscow allowed for it, it would return to a policy of outright repression.

While the elements in Georgian society that sought a gradual, constitutional approach to the question of independence found the ground falling away from under their feet the radical leaders, who were still in prison in the aftermath of the 9 April massacre, formed a Main Committee of National Salvation to unite all the radical forces. The Main Committee for National Salvation proclaimed that independence could only be brought about by a policy of civil disobedience as opposed to participation within the Soviet structures. Civil disobedience included strikes, demonstrations, rallies and, what was to become a feature of Georgian political protest, hunger strikes. For the radicals

Georgia would be considered independent when the 'occupying forces' of the Soviet army had left Georgian territory. Once again, however, the hidden tensions amongst the radical leaders undermined this attempt to give the nationalist movement a coherent organisational form. This time the pretext for the split concerned the reaction to a new ethnic conflict in South Ossetia.

Ossetian feelings had first been inflamed by the publication and approval of the law to strengthen the Georgian language in November 1988. By early 1989 strikes were breaking out in Tskhinvali, the capital of the South Ossetian Auto-nomous Region, in protest at a law to strengthen the position of the Georgian language.[11] In January 1989 a South Ossetian Popular Front, Adaemon Nykhas (Popular Shrine), held its founding meeting at which Alan Chochiev was elected president. Popular Shrine first came to prominence with an open letter of support for the Abkhazians in their campaign against the opening of the branch of Tbilisi University in Sukhumi which was published in March 1989. Popular Shrine also demanded that the South Ossetian Autonomous Region be upgraded in status to that of an autonomous republic and, at some future stage, be united to the North Ossetian Autonomous Republic in the Russian Federation. As tension rose the Georgian minority in South Ossetia began to complain of harassment.

The situation in South Ossetia was discussed in the Main Committee for National Salvation in Tbilisi at the beginning of November but it was divided down the middle.[12] Eventually Gamsakhurdia tried to organise a march of Georgians from Tbilisi to support a demonstration of local Georgians in Tskhinvali on 23 November. A column of several thousand Georgians set out from Tbilisi but it was turned back on the outskirts of Tskhinvali by armed Ossetians and Georgian Internal Ministry troops. Subsequently, through the winter, there was a series of bloody clashes in South Ossetia until Soviet Internal Ministry troops were sent in in January. In Ossetia casualties were more evenly divided between the two communities than in Abkhazia. This was partly due to the appearance of unofficial armed bands of Georgians attached to political organisations. These bands were to become a serious factor in the internal disputes of the Georgian radicals in 1990 but the South Ossetian conflict had a more immediate deleterious impact on the Main Committee for National Salvation.

Tchanturia had opposed Gamsakhurdia's demonstration mainly on the grounds of tactics. Both Gamsakhurdia and Tchanturia regarded the clashes in South Ossetia and Abkhazia as the product of Moscow 'provocations', but the former argued that the rights of Georgians in Ossetia must be determinedly defended whilst the latter claimed that nothing must be allowed to distract Georgians from the goal of national independence. By the beginning of 1990 the Main Committee of National Salvation was no longer active.[13]

The conflict in South Ossetia overshadowed the fact that elections to the republican Supreme Soviet were due in March 1990 but some groups had begun to prepare for this event. The elections to the Congress of People's

Deputies in March 1989 were the first major test of the Popular Fronts in the Baltic republics and they succeeded in electing solid blocs of deputies to the Moscow parliament. The election results in Georgia were in stark contrast; the old Communist apparat was almost uniformly triumphant.[14] However, in Tbilisi groups of citizens had taken it upon themselves to organise the campaigns of three opposition candidates; Akaki Bakradze, Nodar Natadze and Parmen Margvelashvili. Bakradze and Margvelashvili won convincingly but Natadze was prevented from registering as a candidate.[15]

One of the groups involved in the election campaigns for the Congress of People's Deputies held a meeting attended by over 600 people in May 1989 at which it decided to constitute itself as a social organisation; Democratic Elections in Georgia or DAS-i for short. Rezo Shavishvili, like many of the other members of DAS-i, a physicist, was elected president and a board was elected, too. In the meantime DAS-i discovered that there were twelve vacant places in the Georgian Supreme Soviet because the deputies had died but no by-elections had been held. DAS-i helped opposition candidates, including Natadze, gain election. Through these deputies they managed to have changes to the election law raised in the Supreme Soviet.

Over the summer months DAS-i drew up a draft electoral law for the elections to the Georgian Supreme Soviet due to be held in the early part of 1990 which they presented to the electoral commission of the Supreme Soviet in August. As a result they were able to achieve agreement to substantial changes including: the abolition of pre-election meetings, the abolition of reserved places for 'social organisations', the right for all registered organisations to put forward candidates, a reduction in the size of the Supreme Soviet from 300 to 250, and a number of procedural changes. However, the government went back on its agreement and procrastinated over publication of the new draft before it was approved by the Supreme Soviet.[16]

The second half of 1989 witnessed the creation of a large number of new political organisations. The Georgian Green Movement was one of the first independent political organisations to be established in the republic when it was constituted as a section of the Rustaveli Society in the spring of 1988. It worked successfully to raise public consciousness of ecological issues and was able to draw on an impressive array of specialists who contributed to government decision-making. Under the leadership of Givi Tumanishvili the Green Movement adopted a non-political stance and a group of younger members, led by Zurab Zhvania, formed a Green Party in early 1990. Perhaps because its membership only grew slowly to reach around 70 people[17] by the summer of 1991 it remained one of the more stable political organisations in the republic. It successfully sought contacts with European green parties and even received limited financial and material help from them.

In the winter of 1989–90 three parties representing some of the different strands in Georgian political life were established. In November the Georgian Social-Democratic Party held its first conference and elected a former professor at the Communist Party Higher School, Guram Muchaidze, as leader. The party was rapidly recognised by the remnants of the pre-Soviet Social-Democratic Party in exile and was accepted as a member of the Social-Democratic Association, which united many of the new social-democratic organisations that sprang up over the Soviet Union. Despite its past as the ruling party in the Georgian Democratic Republic the Social-Democratic Party had only a limited appeal. Partly, this was due to the popular reaction against anything that was even remotely related to socialism that was felt all over the Soviet Union and partly because the party advocated a moderate line on independence. In March 1990 Muchaidze supported the creation of a new 'union of independent states'.[18]

In December the Stalin Society was set up in the birthplace of Stalin, Gori, about one hundred kilometres west of Tbilisi, led by a retired Lieutenant-General Irakli Jorjadze. The Society inevitably attracted a great deal of coverage in the press outside Georgia but its appeal did not extend outside the city of Gori, where the last statue to Stalin in the Soviet Union still stands, and some people of the older generation, particularly those who had fought in the war.

Also in December a Monarchist-Conservative Party was launched with great enthusiasm, led by Temur Zhorzholiani. The party failed to work out a serious plan for restoring the monarchy in Georgia particularly when there was no official pretender. The party split in the summer of 1990 and one part, called the Union of Georgian Traditionalists and led by Akaki Asatiani, participated in the electoral bloc led by Gamsakhurdia in the October elections whilst the main part, led by Zhorzholiani, concentrated on trying to get the most direct descendant of the last Georgian king, who lived in Spain, to return to Georgia. Monarchism was more popular as an ideal in Georgia than in any other of the former Soviet republics where even some activists with otherwise liberal inclinations saw monarchy as a potentially unifying force in a fractured society.

The nominal ideology of many of these new 'parties', green, national-democratic, social-democratic and so on, reflected the appeal of European models in Georgia but few of the political organisations that were set up as a consequence managed to attract the support of more than a few enthusiasts. At its height the Popular Front was able to claim 15,000 members; at the same time the National Democrats claimed 4,000 members and the Helsinki Union, which was led by Gamsakhurdia, 2,000 members.[19] Apart from this political organisations were very small. The Social-Democratic Party, which was one of the better organised and bigger groups, claimed 780 members in March 1990.[20]

Partly the small number of active members within the organisations reflected an unwillingness to join parties. The Green Movement claimed 5,000 members but the Green Party between thirty and seventy. The success of a political organisation in Georgia depended not so much on its ability to attract formal supporters but on its ability to mobilise the population at public rallies, demonstrations and strikes. The Round Table electoral bloc, which was victorious in the elections to the Supreme Soviet when they were held in October, selected its candidates not by asking its members to stand, as would happen in a British election, but by waiting for someone in a constituency to come forward and convince the bloc that he, or occasionally she, really did support the bloc and had a good chance of winning.[21]

Opposition political organisations also suffered from serious material problems. Some groups such as the Rustaveli Society and the Popular Front, the latter in the Cinema Workers' Union building, managed to obtain premises officially. Other groups seized premises from the authorities; the Popular Forum,[22] for example, occupied the first floor of the Institute of Marxism–Leninism. However, obtaining funds, materials such as newsprint, and premises were almost insurmountable problems. Irakli Tsereteli, rather conservatively, estimated that it would cost three million roubles to finance alternative elections.[23] Some of the most prominent organisations had wealthy backers. Tchanturia said that the National Democratic Party was supported by 'donations from our businessmen and private individuals'.[24] Inevitably the question of funding, particularly when the internal organisation of the political groupings was so poor, led to constant accusations of links with corruption.

In most of the other Soviet republics the majority of political parties were formed by fractions within the Popular Front. Although even these organisations were often small, weak and ephemeral, the experience of work within the Popular Front and their continued contact with an organisation, in the form of the Popular Front, which played a practical and constructive role in the political life of the republic, did provide a relatively substantial basis on which to build a coherent political party. This was even more the case because everywhere the narrow ideologies claimed by the political parties were only of interest to small groups of intellectuals whilst the bulk of public opinion was concerned with the broader issues of independence or breaking the power of the Communist Party apparat. In these circumstances broad Popular-Front-type organisations were a convenient umbrella under which potential politicians could obtain some political experience. The failure of the Georgian Popular Front to play such an integrating role in the emerging Georgian politics meant that Georgian political parties became dominated even more than elsewhere by personalities, by their clashes and their charismatic appeal.

The main beneficiary of this situation was Gamsakhurdia. His presence at public rallies in 1989–90 could be relied on to draw a large crowd. This was despite his tendency to label all his political opponents as 'KGB agents' or 'enemies of the Georgian people'. Gamsakhurdia's popularity was not only due to his undoubted personal charisma and dissident past; he appeared to be one of the few politicians pursuing a consistent political line. More moderate figures were continually being overtaken by events or undermined by Communist Party intransigence. Although his rhetoric gave powerful ammunition to the Abkhazian and Ossetian movements, especially his frequent assertions that they were not the indigenous population which, understandably, made them fear for their future in an independent Georgia, his support for the rights of the Georgian population in the autonomous areas only added to the strength of his standing amongst Georgians in general.

As elections to the republican Supreme Soviet drew near in early 1990 it seemed that despite its relative weakness the Popular Front would probably win a majority of seats. The radical organisations were excluded from direct participation in the elections since only 'social organisations' had the right to put up candidates and a new government dominated by the Popular Front would be a serious blow to their aspirations. Forced to work constructively by this prospect the radicals proposed a boycott of the elections to the Supreme Soviet and took up the idea of the congress movements in Estonia and Latvia and proposed that the nationalist movement begin preparations for the organisation of alternative elections. The radicals' call for a boycott began to gain momentum as it became clear that the Communist Party was attempting to swamp the lists of candidates till there were between ten and twenty-five candidates, with 80 per cent of them being members of the Communist Party, for each place in an attempt to deny the Popular Front victory.[25]

On 13 March a conference of radical organisations was held in the Philharmonia concert hall in the centre of Tbilisi to discuss plans to establish alternative state structures. Natadze was one of the first speakers and he defended the Lithuanian model for achieving independence by holding elections to the Supreme Soviet. However, the mood of the conference was clearly against him and when he said that the creation of the Georgian Soviet Socialist Republic had at least guaranteed the unity of the country he was heckled. His position was further undermined when Tengiz Sigua, a leading member of the Rustaveli Society, announced that Bakradze and the Rustaveli Society had agreed to join the boycott. In the end the radicals' speeches, especially one by Tchanturia, were so pointed that Natadze walked out and was not present when the conference voted to approve a boycott.

The second day of the conference was better-organised. The opening of the first day had been overwhelmed by crowds of people not representing any organisation after a rumour had circulated that 'the more people that come the better'. Gamsakhurdia told participants that its main aim was to prepare for a congress of the Georgian people which could decide on a new constitution and conduct negotiations with Moscow. He told the delegates that elections did not make sense in a one-party system. Irakli Tsereteli read a draft proposal for the creation of a National Forum in order to prepare for the holding of alternative elections to a non-Soviet parliament, the National Congress. Eventually Nodar Tsuleishvili, a representative of the Popular Front, announced that his organisation was now going to call for a postponement of the elections.[26] The postponement of the elections to the end of October was agreed, no doubt with a muffled sigh of relief, shortly afterwards by the Communist Party.[27]

The next three months marked a low point in the prestige in the nationalist movement. At first the radicals, at least, appeared to be united around the congress strategy but even this was thrown into disarray in the middle of May

1990 when Gamsakhurdia walked out of the National Forum after an incident in which shots had been fired at his associates in the street outside. He had been increasingly isolated in the Forum as Tsereteli had gradually moved into a firmer alliance with Tchanturia. Gamsakhurdia now formed a new grouping, the Round Table which was joined by the Society of Saint Ilia the Righteous (headed by Tedo Paatashvili), the Monarchist-Conservative Party and the Merab Kostava Society (headed by Vazha Adamia) which had been founded in Kostava's memory after he had been killed in a car crash in October 1989.[28] The recriminations between Gamsakhurdia and Tchanturia reached new heights. Gamsakhurdia accused Tchanturia of 'terrorism' and Tchanturia, in his turn, accused Gamsakhurdia of having made a secret agreement with the KGB. The conflict was made particularly ominous by the appearance of armed groupings, such as the Mkhedrioni (Warriors) led by Jaba Ioseliani[29] who was a determined opponent of Gamsakhurdia. Supporters of Tchanturia and Gamsakhurdia blockaded each other's newspapers.[30] The atmosphere was further heightened in April when Soviet military helicopters dropped leaflets in Tbilisi calling on non-Georgians to form an Inter-Front on the Baltic model.[31] Articles in the press took on a new desperate tone.[32]

However, only two weeks after Gamsakhurdia left the National Forum the Georgian political scene went through an unexpected transformation. On 31 May students in Tbilisi University went on hunger strike and demanded that Georgia declare independence.[33] The Georgian political log-jam had become particularly painful since even the Russian Federation and Uzbekistan had declared sovereignty. This was a spontaneous rebuke to the nationalist movement but it opened a window of opportunity for Gamsakhurdia. He declared his support for the hunger strike on 6 June but persuaded the students that the existing Supreme Soviet was not morally competent to make a declaration of independence; the students' main demand became a call for multi-party elections.[34] On 8 June Gumbaridze agreed to convene an extraordinary session of the Supreme Soviet to consider the students' demands. The hunger strike was called off on 10 June.[35]

It is unlikely that such an outcome had been in Gamsakhurdia's mind when he walked out of the National Forum, although the example of the Baltic republics where the congresses had been rapidly overshadowed by the Supreme Soviets elected in February and March, particularly after the Lithuanian Supreme Soviet declared independence in March, must have been compelling. On the other hand the Georgian Supreme Soviet had removed Article 6 from the Georgian Constitution, which had enshrined 'the leading role of the Communist Party', in March. This was no doubt an attempt by the Communist Party to make a relatively painless gesture to democratic opinion but it did give the idea of multi-party elections to the Supreme Soviet a greater degree of plausibility.

Opposition groups consisting of DAS-i, the Greens and the Popular Front, along with the Round Table, began negotiations with the Communist Party. The resulting electoral law reflected the struggle between the Communist

Party and the opposition. The main discussion centred around the electoral system to be adopted. The opposition believed that the existing first-past-the-post, constituency system favoured local party bosses who were able to mobilise their patronage. In the end it was agreed that half the places in the Soviet should be elected according to a proportional list system and half according to the existing system. Additionally, independent candidates could stand in constituencies if they could collect the signatures of 500 people. Differences over the number of deputies, the opposition proposing 200 and the communists 300, were resolved with a compromise of 250. If votes for a list did not reach a cut-off level of 4 per cent no candidates from that list would be elected. Originally Gamsakhurdia had demanded that voters should take a test to show knowledge of the Georgian language to qualify.[36] This was not included in the final version but it was laid down that registered organisations must be active over the territory of the whole republic which automatically barred the Abkhazian Popular Forum and the Ossetian Popular Shrine underlining the limits that inter-ethnic conflict placed on democracy in Georgia.[37]

The disarray in the nationalist movement had left Gumbaridze feeling increasingly confident and he clearly believed that the moment had now come to make a stand.[38] Although the draft election law had been agreed he refused to publish it and submit it to the Soviet for approval. Time was running out if it was to be approved in time for elections at the end of October. To force the government's hand the Round Table organised a rail blockade at the vital Samtredia junction at the end of July, the impact of which was multiplied because it was the height of the holiday season.[39] Gumbaridze refused to see members of the opposition whilst he sought help from Moscow. However, Moscow refused to come to his aid and Gumbaridze was forced to back down. The agreed draft electoral law was submitted to the Supreme Soviet and approved on 19 August. The only effect of this desperate manœuvre by Gumbaridze was to convince a large section of Georgian public opinion that only Gamsakhurdia could force the Communist Party to give up power.

At the end of September elections to the National Congress took place. The agreement to hold multi-party elections to the Supreme Soviet inevitably reduced their significance but there were still important organisations involved. In contrast to the congress movements in Estonia and Latvia which represented both the radical wing of the nationalist movements in relation to the Communist Party authorities and in relation to the Russian-speaking minorities, the tone of pronouncements emanating from the Georgian congress movement on inter-ethnic issues were relatively moderate. At a conference of the National Forum held in May representatives of Aidgylara and Adaemon Nykhas had spoken although there was no real debate with the Georgians. The National Democratic Party had changed too, dropping most of its rhetoric about 'theo-democracy', for example. This unexpected development was partly the result of a decision by a group of prominent liberal intellectuals, such as the philosopher

Merab Mamardashvili and others such as the former Popular Front activists Berishvili and Giorgi Zhorzholiani grouped in the Democratic Georgia bloc, to participate in the Forum's deliberations.

Before the elections leaders of the Forum organisations had announced that more than 50 per cent of the electorate would have to take part for the Congress to claim that it represented the will of the people of Georgia. To achieve a 50.8 per cent turn-out the polling stations were reopened on 1 October and 14 October. Added to suspicions of deliberate vote-fixing, technical and material problems made it very difficult for the generally disorganised Georgian opposition to arrange convincing elections on their own.[40] One liberal supporter of the National Congress admitted that not many people realised whether they were voting for the National Congress or Supreme Soviet and described how he had to break into the building where the voting was taking place in his constituency to open it in the morning.[41] An opinion poll conducted in November confirmed that significantly more people felt that the new Supreme Soviet represented the will of the Georgian people than the National Congress.[42]

Despite doubts about the reliability of the results they were regarded as somewhat of a surprise. The largest number of votes, 35.6 per cent, and number of seats, seventy-one, was taken by the National Independence Party which beat the National Democrats and their small ally the Democratic Party into second place. They received 32.6 per cent of the vote and sixty-five seats. The liberal bloc, Democratic Georgia, received 18 per cent of the votes and thirty-seven seats.[43] The first session of the National Congress on 5 November was blessed by the Katolikos, the head of the Georgian Orthodox Church. It became obvious, however, that the role the Georgian National Congress should play in that republic's political life was no more clear than the role that the Baltic congresses should play there.

At the beginning of September strong public concern over the propriety of allowing the Stalin Society to participate in elections to the Supreme Soviet was expressed partly because many Georgians feared that it might secure a small but significant number of votes, casting a cloud over the proceedings. The Central Electoral Commission refused to register the Stalin Society as a participant but the Supreme Court overturned the Commission's decision.[44] Round Table supporters began a hunger strike against the Stalin Society and the Electoral Commission once again refused to register it. Gamsakhurdia's position received a further boost on the eve of polling when Tchanturia was wounded in a shooting incident. Tsereteli immediately went on television and accused Gamsakhurdia of complicity without any evidence in what appeared to many Georgians to be a hysterical attack.

At the start of the campaign for elections to the Supreme Soviet there was a widespread perception that the Communist Party would do well because of the disarray in the nationalist movement. The formation of the Conciliation, Peace and Renewal bloc in August led by Valerian Advadze, a deputy to the Congress of People's Deputies in Moscow whose performance there had stood out in contrast with the mediocrity of the other Georgian deputies, was widely seen as another attempt by the Communist Party to broaden its appeal. In a rather futile appeal Akaki Bakradze called on all opposition forces to sink their differences and unite to defeat the Georgian Communist Party but negotiations soon broke down.

Eleven blocs were registered to take part in the elections but only seven were serious contenders for votes. They were: bloc 1 (Freedom); bloc 3 (Georgian Communist Party); bloc 5 (Conciliation, Peace and Renewal); bloc 7 (Rustaveli Society); bloc 12 (Round Table); bloc 13 (Popular Front) and bloc 14 (Democratic Georgia). All the registered parties were agreed that Georgia must be granted independence but they all, even the Round Table, argued for a transitional period and for no immediate change in the status of the autonomous areas. All the blocs proposed that Georgia should set up a market economy but again cautiously they all argued for a transitional period in which social guarantees would be provided.

Despite the history of the previous two years the organisation of the elections was efficient and conscientious.[45] One of the main points in the electoral law was the creation of an independent Central Electoral Commission.[46] The electoral commission consisted of five representatives of the Supreme Soviet presidium and one representative from each registered political party. The president of the Commission was an academician, Irakli Zhordania and his deputy was Tengiz Sigua from the Rustaveli Society. Similar electoral commissions were set up in each constituency. The Central Electoral Commission administered the 7.5 million roubles that the government had allocated for the elections, distributing them amongst the political parties.[47] Almost all participants were satisfied with the Commission's work.[48] There was a high turn-out of 67 per cent despite boycotts affecting constituencies in Abkhazia and Ossetia. In a few constituencies the activities of the ethnic minorities prevented voting taking place at all.[49] In a number of areas, such as Ajaria, it was reported that electoral commissions had been dominated by the Communist Party and that polling stations had been hung with Communist Party posters but that this and similar reports of irregularities had not affected the overall result.[50]

The election results confirmed the polarised state of Georgian politics. The Round Table–Free Georgia bloc took 54.3 per cent of the votes cast for the party lists and the Communist Party 29.4 per cent. None of the other blocs managed to surmount the four per cent barrier. After run-off elections in those constituencies where no candidate succeeded in gaining 50 per cent of the vote the Round Table held 155 seats in the Supreme Soviet and the Communist Party 64. The other blocs were able to pick up some seats in the constituencies. The Popular Front secured twelve seats and Natadze was elected. Elsewhere Valerian Advadze, from the Conciliation, Peace and Renewal bloc and Eldar Shengelaia from the Democratic Georgia bloc were also elected.

At the first session of the new Supreme Soviet, on 12 November, Gamsakhurdia was elected chairperson of the presidium and Sigua was appointed prime minister of the new government. Although, strictly speaking, the Round Table did not have the two-thirds majority in the Supreme Soviet needed to push through constitutional change, in practice the communist deputies did not oppose the new government. At a congress of the Georgian Communist Party in December, Gumbaridze was replaced as first secretary and the delegates finally voted to break formally with the CPSU.

The most immediate consequence of the elections to the Georgian Supreme Soviet was a sharpening of conflict in South Ossetia. In September the South Ossetian Regional Soviet declared itself to be a democratic republic within the USSR and new elections to the soviet were held at the beginning of December. After the elections, which the Georgian population of the region boycotted, the new soviet elected Torez Kulembekov as its chairperson. The Georgian Supreme Soviet annulled the elections and abolished the autonomous status of the region, renaming it Samachablo. Tskhinvali was all but blockaded and Kulembekov was arrested in January. Heavy fighting continued even after Soviet troops were sent in by Moscow in April and the number of killed was counted in their hundreds. Thousands of Ossetian refugees fled north to North Ossetia in the RSFSR and Georgian refugees southwards to Tbilisi each with stories of persecution that heightened tension and made compromise less and less likely.

A further threat to the stability of the republic was provided by the armed opposition groups who refused to recognise the new government. The best organised and most vociferous of them was Mkhedrioni under Ioseliani. After the group had organised pickets of Soviet military bases the Soviet army occupied their main base just outside Tbilisi in the middle of February.[51] Coming at the same time as the 'conservative' reaction in Moscow and the crack-down and accompanying deaths in Vilnius, the activities of Mkhedrioni appeared increasingly foolhardy. Shortly afterwards Ioseliani was arrested by Georgian government forces and many of his supporters taken into custody.

The fighting in South Ossetia and the activities of the armed extra-parliamentary opposition formed the background to the growing concentration of powers in the presidency. In December Gamsakhurdia was made executive president by the Georgian Supreme Soviet until elections could be held. Asatiani of the Union of Traditionalists took over the post of chairman of the Supreme Soviet. At the end of January the Supreme Soviet passed a law setting up a National Guard. Tengiz Kitovani a supporter of the Round Table was appointed commander. The terms of the new law envisaged conscription and described avoidance of service as 'treacherous for the Republic of Georgia in its fight for freedom and independence'.[52] Enforcing service and arming and equipping the recruits was beyond the resources of the government and its total complement by the summer had fallen far short of the envisaged 12,000 soldiers.

The direct response of the Georgian government to the decision of Moscow to send troops into South Ossetia was to declare independence on 9 April

1991, two years after the massacre. A subsequent referendum on independence, held on 31 May, gave a vote of 98.85 per cent in favour on a 90.3 per cent turn-out, indicating that many non-Georgians outside the autonomous areas had also voted for independence.[53] However, this overwhelming endorsement was not the real reason for the independence declaration. In his early pronouncements Gamsakhurdia's statements on independence had been moderate ruling out immediate declarations and proposing a five-year transition period. The 9 April 1991 declaration represented a continuation of the tactic of facing down communist threats, in the shape of the 'conservative' reaction in Moscow and the sending of Soviet troops into Ossetia, that Gamsakhurdia had employed to defeat the Georgian Communist Party.

On 26 May 1991 elections were held in Georgia for an executive president. Gamsakhurdia won with a massive 86 per cent of the vote, Advadze came in second place with 7 per cent and Natadze was relegated to fourth by the Communist Party candidate. The elections themselves had been held in a relatively free atmosphere.[54] Whilst most of the old official press was in government hands an independent press, such as the commercial newspaper *Shvidi Dgre* (subsequently it changed its name to *Droni*) and newspapers put out by the Popular Front, the Rustaveli Society and the Green Movement, which were frequently highly critical of the government, continued to be published. The television, on the other hand, was heavily and almost exclusively biased in favour of the government. During the election campaign, though, all the candidates were given a broadcast to put forward their views and Advadze and Natadze used theirs to launch fierce attacks on Gamsakhurdia. Nonetheless, unprecedented powers were now concentrated in the hands of the president. The National Guard became directly responsible to him. Local soviets were abolished and replaced with prefects also directly responsible to the president.[55] These prerogatives appeared all the more threatening because Gamsakhurdia continued to use the most provocative language against people who opposed him. The presidential elections marked the high point in Gamsakhurdia's career but the opposition became increasingly vociferous in their attacks on his authoritarian tendencies and, in reality, he was becoming more and more politically isolated.

The National Congress had gradually fallen into a position of complete impotence. The liberals ceased their active participation early in 1991 and Tsereteli quarrelled with Tchanturia over the latter's unwillingness to find any real *modus vivendi* with the government. The 'constitutional' opposition began to regroup. The Popular Front deputies joined by some of the independents, such as Eldar Shengelaia, formed a small but significant fraction in the Supreme Soviet which was joined by two small political parties, the Liberal-Democratic National Party and the Free Democrats, which had participated in the elections to the Supreme Soviet as part of the Freedom and Democratic Georgia blocs but had failed to gain any mandates. The new grouping, called the Democratic Centre, attacked the increasingly centralised nature of political power, the difficulties that the opposition faced in getting their views across in the mass media, and the slowness of the government to put together an economic reform programme.

The 19 August coup attempt in Moscow marked a watershed in Gamsakhurdia's presidency. When news of the events in Moscow reached Tbilisi the government limited its reaction to publishing an appeal for calm and, in an interview, Gamsakhurdia expressed uninterest in the affairs of 'another country'.[56] Many Georgian intellectuals felt that he should have taken a stronger stand in support of El'tsin but it was his decision to disband the National Guard and subordinate it to the militia after the local Soviet military commander threatened to annihilate it that caused the greatest problem when Kitovani refused to obey the president's order and led a group of guards into opposition to the government. The position of the government had been made even weaker by the resignation of Sigua,[57] after Gamsakhurdia had blamed him for not dealing with the economic crisis, and the sacking of the foreign minister Giorgi Khoshtaria a few days before the coup. Immediately after the coup the Supreme Soviet voted to suspend the mandates of the communist deputies in the Supreme Soviet until their possible complicity in the coup could be ascertained. This decision brought an end to the existence of the Georgian Communist Party as a discrete political organisation but the end of Gamsakhurdia's traditional enemy was accompanied by a new surge of oppositional activity by his former comrades in the nationalist movement.

On 2 September a group of National Democrats chanting 'Ceauşescu! Ceauşescu!' tried to organise a demonstration on the steps of the Supreme Soviet building. Shots were fired and at least four people were injured. Gamsakhurdia claimed that the first shots had come from the demonstrators.[58] A month of constant demonstrations in the centre of Tbilisi began.[59] In the middle of September employees of the republican television went on strike and occupied the television centre. This became the main arena for the opposition demonstrations which were now supported by the groups in the Democratic Centre, the Greens, DAS-i and practically every other political organisation in the republic. The central demand of the opposition was the resignation of Gamsakhurdia from the presidency. Sigua made speeches in which he claimed to have evidence that implicated Gamsakhurdia in the August coup in Moscow. In parliament a group of deputies who were members of the Merab Kostava Society, led by Vazha Adamia, and another small group headed by the leader of the Saint Ilia the Righteous Society, Tedo Paatashvili, and deputies close to him, such as Tengiz Dikaminjia and Merab Uridia, split away from the Round Table to boost the opposition although without making any real difference to the domination of pro-Gamsakhurdia deputies in the Supreme Soviet.[60]

At this time activists from the National Democratic Party and the National Independence Party marched down the main Rustaveli Avenue in an attempt to demonstrate in front of the Supreme Soviet but were beaten back by the militia. The following night they commandeered lorries and built barricades across Rustaveli Avenue. On 21 September Gamsakhurdia made an appeal by television for his supporters to come and protect the government building from the opposition. Supporters from Tbilisi were joined by thousands of others bused in from the provinces who proceeded to pull down the barricades and forcibly remove the opposition from their headquarters in the former Institute of Marxism–Leninism. The mobilisation of the government's political supporters and the distribution of weapons to them changed the nature of the conflict as the distinction between political supporters of the government and the forces of the state began to break down, exposing the extreme fragility of the whole state apparatus. Kitovani's fraction of the National Guard rushed to deploy itself by the television centre to ward off any further attacks by supporters of the government. Giorgi Tchanturia was arrested as he tried to fly to Moscow and charged with responsibility for building the barricades on Rustaveli Avenue. An opposition activist and journalist Giorgi Khaindrava was also arrested for his part in organising the occupation of the television centre.

In the evening of 5 October an opposition demonstration set off down Rustaveli Avenue towards the Supreme Soviet building and began a sit-down protest by the buses which had been parked across the road by the government to prevent opposition protests taking place in front of the parliament. In the middle of the night government supporters moved in and began forcibly to remove the demonstrators. At some point gunfire began. By the morning two people had been killed, both of them government supporters, but the opposition had been driven off Rustaveli Avenue and stragglers were being rounded up in the side-streets. The city awoke in a state of shock. After negotiations Kitovani's fraction of the National Guard was allowed to leave the city centre to an encampment by the reservoir that fed Tbilisi where they remained until December. The Supreme Soviet met and, despite vehement protests from the opposition, deputies voted to describe the events of the previous month as an attempted 'putsch'.[61]

For the next two months Georgia gradually sank into a state of paralysis. As Gamsakhurdia's real power ebbed away opposition attacks on his dictatorial tendencies became more and more shrill. Gamsakhurdia made some concessions to opposition demands by giving up some of his prerogatives as president and promising to speed up economic reform but they faded into the growing political chaos and babble. Rumours of mass repressions were rife in the city. The opposition began to prepare for a showdown. Leading figures, including Kitovani, had a series of meetings with politicians, including Eduard Shevardnadze, in Moscow. Discussion included the possibility of obtaining arms.[62]

The conflict in South Ossetia which had died down over the summer flared up again. Abkhazia took advantage of the impotence of Tbilisi. At the end of September elections were held to the Abkhazian Supreme Soviet. Although they made up less than 20 per cent of the population of the autonomous republic the elections were conducted on the basis of separate lists for the different nationalities in such a way that Abkhazians would be guaranteed a veto in the new Supreme Soviet. The new Abkhazian government began a policy of quietly breaking away from Georgia by establishing its own economic independence.

When opposition demonstrations outside the Supreme Soviet building resumed in the middle of December their leaders were much better prepared. Confrontation broke out on the weekend of 20–1 December and guardsmen loyal to Kitovani rapidly took up position, backed up by artillery and rocket launchers, around the Supreme Soviet building where Gamsakhurdia and his supporters were esconced. Heavy fighting ensued for over two weeks in which over a hundred people were killed and large parts of Tbilisi's historic centre were devastated. At the end of December Tchanturia and Ioseliani were freed from prison and Sigua emerged as the opposition's political figurehead and prime minister designate at the head of a Military Council on which were represented both the armed and parliamentary opposition. Gamsakhurdia's position became more and more untenable as a cordon thrown around the city by the heavily armed opposition guardsmen backed up Mkedrioni forces kept Gamsakhurdia supporters out of the city. On 5 January in a last-ditch attempt to reply to opposition demands that he resign, Gamsakhurdia offered to hold a referendum on the question.[63] On the night of 5–6 January 1992 Gamsakhurdia fled first to Armenia and after a brief attempt to rally his forces in western Georgia in the middle of January he finally received asylum in Chechno-Ingushetia in the RSFSR in February.

By early 1992 the prospects for any sort of liberal-democratic regime in Georgia appeared remote. Georgian society was irrevocably fractured and polarised. Gamsakhurdia had managed to unite against him almost all of the numerous political groupings that had grown up in the republic in the previous four years in a remarkable way. On the other hand, although the Military Council was able to establish a superficial order it was clear that Gamsakhurdia still enjoyed considerable popular support, making it difficult for the new regime to call elections. The minority problem showed no sign of easing as both Abkhazia and South Ossetia, with their substantial Georgian populations, gradually slipped out of any control from Tbilisi.

The politicians who emerged in Georgia after 1988 must bear a considerable personal responsibility for the disastrous state that the republic found itself in. Even if there was strong, and even understandable, popular support for Gamsakhurdia's attacks on people who had made successful careers under the Soviet regime and for his championing of Georgian rights in minority areas, it also inevitably risked raising social and political tensions to a point where they could get out of control. The opposition, both parliamentary and paramilitary, did not distinguish itself either. It frequently indulged itself in provocative rhetoric and demands that ratcheted up the already tense political atmosphere. However, even given much wiser leaders the dissolution of communist authority in Georgia was always bound to be particularly difficult. The establishment of three autonomous entities on the territory of one republic (there were none in many less ethnically homogeneous republics), with the concomitant emergence of élites and institutions which could provide rival foci for the articulation of nationalist aspirations, actually turned out not to be the most serious impediment to the realisation of Georgian independence. Rather, it was divisions amongst Georgians themselves that were the result of seven decades of rule from Moscow to which Georgian society had adapted but never accepted.

Notes

1. On 1 January 1989 there were 337,245 Georgian members of the CPSU, which was 8.47 per cent of the total number of Georgians living in the Soviet Union. At the same time the equivalent figure for Russians was 7.87 per cent and for Azerbaijanis, 5.41 per cent. *Vestnik statistiki*, no. 10, 1990; *Izvestiia TsK KPSS*, no. 2, 1989.
2. Ludmilla Alexeyeva, *Soviet Dissent. Contemporary Movements for National, Religious, and Human Rights*, Connecticut, 1985, pp. 106–20.
3. R. Gachechelidze, *Sakartvelos sotsialuri atlasi*, Tbilisi, 1989, pp. 42–5.
4. *Sovetskaia Abkhazia*, 24 March 1989.
5. See below.
6. *Eastern Europe Newsletter*, 22 March 1989, p. 6; *Independent*, 27 February 1989.
7. *Report on the USSR*, 3 November 1989, p. 26; *Independent*, 8 April 1989; *Guardian*, 10 April 1989; *The Times*, 10 April 1989.
8. *Report on the USSR*, 3 November 1989, p. 26.
9. *Eastern Europe Newsletter*, 19 April 1989, p. 3; *Report on the USSR*, 11 August 1989, pp. 31–2.
10. Gumabaridze was widely regarded as a close associate of Shevardnadze. In early December 1988, before he was appointed first secretary, he had been appointed head of the Georgian KGB. His subsequent political tactics bear all the hallmarks of his pedigree. *Summary of World Broadcasts*, 22 December 1988. Adleiba, the Abkhazian first secretary, was sacked by Patiashvili on 6 April 1989. This and the subsequent sackings, which included ethnic Georgians, were for their failure to maintain control of events. *Literaturnaia Gazeta*, 26 July 1989.
11. *Izvestiia*, 29 October 1989.
12. Interview with Irakli Kakabadze, conducted by the author, 6 March 1990.
13. Interview with Vazha Mtavrishvili, conducted by the author, 12 March 1990.
14. 57 per cent of the seats were uncontested and in none of these did the GCP candidate receive less than 50 per cent of the vote. The Georgian government claimed that there was a 97 per cent turn-out. *Eastern Europe Newsletter*, 19 April 1989, p. 2; *Independent*, 16 March 1989.
15. *Demokratiuli archevani sakartvelostvis* ('DAS-i'), Tbilisi, 1990, pp. 3–5.
16. Interview with Kakha Chitaia, conducted by the author, 9 March 1990.
17. Conversation with Irakli Chubinishvili, conducted by the author, May 1991.
18. Interview with Muchaidze, conducted by the author, 10 March 1990.
19. Interviews with Tchanturia and Gamsakhurdia, conducted by the author, 30 March 1990 and 24 June 1990.
20. Interview with Muchaidze, conducted by the author, 10 March 1990.
21. Interview with Vakho Bakhtadze, conducted by the author, 25 October 1990.

22. See below.
23. Meeting of the National Forum Coordinating Centre, attended by the author, 26 June 1990. The Central Electoral Commission for the Supreme Soviet elections distributed 7.5 million roubles to registered parties.
24. Interview with Tchanturia, conducted by the author, 30 March 1990.
25. R. G. Gachechelidze, 'Mnogopartiinye vybory v Gruzii', in *Sotsiologicheskie issledovaniia*, no. 5, 1991, pp. 53–4.
26. This account is taken from notes taken by the author at the conference.
27. *Zaria Vostoka*, 21 March 1990.
28. It is striking that the leaders of all these groups which were regarded as Gamsakhurdia's closest collaborators in the spring of 1990 had become some of his bitterest opponents by the autumn of 1991.
29. Ioseliani had been convicted in his youth for a violent robbery in Leningrad but had returned to Tbilisi after his release to pursue a literary career.
30. *Georgian Film* was generally regarded as supporting the National Forum, and *Young Iberian*, formerly the Komsomol paper *Young Communist*, as supporting the Round Table.
31. *Zaria Vostoka*, 17 April 1990, 21 April 1990 and 24 April 1990.
32. Elizabeth Fuller, *Report on the USSR*, 9 November 1990, p. 19.
33. *Ekspress khronika*, 12 June 1990.
34. *Tbilisi*, 11 June 1990; *Report on the USSR*, 29 June 1990, p. 33.
35. *Ekspress khronika*, 12 June 1990.
36. Interview with Gamsakhurdia, conducted by the author, 24 June 1990.
37. Interview with Rezo Shavishvili, conducted by the author, 2 November 1990; *Sakartvelos sabtchota sotsialisturi respublikis kanoni*, Tbilisi, 1990. The practical significance of this stipulation was less than it might appear since both these organisations had been intending to boycott the March elections. Both organisations decided not to participate in elections to the National Congress, although strong efforts were made to persuade them, and both supported declarations of sovereignty issued by their respective regions in the summer indicating that they were not preparing to participate in any Georgian elections.
38. He may have been encouraged to make a stand when he attended the 28th Congress of the CPSU, held in Moscow in July.
39. *Argumenty i fakty*, no. 35, 1990; *Report on the USSR*, no. 31, 1990, p. 34.
40. Rezo Shavishvili, the leader of DAS-i, which had drawn up the law for election to the National Congress, told the author that the electors to the National Congress should have been asked two questions, at the top of the ballot paper, to ensure that they knew what they were voting for. This was not done. Interview with Rezo Shavishvili, conducted by the author, 2 November 1990.
41. Interview with Berishvili, conducted by the author, 30 October 1990.
42. Poll conducted by the Sociological Laboratory of Tbilisi University in early November 1990.
43. *Tbilisi*, 23 October 1990.
44. The bloc Conciliation, Peace and Renewal, which had also had its registration withdrawn, was successfully reinstated.
45. On the eve of the elections rumours circulated that numbers of ballot papers had gone missing and one person even heard that children had been seen using them as paper darts. As a result it was decided that the president of electoral commissions should endorse all ballot papers with his signature.

46. The Communist Party had wanted the Georgian Council of Ministers to carry out registration. Interview with Tedo Paatashvili, conducted by the author, 25 October 1990.
47. Each party was allowed to spend another four times the amount it received from the Central Electoral Commission from its own resources.
48. Berishvili complained that the election campaign had been too short and that in some areas the electoral commissions were dominated by the Round Table.
49. Press conference of the Central Electoral Commission at the Ajaria Hotel, 2 November 1990.
50. Interview with US and Finnish observers, conducted by the author, 29 October 1990. The author heard reports from Azerbaijanis, 29 October 1990, in the Marneuli district that they had been threatened with deportation if they did not vote for the Communist Party.
51. *The Times*, 19 February 1991.
52. *Independent*, 30 January 1991, 31 January 1991.
53. *Eastern Europe Newsletter*, 15 April 1991.
54. The main event of the campaign concerned the beating-up of Russian body-guards hired by Advadze.
55. Elected assemblies were supposed to provide some local accountability.
56. *Guardian*, 24 August 1991.
57. He was replaced by a leading figure from the Georgian Academy of Sciences, Besarion Gugushvili.
58. *Independent*, 6 September 1991.
59. *Guardian*, 11 September 1991.
60. Subsequently, these deputies and their supporters formed a new oppositional grouping called Charter-91.
61. This account was put together mainly as a result of the author's own observations and conversations made in Tbilisi in September and October 1991.
62. *Eastern Europe Newsletter*, 4 November 1991.
63. *The Times*, 6 January 1992.

7 Popular movements in Estonia
Geoffrey A. Hosking

Of all regions of the Soviet Union, it was natural that the Baltic republics should become the first testing grounds for a more pluralist style of politics. They had been annexed relatively late—only in 1940—after twenty years with some experience of parliamentary democracy, albeit imperfect and curtailed. That democracy had itself grown on quite well-prepared soil, especially in Estonia and Latvia, where two peasant peoples had imbibed German traditions of administrative competence and civic concern, as exemplified by the Baltic nobles. The Lutheran faith, which had come to them from the same source, inspired a committed approach to citizenship along with a spirit of obedience to the legally vested authorities. One testimony to their readiness for democracy is the remarkably high level of literacy which obtained among both people by the end of the nineteenth century: in Estonia, for example, 96 per cent of the population could read, and 75 per cent could both read and write.[1]

The Lithuanians were in rather a different position. Their culture was Polish and Catholic, not German and Lutheran, and they were not simply a peasant people: they had had their own aristocracy in the middle ages (since absorbed into the Polish), and indeed their own kingdom, at one time territorially the largest in Europe. Furthermore, since 1945 they had received fewer immigrants than their Baltic neighbours. They had thus inherited from their past a stronger sense of historical pride and a more homogeneous national identity. What this meant in the post-1985 period was that the Lithuanians were slower than their neighbours to generate an autonomous political culture, but that, once they did so, they asserted it in less restrained, more flamboyant style.

In all three republics, integration into the Soviet Union had brought with it a dramatic and numbing loss of control over national life. Systematic large-scale deportations removed from the homeland members of non-communist political parties, landowners, businessmen, clergy, intellectuals and artists—in fact anyone who might act as a focus for resistance, or might try to sustain the national culture. Thereafter large factories and mines were built, including huge oil-shale mines in Estonia and a nuclear power station billed as the world's largest in Lithuania, producing for all-Union rather than Baltic needs: all of these plants threatened the environment and imported their work-force largely from Russia and Ukraine. The proportion of the indigenous population fell to 60 per cent in Estonia and barely over half in Latvia. Russian increasingly became the language of public life and education, since most educated locals could speak and understand it, whilst few immigrants were able to return the compliment.[2]

The result was what might be called in socio-psychological terms a kind of 'ethnic depression'. As tiny nations in a huge empire, without external support and facing a regime which permitted no organised opposition, the Estonians, Latvians and Lithuanians seemed to accept their lot passively, at least after the end of guerrilla resistance in the early 1950s. There were, it is true, occasional demonstrations of protest (such as followed the self-immolation of Roman Kalanta in Kaunas in 1972) and the odd open letter was smuggled out, but few outside observers thought they represented more than the reaction of a limited circle of intellectuals. As later became clear (and should have been apparent at the time), these manifestations of dissent actually gave vent to the suppressed feelings of whole peoples who could see their languages, their cultures, their customs and their natural environment gradually being undermined or degraded until the question arose whether they could go on surviving as nations at all.

In all three republics, as elsewhere in the Soviet Union, it was scholars and creative artists who first took advantage of the new regime of glasnost, both because they enjoyed a situation of modest privilege and because they were professionally especially sensitive to the dangers posed to their nations.[3] In Latvia, for example, in the autumn of 1986 the so-called Club for the Defence of the Environment circulated a petition calling for the abandonment of plans for a hydro-electric power station on the Daugava River which would have drowned several villages and a good deal of arable land. Coming just after the defeat of the northern rivers diversion project in Moscow, it attracted some 30,000 signatures and the support of the republican government, and under this pressure Gosplan dropped the scheme.[4]

In Estonia the first landmark in the move towards creation of a national liberation movement was an open letter signed by a group of scientists in March 1986: it called attention to the pollution of water by oil-shale mining in the north-east and by leaks from the nuclear submarine base at Paldiski, and also warned of further massive environmental degradation to be caused by planned open-cast phosphate extraction. Cautious reference to these hazards had already been permitted in the press, but the scientists added another, more specifically ethnic dimension to their concern: that large-scale industrial and mining projects tended to bring thousands of immigrants, mainly Russians, into the republic, disturbing the ethnic balance and threatening to make the Estonians a minority in their own homeland. In this connection they pointed particularly to the plan to build a huge oil terminal at Muuga Bay, near Tallinn, and a new town with a population of 20,000 near Rakvere in the north-east.[5]

The Estonian Writers' Union Congress of April 1986 was even bolder (by a curious coincidence it ended on the day of the Chernobyl' explosion). Accounts published at the time show it to have been one of a number of republican writers' congresses then being held, at which censorship and bureaucratic controls over literature were attacked for the first time in public. Only later did it come out that this congress had gone even further and raised the whole question of ethnic and linguistic discrimination. The novelists Mats Traat and Teet Kallas complained that Russian was gradually replacing Estonian as the language of public life, and that Russian-language schools made no more than nominal efforts to teach Estonian. Still more daring, Ingo Normet asked why there was complete silence about the murder and deportation of intellectuals in 1941.[6]

The first open public protests arose from the phosphate-mining project, which combined a number of elements calculated to arouse national feeling. It promised to bring up to 100,000 new immigrants into the republic; it also signalled environmental damage compounded by imperial control, for, being under the control of an all-Union Ministry, it was not subject to the republic's Environmental Protection Act. It was thus an apt target for the first modest public manifestation of discontent. Students at Tartu University carried banners protesting against the phosphate mining at their May Day demonstration of 1987, and this proved to be the initial impetus for the formation of a Green Movement.[7]

Eventually Moscow decided to postpone the project indefinitely, but not before the ripples from it had begun to stimulate public protest about much more sensitive issues underlying the Soviet domination of Estonia. On 23 August 1987, anniversary of the Nazi–Soviet Pact of 1939, a crowd estimated at between 2,000 and 7,000 gathered in the Hirvepark in Tallinn and demanded the publication of the secret protocols of the pact, which had in effect condemned Estonia to Soviet occupation. The meeting was organised by ex-dissenters recently released from prison, but the degree of public support it attracted was remarkable at a time when official victimisation still seemed likely. In the event, treatment of the demonstration in the official press was surprisingly forbearing—a first indication, perhaps, that the Estonian Communist Party leadership might be starting to rethink its strategy.[8] The success of this meeting provided the impetus for the setting up of the Estonian Group for the Publication of the Molotov–Ribbentrop Pact (MRP-AEG).

The growing national pride evident in the capital city was also becoming manifest in the provinces of Estonia. By the end of 1987 an Estonian Heritage Society had been formed. This was a genuine grass-roots movement which had gathered momentum during the year with the formation of small clubs in a number of provincial towns. Its first nation-wide project was the collection of ordinary people's testimony, both written and oral, and of documents and diaries, especially as they reflected people's lives after the Soviet occupation of 1940. The society also set about restoring monuments, especially to the heroes and events of the liberation war of 1918–20, many of which had been destroyed by the Soviets.[9]

Inevitably the work of the Heritage Society soon became politicised, for it was the first mass movement to take up the Estonian national cause. Soon it was agitating together with MRP-AEG for the restoration of the blue-black-white national flag. This agitation merged with the revival of Estonian folksong, also encouraged by the Heritage Society, to produce the main symbolic components of the 'singing revolution' of the following year, first seen on display in Tartu, at a Festival of the Estonian Heritage, on 14–17 April 1988, an event which attracted huge crowds and gave the nation a new sense of self-confidence.[10]

By this time, practical proposals were being discussed to give institutional form to this self-confidence. After the June 1987 Central Committee Plenum of the CPSU, a group of Estonian economists had got together to devise a way in which its recommendation of strengthening the economic powers of local soviets could be implemented. The result, published by four economists in September (the foreign affairs commentators Siim Kallas and Tiit Made, the sociologist Mikk Titma and Edgar Savisaar, an economist from the State Planning Committee), went far beyond that brief: it was actually a proposal for the full economic autonomy of the Estonian republic, and well typified the way in which modest Gorbachevian reform proposals were being radicalised as a result of the strength of public opinion.

The central point of the proposal was that all economic activity in Estonia should be regulated by the authorities of the republic in the interests of its citizens and with regard for the well-being of the environment. It should be a market economy based on a convertible rouble: economic decision-making would be carried out at the level of the individual enterprise and would be based on the signals transmitted by the market, not on the orders of any planning authority.[11]

This concept was soon dubbed IME, which is short for Economically Self-Governing Estonia, but is also by coincidence the Estonian word for 'miracle'. It evoked a very lively response, and was crucial to the development of an Estonian national liberation movement, since it went beyond declarations of principle and offered a practical way of implementing self-determination in the vital field of economics. It was the first step towards generating a full political programme for Estonian sovereignty.

The process was taken a stage further with a joint meeting of leaders of the Estonian cultural unions on 1–2 April 1988. They dispatched two sets of resolutions, one to the forthcoming extraordinary conference of the CPSU, and another to the Estonian Supreme Soviet and leaders of the Estonian Communist Party.

Both resolutions placed the main responsibility for the degraded state of Estonia on the overbearing exercise of power by Moscow:

An all-powerful bureaucracy manifests itself above all in the form of arbitrary actions by all-Union Ministries, which ignore local economic, ecological and socio-cultural interests and needs. This results in an unprofitable economy, uncontrolled migration, increased risk of an ecological catastrophe, and failure to satisfy the population's social and cultural needs.

To provide protection against such abuses, the document proposed the concept of republican citizenship, delineating citizens' rights and responsibilities in relation both to their own republic and to the Union as a whole, and ensuring the republics themselves a proper input into decision-making at the centre. To make possible the full exercise of these rights and responsibilities, secrecy should be eliminated, genuinely free elections guaranteed, and each republic should be given the right to run its own economy and to determine its own cultural and educational policies.[12]

The resolution which the cultural unions presented to the Estonian Supreme Soviet and Communist Party was much more specific and laid much of the blame for current disorders on the Estonian leaders themselves. The very existence of the Estonian nation, it warned, was in jeopardy:

It is self-evident that the ESSR leadership must consider its most important priority the continued existence of the Estonian nation and its need for development . . . From that point of view the joint meeting declares its dissatisfaction with the activities of the ECP Central Committee First Secretary, Karl Vaino, and the Chairman of the ESSR Council of Ministers, Bruno Saul.[13]

By the spring of 1988, then, scholars and artists were taking the lead both in criticising the current leadership and in suggesting what a self-governing Estonia might look like, while a mass movement was beginning to emerge to lend it political weight. What gave these developments decisive significance, however, was the decision of some members of the party-state apparatus to join this emerging consensus. The process began with the preparations for the 19th Conference of the Soviet Communist Party in summer 1988.

When it became apparent that Vaino was behaving in traditional apparatchik style by pushing through his own thirty-two nominees for the thirty-two Estonian places at the conference, a storm of indignation broke out, not only among party members. On 13 April 1988 Edgar Savisaar, a senior planning official and himself a leading communist, appeared on television and appealed for the formation of a mass movement to press from below for the democratisation of party and state decreed from above: he proposed the name of Popular Front for the Support of Perestroika.

The concept of the Popular Front had recently been outlined by Boris Kurashvili of the Institute of State and Law of the Soviet Academy of Sciences. He had pointed out that in a one-party system the competence and probity of the ruling apparatus tends to degenerate unless there is constant monitoring and challenging from what he termed a 'social opposition'. He had proposed the establishment of 'Popular Fronts' to constitute such an opposition, to check on the work of administrators, to criticise legislative drafts and formulate alternatives, and to keep data banks on which the public could draw for informed discussion and continuous input into the political process.[14]

Savisaar's appeal evoked a widespread and immediate response, though, as we shall see, the results did not quite match Kurashvili's vision. Initiative groups and support groups began to spring up in towns all over the republic—2,000–3,000 members were registered in the first few days in Tartu alone.[15] At this stage the generally shared hostility to Vaino's leadership, together with the indignation at the damage inflicted by the command economy, combined to give the initiative groups' slogans and demands irresistible impetus. Even entrenched party officials found it difficult to oppose them, and the reformists in the leadership hastened to embrace them, seeing in them an opportunity to acquire a popular base for their own authority such as had never previously existed.

The result was a series of mass meetings in Tallinn in June, culminating on 17 June with a rally of 150,000 called by the Popular Front to discuss the Estonian Communist Party's platform to the 19th Conference and also its list of delegates to be sent there. In anticipation, the Central Committee of the ECP hurriedly dismissed Vaino, so that the meeting turned into a celebration, complete with folksongs and the blue-black-white flag.[16] His replacement, Vaino Väljas, was a native Estonian speaker, unlike his predecessor, and moved smartly to cement an alliance with the Popular Front.

The Estonian delegates to the 19th Party Conference, headed by Väljas, were sent off as national heroes by a rally of a hundred thousand at the huge 'Singing Field' stadium outside Tallinn, everyone again singing folksongs and waving the national flag. This was the culmination of the so-called 'singing revolution'. The conference delegates took with them a programme which was heavily influenced by the ideas of the Popular Front. They were proposing a new 'union agreement' to ensure that the USSR became a genuine 'union of sovereign republics of equal rights', each with its own citizenship and official language, each owning its own natural resources and with the right to protect or develop them free from outside interference, and each possessing the right to representation in foreign countries and international organisations.[17] By espousing such demands so boldly, the Estonian Communist Party had made itself briefly the spokesman for popular feeling in the republic.

In Latvia a Popular Front emerged in broadly similar fashion, except that public demonstrations played a more important role at an earlier stage. The first was held as early as 14 June 1987, on Riga's Liberty Square, to commemorate those deported by Stalin on the same date in 1941. Its principal organisers were a group called Helsinki-86, originally formed by workers in Liepaja concerned about human rights violations in their country. The demonstration was quite well attended, to many people's surprise was not forcibly dispersed, and proved to be the first in a series of 'calendar demonstrations' reviving the memory of key dates in Latvia's recent past. By March 1988 they had begun to display the national flag. On 1–2 June 1988, a meeting of the leaders of the Latvian creative unions, like their Estonian counterparts two months earlier, put forward a practical programme for moving towards home rule, which shortly afterwards became in essentials the programme of the Popular Front, and precipitated the fall of the Communist Party first secretary, Boris Pugo.[18]

In Lithuania, since demographic pressure was less threatening, ethnic sentiment was somewhat slower to manifest itself publicly, and the Communist Party was able for longer to resist the creation of a Popular Front. Sajudis (or 'movement', the name adopted by the Lithuanian Popular Front) had its origin in a meeting of scholars at the Lithuanian Academy of Sciences in May 1988, and gathered strength during the summer with mass meetings and demonstrations on ecological matters, on the Nazi–Soviet Pact, on the status of the language and the release of political prisoners. Police were still dispersing some of these meetings as late as September 1988. In October, however, the new Communist Party first secretary, Algirdas Brazauskas, came in pledged to work with Sajudis.[19]

By the time the Estonian Popular Front held its founding congress in October, then, all three republics had a similar movement moving towards cooperation with the local Communist Party leadership. At a central committee plenum of the Estonian party held in September, Väljas made a speech which was relayed live on television and confirmed his popularity. He welcomed the appearance of the Popular Front, speaking of it in terms which suggested that the Communist Party now held virtually identical views:

In a situation where the leadership of the Estonian Communist Party was losing the people's confidence, in April this year on the initiative of Communists a new movement emerged: the Popular Front in Support of Perestroika. From the very outset the Front showed itself to be an active force in public life . . . It compels all party and state officials to take notice of public opinion, and helps to clean up the political life of society.

In the one-party system which has taken shape in our country, we need in party and society, as M. S. Gorbachev said at the 19th party conference, a permanent mechanism for comparing and contrasting opinions, for criticism and self-criticism.

Thus far, this was almost universally accepted in the Estonian Republic, but the next part of his speech was more controversial. The Estonian SSR, he asserted, was 'a sovereign national republic, and the Estonians are the basic nation of Soviet Estonia'.[20]

The idea that the primary aim of the proposed reforms should be not so much a law-based state as the survival of the Estonian people had been inherent in the movement right from the beginning and one of its principal sources of impetus, very understandable among a people who had felt their language, culture, natural environment and way of life gradually being undermined and squeezed out by the increasing pressure of immigration, industrial development and centralised control. Marju Lauristin, one of the leaders of the Popular Front, expressed it in dramatic terms: 'The whole people were confronted by Hamlet's question: to be or not to be? There could only be one answer: to be. Then we had to discuss soberly how we should achieve this.'[21]

The founding congress of the Popular Front, held in Tallinn on 1–2 October 1988, showed how varied were the backgrounds of its members: 28 per cent were members of the Communist Party, 19 per cent were from the Estonian Heritage Society, 10 per cent from the Greens, and there were even a few from the MRP-AEG, whose stance was theoretically incompatible with the 'collaborationist' position of the Front.[22] The question of the survival of the Estonian people troubled most of them. Some talked of extending citizenship in the republic only to those who had lived there a certain number of years and could speak Estonian. A few speakers referred to the non-Estonian—and above all Russian—inhabitants of the republic as 'migrants', and talked of schemes through which some of them might be repatriated. Academician Viktor Pal'm warned of the low cultural level of some Estonian 'samostiiniki' (zealots of independence) who 'can only express their national feeling by insulting people of other nationalities'.[23]

All this was not the official policy of the Popular Front, but it was not accidental either. It articulated a mood of ethnic solidarity which had been perhaps the principal emotional cement of the new movement, not only in Estonia but in the other Baltic republics, and elsewhere in the Soviet Union too. The absence of an obvious analogous ethnic target goes some way towards explaining the failure to establish an equivalent Popular Front in Russia. So although the leaders of the Estonian Popular Front wished to emphasise other matters—human rights, a law-based state, economic autonomy, and so on— they found themselves compelled to appeal to ethnic sentiment as well. Boris Kurashvili, the originator of the Popular Front concept, specifically warned against this tendency in an interview for a newspaper.[24]

The actual programme passed at the congress was studiedly moderate. The aim of the Front, it proclaimed, was 'the all-round reconstruction of socialist society on the principles of democracy and humanism and the implementation of the people's will through elected representative organs'. Estonia was to ensure this by claiming 'sovereignty' within the USSR, that is, 'the clearly acknowledged priority of the republic over the Union as a whole'. This sovereignty was to be secured by the recognition of the language of the indigenous people as the official one, by protecting national emblems, and by legalising the concept of citizenship of the republic (rather than of the Union). The economy was to be 'decolonised' and developed in an ecologically responsible manner, to the benefit of the population of the republic. The programme's only element of ethnic discrimination was contained in the stipulation that the Estonians had the right to remain the basic nation of the republic, and therefore to restrict any further growth of the non-Estonian proportion of the population. The congress specifically endorsed the principles proclaimed by the 27th CPSU Congress and the 19th Party Conference and declared readiness to work with the communists to fulfil the promise of 'all power to the soviets'.[25]

No sooner had this agreement between the Popular Front and the ECP been concluded than it was threatened by Gorbachev's attempt to revise the Soviet constitution in such a way as to allow the Union republics more autonomy but abolish their right to secede. The Estonian Supreme Soviet on 16 November 1988 reacted by declaring the republic's 'sovereignty' in the sense in which that was understood by the Front. The vague concept of 'sovereignty' defined the area where the democratic intelligentsia and the apparatchiks felt they could best work together in defiance of Moscow: to the former it meant the realisation of their dreams of national self-determination, to the latter it meant power more real than the pale shadow of it which Moscow had hitherto allowed them. In this respect Estonia pioneered the path which all the Union republics later took. But at this stage Moscow was not having it: a few days later a commission of the USSR Supreme Soviet pronounced the declaration to be unconstitutional.[26] This rejection undermined the very foundation of the cooperation of the Popular Front with the Communist Party and opened the way for the clash of more one-sided forces which took place the following year.

On one side of this clash was Interdvizhenie, or the Internationalist Movement, largely composed of non-Estonians reacting against being treated as 'migrants' and reaffirming their citizenship of the USSR; on the other side was the 'congress' movement, consisting of those Estonians who refused to compromise in any way with Soviet institutions.

Quite a number of Russians and other non-Estonians had participated in the formative stages of the Popular Front, but felt increasingly alienated by what they saw as national animus directed against them. They were especially worried by the restrictions on immigration and by proposals raised at the Popular Front congress (though not passed, at least for the time being) to make Estonian the official language of the republic, and to limit Estonian citizenship to the inhabitants of 1940 and their descendants, thus relegating the great majority of non-Estonians to the status of second-class citizens in the place where some of them had lived all their lives. They could imagine themselves being systematically discriminated against in employment, housing and education.

Once it became apparent that the Estonian Communist Party was taking a line very close to that of the Popular Front, some non-Estonians decided that it was necessary to create a distinct political movement which would reflect their interests.[27] As Evgenii Kogan (a deputy in the USSR Supreme Soviet) put it:

We had got used to relying on our party activists and leaders, we expected and believed that they would put a stop to extremist statements and would decisively denounce nationalist tendencies—in fact simply defend our dignity. After all, we too are part of the people of Soviet Estonia.[28]

The first organisation committed to resisting Estonianisation was the United Council of Work Collectives (OSTK), which was formed in the summer of 1988 among the management and work-force of the mines, transport depots and big all-Union factories of Tallinn and the north-east. This was an economic rather than an ethnic movement and, ironically, it originated in the campaign to create the Popular Front. Its initiator was the Council of Workers' Collectives in the huge *Dvigatel'* motor factory in Tallinn, which published an open letter in June 1988 suggesting that the basic unit of the Popular Front should be not *ad hoc* initiative groups, but the working collectives of enterprises, offices and institutions. They argued that such a structure would make it easier to disseminate the Front's ideas among the working masses. They also recommended that the Front should concentrate more on economic questions, such as defending the population from price rises, monitoring the activities of the new cooperatives, and combating the 'black economy'.[29]

These aspirations were actually very different from those which animated the Popular Front at the time, and revealed the distinct situation of the workers, mostly Russian, concentrated in large enterprises and concerned for the moment mainly with economic problems. The first activities of OSTK were largely economic: defending workers against dismissal, seeking housing for those discriminated against (as they saw it) by the local authorities, organising deliveries of foodstuffs at low prices. They even set up a Russian choir and drama group to stimulate awareness of Russian culture.[30] It soon became apparent, though, that pursuing these economic aims had political implications.

The founding congress of OSTK was held in December 1988, shortly after the Estonian Supreme Soviet had declared sovereignty, and thus in a tense political atmosphere. In the last few days before it opened, there was an attempt at ethnic conciliation: a large number of working collectives of enterprises in medium and light industry, mostly ethnic Estonian, applied to join it. OSTK decided that the premises booked for their congress were too small to accommodate so many newcomers, but suggested that the latter should hold their meeting in parallel elsewhere: if each meeting adopted preliminary versions of its programme and statutes, they could be coordinated at a joint congress later. In the event, however, the differences proved to be too great: the preliminary programme put forward by OSTK was rejected unanimously by their counterparts. The movement of working collectives was thus split irrevocably into Russian and Estonian compartments: the Estonians set up their own organisation, STKE, the Council of Workers' Collectives of Estonia.[13]

The founding congress of Interdvizhenie, as the political spearhead of the non-Estonians, was held in March 1989. It charged the Estonian Communist Party with having permitted the emergence of 'dual power' in the republic: 'Soviet power of the workers and Popular Front power of the nationalists.' It complained of the humiliation of the Soviet flag, of the 'economic separatism' of the IME programme, and of the language and citizenship laws, which 'violated the constitutional principle of equality of citizens'. Finally the congress warned that, if discrimination against the Russian-language population of the republic continued, then Interdvizhenie would 'reserve the right to support the idea of setting up an autonomous republic in north-eastern Estonia in accordance with the right to self-determination'.

In similar manner, in Latvia, non-Latvians alienated by the first congress of the Latvian Popular Front created the Latvian Internationalist Working People's Front (*Interfront*) to combat the tendency to ethnic exclusivity as reflected in the proposals coming forward in the Popular Front on language, immigration and citizenship laws. In Lithuania, Russians and Poles met in Vilnius to form Unity.[32]

In Estonia the political fears of Interdvizhenie were sharply accentuated by the sovereignty declaration of November 1988, by the passage in January 1989 of a lawmaking Estonian the official language of the republic, and in August of a new electoral law. In the case of the language law a distinction must be made between the text of the law and its apprehensive reception among the non-Estonians, who imagined themselves being summarily dismissed from jobs or expelled from educational institutions unless they could speak fluent Estonian. In the case of the electoral law, the provisions themselves were unambiguously discriminatory: inhabitants of the republic were deprived of the vote if they had not lived on the territory of their soviet for at least two years, or in the Estonian SSR for at least five.[33]

Workers in all-Union enterprises, no doubt encouraged by the recent coal-miners' strikes elsewhere in the Soviet Union, decided to take action against the electoral law. In Tallinn, in the north-eastern towns of Sillamäe and Kohtla-Järve, and on the railways, workers laid down their tools. Freight piled up unloaded, blocking the tracks and impeding communications throughout the republic. These were the first ever strikes in the Soviet Union to raise directly political demands, which soon escalated beyond repeal of the electoral law to embrace more generalised grievances. The republican strike committee accused the Estonian leadership of taking over the 'reactionary ideology of the priority of one nation' from the Popular Front and of bringing about 'the complete destruction of everything which has been achieved in Estonia in the years of Soviet rule and turning the republic into a *petit-bourgeois* state on the model of 1920–40'.[34]

The Presidium of the USSR Supreme Soviet pronounced the electoral law unconstitutional, and thereby raised the question of Estonia's sovereignty in stark form. Meanwhile the strike committee, together with OSTK and Interdvizhenie, held negotiations with the government and Supreme Soviet, while delegates of the USSR Soviet of Nationalities acted as intermediaries. In the end, the Estonian government decided not to challenge both the USSR and its own non-Estonian subjects, and recommended to the Estonian Supreme Soviet that the electoral law be reconsidered. In response the latter suspended the residence requirement until a law should be passed defining the require-ments for Estonian citizenship.[35] In this way, the immediate crisis was smoothed over, but the question of principle remained open for future conflict. It was to remain open a long time, for the problem of citizenship proved extremely difficult to deal with.

A few months later Interdvizhenie, having failed to achieve its aims by strikes, presented a direct constitutional challenge to the Estonian Supreme Soviet. In March 1990 some 170 elected soviet deputies from local, regional and republican levels in the north-east convened in Kohtla-Järve to form the Interregional Council of People's Deputies. They announced that they intended to remain faithful to the Soviet Union: to this end they would monitor laws passed by the Estonian Supreme Soviet, and implement only those which conformed to the Soviet constitution. When Gorbachev announced plans for a new Union treaty, they declared that they would sign it, whatever the rest of Estonia did, and if necessary would then claim the status of autonomous republic for north-eastern Estonia.[36]

One is tempted to compare Interdvizhenie to the Ulster Unionists in British politics, with their strong following among Protestants and their claim of separate status for Northern Ireland when the rest of the country left the United Kingdom. Yet it cannot be said that the Interdvizhenie had the same success in rallying all non-Estonians to its cause. According to one estimate, it enjoyed the support of no more than one-third of non-Estonians, and, even in its heartlands, the all-Union enterprises, its members tended to be drawn from the white-collar staff rather than from the workers.[37] Most Estonians suspected it of being artificially created by the apparatus of the CPSU and by the all-Union industrial ministries. They referred to it contemptuously as 'Imperdvizhenie'. Many Russians preferred the prospect of a democratic and prosperous Estonia to what they suspected would be an authoritarian and poverty-stricken Russia. The referendum of March 1991 showed that perhaps 30–40 per cent of non-Estonians took this view. This was a priceless political asset for proponents of Estonian independence, though one which they only gradually learned to cultivate.

Moscow's rejection of Estonian sovereignty gave fresh impetus to those within the Estonian national liberation movement who wanted to proceed without any compromise, either with the Communist Party or with the Soviet Union. In the summer of 1988 the full text of the Nazi–Soviet Pact had at last been published in a daily newspaper. This finally accomplished the purpose for which the MRP-AEG had been set up, and it was disbanded, only to be immediately reconstituted as the Estonian National Independence Party, whose initiative committee had existed since January, and whose founding congress was held in August. This was the first political organisation in Estonia to set itself up in open opposition to the Communist Party, with secession from the Soviet Union its main aim. Its kernel consisted of former dissidents of the 1970s and early 1980s: Mart Niklus, Tunne Kelam, Enn Tarto, Lagle Parek, some of whom had only just been released from labour camp.[38]

In February 1989 the ENIP, together with the Heritage Society and the Estonian Christian Union, called on the population to boycott the elections to the Congress of People's Deputies of the USSR, and to form instead 'citizens' committees', rather like the 'committees of correspondence' which prepared the American revolution in the 1770s, to begin the task of registering all citizens of the pre-1940 republic, together with their descendants. The idea was to proceed from the premise that Estonia had never legally been part of the Soviet Union, having been illegally annexed under the Nazi–Soviet Pact, and that therefore its people should not use Soviet institutions to assert the republic's sovereignty, but should simply reconstitute the overthrown pre-1940 republic. Only registered citizens would have the right to take part in elections: they would elect a new Estonian Congress, which would automatically become the country's legitimate legislature and would appoint a government to re-establish *de facto* independence and to negotiate with Moscow about the removal of military bases.[39]

The ENIP defined the concept of 'Estonian citizen' quite restrictively. Post-1940 immigrants and their descendants could apply for citizenship, but would receive it only if they could demonstrate a reasonable knowledge of the Estonian language and history, avowed loyalty to the Estonian constitution, and renounced citizenship of any other state—usually the USSR. Those who were not full citizens would receive a guarantee of their civil rights, but would not be entitled to vote in elections, still less to become parliamentary deputies or officials.[40] The ENIP programme also called for the restoration of the borders laid down by the Tartu Peace Treaty of 1920 (which would include a section of Pskov oblast' in the RSFSR), an end to immigration from the USSR, the banning of the CPSU as the agency of a foreign power, and the investigation, arrest and trial of those responsible for the crimes committed by the occupation forces.[41]

If, then, the Popular Front represented the 'Herodians', willing to compromise with the empire in order to weaken its dominion, the Estonian Congress movement were the 'zealots', uncompromising in their rejection of all its works. In Latvia likewise the relative moderation of the Latvian Popular Front left scope for a congress movement dedicated to the resurrection of the legal forms of the pre-1940 republic. In Lithuania, by contrast, Sajudis moved swiftly to a total rejection of the Union, and thus absorbed the potential 'zealots'.

In the spring of 1989 most Estonians were still inclined to believe that the 'Herodians' were more likely to achieve their objective. In the election to the USSR Congress of People's Deputies in March 1989, the Popular Front scored a notable triumph. Rejecting the argument that it was absurd to send deputies to the 'parliament of a neighbouring country', the Front urged participation in the election. As an unregistered organisation (till just before the election), it was unable officially to nominate candidates, but it used the mass media to make clear which ones it endorsed. Many of these were tacitly approved by the Estonian Communist Party too. Some 95 per cent of Estonians and 75 per cent of non-Estonians took part in the elections, and candidates backed by the Front won twenty-seven out of the thirty-six seats.[42]

This remarkable success should have cleared the way for cooperation between the Popular Front and the Estonian Communist Party in negotiating far-reaching autonomy for the republic, probably within the framework of a new Union Treaty, such as they were recommending at the time. However, neither Moscow on the one hand nor the Estonian Congress movement on the other was prepared to acquiesce in any such development. Moscow would not hear of a Union Treaty which would acknowledge the sovereignty of the republics. On 26 August 1989 the CPSU Central Committee issued a statement accusing 'nationalist and extremist groups' of 'alienating the Baltic republics from the rest of the country',[43] and in September the long-awaited plenum on the nationality question conceded very little to the republics. These disappointments were followed by the rush of events in Eastern Europe, where communism was largely swept away during the autumn of 1989. In December 1989, moreover, the USSR Congress of People's Deputies finally denounced the Nazi–Soviet Pact, removing the last trace of legitimacy from the Estonian SSR.[44] Suddenly everything seemed possible, and the Lithuanian Communist Party, fortified by its alliance with Sajudis, announced it was breaking with Moscow.

In this atmosphere the policies of the Estonian Congress movement no longer seemed quixotic. Registration of citizens proceeded apace during the winter, and by February 1990 the citizens' committees had some 850,000 names on their books, including more than 60,000 non-Estonians who had satisfied their criteria. At the beginning of March some 600,000 went to the polls to elect the Congress—which, if one disregards minors, suggests a participation rate no lower than that in the elections to the Congress of People's Deputies. More than 1,100 candidates stood in 464 constituencies, while a further thirty-five represented Estonians living abroad. Of those elected, 109 were non-party, 107 supported the Popular Front, 104 the Heritage Society, seventy the ENIP, thirty-nine the ECP, twelve the Estonian Council of Work Collectives, and eleven the Greens. After the election the headquarters of the citizens' committees was burgled, but the thieves did not find the ballot papers, which had been securely hidden.[45]

The Congress proclaimed itself 'the first democratically elected representative body of the citizens of the Republic of Estonia since 1940'. It demanded the withdrawal of 'occupation troops' and an end to the conscription of Estonian citizens into them. It also called for the restitution of state authority to a popularly elected constituent assembly within the Estonian borders agreed at the Tartu Peace Treaty, and appealed to the United Nations and to the CSCE member states to recognise and uphold the independence of Estonia.[45]

The cross-pressures from Moscow, backed by Interdvizhenie, and from the Estonian Congress, together with the demonstration effect from Eastern Europe and Lithuania, tore open the fragile compromise between the Popular Front and the Estonian Communist Party.

Like its counterparts in Latvia and Lithuania, the Estonian Communist Party was losing members rapidly and was on the verge of a split. Throughout 1989 Väljas's priority had been to prevent such a split, a more or less impossible task in the long run, since members of the party included supporters of Interdvizhenie on the one hand and of ENIP on the other. Under mounting pressure from its own members and from society at large, the leadership called an extraordinary party congress (the 20th), which was held in March 1990.

By the time this congress convened, not only had the Lithuanians declared their independence from the USSR, but the CPSU itself had renounced its 'leading role' and opened the way, in principle at least, for a multi-party system throughout the USSR. In Latvia and Lithuania, the cumulative weight of these developments made it impossible to prevent a split into nation-oriented and Union-oriented Communist Parties (the latter popularly known as the 'Communist Parties of the night'). In Estonia, however, this split was masked and delayed for a while.

At the 20th Congress, the ECP for the first time declared its support for full independence, and at the same time announced its own break away from the CPSU. In the past, its statement said, it had underestimated and denied the importance of statehood and of ensuring the preservation of the nation and of freedom, mainly because 'throughout its existence the ECP has not been an independent political force', but 'in essence a regional branch of the CPSU'. Väljas was made party chairman, and was replaced as first secretary by Enn-Arno Sillari, former first secretary of the Tallinn city party organisation.[47]

The response of the Russian delegates to secession was hesitant and disunited. A small group led by A. Gusev, mostly from the big all-Union factories, withdrew and announced that they would remain on the platform of the CPSU. Another group led by V. Mal'kovskii, mostly from the towns of the north-east, reserved their position on controversial points, but tried to prevent a complete split by joining a 'coalition Central Committee'.[48] In attempting conciliation they acted differently from their Russian colleagues in the Lithuanian and Latvian Communist Parties. Maybe the reason for their effort was that they still hoped to be able to promote, with the agreement of the Estonian government, the idea of a free economic zone in the north-east of the republic.

In any event, the compromise did not last long. In December 1990, the Communists loyal to Moscow held their own congress, thus consummating the split, and here Gusev's group was joined by that of Mal'kovskii. Four hundred delegates met, claiming to speak for 33,000 members. Their mood was summed up by Evgenii Kogan: 'Six months ago we had 47,000 members, now we have 33,000. We have lost our property, our Central Committee building and our media outlets. If we carry on concerning ourselves with "principles" and "ideological problems" in this manner, we shall soon lose everything.' (The implication that it was time to defend party property by force became a serious matter in Latvia and Lithuania the following month, when OMON took up the cause.) Another delegate complained of former apparatchiks who had held high positions in the time of 'stagnation', but had now given up their party cards in order to continue enjoying government office. The congress passed a motion of no confidence in the Estonian government, and resolved in favour of preserving the Soviet Union by means of a new Union Treaty.[49]

The Estonian Popular Front, though it had preserved its popularity much better than the Communist Party, also had to face the growing challenge of the Estonian Congress and of the Interdvizhenie. It was able to do so with any prospect of success only by switching its support from mere 'sovereignty' to full secession from the Soviet Union, and by acknowledging the Estonian Congress as a legitimate assembly. In the elections to the Estonian Supreme Soviet of March 1990, the Front made this switch and managed as a result to maintain its unity and to come in as the leading element in a pro-independence bloc of seventy-eight out of 105 seats.[50] It was thus in a position to act as the focus for a majority of moderate Estonian nationalist deputies to support a new non-communist government set up by Edgar Savisaar. On 30 March 1990 the new Supreme Soviet issued a provisional declaration of independence, envisaging a transition period during which the details of secession would be negotiated with Moscow.

All the same, the Popular Front found the period after its electoral triumphs of 1989 and 1990 rather perplexing and frustrating. Its original role had been to mobilise Estonians against rule by Moscow and by the Communist Party apparatus. That task it had fulfilled with striking success. But the very qualities which had enabled it to do so—its flamboyant campaigning style, its openness to people of diverse opinions—rendered it ill suited to tackling the next stage in the country's political development: using its parliamentary dominance to construct a working democracy and market economy while negotiating independence from Moscow. These were undertakings which required patient diplomacy, expert preparation and parliamentary discipline.

Savisaar's government was not in theory a Popular Front government, even though most of its portfolios went to leading members of the Front. Savisaar chose his ministers for their personal merits and included one or two non-Front members. In practice he found himself often unable, because of absences or indiscipline, to rely on stable majorities to back the government's proposals. Thus vital laws on citizenship, on the ownership of land and on the status of pre-1940 property remained blocked, even though their passage was vital to the establishment both of parliamentary democracy and of a market economy.

Because of this uncertain support, Savisaar was in the paradoxical position of sometimes having to seek the support of the Russian deputies, for example by supporting the idea of a special economic zone in north-east Estonia. As a simpler solution to his difficulties, however, he proposed that the Popular Front should be converted from a loose coordinating movement into a more tightly disciplined political party. He argued that democracy in Estonia had not yet matured to the point where a full multi-party system was appropriate, but that it needed an organising force more coherent than the present Popular Front: reorganised as 'a leading party' or 'first among equals', the Front would provide much-needed cohesion.[51]

At the 3rd Congress (13–14 April 1991), where this proposal came up for discussion, a number of speakers commented on the irony of the Front assuming a role which the Communist Party had only just relinquished. Marju Lauristin spoke of her shock at hearing Savisaar speak of political parties 'as little groups that splinter society and bicker among themselves'. Actually, she asserted, Estonian society had 'moved in the direction of cooperation in the past year'. Many delegates were in favour of precisely the opposite way forward: that the Front should accept that its role was ended, and should dissolve into the smaller parties which had grown up under its umbrella.

Overall, however, the congress voted to maintain the Front's status as it was, a coalition and a movement rather than a party, since its function as mobiliser of all the people in an emergency might yet turn out to be very useful.[52]

Meanwhile around the Popular Front, both inside and outside its overall umbrella, embryonic political parties had already formed, with complete political programmes of their own, and ready in principle to pursue a coherent policy if able to take over the reins of government. In practice, however, none of them has more than a few hundred members, their provincial and local organisations are weak, and their press is underdeveloped. They are, moreover, simply too numerous, divided from one another not by serious differences of principle or policy, but rather by personalities and by the circumstances of their creation.

One of the most serious of them is the Social Democratic Party. This is a creation of the 'people of the 1960s', the proponents of 'socialism with a human face', who in their first official jobs in the 1960s tried to work for a reformed Communist Party and for the ultimate achievement of something not unlike Scandinavian Social Democracy. In 1980 forty scholars and scientific workers had sent a letter to the party leadership calling in this spirit for more freedom of speech, greater sensitivity to ethnic aspirations and the introduction of some market mechanisms into the economy. They were the kernel of what later became the 'Social Democratic Party of Independence', whose founding congress was held in March 1989. In September 1990, having absorbed two smaller Social Democratic groups, it renamed itself the Social Democratic Party of Estonia.[53] Despite its name, in Britain it would be considered not much to the left of the Thatcherite Conservative Party, since it emphasises individual property-ownership, private enterprise and wealth creation. It does, however, recognise the importance of social security for the weaker or poorer members of society, and is undoctrinaire about the return of pre-1940 property, recognising that this can in practice often be accomplished only at the cost of considerable upheaval. Its programme stresses 'solidarity' and 'equality of rights and opportunities' as basic principles.[54]

Among the other parties associated with the Popular Front are the Liberal Democrats (who differ more in language than in substance from the Social Democrats), the Greens and the Centre Agrarian Party, which focuses especially on the need to help private farmers establish themselves.

The Christian Union, later renamed the Christian Democratic Union, springs from entirely different roots. It originated among the 'people of the 1970s', those whose early adulthood was marked by the growing conviction that the Communist Party was unreformable, that there was no hope for socialism, and that one must therefore base political activity on entirely different principles. Its origin was in a letter written jointly by three priests, one Lutheran, one Catholic and one Orthodox, to the Tartu newspaper *Edasi* in May 1988, calling on Christians to support perestroika. Initiative groups were set up to respond in a number of regions, and in December a founding congress took place in the hall of the Musicians' Union.[55]

From the outset the Christian Union saw itself as a centre-right party in the tradition of the Italian or German Christian Democrats, stressing individual freedom and property, and aiming at maximal marketisation of the economy, while insisting that, unless entrepreneurs observe ethical principles in dealing with their employees and their customers, then the market-place degenerates into ruthless economic warfare, to the detriment of society and of the individual. One of their leaders, Mart Laar, declared to me that they were 'the only party in Estonia with a philosophy of life', as distinct from a mere political strategy. Since, in their opinion, none of their goals could be achieved inside the Soviet Union, the Christian Union was from the start in favour of complete independence, and worked closely with the ENIP and the Heritage Society to create the Estonian Congress movement.[56]

At the same end of the political spectrum is the Conservative People's Party, founded in January 1990, which takes a radical line on independence, private enterprise and the return of pre-1940 property, but with the underpinning of free-market theory rather than religion. Tactically speaking, the Conservatives were in favour of participation in the Estonian Supreme Soviet elections of March 1990, where the ENIP recommended boycott.[57] Whereas the core of the Conservatives is among the dissidents of the 1970s, the Republican Party, otherwise very close to them in its principles, draws its support more from younger intellectuals and the new entrepreneurs.[58]

An influential group which stands rather on its own is Free Estonia (Vaba Eesti). This is not a party but rather a parliamentary caucus, formed in January 1990, largely from among supporters of the then prime minister, Indrek Toome. Toome, a former ideology chief, had supported Väljas in his reform of the ECP: his support came from officials at the reformist end of the old party-state apparatus who did not wish to identify directly with the Popular Front, yet could see that dependence on the ECP was now electorally hopeless. The outlook of Free Estonia was summarised in the slogan 'Tolerance, Competence, Cooperation', under which they put forward candidates for the elections of March 1990. It was a reaction against populism, nationalism and economic irresponsibility. 'Free Estonia rates highly those politicians who are capable of foreseeing the possible political consequences of their declarations and actions, and possess the capacity to avoid social conflicts and disorders which can impede our democratic development.' It was, in short, a call for confidence in a ruling élite which had been squeezed out by the decline of the ECP, and by the triangle of Popular Front, Estonian Congress and Interdvizhenie. To judge by the election results, it evoked some response.[59]

The March 1990 elections, as we have seen, came just after the Communist Party had renounced its 'leading role' in politics, but before other parties had had a chance to register, still less to organise themselves, nominate candidates and prepare electoral material. Most parties consequently did not nominate candidates directly. The Estonian Popular Front won thirty-three seats, Vaba Eesti, OSTK and the Agrarians twelve each, STKE seven, the ECP and the Estonian Congress Movement five each, the Greens two, Interdvizhenie one. There were twelve independents.[60]

In the Supreme Soviet—or Supreme Council, as it was renamed following the provisional independence declaration of 30 March 1990—no single group thus dominated, though the Popular Front was in a good position to gather allies round itself and steer legislation through. In practice, however, the relative absence of fractional discipline (and the fact that till March 1991 each deputy could belong to two fractions) made the outcome of most votes unpredictable. Consequently, as we have seen, necessary legislation was seriously delayed, and the public began to become impatient with politicians, especially in view of rising prices and of creeping and uncontrolled privatisation, which made it possible for a few to secure quick profits, while arousing resentment among the many.

On the eve of the coup of August 1991, then, the creation of an independent, democratic Estonia was a job only half done. The Estonian people had proved themselves to be courageous, restrained and disciplined, especially at critical times like the attack on the parliament by the Interdvizhenie in May 1990, and the OMON assaults in neighbouring Latvia and Lithuania in January 1991. But the lack of a mature party structure was making it difficult to achieve the second half of the transition to independence and stable democracy.

In the first half year after the coup and the final achievement of independence, some steps were taken towards rectifying this situation, though in a milieu of severe economic crisis, which occasioned the fall of the Savisaar government in January 1992. It was replaced by an interim administration of mainly non-party technocrats pledged to hold new parliamentary elections in the autumn. Under the new constitution, still to be confirmed by referendum, Estonia will be a parliamentary rather than a presidential republic, with deputies elected by a system close to that adopted in the Federal Republic of Germany. The political movements and parties were preparing for the elections by beginning to come together in three main groups, one centred round the old Communist Party and Free Estonia, a second round the Popular Front (including the Social Democrats, the Greens and the Centre Agrarians), and a third round the Estonian Congress movement and the free-market radicals (including the Conservatives, the Republicans, the Christian Democrats and possibly the Liberal Democrats). At the time of writing, this development appears to hold out prospects of evolution towards a normal multi-party system, provided that the economic crisis can be overcome without serious social instability.

Notes

1. E. Jansen, 'Estonian culture—European culture at the beginning of the twentieth century', in A. Loit (ed.), *The Baltic Countries, 1900–14*, University of Stockholm, Centre for Baltic Studies, 1990, pp. 316–17.
2. R. J. Misiunas and R. Taagepera, *The Baltic States: Years of Dependence, 1940–1980*,

London, Hurst, 1983; see also the same authors' article, 'The Baltic states: years of dependence, 1980–86', *Journal of Baltic Studies*, vol. 20, no. i, 1989, pp. 65–85.

3. See G. A. Hosking, *The Awakening of the Soviet Union*, London, Heinemann, 2nd edn, 1991, especially chapters 3 and 4 for general remarks on the situation of scholars and creative artists in Soviet society.

4. N. R. Miuzneks, 'The Daugavpils hydro-station and glasnost in Latvia', *Journal of Baltic Studies*, vol. 18, no. i, 1987, pp. 63–70.

5. Toomas Ilves, 'An open letter of protest from Estonian scientists', *Radio Free Europe Research*, Baltic Area SR/4, 18 July 1986, pp. 5–6.

6. Toomas Ilves, 'Estonian Writers' Union congress calls for greater freedom', *Radio Free Europe Research*, op. cit., pp. 7–11; and 'What the Writers' Union congress really talked about', SR/6, 25 September 1986, pp. 3–6.

7. Interview with Alexei Lotman, of the Green Movement, 26 September 1990; Toomas Ilves, 'Growing opposition and unrest over massive mining project', *Radio Free Europe Research*, Baltic Area, SR/4, 15 June 1987, pp. 5–8.

8. *Radio Free Europe Research*, RAD BR/250, p. 17.

9. Interview with Tõin Särv, on the board of the Estonian Heritage Society, 25 September 1990.

10. Interview with Tõin Särv; Rein Taagepera, 'Estonia's road to independence', *Problems of Communism*, vol. 38, no. vi, 1989, pp. 16–17.

11. Toomas Ilves, 'Conformist Communists propose turning Estonia into closed economic zone', *Radio Free Europe Research*, Baltic Area, SR/7, 28 October 1987, pp. 7–10; Toivo Miljan, 'The proposal to establish economic autonomy in Estonia', *Journal of Baltic Studies*, vol. 20, no. ii, 1989, pp. 149–64.

12. Toomas Ilves, 'Cultural unions adopt resolution on nationality reforms', *Radio Free Europe Research*, Baltic Area, SR/6, 3 June 1988, pp. 3–6.

13. Toomas Ilves, 'The cultural unions' resolution to the leaderships of the ECP and ESSR', *Radio Free Europe Research*, op. cit., pp. 7–14.

14. Vera Tolz, 'Informal groups in the USSR in 1988', *Radio Liberty Research*, 1988, no. 487, 30 October 1988, pp. 6–7; B. Kurashvili, *Bor'ba s biurokratizmom*, Moscow, Znanie, 1988, pp. 55–6.

15. Interview with Petr Vihalemm of the board of the Estonian Popular Front, 10 May 1991.

16. Toomas Ilves, 'Massive demonstrations', *Radio Free Europe Research*, Baltic Area, SR/7, 13 July 1988, pp. 7–8.

17. *Summary of World Broadcasts*, SWB SU/0205, 16 July 1988, B/3–5.

18. Juris Dreifels, 'Latvian national rebirth', *Problems of Communism*, vol. 38, no. 4, 1989, esp. pp. 82–3; Jan Arveds Trapans, 'The sources of Latvia's popular movement', in his *Toward Independence: The Baltic Popular Movements*, Boulder, CO, Westview Press, 1991, pp 25–43.

19. V. Stanley Vardys, 'Sajudis: national revolution in Lithuania', in J. A. Trapans (ed.), *Toward Independence*, pp. 11–24.

20. *Sovetskaia Estoniia*, no. 209 (13607), 10 September 1988, p. 1.

21. *Kommunist Estonii*, xii, 1988, p. 31.

22. *Narodnyi kongress: sbornik materialov kongressa Narodnogo Fronta Estonii, 1–2 okt 1988g.*, Tallinn, Perioodika, 1989, p. 23.

23. *Narodnyi kongress*, ibid., p. 82; Boris Kagarlitsky, *Farewell Perestroika: a Soviet Chronicle*, London, Verso, 1990, pp. 42–3.

24. *Sovetskaia Estoniia*, no. 275–6 (13673–4), 30 November 1988, p. 7.

25. *Narodnyi kongress*, pp. 171–4, 176, 178, 180.
26. Richard Sakwa, *Gorbachev and His Reforms, 1985–90*, London, Philip Allan, 1990, p. 238.
27. Interview with Arnold Sai, member of the Presidium of Interdvizhenie, 9 May 1991.
28. A. V. Gromov and O. S. Kuzin, *Neformaly: kto est' kto*, Moscow, Mysl', 1990, p. 121.
29. Viktor Shirokov, *Neozhidannaia Estoniia: politicheskii reportazh*, Moscow, Politizdat, 1991, pp. 121–2.
30. Interview with Artur Kopytin, chairman of the executive committee of OSTK, 14 May 1991.
31. Interview with Kopytin; Shirokov, *Neozhidannaia Estoniia*, pp. 145–6; *Sovetskaia Estoniia*, no. 278 (13676), 2 December 1988, p. 3.
32. Dreifels, 'Latvian national rebirth', p. 86; Vardys, 'Sajudis', pp. 59–60.
33. *Sovetskaia Estoniia*, no. 183 (13881), 9 August 1989, p. 1.
34. *Sovetskaia Estoniia*, no. 188 (13886), 15 August 1989, p. 2; no. 197 (13895), 25 August 1989, p. 3.
35. *Sovetskaia Estoniia*, no. 192 (13890), 19 August 1989, p. 3.
36. Riina Kionka, 'Identity crisis in Estonian Popular Front', *Report on the USSR*, 10 May 1991, p 19; interview with Arnold Sai, chairman of the third chamber of the Interregional Council, 9 May 1991.
37. Toomas Ilves, 'Reaction: the Intermovement in Estonia', in Trapans (ed.), *Toward Independence*, pp. 81–2.
38. Interview with Enn Tarto, of the board of the Conservative Party, 25 September 1990; with Maris Sarv, press officer of ENIP, 26 September 1990; with Tunne Kelam, chairman of the Estonian Committee, 14 May 1991.
39. Riina Kionka, 'The Estonian citizens' committees', *Report on the USSR*, 9 February 1990, pp. 30–3.
40. *Estonian National Independence Party: Documents*, 1, 1989, p. 2.
41. ibid., 2, 1989, pp. 6–8.
42. Rein Taagepera, 'A note on the March 1989 elections in Estonia', *Soviet Studies*, vol. 42, no. 2, 1990, pp. 329–39.
43. *Pravda*, 27 August 1989, p. 1.
44. *Sovetskaia Estoniia*, no. 296 (13994), 28 December 1989, p. 1.
45. Riina Kionka, 'The Congress convenes', *Report on the USSR*, 23 March 1990, pp. 32–3.
46. Kionka, 'The Congress convenes', ibid., pp. 32–5.
47. *Sovetskaia Estoniia*, no. 73 (14071), 29 March 1990, p. 1.
48. *Sovetskaia Estoniia*, ibid.
49. *Sovetskaia Estoniia*, no. 292 (14290), 19 December 1990, p. 20.
50. Oleg Samorodnii, 'Stanovlenie mnogopartiinosti v Estonii v 1988–90', pp. 10–11. I am most grateful to Mr Samorodnii, of the Institute of Philosophy, Sociology and Law of the Estonian Academy of Sciences, for making this unpublished paper available to me.
51. Riina Kionka, 'Identity crisis in the Estonian Popular Front', *Report on the USSR*, 10 May 1991, p. 21.
52. Kionka, 'Identity crisis', ibid., p. 22; interview with Rein Veidemann, member of the board of the Popular Front, 15 May 1991.
53. Interview with Rein Veidemann, of the board of the Social Democratic Party, 15 May 1991.

54. Interview with Veidemann; *Programma sotsial-demokraticheskoi partii Estonii*, Tallinn, 1990; 'Obshchestvenno-politicheskie organizatsii, partii i dvizheniia v Estonii', *Izvestiia TsK KPSS*, 6, 1991, pp. 98–9; *Ausalt ja avameelselt: Eesti parteidest I*, Tallinn, Perioodika, 1990, pp. 7–14.
55. *Ausalt ja avameelselt: Eesti parteidest II*, Tallinn, Perioodika, 1990, p. 14.
56. Interview with Mart Laar, of the board of the Christian Democratic Union, 15 May 1991; *Ausalt ja avameelselt I*, pp. 16–19.
57. Interview with Enn Tarto, 24 September 1990; *Ausalt ja avameelselt II*, pp. 27–31.
58. Interview with Juri Luik, of the board of the Republican Party, 12 December 1991; *Ausalt ja avameelselt I*, pp. 38–43.
59. Interview with Jaak Kaarma, vice-president of Free Estonia, 13 May 1991; *Osnovnye printsipy demokraticheskogo ob" edineniia 'Vaba Eesti'*, Tallinn, 1990.
60. Samorodnii, 'Stanovlenie', pp. 11–12.

8 Triumph and foreboding

Geoffrey A. Hosking, Jonathan Aves, Peter J. S. Duncan

The movements which form the subject of this volume transformed basic political assumptions in the Soviet Union. The extent to which they had done so was dramatised by the coup of August 1991 and the formation of the Commonwealth of Independent States in December 1991. The notion that the Soviet Union was one polity and that the Communist Party had a natural birthright to rule over it had, apparently quite suddenly, become discredited. Sovereign republics, with elected parliaments and presidents had taken its place as the natural focuses of legitimacy.

Not that that was apparent in the hectic first hours of the coup. Most western journalists and commentators immediately assumed that it would be successful, and began writing obituaries of the Gorbachev era. The usually reliable *Independent* devoted its weekend colour supplement to a post-mortem, which was brusquely upstaged by the sudden revival of the corpse. Decades of living with totalitarian communist systems had accustomed us to the grim moment of truth, when the bright hopes raised by this or that reformer were summarily crushed by tanks.

This time, however, the tanks failed to move in—or did so in such a half-hearted manner that a barricade of trolleybuses was sufficient to restrain them. When it came to the crunch, some army and KGB commanders were not prepared to respond to the traditional call of the Union, or to the familiar slogans of the Communist Party, for now there was a rival source of authority, one moreover with a more cogent claim to legitimacy. The duly constituted Russian parliament and Russia's recently popularly elected president defied the coup and exposed its unconstitutionality, warning that those who collaborated with it would lay themselves open to grave criminal charges. The 'White House' on the bank of the Moscow River became a focus for all those citizens who wished to express their opposition to the junta and to do something effective to resist it. Without this centre of resistance, the coup might well have succeeded, or at least plunged the country into a prolonged and bitter civil war. The Russian parliament and presidency were crucial.

Similarly, when at the beginning of December a considerable majority of Ukrainians voted for their republic's final secession from the Soviet Union, the idea of a commonwealth of independent states, worked out by the democrats, was ready to be taken up. This was important, since, however fragile the Commonwealth looks, it does offer some hope of the orderly liquidation of the

Soviet legacy. If the Soviet Union had simply fallen apart, without any attempt at an inter-republican association, then the resulting chaos in military, economic and ethnic relations would have frustrated everyone's political aspirations.

Revolutions never proceed simply from popular discontent, or even from the discontent of excluded élites. It needs some institution from within the *ancien régime* to break away and to act, sometimes only half intentionally, as a force articulating the mood either of the masses or of disaffected élites. That was the role of the Long Parliament in England in the seventeenth century, of the Estates General in France in 1789, and of the Duma in Russia in 1917. The first scholar to apply this idea to Soviet society was Alex Shtromas. Writing in 1980, he proposed that the Soviet system would only be radically changed if there arose a 'second pivot', an institution from within the system which became 'extra-structural' and began to serve as a focus for the articulation of 'potential dissent'.[1] He identified the technocrats and the military officers as the disaffected professionals who would activate the 'second pivot' and use it to bring about change.[2] In actual fact, as we have seen, the creative and humanitarian intelligentsia was at least as important during the early stages, but the general point stands. Institutions created by the party-state apparatus were taken over, infiltrated or 'infected' by the independent political movements, and proved in the end to be decisive forces for change. Without these institutions, and Gorbachev's attempts to reconstruct them, the recent political transformation would not have taken place. The long-haired youths with guitars protesting about the bulldozing of historical buildings and the pollution of rivers would not have become more than tiny single-issue movements, and young scholars investigating Ukrainian folklore, Armenian church history, American constitutional law and European market economies would have remained confined to their seminar rooms.

The first impulse to combine political clubs and single-issue movements (mostly ecological) into broader mass movements came with the announcement of the more democratic election of delegates to the 19th Party Conference in the summer of 1988. The political reform process instituted by that conference then offered a semi-normal electoral forum for the evolution of the mass movements into electoral blocs. The intermittent but nevertheless striking success of radical candidates in a few constituencies in the election campaign of spring 1989 provided a small number of delegates who formed the Inter-regional Group of Deputies in the Congress of People's Deputies and the Supreme Soviet of the USSR—a potential kernel for an opposition. The Inter-regional Group did not fulfil its potentiality in the short term, swamped as it was by the 'aggressively obedient majority' of old-style nomenklatura nominees in both legislative chambers. But it did provoke the latter into forming their own fraction, *Soiuz*, dedicated to preserving the Soviet Union as a unified great power rather than a loose confederation of republics. The radicals within the CPSU had already begun working out a coherent political programme independent of the leadership, but this was the first time the conservatives had tried to do so, and the formation of *Soiuz* thus widened the incipient split in the Communist Party. This split continued to deepen with the crisis over the elaboration and signing of a Union Treaty during 1990–1.

By this time, in the country at large, electoral blocs were beginning to generate political parties, at first in the Baltic, then in the Caucasus, then in Russia, as can be seen in other chapters. The new-style Russian parliament (like the other parliaments of the Union Republics) was elected before these new political parties could register themselves and take a full legal part in the electoral process. Nevertheless a significant minority of its deputies reached the chamber with the help of the Popular Fronts or voters' associations; and, like a leaven, their attitudes gradually spread to the rump of deputies who had been nominated in traditional style by the apparatus. One result was the formation of a bewildering and shifting kaleidoscope of 'fractions' in the republican Supreme Soviets. A definite, if chaotic, political differentiation was, then, already under way long before the August coup, and it arose inside the 'second pivot', in the reformed Soviet institutions. At the moment, in fact, it seems likely that if effective political parties are formed it will be on the basis of parliamentary fractions, rather than the other way round.

El'tsin as political leader was rescued from the wilderness by the urban Popular Fronts and voters' associations. They ran his election campaigns and began his political re-education from maverick apparatchik to democratic politician. As he says in his autobiography,

Many people asserted that I was making a terrible mistake [in 1989] by choosing as my campaign aides people who were not professionals—not politicians, not experts, but plain, intelligent, decent human beings. I knew none of them before the election campaign started; they either rang up or came to see me, saying that they wanted to be my campaign assistants. I was grateful for this, but warned them that the going would be extremely tough. They knew this, of course, and many were dedicated enough to have taken unpaid leave to help in my campaign. And they worked, without exaggeration, literally night and day.[3]

Without his helpers and advisers from the 'informals', El'tsin would never have become President of Russia. That is not to deny his own skill and courage as a politician. He knew how to seize the opportunities presented, and the long experience of public administration he had gained while serving in the apparatus was also essential to his new role. The 'informals' on their own strength could never have put forward a figure capable of handling power as El'tsin did at several crucial turning points, and especially during the coup. Both the experience of the apparatchik and the zeal of the 'informals' were required to make the 'second pivot' effective. Organisations such as the Democratic Union which have forsworn cooperation with official institutions have condemned themselves to impotence—if colourful and ostentatious impotence.

This confluence of talents points up a general lesson of the events of the last five years. The 'informals' and their successors did more to reshape and eventually destroy the Soviet Union than the Communist Party leadership. But without Gorbachev, and without the tolerance and at times direct participation of sections of the party-state apparatus they could never have broken out of their *kruzhki* into real politics. During their gestation, reformist members of the Communist Party formed an important proportion of their membership, and they were dependent on party and soviet officials for premises, the use of facilities and access to the media.

Gorbachev at first encouraged the 'informals' as allies in his endeavour to reform the apparatus and to make the existing system work better. Later, when he became apprehensive about some of their ideas and activities, it was too late to suppress them resolutely without trampling underfoot everything he stood for. He proposed the abolition of the Communist Party's political monopoly (Article 6 of the Soviet Constitution) in response to the mass pressure they had been able to generate, manifested in two huge street demonstrations in Moscow in February 1990. But at the same time he tried to replace the party's grip on executive power by requesting and obtaining increased powers for himself as President of the USSR.

Meanwhile more and more Communist Party members and even officials, especially of the younger generation, were becoming convinced that their party could never be reformed, and would have to be destroyed or split from within. Even as he assumed his new powers, Gorbachev was becoming the classical *ancien régime* reformer, torn between the forces he had unleashed, which had dragged him immeasurably further than he had ever envisaged, and the siren voices of his old apparat colleagues, increasingly indignant and alarmed at the crumbling of everything they had held dear. In a very real sense, 19 August was a coup of Gorbachev against Gorbachev: he appointed its leaders, and they were carrying out one side of his ambivalent policies. Its failure compelled him to abandon his ambivalence and come down clearly on the side of destroying the old system.

How did the 'informals' obtain such a hold inside a system which to most observers looked unshakeable? They did so not only by articulating the grievances of a disaffected intelligentsia, but also by picking up and reflecting the resentment of broader masses, especially of workers and employees, at the disdain and arrogance with which the party-state apparatus had treated them. Without this input they would never have gained their initially sporadic but increasingly numerous successes in the popular elections of 1989 and 1990. Their great trump card was the generally perceived illegitimacy of the Communist Party of the Soviet Union. What was difficult for at least the Russians among them to perceive in the joy of electoral success was that, without the Communist Party, the Soviet Union could not last much longer either.

The informals' success in reflecting broader moods depended in part on their ethnic closeness to the population. In regions where a variety of discontents could be bundled together under a single, readily recognisable ethnic label, the 'informals' found it particularly easy to attract popular support. They could deploy national symbols, flags, emblems and folk-songs, they could organise national 'happenings' such as the Baltic and Ukrainian 'human chains', and they could impart an ethnic colouring to issues which aroused strong emotions, but which were not in themselves ethnic, such as the environment and the economy. This was a hazardous policy, since it alienated non-indigenous populations whose assistance they would need in establishing sovereign republics; but it did force the local apparatchiks, the proconsuls of empire, to start redoing their calculations about where their political power base lay, a process which led to the creation of 'national communist' fractions in republican Supreme Soviets, and to declarations of sovereignty.

The forms which the national liberation movements assumed depended partly on how far the republics concerned were situated on the rural–urban continuum. The vital interrelationship was the triangle formed by the non-conformist intelligentsia, the reformist members of the Communist Party, and the old nomenklatura apparatus. The initial impulse towards the formation of national liberation movements in the non-Russian republics usually came from the non-conformist intelligentsia, typically starting with writers and other creative artists. Glasnost enabled them to articulate concern about degradation of the environment, belittlement of the indigenous language, culture and history, the poor performance of the local economy, sometimes too about territorial issues or the excessive immigration of outsiders.

The Popular Fronts initially pioneered in the Baltic were movements led by the non-conformist intelligentsia and supported by reformist republican apparatchiks. Their formation was due partly to pressure from below, and partly to republican leaders' perception that, in order to survive perestroika, they needed to rely far more upon the support of their own peoples. Many of these leaders probably accomplished this shift with conviction, liberating long suppressed national feelings in themselves; others will have acted largely out of calculation. Either way, the essence of their policy was to use existing Soviet institutions to bolster their own power, a classical use of the 'second pivot'.

By 1990 this new power relationship was being articulated in declarations of 'sovereignty' and 'independence'. The word 'sovereignty' meant many things to many people, but it had the advantage that it provided a symbol on which intellectuals and republican apparatchiks could agree. For the former, the word embodied their dreams of national self-determination and democracy; for the latter, it meant they would at last have real power—including the power to repel unwelcome measures of perestroika emanating from Moscow.

In some republics the Popular Front quickly emerged as the dominant force in the new political constellation: Estonia, Latvia, Lithuania, Moldavia and Armenia (in the form of the Karabakh Committee and later the Pan-Armenian Movement). In Estonia and Latvia, though, it faced a challenge from those who might be called 'irreconcilables', the 'congress' movements, who wished to ignore Soviet institutions altogether and act as if their republic had never juridically been part of the Soviet Union at all. In Armenia an analogous challenge came from the Armenian National Army, which proclaimed that the Armenian people could not expect effective protection from the Soviet authorities, and must therefore defend themselves. In Lithuania, by contrast, the 'irreconcilables' found a home in Sajudis, the Popular Front, and propelled it towards the first outright declaration of independence from the Soviet Union.

In Moldova, on the other hand, the Popular Front after early successes gradually lost ground to the reformist wing of the party apparatus, partly because of the opposition of collective farmers (in a largely agrarian country) to its land reform, partly because of the relative success of Russians in establishing and maintaining their own institutions. Many Moldovans feared that reunion with Romania, which the Popular Front proposed, would seriously exacerbate ethnic conflict in their republic.

In Georgia, the 'irreconcilables' actually won power with the support of the majority of the population, since the Communist Party proved too inflexible and the Popular Front too moderate to channel the intense desire for independence which gripped the Georgian people after the Tbilisi massacre of April 1989. However, in a striking confirmation of the 'second pivot' theory, Gamsakhurdia and the Round Table did in the end have recourse to the Soviet election system, in order to defeat rival 'irreconcilables'.

Gamsakhurdia's subsequent fate suggested the drawbacks of a purely dissident career as a preparation for a more open politics, and demonstrated how important was the participation of élites formed under the Soviet regime for the smooth transition from central control to republican sovereignty. In December 1991 opponents from the old élites combined with 'irreconcilable' rivals of Gamsakhurdia to overthrow him by force, despite his overwhelming popular mandate.

In Azerbaijan and Central Asia it is the republican Communist Parties which have come best out of the upheavals. In Azerbaijan, which is a relatively urbanised republic, the Popular Front gained widespread public support during 1989, especially among the working class, not least by accusing the communist leadership of pusillanimity on the issue of Nagornyi Karabakh. A large-scale military operation had to be mounted by the Soviet Army in Baku in January 1990 to prevent it coming to power—the only time state violence was successfully used in the perestroika period to reinstall communist rule. Thereafter, the Azerbaijani Communists reasserted their power, partly by using traditional patronage, partly by exploiting martial law, and partly by taking over and manipulating popular grievances over Karabakh. By early 1992, however, it was evident that the Popular Front could still mount an effective challenge to them.

In Central Asia, by contrast, the Popular Fronts were never strong, for the region does not have a developed enough urban, or European, culture to sustain movements of that type. Ethnic conflict there has grown out of very localised issues, such as access to land, water, jobs and housing. The Communist Parties (renamed after August 1991) and their apparats have maintained their grip partly by manipulating these issues through their network of clientelism, but partly also by promoting technological development and foreign investment, espousing more vigorously the cause of the indigenous nation, and in some cases by reaching a cautious accommodation with Islam. An exception is Kyrgyzstan, where President Akaev (former head of the Academy of Sciences) manages to remain independent of the apparatus, basing his power on a working alliance of Kyrgyz and Russian democrats with former communists; while in Kazakhstan President Nazarbaev has taken great care to ensure that the interests of Russians are respected.

In Ukraine and Belorussia, Popular Fronts developed belatedly, mainly because the thrust of the national movements was weakened by the large number of Russians living in each republic, and also by the substantial number of locals who did not feel themselves nationally distinct from the Russians. Rukh and Adradzhenne were not even able to participate fully in the republican soviet elections of spring 1990. All the same, they proved to be the driving force in the republican Supreme Soviets, where their programme of 'sovereignty' (in 1990) and 'independence' (in 1991) was accepted by the great majority of deputies.

The Russians were in a different situation from all other Soviet nations, and for them the formation of a Popular Front was much more problematic; indeed, although several movements bore the name, none of them fulfilled the same role as in the non-Russian republics. The problem was that the Russians themselves were the imperial nation; national liberation for them was not necessarily synonymous with secession from the USSR. On the contrary, most Russian democrats assumed at first that the reforms they were proposing should be applied throughout the USSR, using the centralised state machinery. When the programmes of non-Russian Popular Fronts challenged that assumption, the reactions of Russian democrats were divided: some favoured giving the non-Russians autonomy or even independence, others insisted that the break-up of the USSR would be a disaster for everyone involved.

In the end El'tsin and Democratic Russia resolved in favour of the former course. This decision resulted partly from El'tsin's priorities in the power battle with Gorbachev, and partly from his continuing political re-education. When he entered the Congress of People's Deputies in May 1989, he became one of the leaders of the Inter-Regional Group of Deputies, and met some of the Soviet Union's principal non-conformist intellectuals, such as Sakharov, Afanas'ev, Popov and Sobchak, elected like himself through the efforts of the 'informals'. Their relationship was not easy at first; there were plenty of reasons why a former apparatchik should distrust professors and vice versa. But gradually they learnt to tolerate and even respect one another, and under their influence El'tsin began to put together a liberal programme over the whole range of issues.

Important though it was as a stage in his career, the Inter-regional Group was unsatisfactory to El'tsin as a power base. At a time when all political issues were being ethnicised, it suffered from its multi-national composition. It represented, moreover, only a small minority of deputies in the face of the 'agressively obedient majority'. Accordingly, early in 1990, El'tsin decided to shift his position and take advantage of the upcoming republican soviet elections. His intention was to adopt the tactics of the non-Russian Popular Fronts. With his sure instinct for power he had seen that 'sovereignty', troublesome enough for Gorbachev when claimed in Estonia or Moldavia, would revolutionise Soviet politics completely if declared in Russia. The Russian Supreme Soviet, hitherto a pale legislative shadow, would become an excellent vantage point from which to challenge both the communist apparatus and the Soviet President.

Sure enough, once he had been elected to the Russian Supreme Soviet, El'tsin had the power base he needed to make himself the first popularly elected President of Russia in 1991, again with the support of Democratic Russia. This was the position from which he was able to defeat the coup, accomplish the dissolution of the Soviet Union, and establish the Commonwealth of Independent States.

The widespread dissemination of new political ideas and information would have been impossible without the remarkable flowering of the mass media which began in 1986 and steadily deepened thereafter. It is often assumed that this flowering was decreed by Gorbachev, in the form of glasnost. It is true that without Gorbachev it could not have taken place, but popular television programmes like *Vzgliad*, *Vesti* and *Piatoe koleso*, newspapers like *Atmoda* in Riga, *Literaturna Ukraina* in Kiev and *Literaturuli Sakartvelo* in Tbilisi had constantly to fight and manoeuvre against authorities accustomed to blandness and half-truths. Without the skill and courage of certain campaigning editors, like Vitalii Korotich of *Ogonek*, Egor Iakovlev of *Moskovskie novosti*, Vladislav Starkov of *Argumenty i fakty*, Sergei Zalygin of *Novyi mir*, Grigorii Baklanov of *Znamia*, and later on Vitalii Tret'iakov of *Nezavisimaia gazeta*, real politics would have been impossible, in so far as it rests on the many-sided and well-informed discussion of controversial issues. Where these editors pointed the way, unofficial journals, without access to official presses, but also untrammelled by any official status, strode boldly ahead, campaigning for the oppressed and mapping out a complete political agenda, as well as tearing down the veils of secrecy which still in 1986 obscured the nations' vision of their past.

The 19 August coup demonstrated how vital these publications and the attendant technology had become. El'tsin's grand gesture of clambering on to one of the junta's tanks to issue his defiant proclamation would have gone for nothing had it not been shown on television and had printers and duplicating machines not immediately ensured that his words were posted up at street corners and in Metro stations all over Moscow. Eleven banned newspapers got together to produce a joint issue called *Obshchaia gazeta* (The Common Newspaper), while publishing houses in Estonia and Moldavia helped to rush out special numbers of *Nezavisimaia gazeta* and *Moskovskie novosti*.[4] In the major Russian cities, radio stations improvised to stay on the air when the junta tried to close them down. Meanwhile the BBC, Radio Liberty, the Voice of America and other foreign stations broadcasting in the Soviet languages briefly resumed a leading role in the provision of information such as they had not exercised for years: those in and around the White House, and Gorbachev himself in house arrest in the Crimea, depended on them to keep abreast of events.

Workers, as well as intellectuals and the mass media, have played a major role in the development of the independent political movements. They were mobilised at an early stage in the inter-ethnic conflicts, but, even where national feeling was not dominant, they often gave the democrats the political impetus necessary to move reform forward. In Russia the miners' strike of March–April 1991 played a crucial role in forcing Gorbachev's move away from the alliance he had forged with the 'conservatives' the previous autumn back into an agreement with El'tsin and the reformers.

Nonetheless, the new trade unions in Russia failed to develop into a broad social movement in support of reform, the sort of Soviet Solidarność which some democrats had hoped for. Even when workers were determined they were not always able to break the power of the apparat, as the Belorussian general strike of April 1991 demonstrated. The power of the labour movement was so localised that it could not coordinate a widespread campaign of strikes.

In general, though, contrary to popular wisdom before perestroika, workers have not rallied to the 'conservative' cause either. Their revulsion from the party-state apparatus is so intense that they have on the whole given their support, however hesitant and poorly organised, to the radicals. This support has not generated permanent links, partly because the radicals themselves have been insufficiently organised to sustain such links.

At the moment of his greatest triumph, El'tsin's power base began to demonstrate its weaknesses only too plainly. The radical deputies in the Russian parliament, elected at a time of transition in spring 1990, represented either very tiny parties or none at all. Democratic Russia was an electoral bloc, not a party, and could not provide either the political programme or the voting discipline needed to support the government's reforms. In November 1991 El'tsin tried to deal with the disarray in the parliament by concluding an informal agreement to consult with the major parties of Democratic Russia over legislation and personnel appointments in return for their regular support, especially over his ambitious economic reforms. In practice, the agreement did not work as intended, though the democratic parties (and the non-aligned democrats) in practice normally gave El'tsin their support anyway. In a fast-changing situation, where new laws were urgently needed, the government skimped consultation, and the parties had neither the experience nor the influence to compel it to do otherwise. Lacking an obvious constituency among the population, they were unable to conjure up the threat of mass pressure either. Trade unions, when they took action, did so in isolation and sometimes at odds with Democratic Russia.

Without real parties to act as intermediaries between the government and the various strata of the population, the government has tended to fall back on the traditional weapons of secrecy and privilege in pushing through its programme. Much of its legislation has been by decree. El'tsin's radical advisers, never having quite outgrown the divisive traditions of the *kruzhki* where they began their political careers, tend to squabble publicly among themselves, while remaining intensely suspicious of the ex-apparatchiks on whom he also relies.

Furthermore, the final dissolution of the Soviet Union and the establishment of the Commonwealth of Independent States revealed the deep ambivalence of many Russian democrats about the nature of Russian statehood. Some of El'tsin's erstwhile supporters, from Sobchak to Rutskoi, went on record to express their desire to maintain the Union in some form. In this their position coincided with that of the armed forces leadership, and at times some of them seemed to be manœuvring themselves into positions from which they could one day challenge El'tsin.

Many of the non-Russian republican parliaments are in disarray too, even if they do not experience such ambivalence about the end of the Union. There also elections conducted in spring 1990 without proper political parties have created legislative assemblies with little internal cohesion or discipline, unable effectively either to support their governments or to restrain them when necessary.

Now, as the ex-Soviet political system is finally being totally rebuilt— or, more accurately, refashioned into several systems—the former 'informals' face new and imperfectly understood responsibilities. They must create fully fledged political parties, able to provide the motive power for polities which may not be fully democratic, but will certainly not be dominated any longer by a supranational apparatus. They must outgrow the *kruzhok* mentality and the habit of perpetual opposition. They must learn to drop personal feuds and reach compromise on the less important political problems. They lack the traditions of legality and the experience of functioning democracy. On the other hand, to some extent in compensation for that inexperience, their recent struggles have equipped them with a keen perception of what is really important to political freedom, for which the inhabitants of older democracies, daily beset by media-baked trivia, may sometimes envy them.

There is much to be done, then, in outgrowing *kruzhkovshchina*, in developing links with economic interest groups, in learning to quieten rather than inflame ethnic conflict, in settling to disciplined legislative work. But most political activists are aware of these needs, and they have demonstrated in the past a degree of determination and ingenuity in overcoming communist domination which leads one to hope that they can accomplish the tasks which lie before them now.

At the time of writing (February 1992), it is impossible to give a clear verdict on all the experiments in pluralism which the ex-Soviet republics are conducting, or even on that in Russia alone. The breakdown of an empire and the accompanying economic disorder and ethnic conflict provide an inaus- picious setting for the establishment of democracy, for which in any case many of the institutions and customs are lacking. One can marvel that so much has been achieved in so short a space of time, and yet feel foreboding about the short- and medium-term future.

Notes

1. Alexander Shtromas, *Political Change and Social Development: The Case of the Soviet Union*, Frankfurt-on-Main, Verlag Peter Lang, 1981, pp. 101–5.
2. ibid., pp. 105–22.
3. Boris Yeltsin, *Against the Grain: An Autobiography*, London, Jonathan Cape, 1990, p. 87.
4. Vera Tolz, 'How the journalists responded', *Report on the USSR*, 6 September 1991, pp. 23–8.

Appendix: Main independent political organisations

Organisations are listed alphabetically by area and then by date of foundation. The name is given first in English and then in the language of the main ethnic group that they serve (i.e. Estonian Popular Front is given in Estonian but interfront organisations in Estonia in Russian).

Area	Name in English	Name	Date
All-Union	Crimean Tatar National Movement	Krymsko-tatarskoe natsional' noe dvizhenie	1964
All-Union	Circle of Social Initiatives	Kol' tso obshchestvennykh initsiativ	1987
All-Union	Inter-Regional Association of Democratic Organisations	Mezhregional' naia assotsiatsiia demokraticheskikh organizatsii (MADO)	1989
All-Union	Social Democratic Association	Sotsial-demokraticheskaia assotsiatsiia	1989
All-Union	Inter-Regional Group of Deputies	Mezhregional' naia deputatovskaia gruppa	1989
All-Union	United Front of Workers of the USSR	Ob"edinennyi front trudiashchikhsia SSSR	1989
All-Union	Unity for Leninism and Communist Ideals	Edinstvo dlia leninizma i kommunisticheskikh idealov	1989
All-Union	Union	Soiuz	1990
All-Union	Islamic Party—Renaissance	Islamskaia partiia—Vozrozhdenie	1990
All-Union	Movement for Democratic Reforms	Dvizhenie demokraticheskikh reform	1991
Armenia	Armenian Revolutionary Federation	Hai Heghapokhakan Dashnaktsutiun	1890
Armenia	Armenian Democratic Liberal Party	Hai Ramkavar Azatakan Kusaksutiun	1921
Armenia	Karabakh Committee	Artsakh Gusaghsutiun	1988
Armenia	Armenian Association for Self-Determination	Hai Inknoroshman Miutsun	1988
Armenia	Armenian Pan-National Movement	Haiochs Hamazgayin Sharzhum	1989
Azerbaijan	Popular Front of Azerbaijan	Azerbaijan Khalk Japasi	1989
Azerbaijan	Social Democratic Party	Sosial-Demokratik Partiyosi	1989

Area	Name in English	Name	Date
Azerbaijan	Equality	*Musavat*	1989*
Azerbaijan	Azerbaijani National Independence Party	*Azerbaijan Milli Istiglalijat Partiyesi*	1990
Belarus	Martyrolog (List of Martyrs)	*Martyrolah*	1988
Belarus	Belorussian Language Society	*Tavarystva belaruskai movy*	1989
Belarus	Belorussian Ecological Union	*Belaruskaia ekalahichnyi saiuz*	1989
Belarus	Revival (Belorussian Popular Front)	*Adradzhenne*	1989
Belarus	Belorussian Social Democratic Party	*Satsyial-demakratychnaia partyia Belarusi*	1989
Belarus	Belorussian Social Democratic Society	*Belaruskaia satsyial-demakratichnaia hramada*	1990
Belarus	Belorussian Democratic Party	*Demakratichnaia partyia Belarusi*	1990
Estonia	Estonian Heritage Society	*Eesti Muinsuskaitse Selts*	1987
Estonia	Estonian Green Movement	*Eesti Roheline Liikumine*	1988
Estonia	National Front (Estonian Popular Front)	*Rahvarinne*	1988
Estonia	International Movement	*Interdvizhenie*	1988
Estonia	Estonian National Independence Party	*Eesti Rahvusliku Sôltumatuse Partei*	1988
Estonia	Council of Workers' Collectives	*Töökollektiivide Nôukogu*	1989
Estonia	Estonian Social Democratic Party	*Eesti Sotsiaal-Demokraatlik Partei*	1989
Estonia	United Council of Workers' Collectives	*Ob"edinennyi sovet trudozykh kollektivov*	1989
Estonia	Estonian Christian Democratic Union	*Eesti Kristklik-Demokraatlik Liit*	1989
Estonia	Agrarian Centre Party	*Maakeskerakond*	1990
Estonia	Free Estonia	*Vaba Eesti*	1990
Georgia	Georgian Helsinki Union	*sakartvelos helsinkis kavshiri*	1987
Georgia	Ilia Tchavtchavadze Society	*ilia tchavtchavadzis sazogadoeba*	1987
Georgia	Rustaveli Society	*rustavelis sazogadoeba*	1988
Georgia	Georgian Green Movement	*sakartvelos mtsvaneta modsraoba*	1988
Georgia	Georgian National Independence Party	*sarkartvelos erovnuli damoukideblobis partia*	1988

Country	Name	Native name	Year
Georgia	Georgian National Independence Party	*sarkartvelos erovnul-demokratiuli partia*	1988
Georgia	Georgian Social Democratic Party	*sarkartvelos sotsial-demokratiuli partia*	1989*
Georgia	Georgian Popular Front	*sarkartvelos sakhalkho pronti*	1989
Georgia	Georgian Monarchist Conservative Party	*sarkartvelos monarkistul-konservatiuli partia*	1989
Georgia	Democratic Choice for Georgia	*demokratiuli archevani sakartvelostvis*	1989
Georgia	Round Table	*mrgvali magida*	1990
Georgia	Charter-91	*khartia-91*	1991
Georgia/Abkhazia	Popular Forum	*Aidgylara*	1988
Georgia/South Ossetia	Popular Shrine	*Adaemon Nykhas*	1989
Kazakhstan	Nevada-Semipalatinsk	*Nevada-Semipalatinsk*	1989
Kazakhstan	Azat	*Freedom*	1990
Kyrgyzstan	Democratic Movement of Kyrgyzstan	*Demokraticheskoe dvizhenie Kyrgyzstan*	1990
Latvia	Helsinki-86	*Helsinki 86*	1986
Latvia	Latvian Movement for National Independence	*Latvijas Nacionāla Neatkarības Kustiba*	1988
Latvia	Latvian Popular Front	*Latvijas Tautas Fronte*	1988
Latvia	International Front	*Interfront*	1988
Latvia	Latvian Social Democratic Workers' Party	*Latvijas Sociāldemokrātiskā Strādnieku Partija*	1989*
Latvia	Latvian Social Democratic Party	*Latvijas Sociādemokrātiskā Partija*	1990
Latvia	Equal Rights	*Ravnopravie*	1990
Lithuania	Lithuanian Liberty League	*Lietuvos laisves lyga*	1978
Lithuania	Movement (Lithuanian Popular Front)	*Sajudis*	1988
Lithuania	Unity	*Edinstvo (Vienybe)*	1988
Lithuania	Lithuanian Democratic Party	*Lietuvos demokratu partija*	1988
Lithuania	Lithuanian Social Democratic Party	*Lietuvos social-demokratu partija*	1989*
Lithuania	Lithuanian Christian Democratic Party	*Lietuvos krikscioniu demokratu partija*	1990
Lithuania	Lithuanian Democratic Labour Party	*Lietuvos demokratine darbo partija*	1990
Lithuania	Lithuanian National Union	*Lietuvos tautintu sajunga*	1991

Area	Name in English	Name	Date
Lithuania	Lithuania Liberal Union	*Lietuvos liberalu sajunga*	1991
Lithuania	Lithuania Future Forum	*Lietuvos Ateities Forumas*	1991
Moldova	Movement in Support of Perestroika	*Mişcarea pentru Susţinerea Restructurării*	1988
Moldova	Alexei Mateevici Society	*Cenaclul Alexei Mateevici*	1988
Moldova	Moldovan Popular Front	*Frontul Popular Moldovenesc*	1989
Moldova	Unity	*Edinstvo*	1989
Moldova	United Council of Workers' Collectives	*Ob"edinennyi sovet trudovykh kollektivov*	1989
Moldova/Gagauzia	Gagauz Nation	*Gagauz Khalky*	1990
RSFSR	Popular Labouring Union	*Narodno–Trudovoi Soiuz*	1931
RSFSR	Memory	*Pamiat'*	1979
RSFSR	Club of Social Initiatives	*Klub sotsial'nykh initsiativ*	1986
RSFSR	Commune	*Obshchina*	1987
RSFSR	Memorial	*Memorial*	1987
RSFSR	Federation of Socialist Public Clubs	*Federatsiia sotsialistcheskikh obshchestvennykh klubov*	1987
RSFSR	Democratic Union	*Demokraticheskii soiuz*	1988
RSFSR	Socialist Trade Unions	*Sotsprof*	1989
RSFSR	Union of Constitutional Democrats	*Soiuz konstitutsionnykh demokratov*	1989
RSFSR	Russian Popular Front	*Rossiiskii narodnyi front*	1989
RSFSR	United Front of Workers of RSFSR	*Ob"edinennyi front trudiashchikhsia RSFSR*	1989
RSFSR	Confederation of Anarcho-Syndicalists	*Konfederatsiia anarkho–sindikalistov*	1989
RSFSR	Christian Democratic Union of Russia	*Khristiansko–demokraticheskii soiuz Rossii*	1989
RSFSR	Democratic Russia	*Demokraticheskaia Rossiia*	1990
RSFSR	Democratic Platform of the CPSU	*Demokraticheskaia platforma KPSS*	1990
RSFSR	Social Democratic Party of the Russian Federation	*Sotsial-demokraticheskaia partiia Rossiiskoi Federatsii*	1990

Region	English Name	Russian Name	Year
RSFSR	Russian Christian Democratic Movement	*Rossiiskoe khristianskoe demokraticheskoe dvizhenie*	1990
RSFSR	Democratic Party of Russia	*Demokraticheskaia partiia Rossii*	1990
RSFSR	Free Democratic Party of Russia	*Svobodno–demokraticheskaia partiia Rossii*	1990
RSFSR	Socialist Party	*Sotsialisticheskaia partiia*	1990
RSFSR	Republican Party of the Russian Federation	*Respublikanskaia partiia Rossiiskoi Federatsii*	1990
RSFSR	Peasant Party	*Krest'ianskaia partiia*	1990
RSFSR	Republican Popular Party of Russia	*Respublikanskaia narodnaia partiia Rossii*	1990
RSFSR	Party of Constitutional Democrats	*Partiia konstitutsionnykh demokratov*	1990
RSFSR	Liberal Democratic Party of the Soviet Union	*Liberal' no–demokraticheskaia partiia Sovetskogo Soiuza*	1990
RSFSR	Confederation of Labour	*Konfederatsiia truda*	1990
RSFSR	Popular Party–Free Russia	*Narodnaia partiia 'Svobodnaia Rossiia'*	1991
RSFSR	Socialist Party of Workers	*Sotsialisticheskaia partiia trudiashchikhsia*	1992
RSFSR/Iaroslavl	Iaroslavl Popular Front	*Iaroslavskii narodnyi front*	1989
RSFSR/Kuzbass	Union of Kuzbass Workers	*Soiuz trudiashchikhsia Kuzbassa*	1989
RSFSR/Leningrad	Salvation	*Spasenie*	1986
RSFSR/Leningrad	Epicentre	*Episentr*	1987
RSFSR/Leningrad	Fatherland	*Otechestvo*	1988
RSFSR/Leningrad	Justice	*Spravedlivost'*	1989
RSFSR/Leningrad	Leningrad Popular Front	*Leningradskii narodnyi front*	1989
RSFSR/Leningrad	United Front of Workers of Leningrad	*Ob" edinennyi front trudiashchikhsia Leningrada*	1989
RSFSR/Leningrad	National Democratic Party	*Natsional' no–demokraticheskaia partiia*	1989
RSFSR/Leningrad	Independence	*Nezavisimost'*	1989
RSFSR/Leningrad	Russians	*Rossy*	1989
RSFSR/Leningrad	Democratic Elections-90	*Demokraticheskie vybory–90*	1989
RSFSR/Moscow	Club 'Perestroika"	*Klub 'Perestroika'*	1987
RSFSR/Moscow	Russian Popular Democratic Front– 'Memory' Movement	*Russkii narodno–demokraticheskii front– dvizhenie 'Pamiat' '*	1987
RSFSR/Moscow	Democracy and Humanism Seminar	*Seminar 'Demokratiia i gumanizm' '*	1987

Area	Name in English	Name	Date
RSFSR/Moscow	Democratic Perestroika	*Demokraticheskaia Perestroika*	1988
RSFSR/Moscow	National Patriotic Front 'Memory'	*Natsional'no-patrioticheskii front Pamiat'*	1988
RSFSR/Moscow	Moscow Tribune	*Moskovskaia tribuna*	1988
RSFSR/Moscow	Fatherland	*Otechestvo*	1988
RSFSR/Moscow	Moscow Association of Electors	*Moskovskoe ob"edinenie izbiratelei*	1989
RSFSR/Moscow	Union for National Proportional Representation–'Memory'	*Soiuz za natsional' no-proportsional' noe predstavitel' stvo 'Pamiat'*	1989
RSFSR/Moscow	Moscow Popular Front	*Moskovskii narodnyi front*	1989
RSFSR/Moscow	United Front of Workers of Moscow	*Ob"edinennyi front trudiashchikhsia Moskvy*	1989
RSFSR/Sverdlovsk	Discussion Tribune	*Diskussionnaia tribuna*	1987
RSFSR/Sverdlovsk	Fatherland	*Otechestvo*	1988
RSFSR/Sverdlovsk	Democratic Choice	*Demokraticheskii vybor*	1990
RSFSR/Tatarstan	Tatar Public Centre	*Tatarskii obshchestvennyi tsentr*	1989
RSFSR/Tatarstan	Unity	*Ittifaq*	1990
RSFSR and Ukraine	Independent Miners' Union	*Nezavisimyi soiuz gorniakov*	1990
RSFSR and Kazakhstan and Baltic states	Russian Union	*Russkii soiuz*	1991
Tajikistan	Renaissance	*Rastokhez*	1989
Tajikistan	Democratic Party of Tajikistan	*Demokraticheskaia partiia Tadzhikistana*	1990
Turkmenistan	Unity	*Agzybirlik*	1990
Ukraine	Ukrainian Helsinki Union	*Ukrains' ka hel' sinks' ka Spilka*	1988
Ukraine	Green World	*Zelenyi svit*	1989
Ukraine	Taras Shevchenko Ukrainian Language Society	*Tovarystvo ukrains' koi movy i T. H. Shevchenko*	1989
Ukraine	Ukrainian Popular Movement for Perestroika	*Narodnyi Rukh Ukrainy za Perebudovu*	1989
Ukraine	Union of Independent Youth	*Spilka nezalezhnoi molodi*	1990
Ukraine	Social Democratic Party of Ukraine	*Sotsial–demokratychna partiia Ukrainy*	1990

Ukraine	Ukrainian Republican Party	*Ukrains'ka respublikans'ka partiia*	1990
Ukraine	United Social Democratic Party of Ukraine	*Obiednana sotsial–demokratychna partiia Ukrainy*	1990
Ukraine	Party of the Democratic Renaissance of Ukraine	*Partiia demokratychnoho vidrodzhennia Ukrainy*	1990
Ukraine	Democratic Party of Ukraine	*Demokratychna partiia Ukrainy*	1990
Ukraine/L'viv	Lion Society	*Tovarystvo Lev*	1987
Uzbekistan	Unity	*Birlik*	1988
Uzbekistan	Freedom	*Erk*	1990

* Denotes the re-founding of an organisation

Suggested further reading

For current developments, see *RFE/RL Research Report* (before 1992: *Report on the USSR*); *Moscow News*; *Current Digest of the Post-Soviet Press* (before 1992: *Current Digest of the Soviet Press*); all weekly.

Aves, J. *Paths to National Independence in Georgia, 1987–1990*. London: School of Slavonic and East European Studies, 1991.

Babkina, M. A. (ed.). *New Political Parties and Movements in the Soviet Union*. Commack, NY: Nova Science Publishers, 1991.

Beissinger, M., and Hajda, L. (eds). *The Nationalities Factor in Soviet Society and Politics*. Boulder, Colo.: Westview Press, 1990.

Bialer, S. (ed.). *Politics, Society and Nationality in Gorbachev's Russia*. Boulder, Colo.: Westview Press, 1989.

Bloomfield, J. (ed.). *The Soviet Revolution: Perestroika and the Remaking of Socialism*. London: Lawrence and Wishart, 1989.

Brovkin, V. 'Revolution from Below: Informal Political Associations in Russia 1988–1989'. *Soviet Studies*, vol. 42, no. 2, April 1990, pp. 233–58.

Carter, S. K. *Russian Nationalism: Yesterday, Today, Tomorrow*. London: Pinter, 1990.

Conquest, R. (ed.). *The Last Empire: Nationality and the Soviet Future*. Stanford: Hoover Institution Press, 1986.

Crawshaw, S. *Farewell to the USSR*. London: Bloomsbury, 1992.

Crouch, M. *Revolution and Evolution: Gorbachev and Soviet Politics*. Hemel Hempstead: Philip Allan, 1989.

Dunlop, J. B. *The Faces of Contemporary Russian Nationalism*. Princeton, NJ: Princeton University Press, 1983.

Fehér, F., and Arato, A. (eds). *Gorbachev—The Debate*. London: Polity Press, 1989.

Fish, S. 'The Emergence of Independent Associations and the Transformation of Russian Political Society'. *Journal of Communist Studies*, vol. 7, no. 3, September 1991, pp. 299–334.

Five Years Gorbachev. Amsterdam: Second World Center, 1990.

Gitelman, Z. (ed.). *The Politics of Nationality in the Contemporary Ukraine*. Basingstoke: Macmillan for the International Committee for Soviet and East European Studies, 1991.

Glebov, O., and Crowfoot, J. (eds). *The Soviet Empire: Its Nations Speak Out*. London: Harwood, 1989.

Hasegawa, T., and Pravda, A. (eds). *Perestroika: Soviet Domestic and Foreign Policies*. Beverly Hills, Calif., and London: Sage for the Royal Institute of International Affairs, 1990.

Hewett, E., and Winston, V. (eds). *Milestones in Glasnost and Perestroika*. Vol 2. *Politics and People*. Washington, DC: Brookings Institution, 1991.

Hill, R. J. *Soviet Union: Politics, Economics and Society*. 2nd edn. London: Pinter, 1989.

Hosking, G. *The Awakening of the Soviet Union*. Rev. edn. London: Mandarin, 1991.

—— *A History of the Soviet Union*. Rev. edn. London: Fontana, 1992.

Kagarlitsky, B. *Farewell Perestroika: a Soviet Chronicle*. Trans. Rick Simon. London: Verso, 1990.

Karklins, R. *Ethnic Relations in the USSR: The Perspective from Below*. London: Allen and Unwin, 1986.

Kiernan, B., and Aistrup, J. 'The 1989 Elections to the Congress of People's Deputies in Moscow'. *Soviet Studies*, vol. 43, no. 6, 1991, pp. 1049–64.

Kotkin, S. *Steeltown, USSR: Soviet Society in the Gorbachev Era*. Berkeley: University of California Press, 1991.

Kux, S. 'Soviet Federalism'. *Problems of Communism*, vol. 39, no. 2, March–April 1990, pp. 1–20.

Lacquer, W. *The Long Road to Freedom: Russia and Glasnost*. London: Unwin Hyman, 1989.

Lentini, P. 'Reforming the Electoral System: The 1989 Elections to the USSR Congress of People's Deputies'. *Journal of Communist Studies*, vol. 7. no. 1, March 1991, pp. 69–94.

McCauley, M. *The Soviet Union 1917–1991*. Rev. edn. Longman, due 1993.

—— (ed.). *Gorbachev and Perestroika*. Basingstoke: Macmillan for the School of Slavonic and East European Studies, 1990.

Mandel, D. *Perestroika and the Soviet People: Rebirth of the Labour Movement*. Montreal: Black Rose Books, 1991.

Mandelbaum, M. (ed.). *The Rise of Nations in the Soviet Union: American Foreign Policy and the Disintegration of the USSR*. New York: Council for Foreign Relations, 1991.

Marples, D. *Ukraine under Perestroika*. Basingstoke: Macmillan, 1991.

Melville, A., and Lapidus, G. (eds). *The Glasnost Papers: Voices on Reform from Moscow*. Boulder, Colo.: Westview Press, 1990.

Morrison, J. *Boris Yeltsin: From Bolshevik to Democrat*. London: Penguin, 1991.

'Moscow, August 1991: The Coup de Grace'. *Problems of Communism*, vol. 40, no. 6, November–December 1991, pp. 1–62.

Motyl, A. J. *Sovietology, Rationality, Nationality: Comings to Grips with Nationality in the USSR*. New York: Columbia University Press, 1990.

Nahaylo, B., and Swoboda, V. *Soviet Disunion: A History of the Nationalities Problem in the USSR*. London: Hamish Hamilton, 1990.

Nove, A. *Glasnost in Action: Cultural Renaissance in Russia*. London: Unwin Hyman, 1989.

Olcott, M. B., and Hajda, L. (eds). *The Soviet Multinational State*. Armonk, NY: M. E. Sharpe, 1987.

Problems of Communism, vol. 38, no. 4, July–August 1989, series of articles on nationality politics in the USSR.

Ruble, B. A. *Leningrad: Shaping a Soviet City*. Berkeley: University of California Press, 1990.

Saroyan, M. 'The "Karabakh Syndrome" and Azerbaijani Politics'. *Problems of Communism*, vol. 39, no. 5, September–October 1990, pp. 14–29.

Sakharov, A. *Moscow and Beyond: 1986 to 1989*. Trans. Antonina Bouis. London: Hutchinson, 1990.

Sakwa, R. *Gorbachev and his Reforms, 1985–1990*. Hemel Hempstead: Philip Allan, 1991.

—— *Soviet Politics: An Introduction*. London: Routledge, 1989.

Sedaitis, J., and Butterfield, J. (eds). *Perestroika from Below: Social Movements in the Soviet Union*. Boulder, Colo.: Westview Press, 1991.

Senn, A. E. *Lithuanian Awakening*. Berkeley, University of California Press, 1990.

—— 'Toward Lithuanian Independence: Algirdas Brazauskas and the CPL'. *Problems of Communism*, vol. 39, no. 2, March–April 1990, pp. 21–28.

Shevardnadze, E. *The Future Belongs to Freedom*. London: Sinclair Stevenson, 1991.

Sixsmith, M. *Moscow Coup*. London: Simon and Schuster, 1991.

Slider, D. 'The Politics of Georgia's Independence'. *Problems of Communism*, vol. 40, no. 6, November–December 1991, pp. 63–80.

Smith, G. (ed.). *The Nationalities Question in the Soviet Union*. Harlow: Longman, 1990.

Sobchak, A. *For a New Russia*. London: Harper Collins, 1992.

Szajkowski, B. (ed.). *New Political Parties of Eastern Europe and the Soviet Union*. Harlow: Longman, 1991.

Taagepera, R. 'Estonia's Road to Independence'. *Problems of Communism*, vol. 38, no. 6, November–December 1989, pp. 11–26.

Tarasulo, J. (ed.). *Perils of Perestroika: Viewpoints from the Soviet Press, 1989–1991*. Wilmington, Delaware: Scholarly Resources, 1992.

Temkina, A. A. 'The Workers' Movement in Leningrad, 1986–91'. *Soviet Studies*, vol. 44, no. 2, 1992, pp. 209–36.

Tolz, V. *The USSR's Emerging Multiparty System*. (The Washington Papers 148.) New York: Praeger with the Center for Strategic and International Studies, 1990.

Urban, G. R. (ed.). *Can the Soviet System Survive Reform?* London: Pinter, 1989.

Urban, M. E. 'Boris El'tsin, Democratic Russia and the Campaign for the Russian Presidency'. *Soviet Studies*, vol. 44, no. 2, 1992, pp. 187–208.

—— 'Democrats, Republicans and Socialists in Today's Russia'. *Critique*, no. 23, 1991, pp. 127–41.

—— *More Power to the Soviets: The Democratic Revolution in the USSR*. Aldershot: Edward Elgar, 1990.

White, S. *Gorbachev and After*. 3rd edn. Cambridge: Cambridge University Press, forthcoming 1992.

—— Pravda, A., and Gitelman, Z. (eds). *Developments in Soviet Politics*. Basingstoke: Macmillan, 1990.

Yanov, A. *The Russian Challenge and the Year 2000*. Oxford: Blackwell, 1987.

Yeltsin, B. *Against the Grain: An Autobiography*. Updated edition. London: Cape, 1991.

Among the most useful Russian-language reference volumes are:

Berezovskii, V. N., Krotov, N. I. and Cherviakov, V. V. *Rossiia: partii, assotsiatsii, soiuzy, kluby. Spravochnik*. 2 vols. Moscow: RAU-Press, 1991. (This incorporates material from the earlier publication by two of these authors: Berezovskii, V. N. and Krotov, N. I. *Neformal' naia Rossiia. O neformal' nykh politizirovannykh dvizheniiakh i gruppakh v RSFSR (opyt spravochnika)*. Moscow: Molodaia gvardiia, 1990.)

Bogdanova, M. *Samizdat i politicheskie organizatsii Sibiri i Dal' nego Vostoka*. Moscow: Panorama, 1991.

Glubotskii, A. *Strany Baltii. Politicheskie partii i organizatsii*. Moscow: Panorama, April 1992.

Koval', B.I. (ed.). *Rossiia segodnia. Politicheskii portret v dokumentakh, 1985–1991*. Moscow: Mezhdunarodnye otnosheniia, 1991.

Mikhailovskaia, E. *Ukraina. Politicheskie partii i organizatsii*. Moscow: Panorama, January 1992.

Pribylovskii, V. *Russkaia natsional' no-patrioticheskaia organizatsiia Pamiat'. Dokumenty i teksty*. Moscow: Panorama, 1991.

—— *Slovar' novykh politicheskikh partii i organizatsii Rossii'*. 3rd edn. Moscow: Panorama, November 1991.

Spravochnik periodicheskogo samizdata. Comp. Aleksandr Suetnov. Moscow: Iz glubin, 1990.

Verkhovskii, A. *Sredniaia Aziia i Kazakhstan. Politicheskii spektr*. Moscow: Panorama, January 1992.

Index